Lecture Notes in Computer Science

Lecture Notes in Artificial Intelligence 15923

Founding Editor

Jörg Siekmann

Series Editors

Randy Goebel, *University of Alberta, Edmonton, Canada*
Wolfgang Wahlster, *DFKI, Berlin, Germany*
Zhi-Hua Zhou, *Nanjing University, Nanjing, China*

The series Lecture Notes in Artificial Intelligence (LNAI) was established in 1988 as a topical subseries of LNCS devoted to artificial intelligence.

The series publishes state-of-the-art research results at a high level. As with the LNCS mother series, the mission of the series is to serve the international R & D community by providing an invaluable service, mainly focused on the publication of conference and workshop proceedings and postproceedings.

Tianqing Zhu · Wanlei Zhou · Congcong Zhu

Editors

Knowledge Science, Engineering and Management

18th International Conference, KSEM 2025
Macao, China, August 4–7, 2025
Proceedings, Part V

 Springer

Editors
Tianqing Zhu
City University of Macau
Macau, China

Wanlei Zhou
City University of Macau
Macau, China

Congcong Zhu
City University of Macau
Macau, China

ISSN 0302-9743   ISSN 1611-3349 (electronic)
Lecture Notes in Computer Science
Lecture Notes in Artificial Intelligence
ISBN 978-981-95-3060-1   ISBN 978-981-95-3061-8 (eBook)
https://doi.org/10.1007/978-981-95-3061-8

LNCS Sublibrary: SL7 – Artificial Intelligence

Preface

On behalf of the Conference Committee, we are pleased to present the proceedings of the 18th International Conference on Knowledge Science, Engineering and Management (**KSEM 2025**), held at the Wynn Palace, Macau Special Administrative Region, China, from August 4–7, 2025. KSEM 2025 was the eighteenth event in this well-established series of conferences, founded by Academician Ruqian Lu, which is recognized as a premier international forum for the exchange of research in artificial intelligence, data science, knowledge engineering, AI safety, large language models, and related frontier areas. Over the years, KSEM has provided an important venue for disseminating both theoretical advances and practical innovations, fostering interdisciplinary collaboration between academia and industry.

This year, KSEM 2025 received 354 submissions from authors around the world. Following a rigorous single-blind peer-review process, with an average of 2.82 reviews received per submission, involving 342 Program Committee members and external reviewers, 106 regular papers, 66 short papers, and 16 workshop papers were accepted for inclusion in these proceedings and will be submitted for EI indexing. In addition to the contributed papers, the program featured keynote lectures by distinguished scholars, as well as workshops and tutorials on emerging research topics, offering valuable opportunities for academic exchange and collaboration.

Among the accepted papers, the following were selected for the **Best Paper Awards**:

- *Masked Aggregation Learning for Enhancing Distributed Gradient Boosting Decision Trees* Yuting Zha, Chao Lin, Xinyi Huang, and Dugang Liu
- *Label Inference Attacks against Federated Unlearning* Wei Wang, Xiangyun Tang, Yajie Wang, Yijing Lin, Tao Zhang, Meng Shen, Dusit Niyato, and Liehuang Zhu

The **Best Student Paper Awards** went to:

- *LVLM-FDA: Protecting Large Vision-language Models via Fast Detection of Malicious Attempts* Boxu Chen, Chaoyi Wang, Le Yang, Ziwei Zheng, Cong Wang, Qian Wang, and Chao Shen
- *FATFI: A Framework to Generate Adversarial Traffic with Feature Interpretability* Yikang Wang, Weina Niu, Dujuan Gu, Qingjun Yuan, Jiacheng Gong, Shuangqi Gan, Xin Lin, and Xiaosong Zhang

We would like to express our sincere gratitude to all authors for their valuable contributions, and to the Program Committee members and reviewers for their professional and timely evaluations. We also warmly thank all the volunteers who supported the conference at various stages.

We further extend our appreciation to the following chairs for their invaluable contributions:

- **General Chairs:** Wanlei Zhou, Zhi Jin, Aniello Castiglione
- **Program Chairs:** Tianqing Zhu, Gang Li, Congcong Zhu, Lucia Cimmino

- **Local Chairs:** Wenjian Liu, Minghao Wang, Huajie Chen
- **Publication Chairs:** Lefeng Zhang, Youyang Qu
- **Workshop Chairs:** Jia Gu, Bo Liu, Chi Liu
- **Publicity Chairs:** Yu Huang, Minfeng Qi

We were so honored to have many renowned scholars be part of this conference. Finally, we would like to thank all speakers, authors, and participants for their great contribution to and support for the success of KSEM 2025.

August 2025

Tianqing Zhu
Wanlei Zhou
Congcong Zhu

Committees

General Chairs

Wanlei Zhou	City University of Macau, China
Zhi Jin	Peking University, China
Aniello Castiglione	University of Salerno, Italy

Program Chairs

Tianqing Zhu	City University of Macau, China
Gang Li	Deakin University, Australia
Congcong Zhu	City University of Macau, China
Lucia Cimmino	University of Salerno, Italy

Local Chairs

Wenjian Liu	City University of Macau, China
Minghao Wang	City University of Macau, China
Macau Huajie Chen	City University of Macau, China

Publication Chairs

Lefeng Zhang	City University of Macau, China
Macau Youyang Qu	Shandong Computer Science Center, China

Workshop Chairs

Jia Gu	City University of Macau, China
Bo Liu	University of Technology Sydney, Australia
Chi Liu	City University of Macau, China

Publicity Chairs

Yu Huang	Peking University, China
Minfeng Qi	City University of Macau, China

Contents – Part V

Global Discovery: A Global Graph-RAG Approach for Query-Focused
Multimodal Summarization Across Multiple PDF Papers 1
Chenhan Fu, Guoming Wang, Rongxing Lu, and Siliang Tang

Metric Embedding Initialization-Based Differentially Private
and Explainable Graph Clustering 9
Haochen You and Baojing Liu

M^3Net: Multimodal-Feature-Masked Networks for Fake News Detection 17
Zhaokang Zhang, Xiaorui Luo, Chi Jiang, Ranran Wang, Yiran Wang,
and Yin Zhang

TB-DML4HS: A Task-Based Modeling and Causal Effect Estimation
Method Using DML for Heterogeneous UAV Swarm 25
Jiabao Wang, Guang Yang, Lingzhong Meng, Youdi Gong, and Yuxi Ma

WebGCN: Web Information Extraction Algorithm Based on Graph Neural
Networks 36
Xiaole Wang, Dengcheng Yan, Yuting Wang, Heng Zhang, Xu Wen,
Fangxiang Liu, and Qingren Wang

Federated Rank Learning with Dimensionality Reduction and Clustering
for Electricity Load Forecasting 46
Lei Li, Bing Su, Shichao Zhang, Yuchong Liu, Jianchao Zheng,
Chuan Zhang, and Liehuang Zhu

Context-Aware Vectors: A New Method Integrating Personality Into
LLMs for Enhanced Sentiment Analysis 59
Zhihao Shuai, Kaiwen Li, Guoyu Li, Shengyao Liu, Dandan Li,
and Naisheng Tang

Research on Detection and Reconstruction of Multiple Types of Anomalies
in Wind Speed-Power Data of Wind Farms 67
Shouyi Chen, Yiyi He, Yanfei Guo, Wei Ma, Chung-Lun Wei,
and Chiawei Chu

An LLM-Enabled Data Augmentation Framework for Low-Resource
Scenarios 77
Zhongjian Hu, Peng Yang, Tianwai Zhou, and Kun Song

Lightweight Remote Sensing Tiny Object Detection Model Based
on YOLOv8n Architecture 85
   Jinyin Bai, Wei Zhu, Qinglin Xu, Xiangchen Wang, and Peng Zheng

Causal Encoding Generative Model Based on Attention and KAN 97
   Jing Yang, Xiangbin Meng, Xuanli Qin, Xianjun Xu, and Zhangxiang Hu

TRVP: Transformer-VAE Framework for 3D Point Cloud Instance
Segmentation 105
   Jiangmai Cheng, Bo Jiang, Tianfang Sun, and Boyu Wang

A Metapath-Based Neighborhood Reconstruction Network for Graph
Anomaly Detection 116
   Yanjun Lu and Xinyi Song

DarkFusionNet: A Fusion Neural Network Based Architecture for Darknet
Text Classification 124
   Anyang Xu, Peng Wu, Dong Wang, and Bowen Yang

Key Nodes Evaluation for Human Proximity Networks Based on Gravity
Model 134
   Jian Shu, Weide Huang, Yunan Jiang, Zhenghao Wei, and Linlan Liu

SRViT-MCNet: An IoT Malware Classification Model 143
   *Changguang Wang, Hongxuan Wang, Xi Zhang, Qingru Li,
   and Fangwei Wang*

MultiTEmb: Multi-scale Embeddings for Temporal KG Completion 156
   Junyu Chen, Xingjian Xu, Wenfeng Cui, and Fanjun Meng

Education Distillation: Let the Model Learn in the School 165
   Ling Feng, Tianhao Wu, Xiangrong Ren, Zhi Jing, and Xuliang Duan

A Multi-source Temporal Graph Approach for Reliable Market Forecasting
with LLM Synergy 176
   Yuting Shi

Memory-Enhanced Transformer Adaptive Graph Convolutional Recurrent
Network for Traffic Flow Forecasting 190
   Cheng Jiang and Chun Wang

Investigation into Auto-scaling Mechanisms in Cloud Computing 198
   *Xin Li, Jiming Dong, Wenkang Xiang, Dawei Zhao, Lijuan Xu,
   and Fenghua Tong*

Multi-receptive-Field Feature Fusion Knowledge Graph Embedding
for Link Prediction 210
   Zhehao Hou, Fang Liu, Xikai Ke, Weike Xia, Tongliang Li,
   Hezhong Jiang, and Wei Hu

RAG with Visual Alert: Boosting Multimodal Language Models
for Enhanced Visual Question Answering 219
   Hongze Ou, Xiaoyu Liang, Lianrui Mu, and Haoji Hu

Dynamic Heterogeneous Graph Neural Network for Personality Detection
in Chinese Social Media Texts 228
   Te Wang, Fanjun Meng, and Xingjian Xu

DualCBR: Cross-Modal Collaborative Filtering with Bidirectional
Alignment for Long-Tail Recommendation 237
   Xin Li, Lei Zhao, Dekai Zhang, Dawei Zhao, Lijuan Xu, Chunhui Wang,
   and Fuqiang Yu

Semantic Information Extraction with Language Models for Zero-Day
Attack Detection 248
   Shyamali Sinali Karunarathne, Sutharshan Rajasegarar, and Lei Pan

A Review of Optimization Techniques for Large Language Model Inference ... 257
   Yujia Cao, Xi Tao, Weipeng Cao, Chuanfei Xu, and Zhong Ming

GeoER: A Challenging Benchmark for Geometric Element Recognition 266
   Jiamin Tang, Chao Zhang, Xudong Zhu, and Mengchi Liu

SocioSupplyAlert: Comprehensive Supply Chain Crisis Prediction Using
LLMs and Social Media Data 274
   Meixuan Chen, Chen Wang, Yujun Wu, Wei Kang, and Zaiwen Feng

SKG-LLM: Enhancing Large Language Models with Sentiment
Knowledge Graphs for Fine-Grained Sentiment Analysis 282
   Yixuan Yuan and Bixuan Li

Harnessing Heterogeneous Social Networks for Better Group
Recommendations: An Integrated Approach Towards Cold-Start Problem 291
   Yunwei Zhao, Songtao Peng, Linbo Qiao, Qiwei Ye, Han Han,
   and Shanqing Yu

An Agent-Based Cybersecurity Framework Enhanced by Large Language
Models: Integrating Retrieval-Augmented Generation and Monte Carlo
Tree Search 302
   Tianxiang Xu, Chang Liu, Zihao Wang, Jiahao Li, and Kangsheng Wang

Constrained Multi-agent Reinforcement Learning Approach on Wireless
Charging Scheduling 310
    Yingjun Liu, Fuchun Liu, and Hongzhen Zhu

A Dual-Module System Design and Application for Digital Payment
Fraud Detection 318
    Yingxin Hong, Qingqing Ren, Shijie Cao, and Hualing Liu

Correction to: SocioSupplyAlert: Comprehensive Supply Chain Crisis
Prediction Using LLMs and Social Media Data C1
    Meixuan Chen, Chen Wang, Yujun Wu, Wei Kang, and Zaiwen Feng

Author Index 327

Global Discovery: A Global Graph-RAG Approach for Query-Focused Multimodal Summarization Across Multiple PDF Papers

Chenhan Fu[1], Guoming Wang[1(✉)], Rongxing Lu[2], and Siliang Tang[3]

[1] School of Software Technology, Zhejiang University, Ningbo 315100, China
NB21013@zju.edu.cn
[2] School of Computing, Queen's University, Kingston K7L 3N6, Canada
[3] College of Computer Science and Technology, Zhejiang University,
Hangzhou 310027, China

Abstract. Retrieval-Augmented Generation (RAG) allows large language models to generate summaries focusing primarily on textual content. However, in specialized academic fields, documents often contain multimodal information such as images and tables, which are crucial for fully understanding and deepening the comprehension of the literature. Meanwhile, summary generation methods that focus solely on text are unable to scale to the volume of text that typical RAG systems can index. To overcome this limitation, we introduced a new summary system, Global-Graph RAG Summarizer (GGRS), specifically designed for multiple PDF-format academic documents in the medical field that include not only text but also images and tables. GGRS combines graph-based RAG with LLMs to effectively process and integrate multimodal data, producing high-quality summaries. Evaluation results show that our GGRS system performs exceptionally well in generating semantically rich summaries, achieving win rates of 89% in accuracy and 94% in comprehensiveness compared to GPT-4.

Keywords: Retrieval-Augmented Generation · Query-Focused Summarization · Graph-Based Retrieval · Medical Document

1 Introduction

In various professional academic fields, individuals typically rely on reading and understanding a vast array of scholarly documents to advance research and decision-making, and they need the capability to derive insights that transcend the literal content described in the texts. In the current research landscape, academic documents in these fields are predominantly available in PDF format and contain not just text but also multimodal information such as images and tables. With the advancement of large language models (LLMs), efforts are being made

T. Zhu et al. (Eds.): KSEM 2025, LNAI 15923, pp. 1–8, 2026.
https://doi.org/10.1007/978-981-95-3061-8_1

to automate these complex information processing and reasoning summarization tasks.

Retrieval-Augmented Generation (RAG) [1] provides a framework for addressing queries across an entire corpus, initially retrieving information fragments related to the query from the corpus and then using this information to generate the target text. However, standard RAG methods are more suitable for scenarios where answers can be directly retrieved from local text segments. In contrast, query-focused summarization (QFS [2]), especially query-focused abstractive summarization, is more aligned with our reasoning summarization tasks as it produces natural language summaries, not just a patchwork of summaries [3–5]. Therefore, for professional academic literature that requires a comprehensive understanding and integration of text, images, and tables, traditional RAG methods may not suffice. Developing a new RAG method, specifically for generating global summaries that can simultaneously handle text and multimodal data—elements that often carry crucial supplementary information in documents—is particularly important.

In this paper, we explore the task of generating focused summaries from multiple professional medical academic documents in PDF format. We introduce a new summarization system (Global-Graph RAG Summarizer, GGRS) that not only processes text but also integrates multimodal datas from multiple documents, which overview as shown in Fig. 2. To compensate for the limitations of naive RAG, we employed a pre-indexing form graph to support a global summarization-focused RAG approach. Our method combines graph-based RAG with LLMs, utilizing graphs to capture and represent the relationships and structural information across multiple documents. Initially, we automate the extraction and integration of multimodal information from all PDF documents, converting them into a single modality element to construct a comprehensive information graph covering all literature. Through this graph, our system can more accurately understand and handle complex queries, thereby producing more comprehensive and accurate summaries.

When evaluating our system, we employed various metrics, including accuracy and comprehensiveness, comparing it against other AI systems capable of summarization. The evaluation results demonstrate our system's significant advantages in handling highly specialized and information-dense medical literature, particularly in integrating multimodal information and generating semantically rich summaries.

2   Global-Graph RAG Summarizer

Our Global-Graph RAG method (as shown in Fig. 2) is an innovative framework for multimodal data file retrieval and summarization, designed to extract relevant information from multiple sources (with a focus on PDFs in this paper) and generate comprehensive summaries. Below is a detailed analysis of the data flow of this method and the pipeline of Global-Graph RAG Summarizer (GGRS).

2.1 Source PDF Documents → Docx Documents → Modal Data

Our work focuses on synthesizing information from multiple PDF files, which contain various modalities of data and not just plain text, in response to specific queries. Therefore, in the initial design phase, our core decision was how to extract different modalities of data such as text, images, and tables from PDF files. We first convert PDF files to DOCX format to leverage the more structured characteristics and higher data accessibility of DOCX files, facilitating the extraction of different data modalities.

Once the conversion to DOCX is complete, we can efficiently and accurately extract the required modal data from the documents. For textual data, we utilize XML parsing techniques to extract structured text content from document.xml while also handling related style files to preserve the original document's format information, such as paragraph layout. Image data is obtained by analyzing the files in the word/media directory. By precisely locating the images within the file and analyzing the surrounding text elements, we can identify and extract the corresponding text as the image's caption. Similarly, for table data, by parsing the <w:tbl> tags and their subtags, we reconstruct the row and column structure and the content of the cells. Like images, the caption for tables is also extracted by analyzing text elements closely associated with the table. These methods ensure the integrity and accuracy of data extraction from multimodal documents.

2.2 Modal Data → Text Elements

The basic requirement of this workflow is to extract relevant textual information from three main types of modal data collected: images, tables, and textual content. Each type of data undergoes a specific process for extraction, especially images and tables, as they often contain important information not fully mentioned in the main text.

- **Text:** Processing text data is central to information extraction and analysis. In our workflow, we use a technique called "sentencize" to break continuous text into individual sentences, making the text easier to manage and analyze.
- **Images:** Extracting information from images is crucial as they often contain visual details not fully covered in text. During content extraction, we not only retrieve detailed information from images but also enhance the original captions using a multimodal large model to create deeper, more meaningful descriptions. This ensures that the key visual information is accurately captured and expressed.
- **Tables**: Similar to images, tables often come with titles that summarize or describe their content, usually found above or below the table. These descriptions are key to understanding the table's purpose and context. Tables contain structured data that may not be fully explained in text alone. We first convert table content into plain text while preserving its structure (i.e., rows and columns), then combine it with the original caption and use a large model to generate detailed, explanatory text.

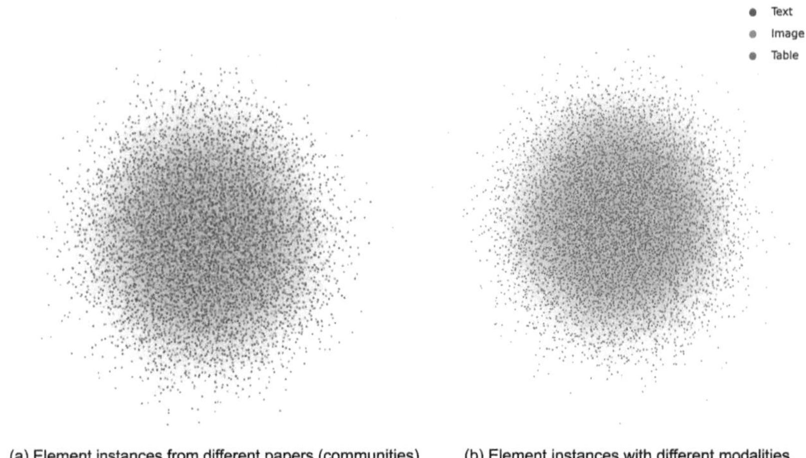

(a) Element instances from different papers (communities)   (b) Element instances with different modalities

Fig. 1. Visualization of element instances in the graph structure. (a) shows instances derived from different papers (communities), with each color representing a distinct paper or community. (b) illustrates instances of elements with different modality types, where colors represent various modalities. The graph highlights both the diversity and interconnectedness of elements across communities and modalities. (Color figure online)

2.3   Text Elements → Global Graph

The core task of this step is to identify and extract nodes and edge instances from the previously extracted textual elements to build a global graph. In this graph, each textual element is viewed as an entity and categorized into one of three modal types: text, image, and table. Text-type nodes are represented using the entity-attribute-value tuple $< id, type, content >$, where id is the index assigned to each sentence during the sentencize process; image-type nodes are represented with the tuple $< base64, type, content >$, where $base64$ is the Base64 encoded string of each image; table-type nodes are denoted by the tuple $< infor, type, content >$, with $infor$ being the table text obtained from the previous step.

The relationships between entities include two main types: one is based on textual references, for example, if a sentence mentions a specific image or table, a reference relationship is established between the node of that sentence and the corresponding image or table node, represented by the entity-relationship-entity tuple $< node, refer\_to, node >$. The other is based on the semantic relationships between the nodes' textual content, where the edge value is the semantic similarity calculated by the model, represented by the tuple $< node, similarity\_value, node >$. This approach not only clarifies the direct connections between different data elements but also delves into their underlying semantic links, as shown in the constructed graph in Fig. 1.

Simultaneously, to optimize the subsequent entity retrieval process, we have created indexes for the Text type's id, the Image type's $base64$, and the Table type's *infor*. The establishment of these indexes significantly enhances the efficiency of queries, allowing for rapid execution of queries based on these key attributes and avoiding a comprehensive scan of the entire database.

2.4   Global Graph → Related Entity → Global Summary

After the construction of the graph is complete, we will receive a user query. A comprehensive search will be conducted across the global graph to identify all nodes that are semantically similar to the query. For each retrieved node, a secondary search is performed within the graph to find nodes that share semantic similarities with the content of the retrieved node, as well as Image and Table nodes that are linked through reference relationships. Subsequently, the content of these Text, Image, and Table nodes is extracted, along with the Base64 encoding of the images and the original text content of the tables that have referential relationships. This aggregated content is then provided as context to a large model, which generates a global summary based on the query.

3   Evaluation

3.1   Dataset

Given our focus on performing query-focused summarization from multiple PDFs and the absence of a suitable dataset in our research, we meticulously created a dataset focusing on medical research papers, considering the following factors: (1) Professional Complexity: Medical literature is filled with specialized terminology and complex concepts; (2) Diversity of Data: Medical literature encompasses a broad spectrum from basic research to clinical practice, including but not limited to drug development, disease diagnosis, treatment plans, and preventive medicine; (3) Currency: Medical research is rapidly evolving, with the latest findings often providing cutting-edge information unavailable in existing large models; (4) Social Impact: The outcomes of medical research significantly influence societal health. Furthermore, the information contained within medical literature is highly valuable to researchers, physicians, and related professionals.

To build our dataset, we first selected 10 common diseases in the medical field, such as Alzheimer's disease and cancer. We then used PubMed to download 10 PDF papers related to each disease. These papers include both broad review articles and in-depth studies on specific subdomains, such as novel treatments and diagnostic techniques.

3.2   Queries

To better assess the effectiveness of the Global Graph RAG system in constructing tasks for broad data meaning, we need to design queries that convey a high-level understanding of the dataset rather than the details of specific texts. We adopted an approach centered around a LLM to automatically generate these queries: after providing a brief description of each disease dataset, we requested the LLM to generate N queries that require an understanding of the entire corpus of papers. In our experiment, we set N = 5, resulting in a total of 50 test queries.

3.3   Metrics

Considering the complexity of evaluating summarization tasks and the lack of gold standard answers for our semantic queries based on global understanding, we have decided to use a head-to-head comparison method with an LLM evaluator. We have carefully selected five target metrics that capture the qualities needed for summarization tasks.

- ***Accuracy.*** Are the answers well-grounded in reliable facts and data with logical and sound reasoning?
- ***Comprehensiveness.*** Do the answers provide sufficient details and background information to cover all key aspects of the question?
- ***Practicality.*** Do the answers offer practical advice or steps that effectively address the question and assist the questioner in their subsequent actions?
- ***Directness.*** Are the answers directly and specifically responding to the question without deviation from the topic?
- ***Readability.*** Are the answers easy to read, using appropriate paragraph divisions, lists, or headings?

To conduct our evaluation, we will present the LLM with a question, target metrics, and a pair of answers, along with a task description instructing the LLM to assess which answer is better based on the given metrics and explain why. If there is a clear winner between the two, the winner will be returned; if both are essentially similar and differences are negligible, it will be deemed a tie. To account for the randomness of the LLM, we will run each pair comparison five times and use the average result.

3.4   Baselines and Configuration

In our work, we chose to use several commercial large-model online interaction platforms as baseline systems, including OpenAI's GPT-4 [6], Alibaba's Qwen [7], and Moonshot's Kimi [8]. These models allow users to directly upload PDF files and perform subsequent information processing and query tasks based on the uploaded PDFs.

In our GGRS system, we use all-MiniLM-L6-v2 [9] from sentence-transformers for calculating sentence similarity, and GPT-4 API from OpenAI (which only accepts text modality) as the underlying large model for generating summaries.

3.5   Results

We conducted a comprehensive evaluation of four different methods—GGRS (GR), GPT-4 (G4), Qwen (QW), and Kimi (KM)—covering five key metrics:

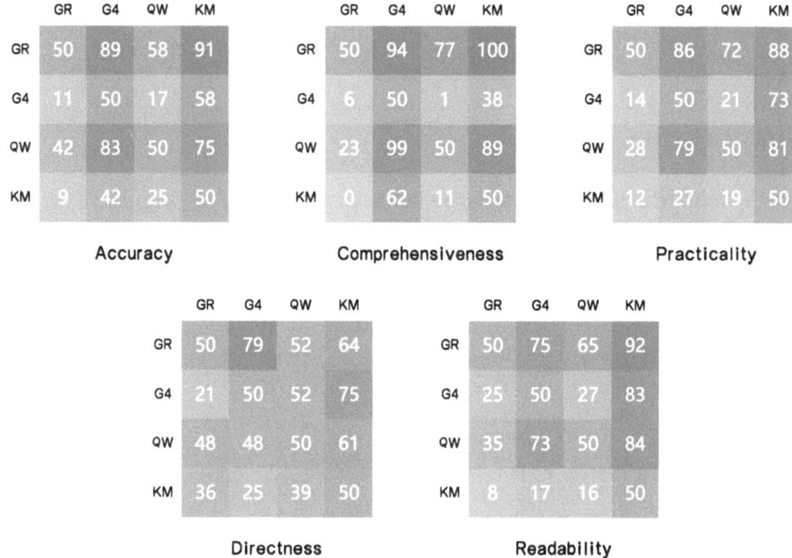

Fig. 2. Comparison Results of GGRS(GR) with GPT-4(G4), Qwen(QW), Kimi(KM) in LLM evaluation, showing the win rates of (row system) over (column system).

accuracy, comprehensiveness, practicality, directness, and readability. The experimental results are shown in Fig. 2.

In terms of accuracy, our GGRS demonstrated a significant advantage, particularly in direct comparisons with other methods, such as against Kimi's generated answers where GGRS achieved a winning rate of 91%. This underscores GGRS's high reliability and precision in understanding and responding to queries. In contrast, GPT-4 performed poorly on this metric, especially in its direct comparison with GGRS, where it only secured a win rate of 11%.

In terms of comprehensiveness, GGRS also demonstrated its exceptional capabilities, achieving a 100% win rate against Kimi, highlighting its ability to cover and process a wide breadth and depth of information when responding to queries. However, GPT-4 performed poorly in this metric compared to GGRS, with only a 6% win rate, and Qwen's performance in comprehensiveness was also significantly lower than its performance in accuracy.

In terms of practicality and directness, GGRS and Qwen performed well in comparisons with GPT-4 and Kimi, with practicality win rates reaching 86% and 88% for GGRS, and 79% and 81% for Qwen, respectively. However, Qwen still falls short of GGRS. The win rates for directness were relatively balanced across systems, with GGRS only having a clear advantage in comparisons with GPT-4 and between GPT-4 and Kimi.

In terms of readability, GGRS consistently outperforms other systems, maintaining a clear advantage. Qwen also ranks well, just behind GGRS, while Kimi lags, consistently trailing the other systems. This highlights GGRS's strengths in delivering information clearly and generating summaries that are easy to understand and accept.

4   Conclusions

We have developed a new system named Global-Graph RAG Summarizer, specifically designed for academic literature containing multimodal information. By combining graph, RAG and LLMs, our system effectively combines text, images and tables to generate high-quality summaries. Experimental results demonstrate that our system excels in both data integration and summary generation, significantly improving the efficiency and accuracy of information retrieval and processing.

5   Limitations and Future Work

Although effective in integrating and summarizing multimodal academic content, the Global-Graph RAG Summarizer faces limitations in computational efficiency and struggles with complex visual elements like dense tables or intricate charts, which may impact summary accuracy. Future work will focus on reducing computational overhead by optimizing algorithms to minimize redundancy in graph generation, retrieval, and summarization, enhancing suitability for low-resource settings. We also plan to improve the handling of complex multimodal data by developing adaptive representations for intricate tables and high-dimensional images, aiming for more comprehensive summaries.

References

1. Lewis, P., et al.: Retrieval-augmented generation for knowledge-intensive NLP tasks. In: Advances in Neural Information Processing Systems, vol. 33, pp. 9459–9474 (2020)
2. Dang, H.T.: Duc 2005: evaluation of question-focused summarization systems. In: Proceedings of the Workshop on Task-Focused Summarization and Question Answering, pp. 48–55 (2006)
3. Baumel, T., Eyal, M., Elhadad, M.: Query focused abstractive summarization: incorporating query relevance, multi-document coverage, and summary length constraints into seq2seq models. arXiv preprint arXiv:1801.07704 (2018)
4. Laskar, M.T.R., Hoque, E., Huang, J.: Query Focused abstractive summarization via incorporating query relevance and transfer learning with transformer models. In: Goutte, C., Zhu, X. (eds.) Canadian AI 2020. LNCS (LNAI), vol. 12109, pp. 342–348. Springer, Cham (2020). https://doi.org/10.1007/978-3-030-47358-7_35
5. Yao, J.G., Wan, X., Xiao. J.: Recent advances in document summarization. Knowl. Inf. Syst. **53**, 297–336 (2017)
6. Achiam, J., et al.: GPT-4 technical report. arXiv preprint arXiv:2303.08774 (2023)
7. Bai, J., et al.: Qwen technical report. arXiv preprint arXiv:2309.16609 (2023)
8. Moonshot: Kimi by moonshot AI (2023). https://kimi.moonshot.cn
9. Hugging Face: sentence-transformers/all-minilm-l6-v2 (2023)

Metric Embedding Initialization-Based Differentially Private and Explainable Graph Clustering

Haochen You[1]($\boxtimes$) and Baojing Liu[2]

[1] Graduate School of Arts and Sciences, Columbia University, New York, USA
hy2854@columbia.edu
[2] School of Artificial Intelligence, Hebei Institute of Communications, Shijiazhuang, People's Republic of China
liubj@hebic.edu.cn

Abstract. Graph clustering under the framework of differential privacy, which aims to process graph-structured data while protecting individual privacy, has been receiving increasing attention. Despite significant achievements in current research, challenges such as high noise, low efficiency and poor interpretability continue to severely constrain the development of this field. In this paper, we construct a differentially private and interpretable graph clustering approach based on metric embedding initialization. Specifically, we construct an SDP optimization, extract the key set and provide a well-initialized clustering configuration using an HST-based initialization method. Subsequently, we apply an established k-median clustering strategy to derive the cluster results and offer comparative explanations for the query set through differences from the cluster centers. Extensive experiments on public datasets demonstrate that our proposed framework outperforms existing methods in various clustering metrics while strictly ensuring privacy.

Keywords: Differential Privacy · Graph Clustering · Interpretability

1 Introduction

Differential Privacy (DP) is a mathematical framework for protecting data privacy, widely applied in fields such as statistical analysis and machine learning [4]. Its core goal is to safeguard individual privacy while providing useful information, ensuring that even with external knowledge, an attacker cannot infer sensitive details about a single individual from query results. DP achieves this by introducing noise through mechanisms such as the Laplace, Gaussian, and exponential mechanisms, and has been widely adopted in real-world scenarios due to strong theoretical guarantees. However, challenges remain in addressing the trade-off between noise-induced utility loss and analysis accuracy, efficiently handling non-standard data, and managing dynamic data like time series [5].

T. Zhu et al. (Eds.): KSEM 2025, LNAI 15923, pp. 9–16, 2026.
https://doi.org/10.1007/978-981-95-3061-8_2

We focus on graph clustering under the framework of differential privacy, an important problem at the intersection of graph theory and data mining [22]. This framework aims to group the nodes in a graph such that nodes within the same group are closely connected, while nodes in different groups are sparsely connected. Graph structures have significant natural advantages in representing data from various modern societal scenarios, but their high dimensionality, sparsity, and scalability pose challenges for designing corresponding algorithms [4].

Spectral methods are one of the key approaches to addressing the above issues, achieving great success in graph clustering problems [1]. However, their application under the differential privacy framework has yet to be deeply explored. Meanwhile, in existing clustering algorithms, particularly those based on iterative optimization, the choice of initial centers is highly sensitive [7,9]. For graph clustering under the framework of differential privacy, there are additional unique challenges, such as high-dimensional data distribution, non-uniformity, high noise, and application-specific requirements (private dataset), which impose even higher demands on the initialization of centers [24].

Our main contributions are given:

(i) We propose a novel graph clustering framework under differential privacy, integrating spectral methods and semidefinite programming.
(ii) We combined HST to provide an initialization scheme for the k-median methods used in graph clustering and presented detailed algorithmic steps.
(iii) We conducted extensive numerical experiments on public datasets, demonstrating the effectiveness and indispensability of each module of our model.

2 Private and Explainable Graph Clustering

Let $G = (V, E)$ be the input graph. Let $u, v \in V$ denote two nodes in the graph. We denote $m = |E|$ as the number of edges and $d_G(u)$ as the degree of node u in G. The parameter $\lambda > 0$ is a user-defined coefficient controlling the trade-off between structural fidelity and cluster separation. The variable b quantifies the balance between cluster volumes. We use SDP to extract the graph clustering structure. Let $\overline{u}, \overline{v} \in \mathbb{R}^d$ denote the vector embeddings of nodes u and v. The optimization expression is as follows:

$$\min \sum_{(u,v) \in E} \|\overline{u} - \overline{v}\|_2^2 + \frac{2 \sum_{u,v \in V} \langle \overline{u}, \overline{v} \rangle^2 \, \mathrm{d}_G(u) \mathrm{d}_G(v)}{\lambda m}$$

$$\text{s.t.} \sum_{u,v \in V} \left(\|\overline{u} - \overline{v}\|_2^2 \, \mathrm{d}_G(u) \mathrm{d}_G(v) \right) \geq 2bm^2, \tag{1}$$

$$\langle \overline{u}, \overline{v} \rangle \geq 0, \text{ for all } u, v \in V; \|\overline{u}\|_2^2 = 1, \text{ for all } u \in V,$$

where $b = \frac{1}{m^2} \sum_{i,j \in [k], i \neq j} \mathrm{vol}_G\left(C_i\right) \mathrm{vol}_G\left(C_j\right) = 1 - \frac{1}{2m^2} \sum_{i \in [k]} \mathrm{vol}_G\left(C_i\right)^2$.

To facilitate efficient optimization, we reformulate the vector-based objective into matrix form. Specifically, we define the unnormalized graph Laplacian as L_G, and the Gram matrix $X \in \mathbb{R}^{n \times n}$ with $X_{i,j} = \frac{1}{n} \overline{v}_i \cdot \overline{v}_j$, where $\overline{v}_i$ is the embedding of node i. Under this formulation, node similarities are captured via inner products, and the trace term $\langle L_G, X \rangle$ corresponds to the spectral cut cost [3]. The regularization term encourages balanced clustering through degree-normalized representations. The resulting optimization problem is:

$$\min_{X \in \mathcal{D}} \langle L_G, X \rangle + \frac{n}{\lambda m} \left\| D_G^{1/2} X D_G^{1/2} \right\|_F^2, \tag{2}$$

where the feasible region $\mathcal{D}$ is defined as:

$$\mathcal{D} := \left\{ \langle D_G L_V D_G, X \rangle \geq \frac{bm^2}{n}, X \succeq 0, X \geq 0, X_{ii} = \frac{1}{n}, \forall i \right\}.$$

We add Gaussian noise W to the matrix and use spectral decomposition to provide a graph embedding for each vertex. The addition of Gaussian noise W to the matrix X_1 ensures (ε, δ)-differential privacy via the Gaussian mechanism. Since the sensitivity of the spectral embedding process is bounded under the Frobenius norm, the noise scale is calibrated accordingly [5].

Algorithm 1. Privacy-Preserving Spectral Embedding.

Input: Global rep. X_1, privacy parameters ε, δ, target number of clusters k

$W \leftarrow \mathcal{N}\left(0, 24(\lambda + 3)m \cdot \frac{\ln(2/\delta)}{\epsilon^2}\right)^{n \times n}$

$X_2 \leftarrow n D_G^{1/2} X_1 D_G^{1/2} + W$

$f_1, \ldots, f_k \leftarrow$ eigenvectors of X_2 for its k smallest eigenvalues

$F(V(G) \rightarrow \mathbb{R}^k) \leftarrow d_G(u)^{-1/2} \left(f_1(u), f_2(u), \ldots, f_k(u)\right)^{\top}$

Output: Embedding representation of vertices F

We utilize the DP exponential mechanism to construct a private ranking set [8], scale the low-dimensional clustering cost to estimate the original high-dimensional cost, and recover the centroid structure. The steps are presented in Algorithm 2. The HST-based initialization introduces Laplace noise to node counts during subtree scoring. As each node query has bounded sensitivity and the Laplace mechanism is applied independently at each level of the tree, the algorithm achieves $(\varepsilon, 0)$-differential privacy.

To implement this initialization strategy, we adopt a HST structure to represent the recursive partitioning of the data space. Specifically, the data point set is recursively divided, with each partition forming smaller subsets. Each node at level i represents a partition of diameter $\Delta/2^{L-i}$, where Δ is the initial diameter and L is the tree depth. The top-level node corresponds to the full dataset, its children represent first-level partitions, and the process continues until each leaf represents a single data point. The resulting HST structure enables both efficient initialization and privacy-preserving subtree scoring [6].

The result of this construction is a well-separated HST, where each node represents a partition, and the leaf nodes represent the specific data points [25]. The detailed steps are presented in Algorithm 3.

Algorithm 2. Critical Set Generation.

Input: Data points $\{x_i\}_n$, primitive dimension d, dimension after reduction d', target # clusters k, privacy parameter ϵ, error parameters λ, α, β, distance parameter p

$\zeta \leftarrow 0.01 \left(\frac{\alpha}{10 \lambda_{p, \alpha/2}} \right)^{p/2}, \Lambda \leftarrow \sqrt{\frac{0.01 d}{\ln(n/\beta) d'}}$

for $i \in \{1, .., n\}$ **do**

    $\tilde{x}_i \leftarrow \Pi_S (x_i)$

    if $\|\tilde{x}_i\| \leq 1/\Lambda$ **then**

        $x_i' = \Lambda \tilde{x}_i$

    else

        $x_i' = 0$

end for

$C \leftarrow PCS^{\epsilon/2}(x_1', \ldots, x_n', \zeta)$ [8], $cost(S_\epsilon) \leftarrow \left(\frac{\ln(n/\beta)}{0.01} \right)^{p/2} NPA(C, k)$ [18]

Output: Critical set C, $cost(S_\epsilon)$

We construct k initial cluster centers from the HST by selecting k high-score nodes as subtree roots, using $score(v) = N_v \cdot 2^{h_v}$, where N_v is the number of data points and h_v is the level of node v. To ensure diversity, selected nodes have no ancestor-descendant relations. If candidates are insufficient, the process repeats. Within each subtree, a center is chosen by greedily descending to the leaf with the highest score. Under differential privacy, Laplace noise is added to node counts before selection. The full procedure is shown in Algorithm 4.

Algorithm 3. Subtree and leaf search.

Input: Hierarchical well-separated tree T, depth of tree L, privacy-protected data point set C', target number of clusters k

$C_0 \leftarrow \emptyset, C_1 \leftarrow \emptyset$

for each node v in T **do**

    $N_v \leftarrow |C' \cap T(v)| + Lap(2^{L - h_v}/\epsilon)$, $score(v) \leftarrow N(v) \cdot 2^{h_v}$

end for

while $|C_1| < k$ **do**

    Add top $(k - |C_1|)$ nodes with highest score to C_1

    for each $v \in C_1$ **do**

    $C_1 = C_1 \backslash \{v\}$, if $\exists \, v' \in C_1$ such that v' is a descendant of v

    end for

for each node v in C_1 **do**

    while v is not a leaf node **do**

        $v \leftarrow \arg_w \max \{N_w, w \in \text{ch}(v)\}$, $ch(v)$ denotes the children nodes of v

    Add v to C_0

end for

Output: Center set of subtree C_0

After completing the aforementioned key steps, we finally introduce the explainability module. Using the original clustering cost from Algorithm 2, we incorporate the fixed-centroid clustering algorithm to restore the clustering structure and cost in the high-dimensional space. The clustering cost is then cal-

---

Algorithm 4. Finding Initial Cluster Centers.

Input: Data point set C
$\triangle \leftarrow \max_{c_1,c_2 \in C} \|c_1 - c_2\|, L \leftarrow \ln \triangle$
Randomly pick a point in C as the root node
for each $c \in C$ **do**
     Set $V_c = [c]$
     for each $c' \in C$ **do**
         Add $c' \in C$ to V_c if $d(c,c') \leq \triangle/2$ and $c' \notin \bigcup_{v \neq c} C_v$
     end for
end for
Set the non-empty clusters V_c as the children nodes of T
for each non-empty cluster V_c **do**
     Run 2-HST $(V_c, L - 1)$ to extend the tree T
     stop until L levels or reaching a leaf node
end for
$C_0 \leftarrow$ **Algorithm 3** (T, L)
Output: Private initial center set $C_0 \subseteq C$

---

culated as a contrastive explanation for query users based on the fixed-centroid results [19]. The final integrated algorithm steps are shown in Algorithm 5.

Algorithm 5. Private and Explainable Graph Clustering.

Input: $G = (V, E)$, target # clusters k, query user set V_s, error parameter β
$X_1 \leftarrow \arg\min_{X \in \mathcal{D}} \langle L_G, X \rangle + \frac{n}{\lambda m} \left\| D_G^{1/2} X D_G^{1/2} \right\|_F^2$
$F \leftarrow$ **Algorithm 1** (X_1)
Critical Set C , $cost(S_\epsilon) \leftarrow$ **Algorithm 2** $(F(u), u \in V)$
Private initial center set $C_0 \subseteq C \leftarrow$ **Algorithm 4** (C)
$\widehat{C}_1, \ldots, \widehat{C}_k \leftarrow$ KMedian $(F(c), c \in C \mid$ Initial center set $C_0)$
$Exp(i) \leftarrow |cost(S_\epsilon) - \left(\frac{\ln(n/\beta)}{0.01} \right)^{\frac{p}{2}} FixedCenter(C, k, x_i)|$ [2,13]
Output: k-partition $\left\{ \widehat{C}_i \right\}$, comparative explanation collection $\{Exp(i) | x_i \in V_s\}$

---

3   Experiments

First, we aim to verify the effectiveness of the metric embedding-based clustering center initialization module (**MEI**), specifically Algorithm 4, through comparative experiments. The baseline models we selected include: **DPFN** [21], **BR-DP** [12], **PP-DOAGT** [10], **QFL-DP** [20], **DNN-SDP** [15]. Due to space limitations, please refer to the arXiv version for detailed experimental setup.

As shown in Fig. 1a and 1b, it can be observed that both the initial cost values at the start of the algorithm and the terminal values at the end of the iterations are significantly lower for our algorithm compared to other similar algorithms.

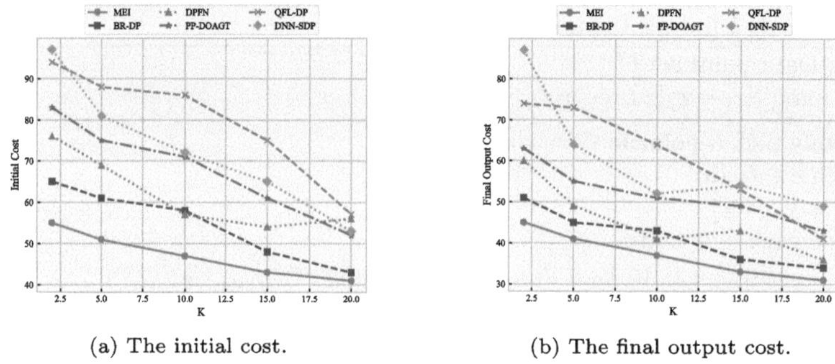

(a) The initial cost.   (b) The final output cost.

Fig. 1. The cost of graph metric experiment.

Table 1. Overall Performance on NMI, Purity, ACC, ARI, and F1.

Method	USPS					Reuters				
(ϵ,δ)-**DP**	0.801	0.638	0.830	0.796	0.805	0.557	0.791	0.714	0.578	0.651
PE	0.831	0.651	0.806	0.819	0.782	0.553	0.766	0.726	0.505	0.629
NpGC	0.829	0.665	0.815	0.802	0.741	0.538	0.782	0.698	0.513	0.673
NMFGC	0.783	0.598	0.835	0.776	0.811	0.496	0.732	0.681	0.577	0.648
SCGC	0.814	0.647	0.825	0.799	0.764	0.510	0.773	0.709	0.582	0.635
Our Model	**0.859**	**0.691**	**0.847**	**0.805**	**0.832**	**0.565**	**0.807**	**0.743**	**0.594**	**0.680**

Method	DBLP					ACM				
(ϵ,δ)-**DP**	0.483	0.462	0.712	0.509	0.740	0.718	0.651	0.933	0.749	0.901
PE	0.479	0.473	0.758	0.496	0.732	0.722	0.610	0.905	0.748	0.881
NpGC	0.466	0.415	0.735	0.478	0.694	0.709	0.617	0.931	0.754	0.908
NMFGC	0.457	0.478	0.764	0.469	0.750	0.688	0.647	0.862	0.771	0.870
SCGC	0.476	0.458	0.741	0.475	0.760	0.727	0.650	0.919	0.764	0.889
Our Model	**0.476**	**0.493**	**0.784**	**0.518**	**0.762**	**0.733**	**0.679**	**0.956**	**0.804**	**0.917**

Method	CiteSeer					HHAR				
(ϵ,δ)-**DP**	0.437	0.554	0.716	0.488	0.647	0.835	0.703	0.870	0.812	0.902
PE	0.418	0.537	0.723	0.499	0.630	0.844	0.666	0.805	0.824	0.873
NpGC	0.426	0.517	0.708	0.517	0.637	0.840	0.705	0.880	0.859	0.891
NMFGC	0.469	0.538	0.719	0.502	0.646	0.811	0.647	0.847	0.845	0.862
SCGC	0.441	0.561	0.732	0.489	0.639	0.0259	0.828	0.867	0.863	0.884
Our Model	**0.471**	**0.584**	**0.749**	**0.528**	**0.657**	**0.853**	**0.726**	**0.895**	**0.879**	**0.904**

This demonstrates its superior ability in identifying good initial clustering centers and providing favorable preconditions for the subsequent clustering process.

Next, we conduct experiments on publicly available datasets. The selected datasets include **USPS** [16], **Reuters** [17], **DBLP**[1], **ACM**[2], **CiteSeer**[3], and **HHAR** [23]. Comparable baselines were selected, including (ϵ, δ)-**DP** [9], **PE** [6], **NpGC** [26], **NMFGC** [11], **SCGC** [14]. From the data in Table 1, it can be seen that our proposed model achieves significant improvements over existing models in most metrics while ensuring privacy protection.

4 Conclusion

We construct a differentially private and interpretable graph clustering framework based on metric embedding initialization and key set construction. Experiments on public datasets demonstrate the effectiveness and indispensability of each component of our model. Our research significantly addressing many of the current challenges and laying a solid foundation for broader applications.

References

1. Bernardi, C., Maday, Y.: Spectral methods. In: Handbook of Numerical Analysis, vol. 5, pp. 209–485 (1997)
2. Charikar, M., Guha, S., Tardos, É., Shmoys, D.B.: A constant-factor approximation algorithm for the k-median problem. In: Proceedings of the Thirty-First Annual ACM Symposium on Theory of Computing, pp. 1–10 (1999)
3. Chen, Y., Sanghavi, S., Xu, H.: Improved graph clustering. IEEE Trans. Inf. Theory **60**(10), 6440–6455 (2014)
4. Dwork, C.: Differential privacy. In: Bugliesi, M., Preneel, B., Sassone, V., Wegener, I. (eds.) ICALP 2006. LNCS, vol. 4052, pp. 1–12. Springer, Heidelberg (2006). https://doi.org/10.1007/11787006_1
5. Dwork, C.: Differential privacy: a survey of results. In: Agrawal, M., Du, D., Duan, Z., Li, A. (eds.) TAMC 2008. LNCS, vol. 4978, pp. 1–19. Springer, Heidelberg (2008). https://doi.org/10.1007/978-3-540-79228-4_1
6. Fan, C., Li, P., Li, X.: K-median clustering via metric embedding: towards better initialization with differential privacy. In: Advances in Neural Information Processing Systems, vol. 36 (2024)
7. Ge, T., et al.: Optimally ordered orthogonal neighbor joining trees for hierarchical cluster analysis. IEEE Trans. Vis. Comput. Graph. (2023)
8. Ghazi, B., Kumar, R., Manurangsi, P.: Differentially private clustering: tight approximation ratios. In: Advances in Neural Information Processing Systems, vol. 33, pp. 4040–4054 (2020)
9. He, W., Fichtenberger, H., Peng, P.: A differentially private clustering algorithm for well-clustered graphs. arXiv preprint arXiv:2403.14332 (2024)
10. Huang, L., Wu, J., Shi, D., Dey, S., Shi, L.: Differential privacy in distributed optimization with gradient tracking. IEEE Trans. Autom. Control (2024)

---

[1] https://dblp.uni-trier.de/.
[2] https://dl.acm.org/.
[3] https://paperswithcode.com/dataset/citeseer.

11. Jannesari, V., Keshvari, M., Berahmand, K.: A novel nonnegative matrix factorization-based model for attributed graph clustering by incorporating complementary information. Expert Syst. Appl. **242**, 122799 (2024)

12. Jiang, B., Du, J., Sharma, S., Yan, Q.: Budget recycling differential privacy. In: 2024 IEEE Symposium on Security and Privacy (SP), pp. 1028–1046. IEEE (2024)

13. Kanungo, T., Mount, D.M., Netanyahu, N.S., Piatko, C.D., Silverman, R., Wu, A.Y.: A local search approximation algorithm for K-means clustering. In: Proceedings of the Eighteenth Annual Symposium on Computational Geometry, pp. 10–18 (2002)

14. Kulatilleke, G.K., Portmann, M., Chandra, S.S.: SCGC: self-supervised contrastive graph clustering. Neurocomputing **611**, 128629 (2025)

15. Kumar, G.S., Premalatha, K., Maheshwari, G.U., Kanna, P.R., Vijaya, G., Nivaashini, M.: Differential privacy scheme using Laplace mechanism and statistical method computation in deep neural network for privacy preservation. Eng. Appl. Artif. Intell. **128**, 107399 (2024)

16. Le Cun, Y., et al.: Handwritten zip code recognition with multilayer networks. In: [1990] Proceedings. 10th International Conference on Pattern Recognition, vol. 2, pp. 35–40. IEEE (1990)

17. Lewis, D.D., Yang, Y., Russell-Rose, T., Li, F.: RCV1: a new benchmark collection for text categorization research. J. Mach. Learn. Res. **5**, 361–397 (2004)

18. Makarychev, K., Makarychev, Y., Razenshteyn, I.: Performance of Johnson-Lindenstrauss transform for K-means and K-medians clustering. In: Proceedings of the 51st Annual ACM SIGACT Symposium on Theory of Computing, pp. 1027–1038 (2019)

19. Nguyen, D., Vetzler, A., Kraus, S., Vullikanti, A.: Contrastive explainable clustering with differential privacy. arXiv preprint arXiv:2406.04610 (2024)

20. Rofougaran, R., Yoo, S., Tseng, H.H., Chen, S.Y.C.: Federated quantum machine learning with differential privacy. In: ICASSP 2024-2024 IEEE International Conference on Acoustics, Speech and Signal Processing (ICASSP), pp. 9811–9815. IEEE (2024)

21. Romijnders, R., Louizos, C., Asano, Y.M., Welling, M.: Protect your score: contact-tracing with differential privacy guarantees. In: Proceedings of the AAAI Conference on Artificial Intelligence, vol. 38, pp. 14829–14837 (2024)

22. Schaeffer, S.E.: Graph clustering. Comput. Sci. Rev. **1**(1), 27–64 (2007)

23. Stisen, A., et al.: Smart devices are different: assessing and mitigating mobile sensing heterogeneities for activity recognition. In: Proceedings of the 13th ACM Conference on Embedded Networked Sensor Systems, pp. 127–140 (2015)

24. Wang, Y., Yu, S., Gu, Y., Shun, J.: Fast parallel algorithms for Euclidean minimum spanning tree and hierarchical spatial clustering. In: Proceedings of the 2021 International Conference on Management of Data, pp. 1982–1995 (2021)

25. You, H.: Prediction and classification model of hornet sighting report in Washington state based on deep learning. Appl. Comput. Eng. **48**, 87–95 (2024)

26. Yu, S., et al.: A non-parametric graph clustering framework for multi-view data. In: Proceedings of the AAAI Conference on Artificial Intelligence, vol. 38, pp. 16558–16567 (2024)

M³Net: Multimodal-Feature-Masked Networks for Fake News Detection

Zhaokang Zhang, Xiaorui Luo, Chi Jiang, Ranran Wang, Yiran Wang, and Yin Zhang$^{(\boxtimes)}$ iD

School of Information and Communication Engineering, University of Electronic Science and Technology of China, Chengdu 611731, China
`zhangyin123@uestc.edn.cn`

Abstract. The proliferation of multi-modal fake news poses an increasing threat to society. To deal with this issue, several algorithms have proposed to detect fake news by infusing multimodal information. However, the high-dimensional nature of multimodal features constrains the efficiency of fake news detection. To address this challenge, this paper proposes a Multimodal-Feature-masked Networks for fake news detection. Specifically, a learnable dimensional mask is proposed to adaptively reduce the interference of irrelevant information, effectively alleviating the adverse effects of high-dimensional features. Additionally, to utilize text-image consistency as a crucial criterion for classification, we devise a two-stage training strategy for cross-modal consistency detection and news veracity classification to enhance detection accuracy. Through extensive experiments on real-world datasets, the proposed approach is validated to achieve higher accuracy and less runtime compared with the previous work.

Keywords: Multi-modal fake news detection · Learnable dimensional mask · Two-stage training strategy

1   Introduction

The prevalence of social media has led to widespread exposure to fake news. Multimodal news, combining images and text, is particularly appealing and spreads rapidly, making multimodal detection increasingly urgent.

The general paradigm involves transforming news into latent representations for binary classification. Existing methods face challenges:

- Feature dilution: Complex content and images dilute discriminative features.
- Cross-modal consistency: This important higher-order feature for judgment is rarely considered.

Pre-trained models (e.g., BERT [5], ResNet [7]) extract high-dimensional features containing task-irrelevant information. High dimensionality can decrease accuracy as task-related semantic information is limited [10]. Furthermore, fake

T. Zhu et al. (Eds.): KSEM 2025, LNAI 15923, pp. 17–24, 2026.
https://doi.org/10.1007/978-981-95-3061-8_3

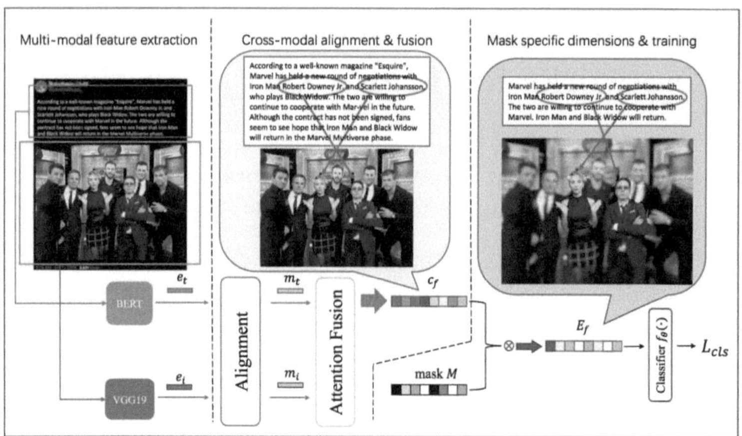

Fig. 1. The functionality of each part of the M^3Net. First, the text and images are encoded by pretrained models. Next, cross-modal consistency is detected and semantic interactions are captured through the alignment and fusion stages. Finally, a learnable dimensional mask is employed to force the model to focus on task-relevant information, detecting the veracity of news.

news often pairs text with misleading images [2], yet consistency is seldom leveraged in detection [15].

In this paper, we propose a staged training model with a masking mechanism, M^3Net, as shown in the Fig. 1. We summarize our main contributions as follows:

– A learnable dimensional mask updated via gradient effects to weaken dimensions with irrelevant information, improving accuracy.
– A staged training strategy separating consistency detection from veracity classification, embedding consistency as a high-order feature for better performance.
– Experiments verify the generalization of consistency judgment for multimodal tasks.

The code for our method is in https://github.com/xawmx/MMMNet.

2 Related Work

2.1 Unimodal Approach

Early methods used single modalities. Text-based approaches evolved from basic CNNs [18] to two-level CNNs [12] and VAEs [4]. Image-based methods like VS [9] detected manipulation signs, improved by MVNN [11] using spatial and frequency features.

2.2 Multimodal Approach

Methods incorporate images and text. EANN [16] used event discriminators. Spot-Fake [14] used BERT and VGG19. MFAN [19] fused text, visual, and social features via attention. SAFE [20] measured text-image correlation. CAFE [3] addressed cross-modal ambiguity. BMR [17] decoupled consistency learning, incorporating image semantics. Alignment of modalities for optimal fusion remains a challenge.

3 Methodology

3.1 Problem Definition

For a given multimodal news dataset $D = \{X, Y\}$, where $X = \{x_1, x_2, \ldots, x_n\}$, and $Y = \{y_1, y_2, \ldots, y_n\}$, with 0 for real news and 1 for fake news. $x^s = \{t^s, i^s\}$ ($text, image$).

Cross-modal Consistency Detection: Binary classification: same news (positive, label=1) vs. different news (negative, label=-1). Construct dataset $D^s = \{X^s, Y^s\}$ from D. The goal is to learn mapping g.

Fake News Detection: Binary classification. Learn function f_θ and a dimensional mask M:

$$y_{pre} = f_\theta(x \otimes M) = \underset{y_i \in Y}{argmax} P(y_i \mid x \otimes M) \tag{1}$$

3.2 Overall Framework

M³Net mainly consists of text and image feature extraction module, an alignment module, a feature fusion module, and a classifier module with masking mechanism.

Feature Extraction Module. Given the text t of a news article, we use the pre-trained BERT [5] model to extract the [CLS] token as the text feature $e_t \in \mathbb{R}^{768}$. For the image i, we use the pre-trained VGG19 [13] model to extract the last layer output as the image feature $e_i \in \mathbb{R}^{1000}$.

Alignment Module. MLPs map to e_t, e_i shared space $m_t, m_i \in \mathbb{R}^{64}$.

Feature Fusion Module. For aligned m_t, m_i: A co-attention mechanism [8] is introduced to compute attention weights:

$$Co-att_{i \to t} = softmax(m_t \times m_i / \sqrt{dim}) \,;\, Co-att_{t \to i} = softmax(m_i \times m_t / \sqrt{dim}) \tag{2}$$

To capture intricate interactions, we compute the interaction matrix between textual and visual features by calculating their outer product:

$$e_f = flatten(\hat{m}_t \times \hat{m}_i) \tag{3}$$

The resulting correlation matrix is flattened into a vector $e_f \in \mathbb{R}^{64}$.

Classifier Module with Masking Mechanism. Apply learnable mask $M \in \mathbb{R}^{64}$(initialized to 1):

$$E_f = e_f \otimes M \tag{4}$$

3.3   Stage 1: Cross-Modal Consistency Detection

In alignment module, we use InfoNCE loss [6] to assess cross-modal consistency:

$$InfoNCE = -\sum_{i=1}^{N} log \frac{exp(sim(z_i, z_i^{+}))}{\exp(sim(z_i, z_i^{+})) + \sum_{j=1,j\neq i}^{N} exp(sim(z_i, z_j^{-}))} \tag{5}$$

In the formula, "sim" is cosine similarity, "z_i^{+}" is a sample with the same label as "z_i" and "z_i^{-}" is the opposite. Update alignment module parameters $g()$ via backpropagation. Freeze alignment module after this stage. Consistency is embedded into aligned vectors m_t, m_i.

3.4   Stage 2: Fusion and Authenticity Classification

Update fusion module, classifier f_θ, and mask M. The first step involves training the classifier $f_\theta()$ by minimizing the loss L_{cls} and using gradient descent to update parameters θ.

$$\theta' = \theta - l_\theta \nabla_\theta L_{cls}(f_\theta(e_f \otimes M)) \tag{6}$$

where l_θ is the learning rate, θ' denotes the model parameters after the first gradient update.

In the second step, regarding the dimensional mask M, we employ a second-order derivative technique to minimize interference.Update based on impact on classifier performance after θ update:

$$\underset{M}{argmin} L_{cls}(f_{\theta'}(e_f \otimes M)) \tag{7}$$

Dimensions with minimal impact on loss are masked (weights reduced), enhancing gradients for discriminative dimensions. Iterate until convergence.

4   Experiments

In this section, we conducted experiments on two real-world multimodal news datasets to evaluate M^3Net. We performed 15 trials per experiment, with results averaged after removing the highest and lowest values.

4.1   Datasets and Baselines

We utilized two multi-modal news datasets from Weibo [8] and Twitter [1]. In the experiments, we configure all baselines consistently with the settings provided in their respective papers, including both unimodal approaches (BERT [5] and MVNN [11]) and multimodal approaches (EANN [16], Spot-fake [14], MFAN [19], CAFE [3] and BMR [17]).

Table 1. The overall performance

	Model	Weibo				Twitter			
		Acc	Pre	Rec	F1-score	Acc	Pre	Rec	F1-score
Uni- modal	BERT	0.7320	0.7274	0.7422	0.7347	0.6902	0.7155	0.6637	0.6814
	MVNN	0.6479	0.6104	0.6599	0.6342	0.6585	0.6256	0.6679	0.6455
Multi- modal	EANN	0.8271	0.8316	0.8203	0.8259	0.7833	0.7707	0.8066	0.7882
	Spot-fake	0.8267	0.8219	0.8334	0.8276	0.7778	0.7722	0.7880	0.7801
	MFAN	0.8890	0.8653	0.9214	0.8925	0.8082	0.8106	0.8044	0.8074
	CAFE	0.8719	0.8647	0.8818	0.8731	0.8159	0.8220	0.8064	0.8141
	BMR	0.8923	0.8829	0.9046	0.8936	0.8346	0.8182	**0.8584**	0.8467
	M^{3}Net	**0.9318**	**0.9241**	**0.9383**	**0.9311**	**0.8612**	**0.8643**	0.8580	**0.8607**

4.2 Comparative Study

The performance of M^{3}Net compared with the aforementioned baselines is shown in Table 1. M^{3}Net achieved excellent performance on both the Weibo and Twitter datasets, outperforming existing baseline models across most evaluation metrics. Multimodal methods consistently outperformed unimodal ones, highlighting the benefits of combining cross-modal information. BMR is the strongest baseline, performs well by balancing cross-modal consistency and semantic information but is surpassed by M^{3}Net in most metrics.

4.3 Ablation Study

To gain insights into the effectiveness of each component in our proposed model, we conduct a series of experiments evaluating the impact of different modules. Specifically, we design experiments comparing M^{3}Net and its variants in Table 2.

Table 2. Ablation experiments results

Methods	Weibo				Twitter			
	Acc	Pre	Rec	F1-score	Acc	Pre	Rec	F1-score
w/o A	0.9103	0.9084	0.9126	0.9106	0.8232	0.8240	0.8220	0.8230
w/o C	0.9127	0.9047	0.9226	0.9135	0.8196	0.8276	0.8074	0.8173
w/o M	0.8833	0.8665	0.9062	0.8859	0.8007	0.8001	0.8018	0.8009
M^{3}Net-cos	0.9257	0.9174	0.9323	0.9248	0.8446	0.8507	0.8320	0.8412
M^{3}Net	**0.9318**	**0.9241**	**0.9383**	**0.9311**	**0.8612**	**0.8643**	**0.8580**	**0.8607**

Ablation experiments shows that removing any module (modality alignment, feature fusion, or dimensional mask) led to performance degradation, emphasizing the contribution of each component. InfoNCE loss outperformed cosine loss as it captures the overall distribution of negative samples.

Experiments on random masking indicated that a small amount of random masking improved performance by concealing irrelevant information, but excessive masking reduced performance by losing valuable information, and even the best random masking performance was inferior to M^{3}Net, validating the effectiveness of the learnable dimensional mask.

4.4   Efficiency Performance Analysis

Table 3. Different backbone models add dimensional mask

-2*Methods	Weibo				Twitter			
	Acc	Pre	Rec	F1-score	Acc	Pre	Rec	F1-score
BERT	0.7320	0.7274	0.7422	0.7347	0.6902	0.7155	0.6637	0.6814
BERT+Mask	0.7927	0.7832	0.8026	0.7904	0.7383	0.7251	0.7723	0.7481
Spot-fake	0.8267	0.8219	0.8334	0.8276	0.7778	0.7722	0.7880	0.7801
Spot-fake+Mask	0.8659	0.8592	0.8709	0.8650	0.7967	0.7926	0.7992	0.8013
CAFE	0.8719	0.8647	0.8818	0.8731	0.8159	0.8220	0.8064	0.8141
CAFE+Mask	0.8942	0.8867	0.9003	0.8934	0.8290	0.8405	0.8215	0.8302
BMR	0.8923	0.8829	0.9046	0.8936	0.8346	0.8182	0.8584	0.8467
BMR+Mask	0.9206	0.9152	0.9251	0.9202	0.8571	0.8635	0.8528	0.8581

M^{3}Net had the shortest training runtime and fewer parameters compared to most baselines in Fig. 2. Introducing the dimensional mask to other baselines in Table 3 improved their performance without significantly increasing parameters or runtime.

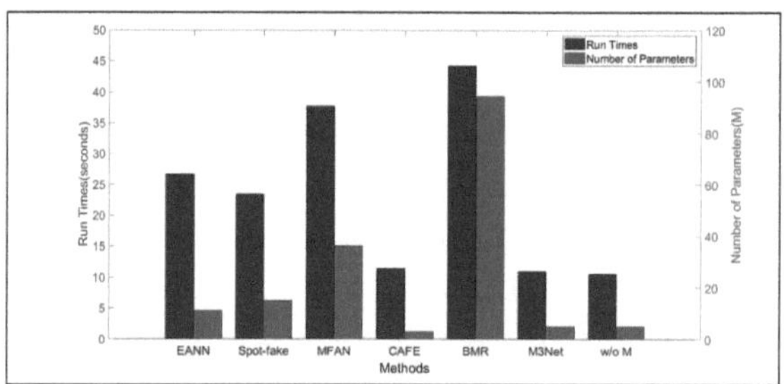

Fig. 2. Running time and the number of model parameters

5 Conclusion

In this paper, a dimensional mask is introduced to multimodal fake news detection to mask the dimensions containing irrelevant information. We designed a staged training strategy that embeds cross-modal consistency as a higher-order feature into the aligned vectors. Experimental evaluations conducted on two real-world datasets underscore the efficacy of our proposed model, it consistently achieves optimal results across a majority of performance metrics, accompanied by the added benefit of minimal runtime.

References

1. Boididou, C., Papadopoulos, S., Zampoglou, M., Apostolidis, L., Papadopoulou, O., Kompatsiaris, Y.: Detection and visualization of misleading content on twitter. Int. J. Multimedia Inf. Retrieval **7**(1), 71–86 (2018)
2. Chatterjee, M., Pal, S.: Busting fake news: need for digital media literacy. In: Rise of the Digital Human, 4th All India Media Conference, Udaipur, Rajasthan. Accessed February, vol. 14, p. 2022 (2019)
3. Chen, Y., et al.: Cross-modal ambiguity learning for multimodal fake news detection. In: Proceedings of the ACM Web Conference 2022, pp. 2897–2905 (2022)
4. Cheng, M., Nazarian, S., Bogdan, P.: VROC: variational autoencoder-aided multi-task rumor classifier based on text. In: Proceedings of the Web Conference 2020, pp. 2892–2898 (2020)
5. Devlin, J., Chang, M.W., Lee, K., Toutanova, K.: BERT: pre-training of deep bidirectional transformers for language understanding. arXiv preprint arXiv:1810.04805 (2018)
6. He, K., Fan, H., Wu, Y., Xie, S., Girshick, R.: Momentum contrast for unsupervised visual representation learning. In: Proceedings of the IEEE/CVF Conference on Computer Vision and Pattern Recognition, pp. 9729–9738 (2020)
7. He, K., Zhang, X., Ren, S., Sun, J.: Deep residual learning for image recognition. In: Proceedings of the IEEE Conference on Computer Vision and Pattern Recognition, pp. 770–778 (2016)
8. Jin, Z., Cao, J., Guo, H., Zhang, Y., Luo, J.: Multimodal fusion with recurrent neural networks for rumor detection on microblogs. In: Proceedings of the 25th ACM International Conference on Multimedia, pp. 795–816 (2017)
9. Jin, Z., Cao, J., Zhang, Y., Zhou, J., Tian, Q.: Novel visual and statistical image features for microblogs news verification. IEEE Trans. Multimedia **19**(3), 598–608 (2016)
10. Li, J., et al.: Metamask: revisiting dimensional confounder for self-supervised learning. arXiv, 16 September 2022. Accessed 30 Nov 2022
11. Qi, P., Cao, J., Yang, T., Guo, J., Li, J.: Exploiting multi-domain visual information for fake news detection. In: 2019 IEEE International Conference on Data Mining (ICDM), pp. 518–527. IEEE (2019)
12. Qian, F., Gong, C., Sharma, K., Liu, Y.: Neural user response generator: fake news detection with collective user intelligence. In: IJCAI, vol. 18, pp. 3834–3840 (2018)
13. Simonyan, K., Zisserman, A.: Very deep convolutional networks for large-scale image recognition. arXiv preprint arXiv:1409.1556 (2014)

14. Singhal, S., Shah, R.R., Chakraborty, T., Kumaraguru, P., Satoh, S.: Spotfake: a multi-modal framework for fake news detection. In: 2019 IEEE Fifth International Conference on Multimedia Big Data (BigMM), pp. 39–47. IEEE (2019)
15. Tufchi, S., Yadav, A., Ahmed, T.: A comprehensive survey of multimodal fake news detection techniques: advances, challenges, and opportunities. Int. J. Multimedia Inf. Retrieval **12**(2), 28 (2023)
16. Wang, Y., et al.: EANN: event adversarial neural networks for multi-modal fake news detection. In: Proceedings of the 24th ACM SIGKDD International Conference on Knowledge Discovery and Data Mining, pp. 849–857 (2018)
17. Ying, Q., Hu, X., Zhou, Y., Qian, Z., Zeng, D., Ge, S.: Bootstrapping multi-view representations for fake news detection. In: Proceedings of the AAAI Conference on Artificial Intelligence, vol. 37, pp. 5384–5392 (2023)
18. Yu, F., Liu, Q., Wu, S., Wang, L., Tan, T., et al.: A convolutional approach for misinformation identification. In: IJCAI, pp. 3901–3907 (2017)
19. Zheng, J., Zhang, X., Guo, S., Wang, Q., Zang, W., Zhang, Y.: MFAN: multi-modal feature-enhanced attention networks for rumor detection. In: IJCAI (2022)
20. Zhou, X., Wu, J., Zafarani, R.: Safe: similarity-aware multi-modal fake news detection (2020). Preprint. arXiv **200304981**, 2 (2020)

TB-DML4HS: A Task-Based Modeling and Causal Effect Estimation Method Using DML for Heterogeneous UAV Swarm

Jiabao Wang, Guang Yang, Lingzhong Meng, Youdi Gong, and Yuxi Ma[(✉)]

Institute of Software Chinese Academy of Sciences, Beijing, China
{wangjiabao2023,yangguang,lingzhong,gongyoudi,mayuxi}@iscas.ac.cn

Abstract. Heterogeneous UAV swarms demonstrate exceptional practical value and scalability in complex scenarios. However, challenges such as the difficulty in modeling heterogeneous UAV swarm tasks and the unclear intrinsic collaboration mechanisms have hindered the optimization of swarm configurations. To address these issues, we propose TB-DML4HS, a task-based, node-level modeling and causal effect analysis method using Double Machine Learning (DML) for heterogeneous UAV swarms. Specifically, TB-DML4HS first decomposes task objectives and events for heterogeneous swarm tasks and constructs a node-level network-structured model. It then employs the DML method to estimate causal effects among various events during task execution, analyzes the contribution rates of heterogeneous nodes within the swarm, and provides optimization suggestions for node configurations to ultimately enhance swarm task performance. Experimental results demonstrate that TB-DML4HS effectively estimates the overall performance with an expected error of less than 5%, and the proposed optimizations significantly improve the specific performance of UAV swarms in current tasks.

Keywords: Heterogeneous UAV Swarm · Causal Effect Estimation · Double Machine Learning · Network-Structured Task Modeling

1 Introduction

In recent years, heterogeneous UAV swarms, as a representative of swarm intelligence technologies, have undergone rapid development, marking the entry of swarm intelligence into a new era characterized by multi-modal collaboration [1,2].

However, research on heterogeneous UAV swarms also faces significant challenges. First, the control strategies for heterogeneous UAV swarms typically involve decentralized decision-making, where interactions between different types of individuals are complex, dynamic, and time-varying [5,6]. Second, the underlying intelligent mechanisms and collaboration dynamics within UAV swarms, as

T. Zhu et al. (Eds.): KSEM 2025, LNAI 15923, pp. 25–35, 2026.
https://doi.org/10.1007/978-981-95-3061-8_4

well as the impact of specific swarm rules on task performance, remain black-box states to researchers [3]. Obscure collaboration mechanisms and the latent effects of swarm rules lead to challenges in optimizing swarm configurations, especially in heterogeneous UAV swarms [4].

Motivated by these objectives, we propose TB-DML4HS, a novel node-level modeling and contribution analysis framework for heterogeneous UAV swarm tasks. Our key contributions are as follows:

- We propose TB-DML4HS—a task-based modeling and causal effect analysis method using Double Machine Learning (DML). By decomposing task objectives and events and integrating node-level network-structured modeling, this framework pioneers the application of DML to causal inference in heterogeneous UAV swarms, thereby addressing the challenges of modeling heterogeneous swarm tasks and analyzing collaboration mechanisms.
- By decomposing task events into sub-events and constructing a network-structured causality graph, TB-DML4HS achieves transparent modeling of the task execution process. At the node level, it establishes associations among environmental variables, node attributes, and task performance, thereby enhancing the interpretability of complex collaboration mechanisms and providing a structured causal basis for configuration optimization.
- TB-DML4HS achieves an expected error of $<5\%$ in estimating the overall performance, significantly outperforming traditional methods. Additionally, the optimization suggestions based on causal effects improve swarm performance in specific tasks (e.g., task success rate, energy efficiency), offering quantifiable decision support for dynamic resource allocation in heterogeneous swarms.

2   Related Work

2.1   UAV Swarm Evaluation Methods

With the rapid progress of UAV swarm tech, evaluating UAV swarms has become a key research focus [8]. As swarms grow larger, evaluating and optimizing whole swarm performance is a major challenge [9,10]. Traditional methods use metrics like reliability [11], resilience [12], and robustness [13], along with statistical analysis and simulations based on empirical data. Some studies propose multi-objective optimization models to assess resource allocation and collaboration efficiency during tasks [14–16]. These methods analyze swarm performance in detail but struggle to accurately capture UAV collaboration and its effect on overall outcomes.

2.2   Causal Effect Estimation Methods

Current research on causal effect estimation methods primarily centers on managing various data types and selecting suitable causal inference models. Classical methods like Propensity Score Matching (PSM) and Inverse Probability

Weighting (IPW) are common in social sciences and healthcare but struggle with continuous treatments. To address this, Huling et al. proposed a new weighting method for robust causal effect estimation with continuous variables [17]. Meanwhile, Chernozhukov et al. introduced Double Machine Learning (DML), combining machine learning and causal inference to handle confounding when randomized trials are not feasible [18]. Consequently, integrating these methods with UAV swarm task evaluation presents a promising yet under-explored research avenue.

3   Methodology

3.1   Overview

This study attempts to apply causal effect estimation methods and task decomposition techniques to perform node-level contribution analysis for large-scale heterogeneous UAV swarms. We propose the TB-DML4HS, which automatically analyzes historical data, constructs, and fills an event-benefit causal graph, and then uses this graph to assess the contribution of UAV nodes during task execution, as shown in Fig. 1.

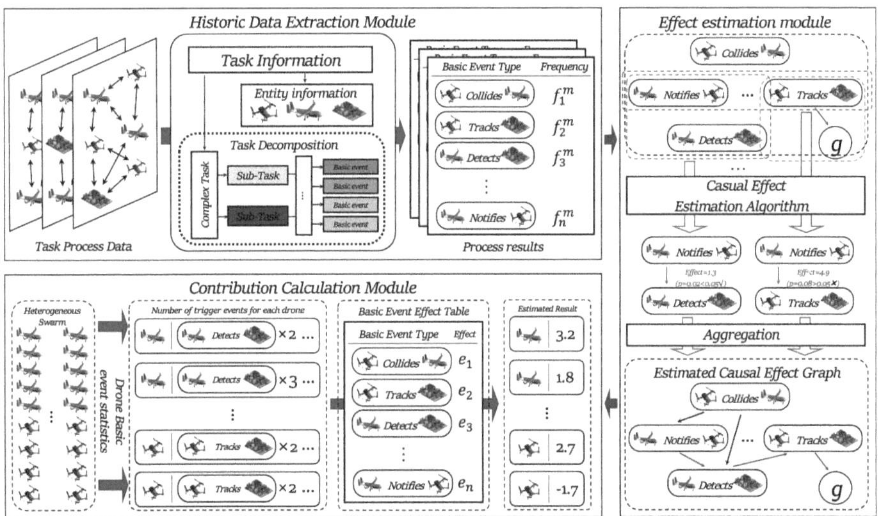

Fig. 1. The overall framework of TB-DML4HS.

3.2   Historic Data Extraction Module

The UAV swarms' tasks typically involve one or more task objectives, which are often challenging and composed of multiple basic events. Direct analysis of such complex task execution processes is difficult. Therefore, we decompose the complex task execution process to derive multiple basic tasks that constitute the complex task. The extraction process involves four main steps: entity information organization, basic event type statistics, event quantification, and basic event statistics. A specific example of task decomposition is illustrated below.

Assume the current task is: constructing a UAV swarm composed of 500 reconnaissance UAVs (RUs) and 500 patrol UAVs (PUs) to track moving targets in a target area. The PUs conduct carpet search in the target area and report suspicious targets to the nearest RU within communication range. The RUs roam within the target area and, upon receiving a report from a PU, proceed to track the suspicious target. If a RU locks onto the target and follows it for more than 20 s, it is considered a successful track, and the task score is increased by 10. During task execution, avoiding any unnecessary collisions is a priority.

- **Entity Information Organization:** This process involves recording all entities that appear in the complex task to ensure no otasks when later conducting basic event type statistics. The entities involved in the current complex task include RUs, PUs, suspicious targets, and external entities.
- **Basic Event Type Statistics:** This process extracts possible basic event types that may occur in the complex task. A basic event can be represented by a triplet ¡s, r, t¿, where s and t are the subject and object of the event, respectively, and r represents the relationship.
- **Event Quantification:** Event quantification represents all basic event types in a measurable format, making it easier for the system to classify entities and judge relationships. Entity classification is mainly performed by recognizing the category of the entity.
- **Basic Event Nature Classification:** Among the decomposed basic events, some directly influence the final task score and are termed direct events. The subsequent analysis focuses on estimating the causal effect between indirect events and direct events, as well as between different indirect events, to evaluate and calculate the contribution of UAV nodes.
- **Basic Event Statistics:** After completing the above steps, the system can traverse historical data and count the occurrences of each type of basic event.

3.3 Effect Estimation Module

The main function of this module is to construct the basic event causal effect graph based on the historical experience data provided by the data extraction module. This causal effect graph serves as the basis for subsequent UAV node contribution analysis. Effect estimation is carried out in two main steps: basic event causal effect graph initialization and basic event causal effect graph filling.

To make the following explanations clearer, let the variables in the data provided by the data extraction module be denoted as $D = \langle g, P, S \rangle$, where g represents the task score, $P = \{p_1, p_2, ..., p_n\}$ is the set of direct events, and $S = \{s_1, s_2, ..., s_m\}$ is the set of indirect events.

Below, the steps for effect estimation will be demonstrated using the task described earlier as an example:

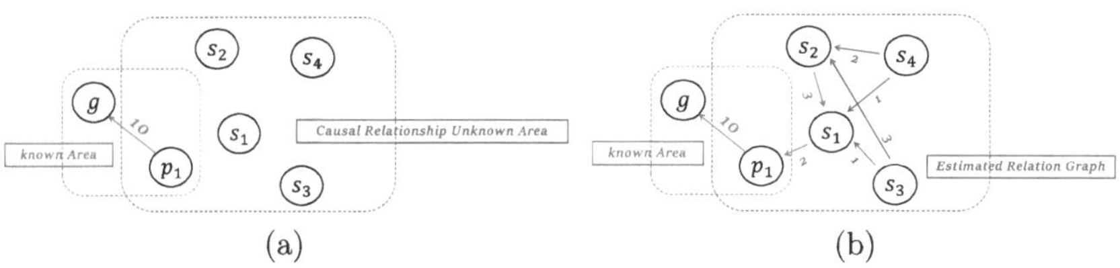

Fig. 2. Causal Effect Diagram. (a) Origin graph of effect casual diagram. (b) Finished graph of effect casual diagram.

- **Basic Event Causal Effect Graph Initialization:** This step aims to preliminarily construct the structure of the basic event causal effect graph. These events are labeled as p_1, s_1, s_2, s_3, s_4, respectively. Therefore, the initial basic event causal effect graph can be constructed as shown in Fig. 2(a).
- **Filling the Basic Event Causal Effect Graph:** This step aims to uncover causal relationships and their effects between direct and indirect basic events. An edge is drawn between X and Y with the estimated effect value as its weight. This process is shown in Fig. 2(b).

DML excels in heterogeneous UAV swarm tasks by eliminating confounding effects, adapting to complex data, supporting continuous variables and multitasking, enhancing robustness, and quantifying causal effects for node optimization. Therefore, we integrate DML into the TB-DML4HS framework for causal effect estimation.

3.4 Contribution Calculation Module

This module consists of three main steps: basic event effect calculation, contribution value calculation, and providing optimization suggestions.

- **Basic Event Effect Calculation:** This step calculates the impact of each type of basic event on the task score based on the basic event causal effect graph. Taking variable X as an example, the graph is traversed to search for all paths starting from X and ending at s, and the sum of the weights of all these paths is considered the effect of X.
- **Contribution Value Calculation:** For a given test task, all basic events are statistically analyzed. During this process, the ID of the subject of each event is recorded and tabulated, as shown in the table below. After completing the statistics, the contribution value of each event subject is calculated based on the effect values of each type of basic event.
- **Providing Optimization Suggestions:** Based on the effect values of different types of basic events, optimization suggestions for the swarm are provided.

4   Experiment Results

4.1   Environmental Setup

To assess the efficacy of TB-DML4HS, this study employs Unreal Engine 5 (UE5) to simulate the autonomous operation of large-scale heterogeneous drone swarms in reconnaissance missions.

The experimental scenario is set in a 2km × 2km suburban housing area, featuring numerous trees and a few buildings with nearby staff. The simulation starts with 200 moving small vehicles, each beginning at a random position and selecting a destination 100 m away, using the A* algorithm for pathfinding. To prevent collisions, vehicles halt when within 3 m of each other and then choose a new destination.

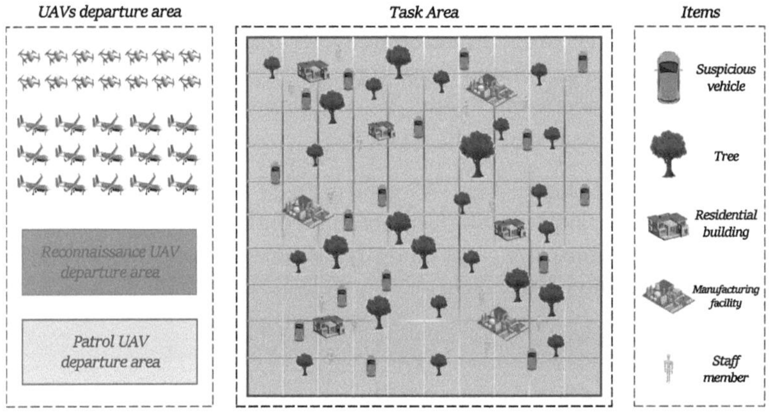

Fig. 3. Schematic Diagram of Task Rules for Simulation Experiment.

The UAV swarm, comprising 300 patrol and 700 RUs, is responsible for tracking and reconnoitering the vehicles. A successful reconnaissance, where a RU follows a target for over 20 s, earns 10 points. Avoiding unnecessary collisions between UAVs and external entities is crucial, and the task score is the sole evaluation metric. The task rules are depicted in Fig. 3.

4.2   Event Causality Diagram Construction

A total of 1000 simulation experiments were conducted as analysis data. Data extraction is performed based on TB-DML4HS for the current task, and the results of basic event type extraction and basic event property classification are shown in Table 1.

Table 1. Basic event type sample illustration table.

Subject	Relation	Object	Event type	Symbol	Effect Value
RU	Tracks	Suspicious Target	Primary Event	p_1	10.00
PU	Notifies	RU	Secondary Event	s_1	8.60
PU	Detects	Suspicious Target	Secondary Event	s_2	7.83
RU	Collides	RU	Secondary Event	s_3	-3.80
RU	Collides	PU	Secondary Event	s_4	-3.83
PU	Collides	PU	Secondary Event	s_5	-2.74
RU	Collides	External Entity	Secondary Event	s_6	-2.10
PU	Collides	External Entity	Secondary Event	s_7	-1.49

4.3   Causal Effect Estimation Result Analysis

The Double Machine Learning method is chosen as the causal effect estimation method, and the p-value of the effect estimate is calculated to infer whether a causal relationship exists. When the p-value is less than 0.05, the causal relationship is considered to exist, and the null hypothesis H_0 (no causal relationship) is rejected. Otherwise, the null hypothesis cannot be rejected, and to avoid misjudgment, the null hypothesis is accepted. The results of the benefit values calculated for each event type on the task score g are shown in Table 1.

From Table 1, it's clear that all collision types negatively affect the task score. So, minimizing UAV collisions is a key optimization goal for the swarm. To verify this, we reduce the patrolling UAVs' radius by 5 m and increase the RUs' by 10 m. This changes the frequency of two event types: s_6 and s_7. We run 100 simulations before and after the change. Results are in Fig. 4 and Table 2.

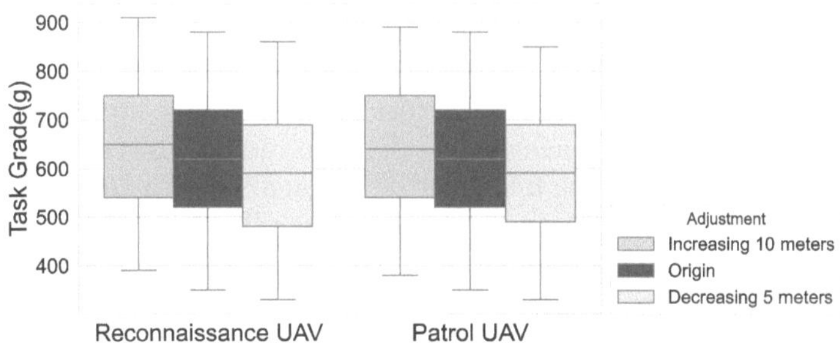

Fig. 4. Experimental Effective of TB-DML4HS.

As shown in Fig. 4, adjusting the recognition radius of UAVs for external entities results in a significant change in the task score. For both RUs and PUs, a 10-m increase in recognition radius raises the task score by 20–30 points, while a 5-m decrease lowers it by a similar amount. Upon closer observation, it can be seen that adjusting the recognition radius for the RU has a greater impact on the task score compared to the PU. To further validate the correctness of the evaluation results, we calculated the mean value of frequency change for basic events of each type, as well as the error between the actual task scores and the evaluated scores, as shown in Table 2. Additionally, the basic event types that are expected to exhibit significant changes are illustrated in Fig. 5.

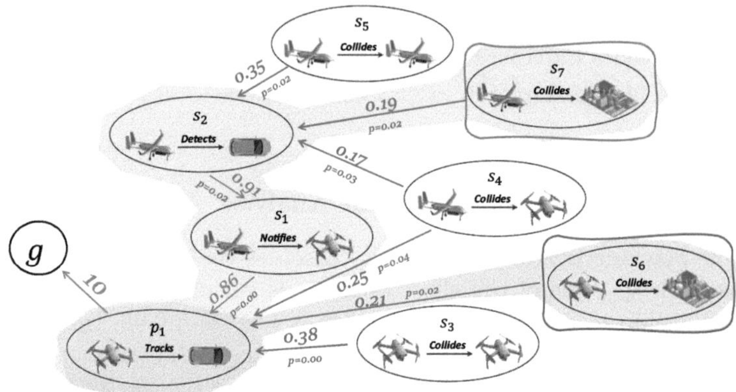

Fig. 5. Expected Major Changes in Basic Events. Cyan: Basic events prone to significant change with patrol aircraft recognition radius adjustment. Burgundy: Basic events prone to significant change with reconnaissance aircraft recognition radius adjustment. Boxed: Basic events directly impacted by recognition radius adjustments. (Color figure online)

As shown in Table 2, when the recognition radius of RU and PU is reduced by 5 m, the mean occurrence frequencies of s_6 and s_7 increase by 15.03 and 15.07, respectively. Conversely, when the recognition radius is increased by 10 m, their frequencies decrease by 14.96 and 14.99, respectively. When adjusting the recognition radius of RUs, the frequencies of other indirect basic events remain mostly stable. However, for PUs, reducing the recognition radius raises the frequency of s_7 (by 15.07), which lowers the frequency of s_2 (by 3.33, with an estimated 2.86 decrease) and subsequently decreases s_1's frequency (by 3.00, with an estimated 2.60 decrease). Conversely, increasing the PUs' recognition radius reduces s_7's frequency (by 14.99), increasing s_2's (by 2.77, with an estimated 2.85 increase) and then s_1's (by 2.49, with an estimated 2.59 increase). As for the task score, the maximum estimation error across different settings is 4.53, and the minimum is 0.09. Despite the estimation errors introduced by TB - DML4HS, their magnitude is relatively small compared to the total score, suggesting that the benefit estimation results are quite accurate.

To further validate the effectiveness of the framework, we meticulously calculated the single-node contribution values of UAVs for each adjusted round. Subsequently, we aggregated the contribution value assessments of all UAV nodes

Table 2. Final Score Error Table. The original mean task score from 1000 simulation rounds is 617.525. Abbreviations: AO (Adjusted Object), AR (Adjust Range), MVFCBE (Mean Frequency Change of Basic Events), TRGA (True Risk Grade Avg), ERG (Estimated Grade).

AO	AR	MVFCBE$((p_1|s_1,...,s_7))$	TRGA	ERG	Error	$avg(e)$	$std(e)$
RU	−5	$(−3.04 — −0.07, −0.08, −0.02, −0.08, −0.03, 15.03, 0.07)$	587.09	585.96	1.13	7.31	3.14
RU	10	$(2.83 — −0.20, −0.22, −0.01, 0.00, 0.06, −14.96, −0.01)$	645.78	648.94	3.16	8.97	4.71
PU	−5	$(−2.70 — −3.00, −3.33, −0.03, 0.00, 0.07, 0.02, 15.07)$	590.54	595.07	4.53	6.53	4.10
PU	10	$(2.22 — 2.49, 2.77, −0.02, 0.03, 0.03, 0.09, −14.99)$	639.77	639.86	0.09	10.81	5.09

and computed the deviation from the actual scores, as illustrated in the following equation:

$$e = \left| g - \sum_{i=1}^{n} g_i \right| \tag{1}$$

where, n represents the number of UAVs within the UVA swarms, g_i denotes the contribution value of the ith UAV, and g signifies the task score achieved in that particular simulation round.

Table 2 clearly presents the error of the total contribution from single nodes, which is indeed larger compared to the error from directly evaluating the final score. However, it is noteworthy that the maximum mean error does not exceed 11, and the maximum standard deviation is only 5.09. Given that this error does not surpass 5% of the total score, we can confidently conclude that the evaluation results are of high accuracy.

5   Conclusion

In this paper, we introduces a novel, task-based evaluation framework, TB-DML4HS, which incorporates causal effect estimation methods. We propose to decompose complex UAV tasks step by step, organize basic event types, and use DML to calculate the causal effect values between basic event types. The causal effect relationship graph between the basic event types is constructed based on the p-value. Using the causal effect relationship graph of the basic event types, we calculate the benefit of each event type on the final evaluation metric, thus providing optimization suggestions for the swarm. In addition, the contribution of each UAV to the task can also be computed. The experimental results show that the optimization suggestions proposed by the framework can effectively improve the overall performance of the swarm and provide accurate benefit estimation results. We believe that this research can offer valuable assistance in the study of UAV swarms. Our future work will focus on discovering deeper causal relationships through causal effect estimation methods and automating the identification of basic event types embedded in complex tasks.

References

1. Alqudsi, Y., Makaraci, M.: UAV swarms: research, challenges, and future directions. J. Eng. Appl. Sci. **72**(1), 12 (2025)
2. Kurt, A., Saputro, N., Akkaya, K., Uluagac, A.S.: Distributed connectivity maintenance in swarm of drones during post-disaster transportation applications. IEEE Trans. Intell. Transp. Syst. **22**(9), 6061–6073 (2021)
3. Na, S., Niu, H., Lennox, B., Arvin, F.: Bio-inspired collision avoidance in swarm systems via deep reinforcement learning. IEEE Trans. Veh. Technol. **71**(3), 2511–2526 (2022)
4. Tang, J., Liu, G., Pan, Q.: A review on representative swarm intelligence algorithms for solving optimization problems: applications and trends. IEEE/CAA J. Autom. Sin. **8**(10), 1627–1643 (2021)
5. Li, K., Yan, X., Han, Y.: Multi-mechanism swarm optimization for multi-UAV task assignment and path planning in transmission line inspection under multi-wind field. Appl. Soft Comput. **150**, 111033 (2024)
6. Hazarika, B., et al.: Generative AI-augmented graph reinforcement learning for adaptive UAV swarm optimization. IEEE Internet Things J. (2025)
7. Javed, S., et al.: State-of-the-art and future research challenges in UAV swarms. IEEE Internet Things J. **11**(11), 19023–19045 (2024)
8. Jiang, Z., Sun, J., Cai, Z., Wang, Y., Wu, K.: Distributed coordinated control scheme of UAV swarm based on heterogeneous roles. Chin. J. Aeronaut. **35**(1), 81–97 (2022)
9. Zhang, Z., Zhou, D., Li, A., Li, Y.: Comprehensive resilience evaluation method for UAV swarm based on multiple performance parameters. In: Yan, L., Duan, H., Deng, Y. (eds.) ICGNC 2022. LNCS, vol. 845, pp. 6107–6116. Springer, Singapore (2022). https://doi.org/10.1007/978-981-19-6613-2_590
10. Bai, G., Li, Y., Fang, Y., Zhang, Y.-A., Tao, J.: Network approach for resilience evaluation of a UAV swarm by considering communication limits. Reliab. Eng. Syst. Saf. **193**, 106602 (2020)
11. Zaitseva, E., Levashenko, V., Mukhamediev, R., Brinzei, N., Kovalenko, A., Symagulov, A.: Review of reliability assessment methods of drone swarm (fleet) and a new importance evaluation based method of drone swarm structure analysis. Mathematics **11**(11), 2551 (2023)
12. Zhang, P., Wu, T., Cao, R., Li, Z., Xu, J.: UAV swarm resilience assessment considering load balancing. Front. Phys. **10**, 821321 (2022)
13. Wu, J., Jiang, Y., Tang, J., Ding, L.: Optimal saturated information load analysis for enhancing robustness in unmanned swarms system. Complex Intell. Syst. **10**(5), 7127–7142 (2024)
14. Li, H., Sun, Q., Zhong, Y., Huang, Z., Zhang, Y.: A soft resource optimization method for improving the resilience of UAV swarms under continuous attack. Reliab. Eng. Syst. Saf. **237**, 109368 (2023)
15. Zhao, B., Huo, M., Li, Z., Yu, Z., Qi, N.: Graph-based multi-agent reinforcement learning for large-scale UAVs swarm system control. Aerosp. Sci. Technol. **150**, 109166 (2024)

16. Wang, Z., Li, J., Li, J., Liu, C.: A decentralized decision-making algorithm of UAV swarm with information fusion strategy. Expert Syst. Appl. **237**, 121444 (2024)
17. Huling, J.D., Greifer, N., Chen, G.: Independence weights for causal inference with continuous treatments. J. Am. Stat. Assoc. **119**(546), 1657–1670 (2024)
18. Chernozhukov, V., et al.: Double/debiased machine learning for treatment and structural parameters. Econom. J. **21**(1), C1–C68 (2018). https://doi.org/10.1111/ectj.12097

WebGCN: Web Information Extraction Algorithm Based on Graph Neural Networks

Xiaole Wang[ID], Dengcheng Yan[✉][ID], Yuting Wang[ID], Heng Zhang[ID], Xu Wen[ID], Fangxiang Liu[ID], and Qingren Wang[ID]

School of Computer Science and Technology, Anhui University, Hefei 230601, China
{wxl,e23301205}@stu.ahu.edu.cn, {yanzhou,wqr}@ahu.edu.cn, i@2git.cn

Abstract. E-commerce platforms have complex and dynamically changing webpage structures. Traditional web crawlers and rule-based information extraction methods struggle to adapt to these challenges, resulting in high maintenance costs and low extraction efficiency. To address this issue, this paper proposes a Graph Neural Network (GNN)-based web information extraction algorithm, WebGCN, which effectively leverages the HTML structure by integrating it into the web document representation and incorporates graph attention, sparse attention, and local attention mechanisms to reduce global computational complexity while enhancing extraction accuracy. Experiments on multiple real-world e-commerce datasets demonstrate that WebGCN achieves state-of-the-art performance.

Keywords: E-commerce Webpages · Information Extraction · Graph Neural Networks

1 Introduction

Extracting structured information from e-commerce web pages is essential for market analysis and decision-making. However, these platforms feature dynamic content and complex HTML structures. Traditional rule-based methods (e.g., XPath) are costly to maintain, and despite advancements in NLP and deep learning, challenges persist with complex e-commerce pages.

Structural Underutilization: Existing models (e.g., BiLSTM-CRF [8], transformers [5,7]) treat web pages as linear text, ignoring the hierarchical structure in DOM trees that encode element relationships.

X. Wang—This work is supported by the Key Project of Natural Science Research for Universities of Anhui Province of China (Nos. 2022AH040019, 2022AH05008637), the Anhui Provincial Natural Science Foundation (No. 2208085QF197), the National Natural Science Foundation of China (No. 62006003), and the Special Fund for Key Program of Science and Technology of Anhui Province (No. 202203a07020008).

Computational Inefficiency: E-commerce pages are long and cluttered with irrelevant text (e.g., ads), making global attention in transformers costly and inefficient for large-scale extraction. To address these limitations, this paper proposes WebGCN, a GNN-based algorithm for e-commerce information extraction. WebGCN models the DOM tree with graph attention networks (GATs) to capture node relationships and uses sparse and local attention to focus on relevant text while reducing computation. Experiments on three datasets show that WebGCN outperforms state-of-the-art methods, with notable gains in Exact Match and F1 scores.

2   Problem Definition

This paper defines the problem of extracting information from web documents, which are represented as a DOM tree with text and HTML nodes. The text nodes form a sequence $T = (t_1, t_2, \ldots, t_k)$, where t_i represents the i-th text node and contains n_i words. The DOM tree is represented as $G = (V, E)$, with V as the set of nodes and E as the edges.

3   WebGCN

3.1   Model Framework

The WebGCN model consists of three components: the input, encoder, and decoder layers (Fig. 1). The input layer generates embeddings for HTML tokens from the DOM tree G and TEXT tokens from the sequence T. The encoder captures structural information using Graph Attention and extracts key content with Local and ProbSparse Attention. The decoder fuses text T and attributes F via Cross Attention, predicts text ranges, and computes loss against ground truth. Self-supervised signals predict HTML node relationships, contributing to the overall loss. The model is trained via gradient descent.

3.2   Input Layer

In WebGCN, each DOM node corresponds to a token: HTML tokens capture the structure of descendant nodes, while TEXT tokens represent textual content. Before encoding, tokens are mapped to embedding vectors with positional encodings added to preserve the order among sibling nodes, as shown in equations (1) and (2).

$$x^{HT} = \sigma(W^{(H2N)}x^{HP} + x^{(POS)}), \tag{1}$$

$$x^{TE} = \sigma(W^{(T2N)}x^{TP} + x^{(POS)}) \tag{2}$$

where x^{HP} is the initial HTML token embedding (randomly initialized), x^{TP} is the initial TEXT token embedding (initialized with BERT), and $x^{(POS)}$ is the positional embedding among siblings. $W^{(H2N)}$ and $W^{(T2N)}$ are learnable projection matrices, and $\sigma(\cdot)$ denotes a non-liner activation function. The

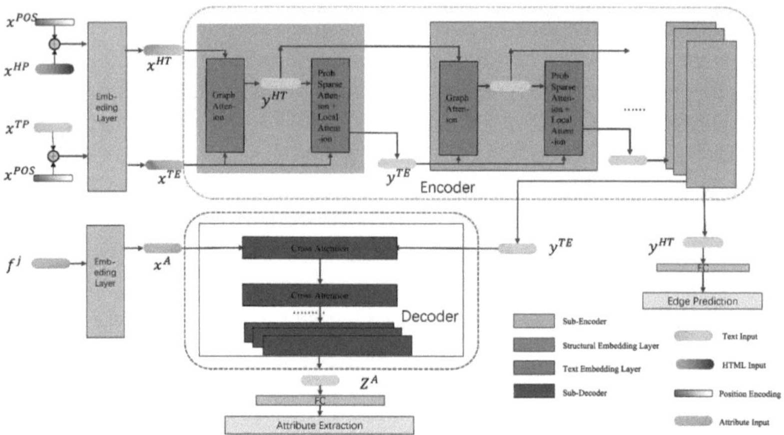

Fig. 1. Overall architecture of the model.

resulting vectors x^{HT} and x^{TE} then used as encoder inputs. For an attribute $f_j = (w_1, w_2, \ldots, w_n)$, its embedding is computed using BERT as:

$$x^A = CLS(TextEncoder([CLS], w_1, w_2, \ldots, w_n)) \tag{3}$$

where $TextEncoder(\cdot)$ represents the BERT encoder, and CLS denotes the special classification token whose output embedding is used as the representation of the attribute.

3.3 Encoder

The WebGCN encoder consists of L stacked sub-encoders, each composed of two layers designed to capture both the hierarchical structure and the rich textual content of web documents. These two layers are:

1. Structural Information Embedding Layer: Web pages are structured as DOM trees, where HTML and TEXT tokens correspond to nodes. To capture such structure, this layer applies a Graph Attention Network (GAT).

(a) For HTML-to-HTML (H2H) relationships: each HTML node aggregates information from its neighbors. The attention score is computed as:

$$\alpha_{ij}^{H2H} = \frac{exp\left(e_{ij}^{H2H}\right)}{\sum_{m \in \mathcal{N}(x_i^{HT})} exp\left(e_{im}^{H2H}\right)}, for\, j \in \mathcal{N}\left(x_i^{HT}\right), \tag{4}$$

$$e_{ij}^{H2H} = \frac{x_i^{HT} W_Q^{H2H} \left(x_j^{HT} W_K^{H2H}\right)^T}{\sqrt{d}} \tag{5}$$

where $N\left(x_i^{HT}\right)$ denotes the neighbors of HTML node x_i^{HT}, and W_Q^{H2H}, W_K^{H2H} are learnable weight matrices. d denotes the embedding dimension.

(b) For HTML-to-TEXT (H2T) interactions:

$$\alpha_{ij}^{H2T} = \frac{exp(e_{ij}^{H2T})}{\sum_{m\in S(x_i^{HT})} e\,xp(e_{im}^{H2T})}, for\, j \in S(x_i^{HT}), \qquad (6)$$

$$e_{ij}^{H2T} = \frac{x_i^{HT} W_Q^{H2T} \left(x_j^{TE} W_K^{H2T}\right)^T}{\sqrt{d}} \qquad (7)$$

where $S(x_i^{HT})$ represents the TEXT neighbors of x_i^{HT}, and W_Q^{H2T} and W_K^{H2T} are learnable parameters. The updated HTML embedding y_i^{HT} combines H2H and H2T as:

$$y_i^{HT} = \sum_{j\in N(x_i^{HT})} \alpha_{ij}^{H2H} x_j^{HT} W_V^H + \sum_{k\in S(x_i^{HT})} \alpha_{ij}^{H2T} x_k^{TE} W_V^T, \qquad (8)$$

where W_V^H and W_V^T are learnable output projections.

2. Textual Information Embedding Layer: Web pages often contain a large amount of text that is irrelevant to information extraction tasks. To effectively identify task-relevant textual information, this study employs ProbSparse Attention for TEXT-to-HTML (T2H) interactions and Local Attention for TEXT-to-TEXT (T2T) interactions. This approach reduces the computational complexity from the original $O(n^2)$ to a more efficient approximation.

(a) T2H Attention: ProbSparse Attention for TEXT to HTML: To focus on useful textual content, a subset of HTML token vectors is randomly sampled for each TEXT token embedding x_i^{TE}, and attention scores are computed as follows:

$$e_{ij}^{T2H} = \frac{x_i^{TE} W_Q^{T2H} (y_j^{HT} W_K^{T2H})^T}{\sqrt{d}}, for\, j \in P(x_i^{TE}) \qquad (9)$$

where $P(x_i^{TE})$ denotes the randomly sampled subset of HTML token vectors, and W_Q^{T2H} and W_K^{T2H} are the linear projection matrices for query and key, respectively. To identify effective TEXT tokens, the deviation of their attention score distribution from a uniform distribution is calculated:

$$M(x_i^{TE}, P(x_i^{TE})) = \max_j\{e_{ij}^{T2H}\} - \frac{1}{K_{len}} \sum_{j\in P(x_i^{TE})} e_{ij}^{T2H} M(x_i^{TE}, P(x_i^{TE})) \qquad (10)$$

where $M(x_i^{TE}, P(x_i^{TE}))$ represents the difference between the attention score distribution of x_i^{TE} and the sampled vectors in $P(x_i^{TE})$ compared to a uniform distribution. This study selects the top u vectors with the greatest difference as effective vectors, where $u = c \cdot lnL_{TEXT}$, and c is the sampling coefficient. Subsequently, these effective vectors perform global attention calculations with all y_j^{HT}:

$$\alpha_{ij}^{T2H} = \frac{exp(e_{ij}^{T2H})}{\sum_m^{L_{HTML}} exp(e_{im}^{T2H})}, for\, i \in U \qquad (11)$$

$$e_{ij}^{T2H} = \frac{x_i^{TE} W_Q^{T2H} (y_j^{HT} W_K^{T2H})^T}{\sqrt{d}} \tag{12}$$

TEXT token updates are then performed as follows:

If $i \in U$ (effective TEXT token):

$$x_i^{T2H} = \sum_j^{L_{HTML}} \alpha_{ij}^{T2H} x_i^{TE} W_V^T + y_{parent}^{HT} \tag{13}$$

If $i \notin U$, then:

$$x_i^{T2H} = Mean(x_i^{TE} W_V^T) + y_{parent}^{HT} \tag{14}$$

where x_i^{T2H} represents the updated vector of x_i^{TE}, and $Mean(\cdot)$ denotes the average of all vectors. y_{parent}^{HT} is the embedding of the parent HTML token corresponding to x_i^{TE}, which propagates short-range structural information from the webpage to the TEXT tokens via its parent node, while long-range structural information is captured using ProbSparse Attention.

(b) T2T Attention: Local Attention for TEXT Tokens: To further model local relationships between TEXT tokens, this study adopts a local attention mechanism inspired by BigBird. Each TEXT token attends only to tokens within a fixed radius r:

$$\alpha_{ij}^{T2T} = \frac{exp\left(e_{ij}^{T2T}\right)}{\sum_{i-r \le l \le i+r} exp\left(e_{il}^{T2T}\right)}, for\ i - r \le j \le i + r \tag{15}$$

$$e_{ij}^{T2T} = \frac{x_i^{TE} W_Q^{T2T} (x_j^{TE} W_K^{T2T} + b_{i-j}^{T2T})^T}{\sqrt{d}} \tag{16}$$

where W_Q^{T2T} and W_K^{T2T} are learnable attention weight matrices, and b_{i-j}^{T2T} is the learnable relative position encoding, which represents the relative position between two text tokens. Note that there are $2r + 1$ possible relative position encodings,i.e., $(i-j) \in -r, \ldots, -1, 0, 1, \ldots, r$. Finally, the embedding calculation for the next layer's TEXT token is as follows:

$$y_i^{TE} = x_i^{TH} + \sum_{i-r \le j \le i+r} \alpha_{ij}^{T2T} x_i^{TE} W_V^T \tag{17}$$

where, W_V^T are learnable parameter matrices, and y_i^{TE} is the updated embedding vector of the TEXT token.

3.4 Decoder

Given inputs x^{HT} and x^{TE}, the encoder outputs y^{HT} and y^{TE}, respectively. This study leverages self-supervised signals for predicting edge types between HTML tokens and employs supervised signals to enhance attribute extraction performance. For the HTML token relation prediction task, a set of directed edge types is defined as $re = self, link, brother, others$. Node pairs with the relationships self, link, and brother are randomly sampled as positive examples, while those with the others relationship serve as negative examples. The sampling ensures a balanced ratio between positive and negative samples. The model is trained by minimizing the cross-entropy loss between the predicted relations and the ground truth. The loss for positive samples is computed as:

$$Loss_{pos} = \sum_{(i,j) \in sample} CrossEntropy(SoftMax(W, Concat(Y_{pos(i)}^{HT}, Y_{pos(j)}^{HT})), re_{true})) \tag{18}$$

where $Concat(\cdot)$ denotes the concatenation operation, $CrossEntropy(\cdot)$ is the cross-entropy loss function, $Y_{pos(i)}^{HT}$ and $Y_{pos(j)}^{HT}$ are the representations of nodes i and j, re_{true} is the ground truth edge label, and W_r is the weight matrix projecting the concatenated features to the output space. The loss for negative samples, $Loss_{neg}$, is calculated in the same manner. The total relation prediction loss is defined as:

$$Loss_{re} = Loss_{pos} + Loss_{neg} \tag{19}$$

For the attribute extraction task, both the attribute representation x^A and the encoded text representation y^{TE} are input into the decoder. The decoder comprises multiple stacked sub-decoders, each applying a full cross-attention mechanism to compute attention scores between x^A and y^{TE}, producing the final attribute representation Z^A. The probabilities of the start and end positions of the attribute are predicted as:

$$Begin_b = softmax(W_b Z^A), End_e = softmax(W_e Z^A) \tag{20}$$

where $Begin_b$ and End_e denote the probability distributions over tokens for the start and end positions, respectively. W_b and W_e are the corresponding weight matrices. The attribute extraction loss is computed using cross-entropy and denoted as $Loss_A$. The overall training objective combines both tasks:

$$Loss_{total} = Loss_{re} + Loss_A \tag{21}$$

Model parameters are updated via gradient descent.

4   Experiments

4.1   Experimental Setup

Datasets: The evaluation includes three datasets: SWDE [3], Common Crawl, and Amazon. Specific details are shown in Table 1.

Evaluation: We evaluate WebGCN using two standard metrics: Exact Match (EM), which measures the proportion of predictions that exactly match the ground truth, and F1 Score, which captures the token-level overlap by balancing precision and recall.

Hyperparameter Settings: In preprocessing, LXML parses web pages to construct the DOM tree and extract text node sequences. BERT initializes word embeddings. WebGCN has 6-layer sub-encoders and sub-decoders with a hidden dimension of 768. ProbSparse Attention's sampling rate is 20, and Local Attention's window radius is 32. The max text length is 2048, and max HTML tokens are 256. The model is trained with Adam optimizer, a learning rate of 3×10^{-5}, and a batch size of 32.

Table 1. Datasets statistics tables.

	SWDE	Common Crawl	Amazon
Page Count	63240	102156	7215
Domain Count	8	2	1
Domain	Car, Book, Job, Movie, ...	Movie, Product	Product

4.2 Baseline

To evaluate WebGCN, this paper compares it with several methods:

- **SimpleDOM** [9]: Treats the task as DOM node labeling, using LSTM to encode node and text features.
- **OpenTag** [8]: Uses BiLSTM-Attention-CRF for sequence labeling but requires a separate model for each attribute.
- **AVEQA** [6]: Frames attribute extraction as a QA task, leveraging BERT to encode attributes and documents jointly.
- **H-PLM** [1]: Employs ELECTRA [2] to encode sorted HTML nodes and text, enhancing structural understanding.
- **MarkupLM** [4]: Jointly encodes HTML and text, using masked language modeling to capture web page structure.

4.3 Overall Performance

The evaluation results in Table 2 show that WebGCN outperforms all baselines across datasets, driven by two key innovations: (1) a structural embedding layer using a graph neural network to capture web page structures, and (2) a textual embedding layer combining ProbSparseAttention for key textual information and Local Attention for fine-grained dependencies, improving both accuracy and efficiency in information extraction.

To evaluate the impact of text sequence length on model performance, test instances were grouped into four ranges: 0–512, 512–1024, 1024–2048, and 2048 and above. EM scores for various methods were evaluated across these groups, as shown in Fig. 2 for datasets SWDE (Fig. 2a), Common Crawl (Fig. 2b), and Amazon (Fig. 2c). Results indicate that WebGCN maintains stable performance across different lengths, unlike other methods (OpenTag, AVEQA, SimpleDOM,

Table 2. Performance of the model on different datasets.

	SWDE		Products		Movies		Amazon	
Method	EM	F1	EM	F1	EM	F1	EM	F1
OpenTag	81.13	86.27	72.39	77.80	80.26	85.03	73.42	76.71
AVEQA	83.31	88.67	74.75	79.48	83.81	88.49	75.21	79.45
SimpleDOM	84.65	90.24	75.08	78.12	82.58	87.73	75.44	79.18
H-PLM	83.47	89.01	76.23	81.08	83.71	89.23	78.37	82.24
MarkupLM	85.23	90.42	79.18	82.07	83.79	90.01	**81.72**	84.42
WebGCN	**87.58**	**93.48**	**80.98**	**84.05**	**85.89**	**91.05**	80.78	**85.33**

H-PLM, MarkupLM), whose performance declines as length increases. This stability is attributed to WebGCN's Local and ProbSparse Attention mechanisms, which effectively capture long-range dependencies and structural information, ensuring robust encoding of long web documents.

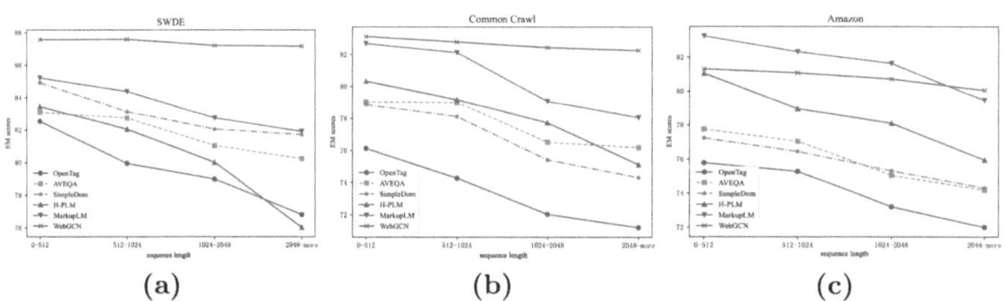

Fig. 2. The impact of different input sequence lengths on model performance.

4.4 Hyperparameter Analysis

To thoroughly assess the impact of the ProbSparse Attention sampling factor c and the Local Attention window radius r on the performance of the WebGCN model, experiments were conducted on the SWDE dataset. Specifically, the effect of c is shown in Fig. 3a, while Fig. 3b illustrates the influence of r. The results indicate that low c values (e.g., 5) hinder the model's ability to capture structural information, whereas high c values introduce noise. Similarly, small r values limit contextual understanding, while large r values increase computational cost without notable performance gains. The optimal hyperparameters were found to be $c = 20$ and $r = 32$, striking a balance between performance and efficiency.

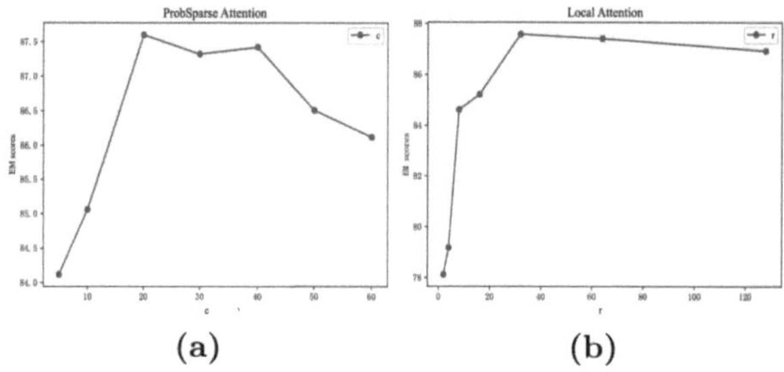

(a)   (b)

Fig. 3. The impact of parameters c and r on model performancel performance.

5   Conclusion

This paper proposes a graph neural network-based method that effectively captures the structural information of web pages using self-supervised signals. To address the high time complexity of global attention in large-scale e-commerce web documents, it introduces sparse and local attention mechanisms. These not only reduce computational overhead but also enhance the extraction of key textual information. Experiments on three real-world datasets demonstrate the method's efficiency and accuracy in handling complex web page structures.

References

1. Chen, X., et al.: WebSRC: a dataset for web-based structural reading comprehension. In: Proceedings of the 2021 Conference on Empirical Methods in Natural Language Processing, pp. 4173–4185 (2021)
2. Clark, K., Luong, M.T., Le, Q.V., Manning, C.D.: Electra: pre-training text encoders as discriminators rather than generators. In: International Conference on Learning Representations (2020)
3. Hao, Q., Cai, R., Pang, Y., Zhang, L.: From one tree to a forest: a unified solution for structured web data extraction. In: Proceedings of the 34th International ACM SIGIR Conference on Research and Development in Information Retrieval, pp. 775–784 (2011)
4. Li, J., Xu, Y., Cui, L., Wei, F.: Markuplm: pre-training of text and markup language for visually rich document understanding. In: Proceedings of the 60th Annual Meeting of the Association for Computational Linguistics (Volume 1: Long Papers), pp. 6078–6087 (2022)
5. Vaswani, A., et al.: Attention is all you need. In: Advances in Neural Information Processing Systems, vol. 30 (2017)
6. Wang, Q., et al.: Learning to extract attribute value from product via question answering: a multi-task approach. In: Proceedings of the 26th ACM SIGKDD International Conference on Knowledge Discovery and Data Mining, pp. 47–55 (2020)
7. Xu, Y., et al.: Layoutlmv2: multi-modal pre-training for visually-rich document understanding. In: Proceedings of the 59th Annual Meeting of the Association for Computational Linguistics and the 11th International Joint Conference on Natural Language Processing (Volume 1: Long Papers), pp. 2579–2591 (2021)

8. Zheng, G., Mukherjee, S., Dong, X.L., Li, F.: Opentag: open attribute value extraction from product profiles. In: Proceedings of the 24th ACM SIGKDD International Conference on Knowledge Discovery and Data Mining, pp. 1049–1058 (2018)
9. Zhou, Y., Sheng, Y., Vo, N., Edmonds, N., Tata, S.: Simplified om trees for transferable attribute extraction from the web. arXiv preprint arXiv:2101.02415 (2021)

Federated Rank Learning with Dimensionality Reduction and Clustering for Electricity Load Forecasting

Lei Li[1], Bing Su[2,3,4], Shichao Zhang[1], Yuchong Liu[5], Jianchao Zheng[6], Chuan Zhang[5(✉)], and Liehuang Zhu[5]

[1] State Grid Shandong Electric Power Company, Jinan 250013, Shandong, China
{lilei,zhangshichao}@sd.sgcc.com.cn
[2] State Grid Shandong Electric Power Research Institute, Jinan 250003, Shandong, China
[3] Shandong Smart Grid Technology Innovation Center, Jinan 250003, Shandong, China
[4] Shandong Key Laboratory of Energy Industry Internet Big Data Technology, Jinan 250003, Shandong, China
[5] Beijing Institute of Technology, Beijing, China
{kka132,chuanz,liehuangz}@bit.edu.cn
[6] The Academy of Military Science, Beijing, China

Abstract. Power load forecasting is crucial for power companies' planning and power dispatching. With the development of machine learning, power forecasting has adopted artificial intelligence techniques based on machine learning. In this paper, we propose a novel forecasting scheme, FRLDRC, which combines the UMAP dimensionality reduction method, the K-means clustering algorithm, and ranking-based federated learning techniques. This approach allows us to obtain a forecasting model while ensuring data privacy, as the data does not leave its domain. To validate the effectiveness of the proposed model, we design experiments using over two million real household electricity consumption data points spanning four years. The experimental results demonstrate that data clustering with dimensionality reduction improves the performance of the baseline model. Additionally, the federated learning-based approach ensures data security, and the ranking federated technique further reduces communication overhead.

Keywords: Dimensionality Reduction · Clustering · K-means · Federated Rank Learning · Electricity Load Forecasting

This research is sponsored by the project of State Grid Shandong Electric Power Company Science and Technology Program, ERP Number: 520626240006.

1   Introduction

The Importance of Power Load Forecasting refers to the practice of predicting electrical demand to ensure efficient and reliable operation of power systems. Load forecasting is crucial for utility companies and grid operators, as it helps balance supply and demand, optimize resource allocation, and minimize operational costs [1]. Accurate load predictions facilitate effective energy management strategies, especially in the context of increasing reliance on renewable energy sources and the complexities introduced by emerging technologies such as electric vehicles and smart meters. Notably, the significance of power load forecasting extends beyond operational efficiency; it impacts financial performance within competitive energy markets. Forecasting errors can lead to substantial economic losses, with studies indicating that even a 1% increase in forecasting error could cost utilities between $300,000 to $1.6 million annually [2].

Short-term load forecasting predicts electricity demand within 24 h to a few days, crucial for real-time grid operations and decisions on power generation scheduling and system stability during peak demand periods. Techniques like ARIMA and LSTM are commonly used for high-accuracy predictions. Medium-term forecasting, covering weeks to months, supports operational planning, maintenance scheduling, and energy procurement strategies, utilizing methods like multiple linear regression and hybrid AI models. Long-term forecasting, spanning years to decades, helps in strategic planning, infrastructure development, and renewable energy projects, relying on demographic trends and economic indicators [3].

The transformation of power forecasting schemes from traditional statistical methods to contemporary machine learning techniques marks a significant evolution in predictive modeling within the energy sector. Historically, traditional statistical methods, such as exponential smoothing and the Theta method, provided reliable benchmarks for time series forecasting, particularly in stable environments. However, these methods often struggle with the complexities and nonlinearities inherent in modern power load data. The advent of machine learning (ML) has brought about a paradigm shift in power forecasting, with algorithms like Recurrent Neural Networks (RNN) and Long Short-Term Memory (LSTM) networks demonstrating superior accuracy and adaptability in handling large, complex datasets. By leveraging vast amounts of data generated through advanced sensor technologies, ML methods can uncover intricate patterns that traditional approaches may overlook, leading to improved forecasting accuracy and operational efficiency in power systems [4]. This transition is particularly notable in the context of renewable energy forecasting, where the ability to capture nonlinear relationships is critical for effective prediction [5]. Despite these advancements, the integration of machine learning in power forecasting has not been without challenges. Economic constraints, regulatory hurdles, and geographical variations can complicate the deployment of these advanced techniques, necessitating ongoing research to refine model applicability and enhance data quality. Moreover, while machine learning methods excel in prediction accuracy, they often sacrifice interpretability and can be more resource-intensive compared to traditional models, raising questions about their practical implementation in diverse operational contexts [6]. The shift from traditional statistical forecasting to machine learning methodologies represents both an opportunity and a challenge for the energy sector, as stakeholders seek to balance accuracy, interpretability, and resource efficiency. Ongoing research into hybrid approaches and ensemble learning strategies aims to bridge the gap between these methodologies, potentially leading to more robust and adaptable forecasting solutions that can meet the evolving demands of a rapidly changing energy landscape [7].

With the emergence of ML technologies, the field of power forecasting has undergone significant transformations. Machine learning techniques have been integrated into predictive modeling to enhance both accuracy and efficiency. While traditional statistical methods are useful, they often struggle to manage the complexity and non-linearity inherent in power load data. Compared to other traditional forecasting models, power system data has the following three distinct characteristics: 1. Large Data Volume: Since the inception of power systems, data has been continuously generated and collected. The dataset used in this study contains more than 2 million records. 2. Data Complexity: The relationships in power system data are intricate, with non-linear structures underlying the data, rather than simple linear correlations. 3. Localized Data Storage: The data is stored locally, with headquarters having limited storage capacity. If data from all subsidiaries were to be uploaded, the communication and storage overhead would exceed expectations.

To validate the proposed solution, the dataset used consists of over 2 million records, spanning four years of electricity usage data. Dimensionality reduction and clustering are common methods for data processing. In the context of the power grid scenario, we propose the use of ranking federated learning to protect data privacy while significantly reducing communication overhead.

The remainder of the paper is structured as follows. Section 2 presents the preliminaries of our scheme. In Sect. 3, we give a problem formulation of our scheme, including the system model and design goals. We give the scheme details in Sect. 4, followed by a experiment analysis in Sect. 5. Next, related work is discussed in Sect. 6. Finally, we conclude this paper in Sect. 7.

2   Background Knowledge

In this section, we will introduce three key techniques: UMAP, K-means, and ranking federated learning to build a predictive model for power grid data. UMAP is a dimensionality reduction method that preserves nonlinear structures, maintaining both local and global relationships within the data. K-means is a classic clustering technique, which is applied to the data after dimensionality reduction with UMAP. Ranking federated learning is a variant of federated learning that, compared to traditional federated learning, substantially reduces communication overhead.

2.1 UMAP

Dimensionality reduction aims to represent data more effectively in two or three-dimensional spaces. In the processing of high-dimensional data, it has been observed that high-dimensional data not only involves high computational complexity but is also difficult to visualize and interpret. As a result, dimensionality reduction techniques are commonly employed in machine learning and data analysis to handle high-dimensional data. Common dimensionality reduction techniques include PCA, ICA, t-SNE, and UMAP. Among these, both t-SNE and UMAP are capable of preserving the nonlinear structure of data. Compared to t-SNE, UMAP is more computationally efficient. For instance, in the dimensionality reduction task of the MNIST dataset, UMAP takes less than 3 min, whereas t-SNE requires 45 min. Furthermore, UMAP is better at preserving the global structure of data. Its robust theoretical foundation allows users to balance the preservation of both global and local structures, whereas t-SNE primarily retains local structure relationships.

Specifically, UMAP dimensionality reduction occurs in two steps. The first step is "Learning the manifold structure," which involves two tasks: the first task is "Finding nearest neighbors," and the second task is "Constructing a neighbor graph." To accomplish the second task, several methods are employed, including varying distance, local connectivity, fuzzy areas, and merging of edges. The second step is "Finding a low-dimensional representation," which also involves two tasks: "Minimum distance" and "Minimizing the cost function." The core of this process is minimizing the cost function (cross-entropy), which serves as the mathematical foundation for finding an optimal low-dimensional manifold representation under the constraint of the specified minimum distance.

$$CE = \sum_{e \in E} w_h(e) \log\left(\frac{w_h(e)}{w_l(e)}\right) + (1 - w_h(e)) \log\left(\frac{1 - w_h(e)}{1 - w_l(e)}\right)$$

Where CE means cross-entropy, $w_h(e)$ known as weights of edges from high-dimensional manifold approximation. $w_l(e)$ is defined as weights to be discovered for low-dimensional representation.

2.2 K-Means

Clustering algorithms are commonly used for datasets that lack predefined labels but exhibit inherent similarities among samples. K-means is a widely used clustering algorithm and a typical example of a distance-based, non-hierarchical clustering approach. It operates by partitioning the data into a specified number of clusters, denoted as K, through the minimization of an error function. The distance between objects is employed as a measure of similarity, such that the closer two objects are, the higher their similarity is considered to be.

The basic steps of the K-means algorithm are as follows:

(1) Select k initial samples as the initial cluster centers, denoted as $a = a_1, ..., a_k$;

(2) For each sample x_i in the dataset, compute its distance to the k cluster centers and assign it to the cluster corresponding to the closest center;

(3) For each cluster a_j, recalculate its center as $a_j = \frac{1}{|c_i|} \sum_{x \in c_i} x$, which is the centroid of all samples belonging to that cluster;

(4) Repeat steps (2) and (3) until the termination condition is met, such as reaching the maximum number of iterations or a minimal change in error.

2.3   Federated Rank Learning (FRL)

Federated Rank Learning (FRL) is a technology that combines federated learning and ranking learning, designed to perform distributed ranking tasks while preserving user privacy. By locally training models on multiple client devices and sharing the updated model parameters with a central server, FRL avoids centralized data storage, thus ensuring the privacy of user data. This technology is primarily applied in fields such as personalized recommendation systems, search engine ranking, and advertisement ranking. It enhances the effectiveness of ranking tasks by learning user behavior data from client devices, all while maintaining privacy protection.

In terms of implementation, FRL follows the basic framework of federated learning, combining the local data training process on multiple clients with the global model update. Each client computes the model parameter updates based on its local data and sends these updates to the central server, instead of uploading raw data. The central server aggregates the updates from the various clients to generate a globally optimized model. Specifically, for ranking tasks, the objective function is defined as:

$$\mathcal{L}(\theta) = \sum_{i=1}^{N} \sum_{j=1}^{K} \ell(f(x_{ij}; \theta), y_{ij})$$

In this formula, $\mathcal{L}(\theta)$ represents the global loss function, θ denotes the model parameters, x_{ij} refers to the feature of the sample on client i, y_{ij} is the ranking label of the sample, $f(x_{ij}; \theta)$ is the model's prediction for the sample x_{ij}, ℓ is the loss function. Each client computes the local gradient based on its own data and aggregates it with the gradients from other clients. Ultimately, the global model parameters are updated through an aggregation algorithm to progressively optimize the ranking task's performance. This method effectively handles data heterogeneity, and since only model updates, rather than raw data, are shared, it ensures the privacy of the data.

3   Problem Formulation

3.1   System Model

In our system model, there are numerous small participants, denoted as $a_1, ..., a_n$, clustered into two servers: Cluster Server A and Aggregation Server B. The participants, a_i, act as data generators, and due to their large numbers, they directly send their data to Cluster Server A. After collecting the data, Cluster Server A applies UMAP for dimensionality reduction, followed by K-means clustering. The resulting clustered data is then utilized in conjunction with Aggregation Server B to perform ranking federated learning, which generates the predictive model (Fig. 1).

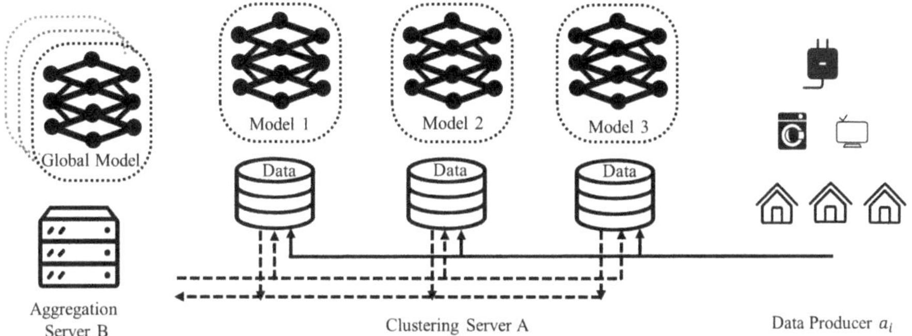

Fig. 1. System model.

Data producer. The data producer, represented by a_i, refers to entities within the power grid system, such as households or small devices. These entities continuously generate electricity usage data and upload this information to the clustering server A for further processing.

Clustering server A. The clustering server A is primarily responsible for the preprocessing and clustering of the electricity usage data it receives from the data producers. It handles the dimensionality reduction, clustering, and other necessary data processing tasks.

Aggregation server B. The aggregation server B is responsible for receiving the ranked aggregation results from multiple clustering servers A. It then uses federated learning techniques to aggregate and update the global model. The aggregation server B focuses solely on the global model aggregation, while A takes care of data processing and clustering tasks.

In this model, clustering servers A are divided based on jurisdiction, while the aggregation server B represents the central authority or headquarters overseeing the global model aggregation process.

3.2 Design Goals

The objectives of our design are as follows:

Prediction Model for Power Consumption: Ensure that the central power authority receives an accurate predictive model of the total electricity consumption, providing essential insights for effective management.

Communication Efficiency: Given the large volume of data, ensure that communication overhead does not interfere with the normal operation of the entire system, optimizing the balance between data transmission and system performance.

Privacy Protection: The central power authority's primary goal is to obtain the predictive model, focusing on the value of the data rather than the raw data itself. Therefore, it is unnecessary for the branches to upload sensitive data to the headquarters, ensuring privacy and minimizing the risk of unauthorized access.

4   Detailed Construction

4.1   The Basic Components of FRLDRC

In this model, as depicted in the diagram, there are three key components that work together to process and analyze electricity consumption data efficiently. Each component serves a specific function and operates sequentially to achieve accurate predictions. Initially, the data is transmitted from the data producers a_i to the clustering server A, where the process begins.

Data Producer a_i: The data producer, represented by a_i, refers to the entities that generate electricity usage data. This data is transmitted through a private communication channel to the clustering server A. The data includes various power consumption readings along with timestamps for accurate tracking.

Clustering Server A: Clustering server A is responsible for preprocessing and clustering the received data. Each clustering server A processes the raw data received from the data producers by performing dimensionality reduction using the UMAP algorithm. UMAP helps retain the global structure of the data and makes the subsequent clustering more interpretable. Based on the reduced two-dimensional data, server A applies the K-means algorithm to cluster the data. The number of clusters, K, is preset to 4, assuming that electricity usage behavior can be categorized into four primary patterns corresponding to seasonal variations. The results of the clustering are then sent for ranking and federated learning with the aggregation server B.

Aggregation Server B: The aggregation server B represents the central power authority and collaborates with multiple clustering servers through federated learning. In this process, complex raw data is not transmitted. Instead, the ranking information of the model parameters is shared. The central authority uses this information to aggregate and update the global model. As a result, the power authority receives an accurate prediction model for electricity consumption based on the aggregated data.

4.2 A Simple Example

As illustrated in the Fig. 2. Once data is generated on the user's device, it is transmitted to clustering server A. At server A, the data undergoes a dimensionality reduction process using UMAP, followed by clustering using the K-means algorithm. This process results in a well-defined classification of the data. Next, a machine learning method is applied to the classified data for further processing. In this case, a random forest algorithm is used as well as FRL.

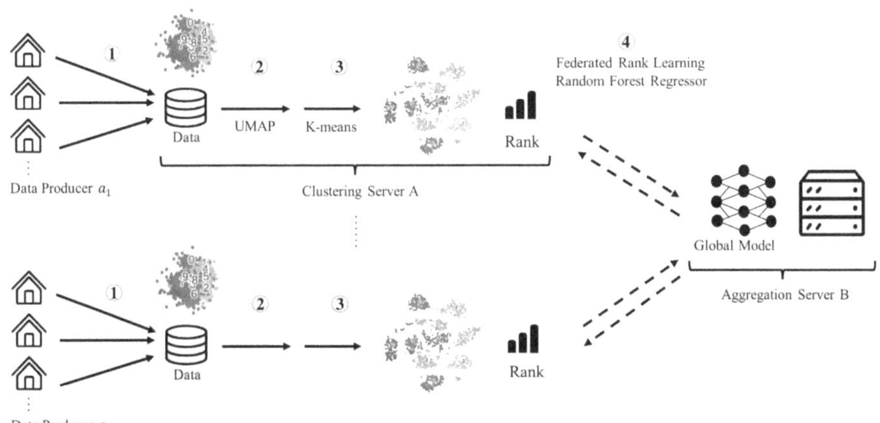

Fig. 2. Example of FRLDRC.

It is important to note that the figure only shows a single clustering server, but in practical applications, there are typically multiple clustering servers. Each of these servers communicates with the aggregation server, aligning their data using timestamps as a synchronization metric. The final step involves federated learning, which aggregates the results from all the clustering servers and generates a predictive model. This approach ensures that the model is built collaboratively across multiple servers, without the need to share sensitive data directly.

5 Experiment Analysis

5.1 Experimental Setup

For the purpose of accuracy evaluation, we implemented FRLDRC using Python on a laptop with the following hardware specifications: 16.0 GB of RAM and an Intel Core i9 2.20 GHz.

The dataset used in this experiment is the Individual Household Electric Power Consumption Data Set. This dataset is a multivariate time-series dataset that records the electricity consumption of a household in Paris, France, over nearly four years (from December 2006 to November 2010), with a sampling interval of one minute.

Although the experimental data pertains to the electricity consumption of a single household, the prediction of household electricity consumption serves merely as an introductory example. In practice, with power grid data, it is possible to transfer and develop models tailored to specific business requirements. For instance, by forecasting electricity consumption across different time periods and regions, the model could assist the power grid in optimizing energy scheduling. Thus, we have chosen this dataset for our experiment.

In the data preprocessing phase, the data was divided by year and processed accordingly for each year in the following sequence: First, UMAP was applied for dimensionality reduction. To ensure data visualization while retaining local structure, the dimensionality was reduced to two, and the number of nearest neighbors was set to 30. Subsequently, clustering was performed using the K-means algorithm, where the number of clusters was set to 4 for this experiment. After completing the data processing, the next step, FRL was carried out. In this stage, we implemented a Random Forest algorithm under the FRL framework for the experiment. Ultimately, We obtained the forecast data for 2011.

5.2 Experimental Results

This section presents our experimental results. The left column displays the UMAP dimensionality reduction and K-means clustering results of the annual data, while the right column shows the daily average electricity consumption for each cluster over the years. The data from 2006 to 2010 are presented from top to bottom. Except for the year 2007, the results from the remaining four years exhibit clear clustering patterns in the top-left, top-right, bottom-left, and bottom-right quadrants. The average electricity consumption displayed on the right shows a noticeable hierarchical structure across all five years. However, the data for 2006 appears slightly lacking due to the much smaller sample size compared to the other years.

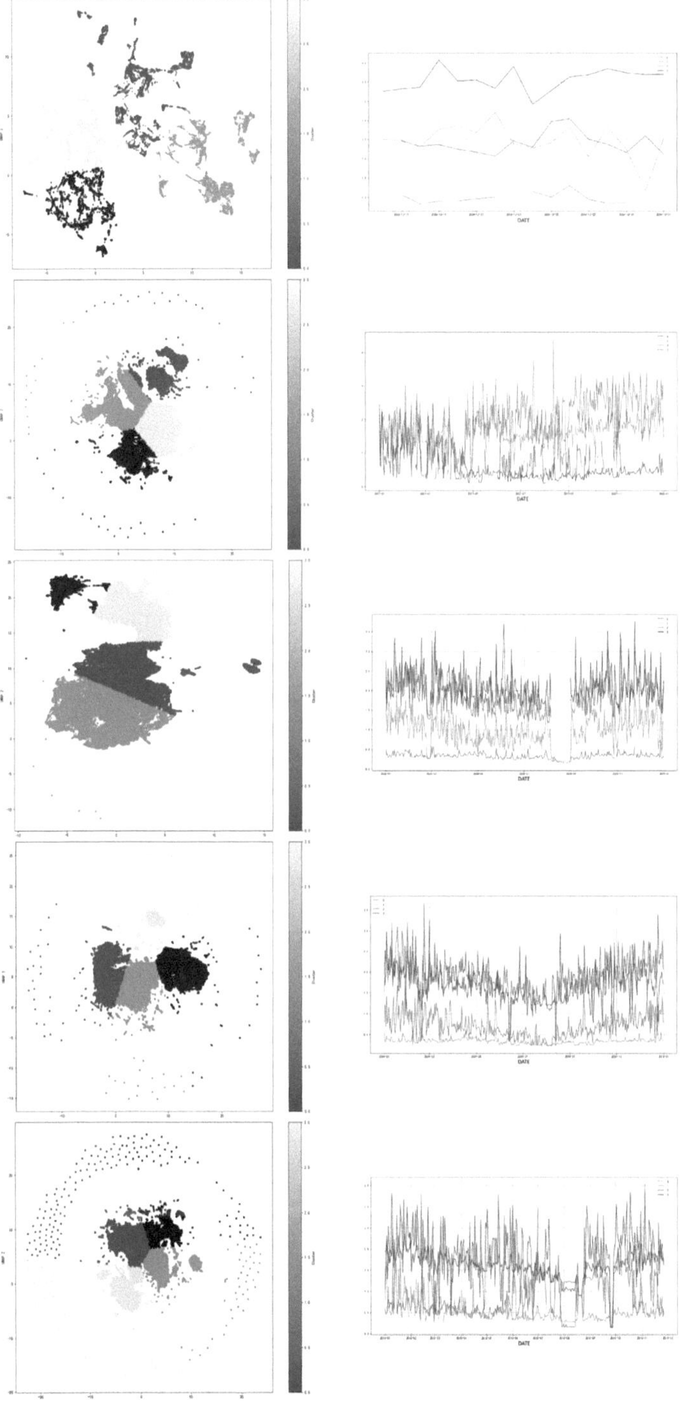

6   Related Works

This section mainly introduces related work, time series forecasting can be categorized into three main types: statistical models, machine learning models, and hybrid models.

Statistical models are mathematical models that reflect the statistical assumptions of sample data. They are typically defined as the mathematical relationships between one or more random variables and other non-random variables. The Autoregressive (AR) model is a time series analysis model that assumes the current value is only related to the values from previous time steps [3]. It predicts the current value by multiplying past data values by coefficients and adding an error term. The Moving Average (MA) model is a time series model that forecasts the current value using the weighted average of past error terms. It assumes that the current observation is influenced by past random disturbances, and is suitable for handling random fluctuations in time series data. The Autoregressive Moving Average (ARMA) model combines both the AR and MA models [8]. It considers past observations as well as past error terms. It is used for modeling stationary time series and makes predictions by utilizing both historical data and errors. The Autoregressive Integrated Moving Average (ARIMA) model is an extension of the ARMA model that incorporates differencing to handle non-stationary time series [9]. By differencing the data to achieve stationarity, ARIMA combines the characteristics of AR and MA models, and is used for forecasting time series with trends or seasonality.

Hus and KL [10] propose a fuzzy expert system for short-term load forecasting, incorporating operators' heuristic rules to improve the accuracy of forecasted hourly loads, particularly by addressing uncertainties in weather variables. Sina and Kaur [11] present a hybrid model combining kernel support vector regression with the social spider optimization algorithm to improve accuracy in short-term load forecasting. Zhu *et al.* [13] proposes a hybrid prediction model using pattern sequence matching and XGBoost to forecast holiday load, aiming to improve accuracy in electricity load predictions. Hu *et al.* [12] introduced a novel short-term load forecasting method, which integrates fuzzy C-mean clustering and weighted support vector machines, focusing on the significance of recent data for more accurate forecasting. Chen *et al.* [15] proposed bidirectional long short-term memory, which is based on Empirical Mode Decomposition (EMD) and Hunter-Prey Optimization (HPO) algorithms. This model aims to address the issue of low prediction accuracy caused by the randomness and nonlinearity of power load. Han *et al.* [16] proposed a short-term power load prediction model based on Whale Optimization Algorithm-Attention Mechanism-Gated Recurrent Unit, which is designed to address the complexity, diversity, and inherent regularities of short-term power load data.

Hybrid models blend the strengths of both statistical and AI methodologies, leveraging the interpretability of statistical models with the adaptability of machine learning techniques. Groß *et al.* [14] introduced a approach, this approach is particularly effective in accounting for seasonal trends while integrating external influences, such as temperature and occupancy levels.

7   Conclusion

In this paper, we proposed FRLDRC, a power consumption prediction scheme under ranking federated learning, which combines data dimensionality reduction and clustering algorithms to address the challenges of complex data types and massive data volumes in power grid scenarios. The scheme integrates data dimensionality reduction and clustering while preserving spatial relationships between data points, reducing computational overhead. By introducing federated learning, the scheme ensures that data remains local, safeguarding privacy and avoiding unnecessary communication costs. Furthermore, the incorporation of ranking federated learning further reduces communication overhead. Experimental validation using a household dataset demonstrated the effectiveness of the proposed scheme. We believe that when applied to real-world power grid data, FRLDRC will also exhibit strong performance, and this is a direction for future exploration and verification.

References

1. Zhuang, L.: Short-term load forecasting for power systems based on BP neural networks. Shandong Electric Power **50**(11), 51–59 (2023). https://doi.org/10.20097/j.cnki.issn1007-9904.2023.11.007
2. Nti, I.K., Teimeh, M., Nyarko-Boateng, O., Adekoya, A.F.: Electricity load forecasting: a systematic review. J. Electr. Syst. Inf. Technol. **7**(1), 1–19 (2020). https://doi.org/10.1186/s43067-020-00021-8
3. Kuster, C., Rezgui, Y., Mourshed, M.: Electrical load forecasting models: a critical systematic review. Sustain. Cities Soc. **35**, 257–270 (2017)
4. Jain, A., Gupta, S.C.: Evaluation of electrical load demand forecasting using various machine learning algorithms. Front. Energy Res. **12**, 1408119 (2024)
5. Song, X., et al.: Comparison of machine learning techniques with classical statistical models in predicting health outcomes. In: MEDINFO 2004. IOS Press (2004)
6. Jaramillo, M., Pavón, W., Jaramillo, L.: Adaptive forecasting in energy consumption: a bibliometric analysis and review. Data **9**(1), 13 (2024)
7. Martin, L.-C.: Machine learning vs traditional forecasting methods: an application to South African GDP. Stellenbosch Economic Working Papers: WP12/2019 (2019)
8. Agrawal, R.K., Adhikari, R.: An introductory study on time series modeling and forecasting, pp. 200–212. Nova York: CoRR (2013)
9. Jetcheva, J.G., Majidpour, M., Chen, W.-P.: Neural network model ensembles for building-level electricity load forecasts. Energy Buildings **84**, 214–223 (2014)
10. Hsu, Y-Y., Ho, K-L.: Fuzzy expert systems: an application to short-term load forecasting. IEE Proc. C (Gener. Transm. Distrib.) **139**(6) (1992)
11. Sina, A., Kaur, D.: Short term load forecasting model based on kernel-support vector regression with social spider optimization algorithm. J. Electr. Eng. Technol. **15**(1), 393–402 (2020)
12. Hu, G., Zhu, F., Zhang, Y.: Short-term load forecasting based on fuzzy c-mean clustering and weighted support vector machines. In: Third International Conference on Natural Computation (ICNC 2007), vol. 5. IEEE (2007)
13. Zhu, K., Geng, J., Wang, K.: A hybrid prediction model based on pattern sequence-based matching method and extreme gradient boosting for holiday load forecasting. Electric Power Syst. Res. **190**, 106841 (2021)

14. Groß, A., Lenders, A., Schwenker, F., Braun, D.A., Fischer, D.: Comparison of short-term electrical load forecasting methods for different building types. Energy Inform. **4**(3), 1–16 (2021). https://doi.org/10.1186/s42162-021-00172-6
15. Chen, X., Wu, J., Cai, J., Tang, W., Long, Y., Wang, Z.: Short-term load prediction based on BiLSTM optimized by hunter-prey optimization algorithm. Shandong Electric Power **51**(4), 64–71 (2024). https://doi.org/10.20097/j.cnki.issn1007-9904.2024.04.007
16. Han, M., et al.: Research on short-term electric load forecasting method based on WOA-AM-GRU. Shandong Electric Power **51**(4), 64–71 (2024). https://doi.org/10.20097/j.cnki.issn1007-9904.2024.12.004

Context-Aware Vectors: A New Method Integrating Personality Into LLMs for Enhanced Sentiment Analysis

Zhihao Shuai[1]([✉]) [iD], Kaiwen Li[2] [iD], Guoyu Li[3] [iD], Shengyao Liu[4] [iD], Dandan Li[1] [iD], and Naisheng Tang[3] [iD]

[1] The Hong Kong University of Science and Technology (Guangzhou), Guangzhou, China
zhihaoshuai@hkust-gz.edu.cn
[2] South China University of Technology, Guangzhou, China
[3] University of Electronic Science and Technology of China, Chengdu, China
[4] Guangdong Ocean University, Zhanjiang, China

Abstract. This research is dedicated to surmounting the limitations of Large Language Models (LLMs) in sentiment analysis. By delving into Myers-Briggs Type Indicator (MBTI) traits, we put forward an innovative Context-Aware Vectors method. Departing from traditional approaches such as rule-setting or data fine-tuning, we explore the latent interpretability of personality traits within LLMs. We conduct experiments on Meta-LLaMA-3.1-8B, employing the SCIFACT dataset devoid of personality bias and carefully crafted prompts. This enables us to extract context-aware vectors, by calculating the differences in the outputs of a specific layer under different MBTI Traits styles. When evaluated on the SemEval dataset, LLMs integrated with context-aware vectors, especially the INFJ-LLM, achieve state-of-the-art (SOTA) performance in comparison to 15 baseline models. Ablation experiments further verify the significance of each component of our context-aware vectors. In summary, this work offers a novel approach to integrating MBTI traits into LLMs, expands the scope of LLM interpretability research, and notably enhances LLMs' performance in sentiment analysis.

Keywords: Large Language Models · Sentiment Analysis · MBTI Traits

1 Introduction

LLMs have shown remarkable growth but still face challenges in sentiment analysis, especially in detecting subtle emotional tones, which affects personalized interactions such as intelligent customer service [1]. Researchers have explored methods to improve LLMs' performance in emotional classification, with MBTI personality traits playing a key role. These traits are linked to emotional processing mechanisms [2], where different personality types, such as INFJs, demonstrate better emotional acuity [3]. Integrating such traits into LLMs may improve emotional intelligence.

T. Zhu et al. (Eds.): KSEM 2025, LNAI 15923, pp. 59–66, 2026.
https://doi.org/10.1007/978-981-95-3061-8_7

Traditional methods such as rule-based systems [4] or fine-tuning on high-quality datasets [5] have limitations. Rule-based systems are rigid and lack interpretability, while fine-tuning is complex and prone to overfitting, with high costs for data collection [6]. These issues motivate the search for more efficient, flexible, and interpretable methods for infusing LLMs with personality traits.

Our study introduces the **Context-Aware Vectors** method, which avoids predefined rules and large-scale fine-tuning. Instead, it explores the interpretability of MBTI traits in LLMs by analyzing model layers' outputs under various MBTI prompts. Visualization techniques reveal underlying personality patterns, and statistical analysis helps quantify the model's ability to distinguish MBTI types. Context-aware vectors, representing the model's understanding of these traits, are built using key features and statistical characteristics.

To validate our method, we conduct experiments on a sentiment analysis dataset [8] across diverse scenarios. We compare LLMs integrated with context-aware vectors to previous models [9] and perform ablation experiments to assess performance changes. The results show significant improvements in accuracy and F1-Score, demonstrating enhanced emotional understanding.

In summary, the key contributions of our work are as follows:

- Introducing the Context-Aware Vector method to integrate MBTI traits into LLMs, overcoming limitations of traditional methods.
- Exploring the interpretability of MBTI traits in LLMs, expanding research in LLM interpretability.
- Enhancing LLM performance in sentiment analysis, benefiting practical applications like intelligent customer service.

2   Methodology

In the field of artificial intelligence, enhancing the sentiment analysis capabilities of LLMs is one of the important research directions at present. As shown in Fig. 1, our study focuses on general-purpose LLMs and adopts a rigorous and innovative methodology. Firstly, through multi-dimensional evaluations, the Meta-LLaMA-3.1-8B model is selected as the research vehicle. Its powerful processing capabilities and adaptable architecture provide a good foundation for a profound exploration of the representation of MBTI personality traits within the model. Secondly, complex vector analysis algorithms and advanced visualization techniques are employed to analyse of the vectors related to MBTI traits in the Transformer layers of the model, aiming to clarify their activation and discrimination mechanisms in different contexts. Then, based on the analysis results, a carefully designed extraction process is utilized to obtain key context-aware vectors. These vectors are precisely integrated into specific layers according to the characteristics of the model, endowing the model with predefined MBTI traits and thus optimizing its emotional analysis function.

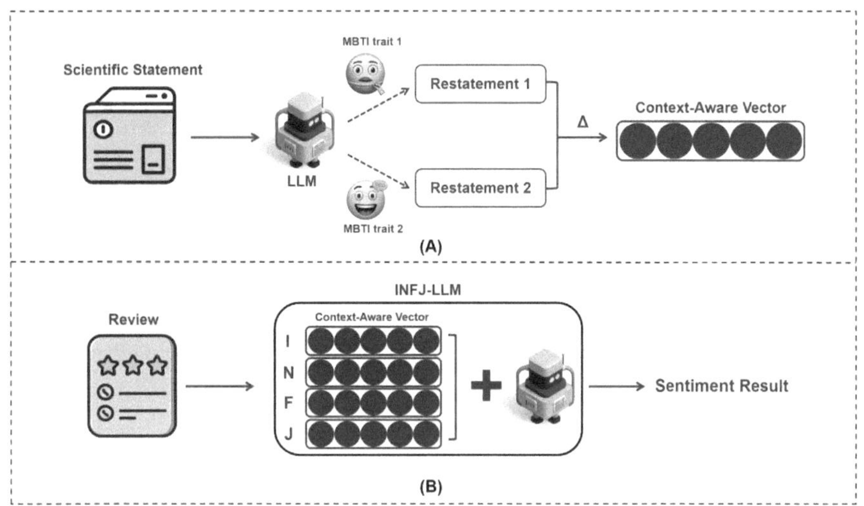

Fig. 1. The framework of our method. (A) describes the extraction process of the Context-Aware Vector. (B) illustrates the process of conducting sentiment analysis after incorporating the MBTI Traits into the LLMs.

2.1 Data Processing.

We utilized the SCIFACT dataset [7] for our study, which is specifically designed for scientific claim verification and does not contain any expressions with MBTI. The dataset contains 1.4K expert-written scientific claims paired with evidence-containing abstracts, annotated with labels and rationales, across specialized domains. To facilitate the model's reasoning capabilities, we designed meticulously constructed prompts. These prompts directed the large language model (LLM) to rewrite sentences in a way that integrated diverse MBTI traits illustrated in Fig. 2.

```
Prompt:
f "Rewrite the following sentence to reflect the '{style}' style in the
MBTI personality framework:\n\n"
f "Sentence: \"{sentence}\"\n\n"
f "Rewritten Sentence:"
```

Fig. 2. Prompt design for guiding the LLMs in sentence rewriting.

In the prompt design, we specify styles corresponding to the MBTI dimensions such as Extroversion (E), Introversion (I), Feeling (F), Thinking (T), and others. Through this prompt-based guidance, we aim to analyze the activation vectors generated within the transformer layers, assessing the model's ability to differentiate and systematically activate internal representations of these vectors. This analysis sets the foundation for future work, where we plan to delve deeper into the model's capability to distinguish between different types of personality traits based on these internal activations.

2.2   Context-Aware Vectors Extraction.

To identify the specific transformer layers where context-aware vectors are most effectively activated, we first aim to maximize the similarity between vectors corresponding to the same MBTI trait and minimize the similarity between vectors from different traits. We employ cosine similarity to measure this similarity, which is defined as:

$$\text{cosine\_similarity}(\mathbf{h}_i^{(l)}, \mathbf{h}_j^{(l)}) = \frac{\mathbf{h}_i^{(l)} \cdot \mathbf{h}_j^{(l)}}{\|\mathbf{h}_i^{(l)}\| \|\mathbf{h}_j^{(l)}\|}, \tag{1}$$

Formally, our objective is to:

$$\max\left(\bar{s}_{i,i}^{(l)} + \bar{s}_{j,j}^{(l)}\right) \quad \text{and} \quad \min\left(\bar{s}_{i,j}^{(l)} + \bar{s}_{j,i}^{(l)}\right), \tag{2}$$

where $\bar{s}_{i,j}^{(l)}$ represents the average cosine similarity between vectors of different traits i and j at layer l, defined as:

$$\bar{s}_{i,j}^{(l)} = \frac{1}{N} \sum_{k=1}^{N} \text{cosine\_similarity}(\mathbf{h}_i^{(l)}, \mathbf{h}_j^{(l)}), \tag{3}$$

where $\mathbf{h}_i^{(l)}$ and $\mathbf{h}_j^{(l)}$ are the hidden state vectors at layer l, corresponding to the input samples associated with concepts i and j, respectively [10]. These hidden state vectors are the representations learned by the transformer model at each layer for different input MBTI traits.

From this objective, we derive the following expression:

$$\max\left(\Delta S^{(l)}\right) = \max\left(\bar{s}_{i,i}^{(l)} + \bar{s}_{j,j}^{(l)}\right) - \min\left(\bar{s}_{i,j}^{(l)} + \bar{s}_{j,i}^{(l)}\right), \tag{4}$$

where $\Delta S^{(l)}$ quantifies how well the model distinguishes between different traits at layer l. It is defined as:

$$\Delta S^{(l)} = \left(\bar{s}_{i,i}^{(l)} + \bar{s}_{j,j}^{(l)}\right) - \left(\bar{s}_{i,j}^{(l)} + \bar{s}_{j,i}^{(l)}\right). \tag{5}$$

This definition captures the difference between the similarity within the same trait and the similarity across different trait. By maximizing $\Delta S^{(l)}$, we can identify the layers where the model best differentiates between MBTI traits.

Once the specific layers are identified, we proceed to calculate the context-aware vectors for these layers. The vectors are computed as the average difference between the hidden state vectors corresponding to different MBTI traits in the identified layers, defined as:

$$\mathbf{c}^{(j-i)} = \frac{1}{2N} \sum_{i=1}^{N} \left(\mathbf{h}_j^{(l)} - \mathbf{h}_i^{(l)} \right).$$ (6)

2.3 Personality Infusion

After determining the context-aware vectors and identifying the specific transformer layers, we integrate these vectors into the corresponding layers of the respective LLMs. This process involve augmenting the model's parameters with the extracted vectors through the following formula:

$$\mathbf{h}^{(l)} \rightarrow \mathbf{h}^{(l)} + \sum_{k} w^k \cdot \mathbf{c}^k,$$ (7)

where $\mathbf{h}^{(l)}$ is the hidden state at layer l, $\mathbf{c}_k$ are the context-aware vectors (e.g., $\mathbf{c}^{I-E}, \mathbf{c}^{N-S}, \mathbf{c}^{F-T}, \mathbf{c}^{J-P}$), and w^k are the corresponding weights. This effectively modify the model's behavior to exhibit predefined MBTI traits.

3 Results

3.1 Experimental Environment

To evaluate the enhancement of Context-Aware Vectors on the sentiment analysis ability of LLMs, we took Meta-LLaMA-3.1-8B as an example. These experiments were executed on our experimental platform, which features 72 GB of RAM, an Intel Xeon Processor with 10 vCPU, and an A100-PCIE-40 GB GPU. The platform runs on the Ubuntu 20.04 operating system, and the experiments are conducted using the PyTorch 1.11.0 deep learning framework with Cuda 11.3. Then, we collected 14 advanced models from recent research for baseline comparison and conducted ablation experiments on our approach.

3.2 Dataset

In our experiments, we employed two datasets to comprehensively assess our approach. We first utilized the SCIFACT dataset [7], which is designed for scientific claim verification. This dataset contains 1,400 claims crafted by experts, each paired with an abstract containing evidence, covering diverse fields such as biology, physics, and chemistry. Each claim abstract pair comes with labels and rationales indicating the claim's veracity. Our unique approach involved rewriting these scientific claims in styles corresponding to different MBTI traits. By analyzing these rewritten versions, we were able to extract context-Aware vectors specific to each MBTI trait. To evaluate the effectiveness of these MBTI trait based context Aware vectors in sentiment analysis, we selected the SemEval dataset [8]. This mainstream dataset encompasses real-world scenarios like product reviews and dining experiences. It provides sentiment labels, allowing us to measure the enhancement in LLMs' sentiment analysis performance after integrating the context-Aware vectors derived from the SCIFACT dataset rewrite.

3.3 Baseline Comparison and Analysis

In an effort to more comprehensively appraise the significance of this research, we meticulously handpicked and contrasted 15 open-source baseline models that are highly representative in recent years. These models span from traditional classic architectures to innovative algorithms, reflecting diverse technical approaches and design philosophies. Given that large-scale experiments invariably consume substantial computational resources and demand a significant investment of time, while maintaining the scientific integrity and comparability of our study, for the evaluation outcomes of certain baseline models, we referenced the relevant data that had been rigorously validated by experiments in TextGT [9]. This paper shares a high degree of compatibility with our current research in aspects such as the experimental setting, dataset utilization, and selection of evaluation metrics. The results presented in this paper are authoritative and carry substantial reference value, thus effectively complementing and refining our comparative analysis.

As shown in Table 1, our model achieves the highest accuracy among all models for sentiment analysis in both commodity and dining scenarios. Notably, in the more common dining scenario, compared with the previous SOTA model TextGT [9], our model improves accuracy by 4.72% points and Macro-F1 by 5.46% points. This clearly demonstrates the value and high efficiency of our method in daily usage.

3.4 Ablation Experiment and Analysis

To further validate the effectiveness of the context-aware vectors and the specific role that each MBTI trait plays in it, we carried out ablation experiments. In each experiment, one of the traits among I, N, F, and J was excluded. As shown in Table 2, for laptop review sentiment analysis, removing traits I, N, or F significantly reduces accuracy and Macro-F1. For restaurant review sentiment analysis, ablating traits I and N has the greatest impact. Consequently, it becomes evident that the trait of concentrated pondering, as denoted by I, and the trait of attaching importance to the comprehensive comprehension of things, represented by N, are capable of exerting a substantial influence in the sentiment analysis task. The experimental results in Table 3 also demonstrate that, by referring to the research findings on MBTI, the method of injecting the INFJ personality into the LLMs using the context-aware vector can indeed enhance the model's sentiment analysis capabilities.

4 Conclusion

In this study, we developed the Context-Aware Vectors method to enhance LLMs' sentiment analysis using MBTI traits. Experiments on Meta-LLaMA-3.1-8B allowed us to extract context-aware vectors, uncovering latent MBTI-related interpretability in LLMs. Results on the SemEval dataset revealed that LLMs

Table 1. Comparison on the benchmark datasets. The best results are highlighted in boldface, and lacking results are marked as "âĂŞ".

Models	Restaurant		Laptop	
	Accuracy↑	Macro-F1↑	Accuracy↑	Macro-F1↑
IAN (IJCAI, 2017)	78.60	–	72.10	–
RAM (EMNLP, 2017)	80.23	70.80	74.49	71.35
MGAN (EMNLP, 2018)	81.25	71.94	75.39	72.47
TNet (ACL, 2018)	80.69	71.27	76.54	71.75
ASGCN (EMNLP, 2019)	80.77	72.02	75.55	71.05
CDT (EMNLP, 2019)	82.30	74.02	77.19	72.99
BiGCN (EMNLP, 2020)	81.97	73.48	74.59	71.84
kumaGCN (EMNLP, 2020)	81.43	73.64	76.12	72.42
InterGCN (COLING, 2020)	82.23	74.01	77.86	74.32
R-GAT (ACL, 2020)	83.30	76.08	77.42	73.76
DGEDT (ACL, 2020)	83.90	75.10	76.80	72.30
DualGCN (ACL, 2021)	84.27	78.08	78.48	74.74
SSEGCN (NAACL, 2022)	83.29	76.31	77.22	73.53
AG-VSR (KBS, 2022)	83.45	76.05	78.16	74.77
TextGT(AAAI, 2024)	85.17	**79.70**	78.64	74.91
INFJ-LLM	**86.91**	78.68	**83.36**	**80.38**

Table 2. Ablation results on the benchmark datasets.

Bias Configuration	Restaurant		Laptop	
	Accuracy	Macro-F1	Accuracy	Macro-F1
INFJ-LLM	**86.91**	**78.68**	**83.36**	**80.38**
w/o I	86.01	77.11	82.73	79.52
w/o N	86.00	77.26	82.57	79.31
w/o F	86.02	77.05	83.20	80.10
w/o J	86.45	77.73	82.91	79.80

integrated with these vectors, particularly INFJ-LLM, outperformed 15 baseline models. Our work contributes by presenting a novel integration method, expanding LLM interpretability, and improving sentiment analysis performance for real-world applications. Importantly, the current method has the advantage of not requiring training with personality traits data nor the formulation of response rules, making it more efficient and flexible. Our work contributes by presenting a novel integration method, expanding LLM interpretability, and improving sentiment analysis performance for real-world applications. Looking ahead, future research could extend this approach to other LLMs and natural language processing tasks. Notably, this research can be extended to personality traits such as occupation, ideology, and emotion, in addition to MBTI. This potentially unlocks new dimensions of enhancing LLMs' capabilities in understanding.

References

1. Zhang, W., Deng, Y., Liu. B., et al.: Sentiment analysis in the era of large language models: A reality check[J]. arXiv preprint arXiv:2305.15005 (2023)
2. Higgs, M.: Is there a relationship between the Myers-Briggs type indicator and emotional intelligence? J. Manag. Psychol. **16**(7), 509–533 (2001)
3. Drenth, A.J.: The 16 personality types. Theory, & Type Development, Profiles (2013)
4. Jiang, G., Xu, M., Zhu, S.C., et al.: Evaluating and inducing personality in pretrained language model. Adv. Neural. Inf. Process. Syst. **36**, 10622–10643 (2023)
5. Zeng Z, Chen J, Chen H, et al. Persllm: a personified training approach for large language models. arXiv preprint arXiv:2407.12393 (2024)
6. Yu, X., Zhang, Z., Niu, F., et al.: What makes a high-quality training dataset for large language models: a practitioners' perspective. In: Proceedings of the 39th IEEE/ACM International Conference on Automated Software Engineering, pp. 656-668 (2024)
7. Wadden, D., Lin, S., Lo, K., et al.: Fact or fiction: verifying scientific claims. arXiv preprint arXiv:2004.14974 (2020)
8. Pontiki, M., Galanis, D., Pavlopoulos, J., Papageorgiou, H., Androutsopoulos, I., Manandhar, S.: SemEval- 2014 Task 4: aspect based sentiment analysis. In: International Workshop on Semantic Evaluation, pp. 27–35 (2014)
9. Yin, S., Zhong, G.: Textgt: a double-view graph transformer on text for aspect-based sentiment analysis. In: Proceedings of the AAAI conference on artificial intelligence, vol. 38(17), pp. 19404-19412 (2024)
10. Tenney, I., Das, D., Pavlick, E.: Bert rediscovers the classical nlp pipeline. In: Proceedings of the 57th Annual Meeting of the Association for Computational Linguistics (2019)

Research on Detection and Reconstruction of Multiple Types of Anomalies in Wind Speed-Power Data of Wind Farms

Shouyi Chen[1]([✉]) [iD], Yiyi He[1] [iD], Yanfei Guo[2] [iD], Wei Ma[1] [iD], Chung-Lun Wei[1] [iD], and Chiawei Chu[1]

[1] Data Science College of City, University of Macau, Macau, China
`d23091100427@cityu.edu.mo`
[2] New Energy Product Dept of Shenzhen Nari Technology, ShenZhen, China

Abstract. The suboptimal environment of wind farms poses significant challenges for maintenance and results in the generation of complex abnormal data in the transmitted signals. This issue is particularly severe due to the accumulation of large volumes of abnormal data caused by wind sensor failures and power limitations. In our work, we analyze the mechanisms behind various types of abnormal data (anomalies) generation and outline the structure of the proposed solution. To detect anomalies and reconstruct wind speed-power data, our approach integrates iterative curve fitting for outlier removal, linear interpolation, and density clustering. Tailored strategies are developed to address different types of abnormal data, and the effectiveness of the proposed anomaly detection method is validated through real-world case studies.

Keywords: Wind Farm · Anomaly Detection · Iterative Fitting · Reconstruction · Density Clustering

1 Introduction

1.1 Background

With growing emphasis on environmental protection, energy optimization, and carbon emission reduction, wind energy has garnered global attention for its continuous power generation, low environmental impact, and minimal land use [1]. However, suboptimal wind farm operating conditions challenge both maintenance and the stability of SCADA (Supervisory Control and Data Acquisition) data [2], leading to complex anomalies in wind speed-power distributions. These anomalies significantly hinder power prediction and research, making anomaly detection in wind farm data a critical task [3].

1.2 Related Work

To address this issue, numerous researchers have conducted studies on anomaly detection in wind farm data. In 2020, Wang et al. applied a phased approach combining density

© The Author(s), under exclusive license to Springer Nature Singapore Pte Ltd. 2026
T. Zhu et al. (Eds.): KSEM 2025, LNAI 15923, pp. 67–76, 2026.
https://doi.org/10.1007/978-981-95-3061-8_8

clustering, truncation methods, slope control methods, and kernel density estimation to detect anomalies in wind speed-power data [4]; In 2023, Li et al. utilized DBSCAN (Density-Based Spatial Clustering of Applications with Noise) combined with the Lidar quasi-measurement method to detect abnormal data [5]. However, these approaches were ineffective in handling accumulated anomalies.

In 2024, Phong B. Dao et al. proposed an interval stationary analysis method based on the sliding window principle for monitoring and anomaly detection in wind turbines. Due to its reliance on the sliding window mechanism, this method struggled to effectively address long-duration anomalies [6]. In 2022, Long et al. introduced a novel image-based algorithm that combined the Hough transform and Canny edge detection to automatically locate stacked outliers [7]. However, this image-based anomaly detection methods faced challenges in effectively handling large areas of stacked abnormal data.

In summary, while various methods have been developed for anomaly detection in wind speed-power data, effective solutions for complex stacked anomalies—especially those caused by anemometer failures—remain limited [8]. This paper focuses on multiple types of stacked anomalies and proposes targeted strategies to develop a more comprehensive anomaly detection framework.

2   Wind Speed-Power Abnormal Data

SCADA data is transmitted through a system consisting of multiple components, including anemometers, various sensors, and wiring [9]. Due to the suboptimal environmental conditions in wind farms, the system is affected by a range of natural and anthropogenic factors, including mechanical failures, aging, magnetic fields, extreme weather, and human interventions. These factors result in diverse abnormal data distribution patterns that vary depending on the specific influencing factor [10], as illustrated in Fig. 1.

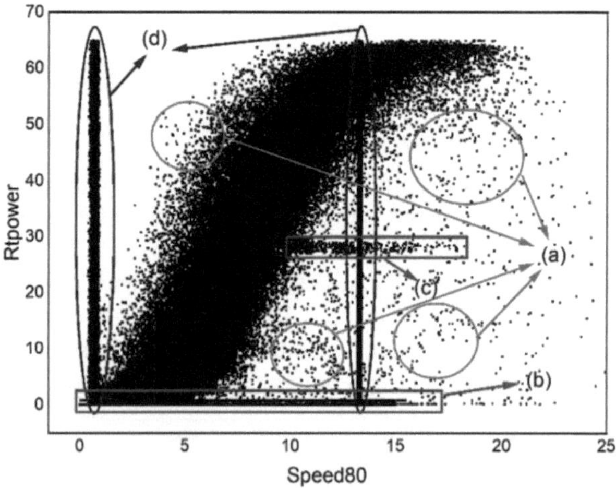

Fig. 1. Typical abnormal data types.

1. Anomaly (a) is primarily caused by factors like hardware malfunctions, magnetic fields, and extreme weather, leading to irregular discrete data anomalies.
2. Anomaly (b) is primarily caused by wind energy curtailment, exhibiting a banded accumulation pattern near the lower boundary of the data.
3. Anomaly (c) is primarily caused by human-imposed power restrictions, presenting a banded accumulation structure extending from the main data distribution.
4. Anomaly (d) is primarily caused by anemometer failures, resulting in wind speed data that cannot be recorded properly, manifesting as a columnar accumulation pattern.

Anomaly (a) is commonly referred to as outliers, while Anomaly (b), (c), and (d) are collectively categorized as stacked anomalies [3]. Among these anomalies, stacked anomalies are critical to data quality.

In the following sections, we will detail the structure and process of the proposed anomaly detection method and further elaborate on the detection and handling strategies for stacked anomalies and outliers.

3 Model Framework: Components and Principles

The proposed anomaly detection model consists of three primary components:

(1) Calculate the mean angle values of continuous data intervals and identify abnormal intervals during the iterative curve fitting process.
(2) Linear interpolation is performed to reconstruct the identified abnormal data intervals.
(3) The DBSCAN algorithm is applied to detect and remove outliers from the interpolated data.

In the following sections, we will elaborate on the implementation details of each component and discuss their contributions to the overall anomaly detection framework.

3.1 Mean Angle of Intervals

The wind speed-power data are segmented into intervals using wind speed and power as criteria, achieving intervalization in both dimensions. For each interval, the angle values of the data points are computed, which yield two arrays of angle values. Proper interval division effectively separates stacked anomalies characterized by distinct structural patterns, as illustrated in Fig. 2.

As shown in Fig. 2(a), wind speed-based interval segmentation effectively isolates the Anomaly (d) data previously described. Specifically, the calculated angle origin is set at $(V_{min} - 5, 0)$. Similarly, Fig. 2(b) demonstrates that power-based interval segmentation effectively isolates the Anomaly (b) and Anomaly (c) data, and the calculated angle origin is set at $(0, P_{max} + 5)$. When calculating the mean angle for each interval, the origin dynamically adjusts with changes in the intervals to emphasize the trend in angle variation.

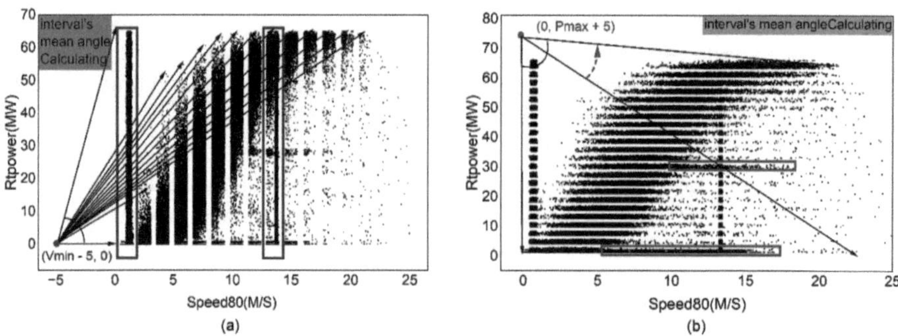

Fig. 2. Data Interval Segmentation Diagram.

3.2 Iterative Curve Fitting for Outlier Removal

The Iterative Curve Fitting for Outlier Removal method, referred to as the iterative removal method, is utilized in this study. Specifically, the logistic growth curve and the logarithmic curve are selected as the target fitting models. Two variations of the iterative removal method are applied in this process.

1. In the wind speed-based data segmentation process, the logistic growth curve is adopted, as expressed in Eq. (1), supported by relevant studies showing that the power output curve of wind farms resembles this growth pattern [11].

$$f(x) = \frac{L}{1 + e^{-k(x-x_0)}} \tag{1}$$

2. In the power-based interval segmentation process, wind farm data tend to cluster near the lower region in a two-dimensional space [12], where lower power often corresponds to a larger range of wind speeds. Consequently, the logarithmic curve, characterized by an initially rapid growth followed by a slower increase, is more suitable as the predefined fitting curve in this context. The mathematical expression for the logarithmic curve is provided in Eq. (2).

$$F(x) = a\log_b x + c \tag{2}$$

This method is further explained as follows: Since stacked anomalies can influence the trend of angle variation within intervals and easily introduce outliers during the fitting process, the proposed approach for identifying anomalous intervals involves iteratively removing a small number of points to optimize the predefined target function. A maximum number of anomaly intervals, denoted as σ, is specified to ensure that no more than σ intervals are removed during the curve fitting process. The method also includes calculating the mean squared error (MSE) after each fitting iteration. At the conclusion of the iterations, the removal configuration yielding the smallest MSE is selected, thereby identifying the outliers in the interval angle variation curve. Finally, the anomalous data intervals are identified, facilitating the reconstruction of these intervals [13–15].

3.3 Linear Interpolation

Linear interpolation is adopted as the data reconstruction method, which estimates values between two known data points based on a linear relationship. This approach effectively captures the linear relationship between wind speed and power output. Specifically, interpolation is performed within the target anomalous interval by utilizing the two adjacent non-anomalous intervals. For a given wind speed value set RAM_V in the target interval, power values are interpolated as shown in Eq. (4). The interpolated power value corresponding to a wind speed aim_v is denoted as aim_{vp}. $x_0^{aim_v}$ and $x_1^{aim_v}$ represent the nearest wind speed values in the preceding and following intervals, while $y_0^{aim_v}$ and $y_1^{aim_v}$ are their respective power values.

If the first data interval is anomalous, auxiliary intervals are constructed to enable interpolation. These auxiliary intervals, corresponding to wind speed and power, are denoted as IV and IP, respectively, as shown in Eqs. (4) and (5). Here, i_{1max}^{v} and i_{1max}^{P} represent the maximum wind speed and power values of the first interval, while i_{2max}^{v} denotes the maximum wind speed value of the second interval.

$$\sum aim_{vp} = y_0^{aim_v} + \frac{\left(y_1^{aim_v} - y_0^{aim_v} \right)}{\left(x_1^{aim_v} - x_0^{aim_v} \right)} \times \left(\sum aim_v - x_0^{aim_v} \right), aim_v \in RAM_V \tag{3}$$

$$I_V = \{(x, y) | x \in [-i_{1max}^{v}, 0], y \in [-2, 0]\} \tag{4}$$

$$I_P = \{(x, y) | x \in [-(i_{2max}^{v} - i_{1max}^{v}), 2i_{1max}^{v} - i_{2max}^{v}], y \in [-i_{1max}^{P}, 0]\} \tag{5}$$

3.4 DBSCAN Algorithm

DBSCAN is a widely used density-based clustering algorithm [16] in data mining and clustering analysis. It effectively identifies clusters of arbitrary shapes and demonstrates robustness to noise. The algorithm is governed by two key parameters: ε (eps) and MinPts. The parameter ε (eps) defines the neighborhood radius within which points are considered "density reachable." MinPts specifies the minimum number of points (including the point itself) required for a point to be classified as a core point. Based on these two parameters, the data points are categorized into three types:

- **Core Point:** A point with at least MinPts points (including itself) within a given radius ε.
- **Border Point:** A point that is not a core point but lies within the ε-radius of a core point.
- **Noise Point:** A point that does not qualify as either a core point or a border point.

By classifying data into these three types, DBSCAN partitions the dataset into clusters based on point density while identifying noise points as outliers. This enables the algorithm to effectively perform anomaly detection.

3.5 Model Process

The algorithm primarily consists of four main components: interval segmentation and angle calculation, anomaly interval detection, data reconstruction, and DBSCAN-based outlier detection. The detailed workflow is illustrated in Fig. 3.

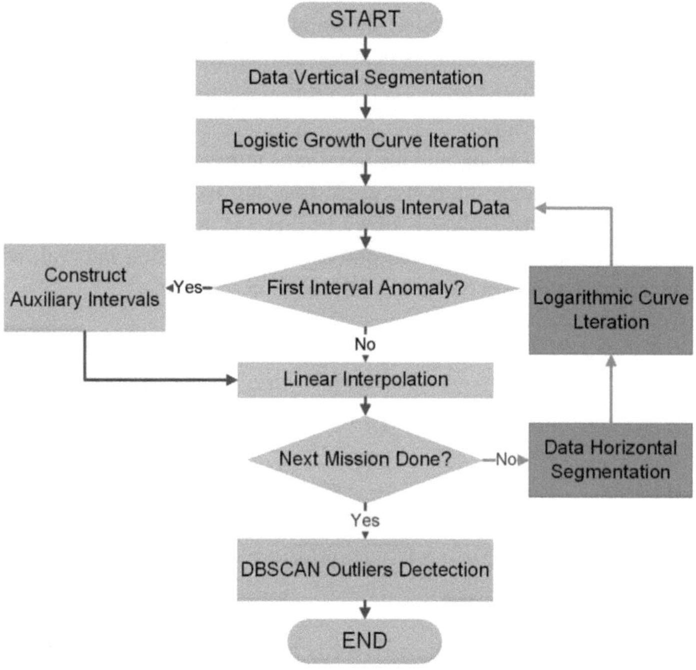

Fig. 3. Flowchart.

As shown in the figure, the first part focuses on anomaly interval detection and interpolation based on wind speed, using a predefined logistic growth curve as the fitting model. This step is aimed at detecting anomaly (d) data. The second part focuses on anomaly interval detection and interpolation based on power, employing a predefined logarithmic curve as the fitting model. This step is designed to detect anomaly (b) and (c) data. Finally, the third stage leverages the DBSCAN algorithm to detect and remove outliers.

4 Experiment Description

To validate the proposed method, wind speed-power data collected from a wind turbine in North China were selected as the experimental dataset. The dataset covers a time span of the past 1.5 years, with measurements recorded every 5 min, including 161,912 data points, of which 44,923 are abnormal data points, accounting for 27.7% of the total. Wind speed data were collected from a meteorological tower at a height of 80 m. The wind farm has an installed capacity of 65 MW, with a cut-in wind speed of 2 m/s, a rated wind speed of 13 m/s, and a cut-out wind speed of 25 m/s. The site is located at an elevation of 1,365 m in a mountainous region. The distribution of the data is illustrated in the figure below (Fig. 4).

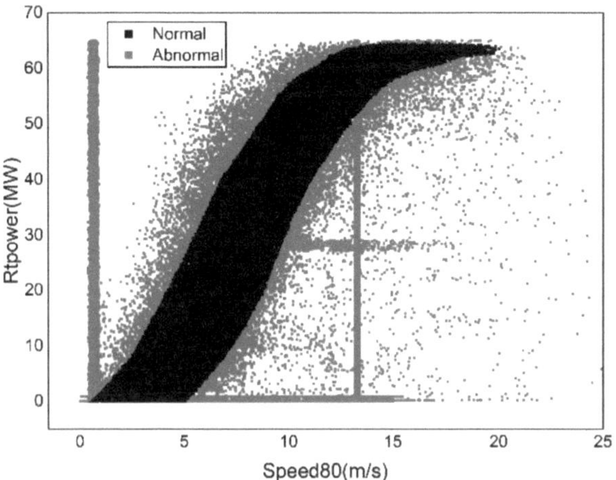

Fig. 4. Distribution of Original Data.

The selected dataset includes anomaly (a), (b), (c), and (d). In the initial stage of the algorithm, anomaly detection and interpolation are first performed. During this step, the data are segmented based on wind speed, and the mean angle is calculated for each segment. The dataset is divided into 15 segments, and intervals containing less than 0.5% of the total data volume are excluded. This results in the retention of the first 11 continuous intervals. The segmentation results and the trend of angle changes are shown in Fig. 5.

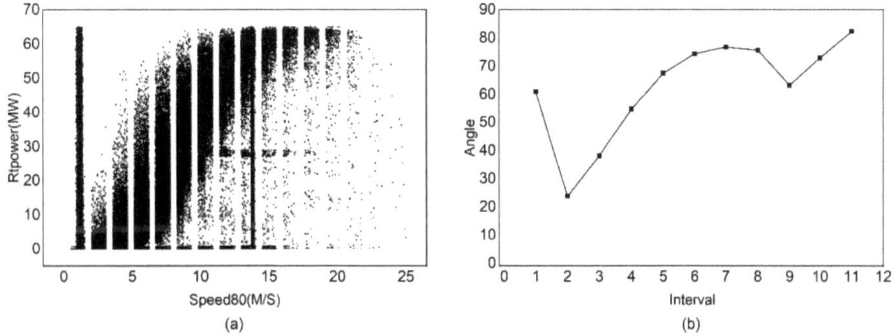

Fig. 5. Wind Speed-based Segmentation and Interval Angle Variation Diagram.

After obtaining the interval angles, logistic curve fitting is applied. The maximum number of anomaly intervals (σ) is set to 2. Among a total of 66 fittings, the result with

74   S. Chen et al.

the smallest mean squared error is selected, identifying anomaly intervals 1 and 9, as shown in Fig. 5(a) and (b). Subsequently, interpolation is carried out for the identified anomaly intervals, as illustrated in Fig. 5(c) and (Fig. 6).

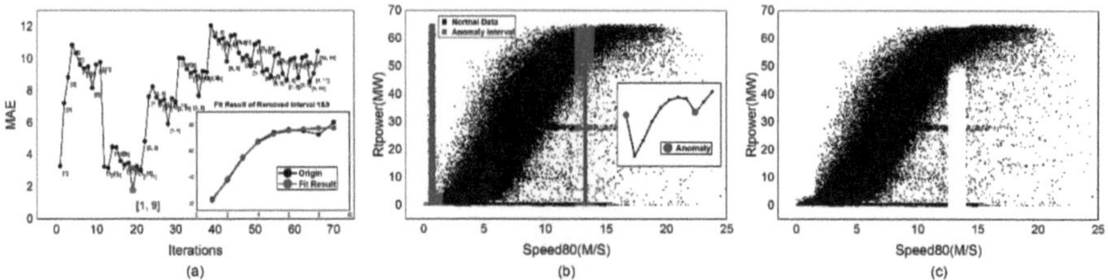

Fig. 6. Abnormal Intervals Detection and Interpolation Results.

Next, the second phase of anomaly detection and interpolation is carried out. In this stage, the data are segmented into 49 intervals, excluding those with 222excessively small data volumes. Ultimately, 49 valid intervals are obtained. The segmentation results and the trend of interval angle variations are illustrated in Fig. 7.

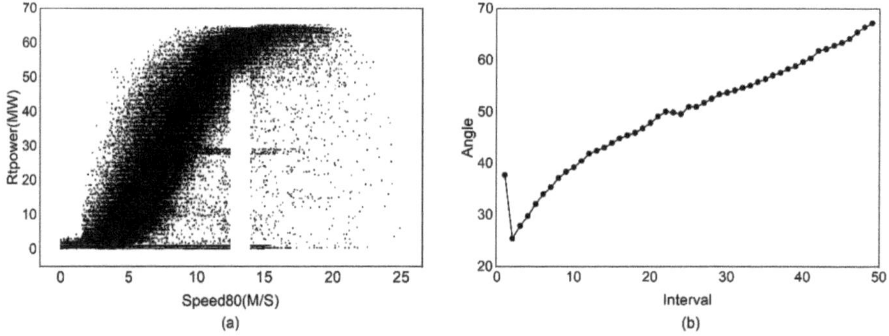

Fig. 7. Power-based Segmentation and Interval Angle Variation Diagram.

After obtaining the interval angles, logarithmic curve fitting is applied, with the maximum number of anomaly intervals (σ) set to 1. Out of 49 fittings, the result with the smallest mean squared error is selected, identifying anomaly interval 1, as depicted in Fig. 8(a) and (b). Subsequently, interpolation is carried out for this interval, as illustrated in Fig. 8(c).

Notably, the stacked anomalies associated with intervals 22 and 23 were not removed in this section, as illustrated in Fig. 8(c). This is because the number of anomalies in this part is small and does not significantly affect the interval angle variations or the overall curve fitting. Moreover, due to their limited quantity, these anomalies can be effectively handled during the DBSCAN anomaly detection phase.

The final step involves applying the DBSCAN algorithm for outlier detection on the data, following two rounds of anomaly detection and interpolation. The DBSCAN

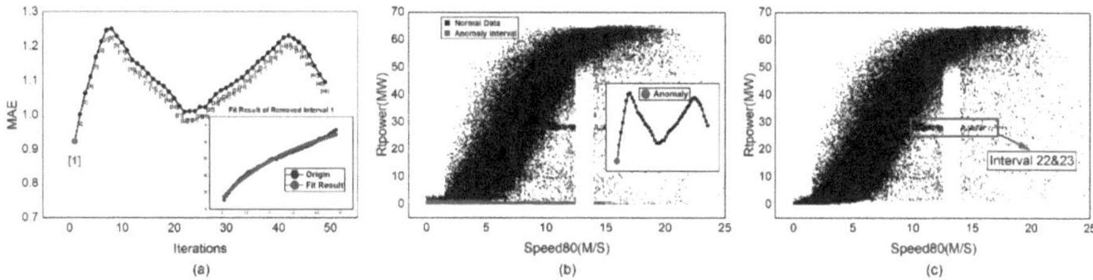

Fig. 8. Abnormal Intervals Detection and Interpolation Results.

algorithm parameters are set to eps $= 0.5$ and min_samples $= 80$, with only the largest data cluster retained. The final results are presented in Fig. 9(b), demonstrating that the stacked anomalies associated with intervals 22 and 23 have been successfully detected.

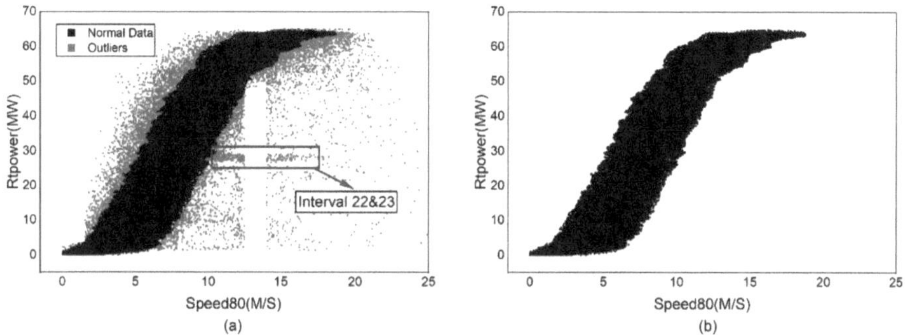

Fig. 9. DBSCAN Outlier Detection Result.

Furthermore, the final wind speed versus power data exhibits a well-defined distribution pattern and maintains a consistent physical relationship, and the proportion of anomalies ultimately decreased from 27.7% to 5.8%.

5 Conclusion

The anomaly detection method proposed in this study integrates iterative removal, linear interpolation, and the DBSCAN algorithm. The method begins by performing targeted detection of two types of stacked anomalies and reconstructs the true physical relationship between wind speed and power through linear interpolation. Subsequently, the DBSCAN algorithm is applied to identify and eliminate outlier anomalies.

Case studies demonstrate that the proposed method effectively detects complex, multi-type stacked anomalies within the wind speed-power relationship. The detection results reveal a well-structured distribution pattern between wind speed and power, thereby validating the effectiveness of the proposed method. This highlights the method's potential for addressing similar anomaly detection challenges in other physical systems or datasets.

References

1. G.W.E. Council, GWECl global wind report 2021, Global Wind Energy Council, 80, Brussels, Belgium (2021)
2. Badrzadeh, B., et al.: Wind power plant SCADA and controls. In: 2011 IEEE Power and Energy Society General Meeting, pp. 1–7. IEEE (2011)
3. Yongbin, W., Jianzhong, Z., Zhengxi, Y.: Others, review on identification and cleaning of abnormal wind power data for wind farms. Power Syst. Technol 47, 2367–2380 (2023)
4. Wang, Y., Liu, H., Song, P., Hu, Z., Deng, X., Wu, L.: Data cleaning method for abnormal operation of wind turbines based on multi-stage progressive identification. Renew. Energy 38, 1470–1476 (2020). https://doi.org/10.13941/j.cnki.21-1469/tk.2020.11.008
5. Lim, J., Kook, J., Kim, J.: DBSCAN-D: a density-based clustering method of directionality. Int. J. Appl. Eng. Res. 12, 3927–3932 (2017). https://doi.org/10.1007/s11634-024-00616-3
6. Dao, P.B., Barszcz, T., Staszewski, W.J.: Anomaly detection of wind turbines based on stationarity analysis of SCADA data. Renew. Energy 232, 121076 (2024)
7. Long, H., Xu, S., Gu, W.: An abnormal wind turbine data cleaning algorithm based on color space conversion and image feature detection. Appl. Energy 311, 118594 (2022)
8. Bilendo, F., Meyer, A., Badihi, H., Lu, N., Cambron, P., Jiang, B.: Applications and modeling techniques of wind turbine power curve for wind farms—a review. Energies 16, 180 (2022). https://doi.org/10.3390/en16010180
9. Reder, M.D., Gonzalez, E., Melero, J.J.: Wind turbine failures-tackling current problems in failure data analysis. J. Phys. Conf. Ser. 072027. IOP Publishing (2016)
10. Modhagala, V.B.: Classification of Root Causes for Wind Turbine Failures, Utica College (2020)
11. Carrillo, C., Montaño, A.O., Cidrás, J., Díaz-Dorado, E.: Review of power curve modelling for wind turbines. Renew. Sustain. Energy Rev. 21, 572–581 (2013)
12. Katinas, V., Gecevicius, G., Marciukaitis, M.: An investigation of wind power density distribution at location with low and high wind speeds using statistical model. Appl. Energy 218, 442–451 (2018)
13. Jing, B., Pei, Y., Qian, Z., Wang, A., Zhu, S., An, J.: Missing wind speed data reconstruction with improved context encoder network. Energy Rep. 8, 3386–3394 (2022)
14. Bokde, N.D., Feijoo, A., Al-Ansari, N., Yaseen, Z.M.: A comparison between reconstruction methods for generation of synthetic time series applied to wind speed simulation. IEEE Access 7, 135386–135398 (2019)
15. Yang, M., Peng, T., Zhang, W., Su, X., Han, C., Fan, F.: Abnormal data identification and reconstruction based on wind speed characteristics, CSEE. Power Energy Syst. (2023)
16. Ester, M., Kriegel, H.-P., Sander, J., Xu, X.: Density-based spatial clustering of applications with noise. Int. Conf. Knowl. Discovery Data Min. (1996)

An LLM-Enabled Data Augmentation Framework for Low-Resource Scenarios

Zhongjian Hu[1,2], Peng Yang[1,2(✉)], Tianwai Zhou[2], and Kun Song[2]

[1] School of Computer Science and Engineering, Southeast University, Nanjing, China
`{huzj,pengyang}@seu.edu.cn`
[2] Key Laboratory of Computer Network and Information Integration, Southeast University, Ministry of Education, Nanjing, China
`songkun@seu.edu.cn`

Abstract. Existing Data Augmentation (DA) methods face key limitations: traditional approaches like Easy Data Augmentation (EDA) may introduce semantic distortions, while Pretrained Language Models (PLMs) often generate insufficiently diverse data. To address these challenges, we propose a Large Language Model (LLM) based framework that integrates EDA, PLM-based augmentation and LLM-based generation to produce the augmented data. Our method incorporates a reranking mechanism to filter generated samples, ensuring semantic consistency while maintaining diversity. Additionally, we utilize EDA and PLM-generated data as prompts to guide the LLM, leveraging its capabilities to further enrich the augmented data. Experiments demonstrate that our framework significantly improves the performance, achieving accuracy gains of 3.48 and 0.50 on the STSA and SNIPS datasets.

Keywords: Data augmentation · Pre-trained language model · Large language model · Easy data augmentation · Similarity reranking

1 Introduction

Data Augmentation (DA) techniques [1,2] are widely utilized in low-resource scenarios [3]. In low-resource Natural Language Processing (NLP), prior studies have delved into various Easy Data Augmentation (EDA) methods [4]. However, these methods often introduce alterations to sentence structure and may affect semantics. Inspired by Zhao et al. [5], we design a similarity calculation method to assess the similarity between augmented and original samples. Subsequently, we rerank the augmented samples based on the similarity scores, prioritizing the retention of augmented samples with higher similarity. Additionally, Pretrained Language Model (PLM)-based approaches have been proposed for DA. Kumar et al. [6] explore both BERT-based and BART-based models for DA. With the emergence of Large Language Models (LLMs), researchers have started utilizing LLMs for DA. Møller et al. [7] utilize LLMs for DA in classification tasks. Motivated by prior works, we adopt LLMs for DA in low-resource scenarios.

T. Zhu et al. (Eds.): KSEM 2025, LNAI 15923, pp. 77–84, 2026.
https://doi.org/10.1007/978-981-95-3061-8_9

Specifically, we randomly select a subset of examples from the samples generated by EDA and PLM methods to construct prompts, which aid the LLM in generating augmented data. This paper introduces a novel framework tailored for low-resource scenarios, which integrates EDA, PLM-based methods, and LLM-based methods. The main contributions are as follows:

1) We propose a novel DA framework that integrates EDA method, PLM-based method and LLM-based method to generate rich augmented data.
2) We incorporate a similarity reranking mechanism to mitigate the potential issue of semantic alterations in augmented samples.
3) We integrate the LLM into the proposed framework, utilizing in-context learning to prompt the LLM to generate augmented data.

2   Related Work

DA methods have been explored in existing works [8]. Popular methods include EDA, Back Translation (BT), PLM-based methods, and others. Wei et al. [4] introduced EDA methods, comprising Synonym Replacement (SR), Random Swap (RS), Random Insertion (RI), and Random Deletion (RD). Wu et al. [9] propose the CBERT. However, it may not be suitable for other PLMs lacking segment embeddings. Kumar et al. [6] implement BERT-based and BART-based models for DA. They applied DA to various tasks, including intent classification, sentiment classification, and question classification. The emergence of LLMs [10–12] has ushered in a new era of NLP. Consequently, some researchers have explored the use of LLMs for DA.

3   Methodology

Figure 1 shows an overview of the proposed framework. Our approach starts with EDA, followed by a reranking mechanism that selects augmented samples most similar to the originals. In parallel, we employ the PLM to generate additional augmentations. A subset of samples from both EDA and PLM is then used as prompts to guide the LLM in producing further augmentations. Finally, we aggregate all augmented samples from EDA, PLM, and LLM to form a comprehensive augmentation set.

3.1   EDA

For input text T_o, we will augment the input data. We improve the EDA. We add a similarity reranking mechanism to ensure priority in obtaining augmented samples with higher similarity to the original sample.

We first use EDA module for DA. After that, we get the output TE.

$$TE = EDA\ (T_o) \tag{1}$$

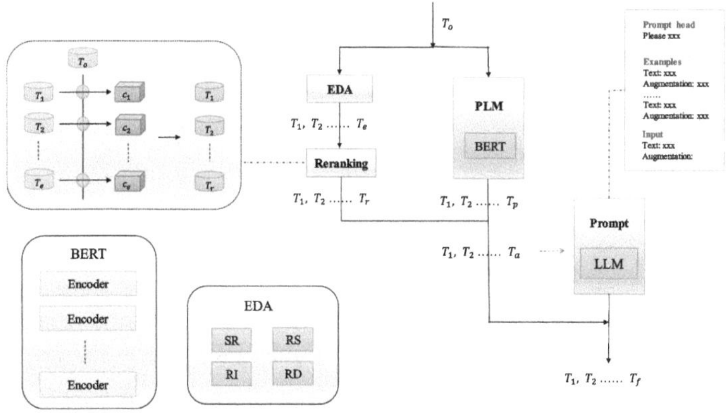

Fig. 1. Overview of the proposed framework.

where $TE = (T_1, T_2, ..., T_e)$ denotes the augmented output through EDA. Then we will rerank according to the similarity to get the output TR.

$$TR = Reranking\ (TE) \tag{2}$$

where $TR = (T_1, T_2, ..., T_r)$ denotes the output after reranking.

Reranking. We rerank the augmented texts according to their similarity with the original text. We design a similarity calculation method. We first obtain the augmented samples. Then we calculate the cosine similarity and the common similarity between the augmented and original samples, and combine the two as the final similarity. Next, we rerank the augmented samples based on the similarity and obtain the final augmented samples.

We calculate the cosine similarity between each augmented text and the original text.

$$D = Cosine\ (TE, T_o) \tag{3}$$

where $D = (d_1, d_2, ..., d_e)$ denotes the corresponding cosine similarity. Then we calculate the common similarity.

$$D' = Common\ (TE, T_o) \tag{4}$$

where $D' = (d'_1, d'_2, ..., d'_e)$ denotes the corresponding common similarity. Then we obtain the final similarity.

$$C = w_1 * D + w_2 * D' \tag{5}$$

where $C = (c_1, c_2, ..., c_e)$ denotes the final similarity, and $w_1 = w_2 = 0.5$ denotes the weights. We rerank based on the final similarity and obtain the returned augmented samples.

For any T_i and T_j, the calculation formulas of the common similarity are as follows:

$$CN = |T_i \cap T_j| \tag{6}$$

$$CR = |T_i| - |T_i \cap T_j| \tag{7}$$

$$CL = |T_j| - |T_i \cap T_j| \tag{8}$$

$$com\_similarity = \frac{2 * CN}{CR + CL + 2 * CN} \tag{9}$$

where CN denotes the number of common words between T_i and T_j, and $|T_i|$, $|T_j|$ denotes the number of words of T_i, T_j. CR denotes the number of words in T_i that are not included in T_j. CL denotes the number of words in T_j that are not included in T_i.

3.2 PLM

For PLM module, we generate augmented texts through pre-trained models, such as BERT.

$$TP = PLM\ (T_o) \tag{10}$$

where $TP = (T_1, T_2, ..., T_p)$ denotes the augmented texts. Finally, we combine the outputs of EDA module and PLM module to get the final output.

$$TA = TR + TP \tag{11}$$

where $TA = (T_1, T_2, ..., T_a)$ denotes the augmented output by EDA and PLM modules. We do not mean to concatenate sentences, but to generate augmented samples for each original sentence. The samples generated by the different methods are then put together.

3.3 LLM

We use in-context learning of LLM to generate augmented data. The in-context learning paradigm generally includes the prompt head, in-context examples, and the input. The prompt head is the description of the task. The in-context examples are some examples for the task, including source text and augmented text. The format of input is similar to the in-context example, but the augmented text will be left blank for the LLM to generate. The in-context examples are randomly selected from the texts generated by EDA and PLM modules. The in-context learning paradigm is as follows:

$$\mathcal{Y} = LLM(\mathcal{H}, \mathcal{C}, \mathcal{X}) \tag{12}$$

where $\mathcal{H}$ denotes the prompt head, $\mathcal{C}$ denotes the in-context examples, and $\mathcal{X}$ denotes the test input.

We integrate the output of LLM, EDA and PLM to get the final output TF.

$$TF = LLM(T_o) + TA \tag{13}$$

where $TF = (T_1, T_2, ..., T_f)$ denotes the final augmented output.

4 Experiments

4.1 Evaluation and Datasets

We use the STSA (SST-2), SNIPS, and TREC datasets. STSA [13] is a sentiment classification dataset with positive and negative labels. SNIPS [14] is an intention classification dataset containing seven intentions. TREC is a dataset of question classification containing six question types [15]. For these datasets, we use the versions of Kumar et al. [6]. For low-resource scenarios, Kumar et al. [6] build a small training set by randomly selecting ten samples for each class. We follow their steps to simulate low-resource scenarios. Our evaluation metrics also follow theirs. The main experiments are repeated 15 times. We randomly sample on the training and dev sets to simulate low-resource regime for each experiment. We adopt the full test set for evaluation.

4.2 Baseline Methods and Implementation Setup

Apart from the results of LLM-based methods, the baseline results are mainly drawn from the work of Kumar et al. [6], including EDA, BT, BERT, CBERT, BART, and others. For EDA, we mainly follow the implementation of [4,6]. For BERT based DA, we use the "bert-base-uncased" model. The parameters of the BERT model follow the default parameters provided in the huggingface. The model is trained for ten epochs. We set the learning rate to 4e−5. For LLM, we use the LLaMA [10] 7B version. For base classifier, we use the "bert-base-uncased" model. The model is trained for eight epochs. We set the initial learning rate to 4e−5.

4.3 Experimental Results

Table 1 shows the results. It can be found that our method outperforms most baselines in the overall evaluation. Specifically, our method outperforms EDA methods on STSA, SNIPS and TREC. This indicates that our method can improve the EDA. By prioritizing the retention of augmented samples with higher similarity to the originals through a reranking mechanism, our approach ensures that the augmented samples closely resemble the originals. Furthermore, our method outperforms BT methods, PLM-based methods, and LLM-based methods on the STSA, SNIPS, and TREC datasets, which demonstrates its effectiveness. The proposed framework combines multiple methods to generate rich data, thereby yielding superior results.

Table 1. Main results

Method	STSA	SNIPS	TREC
EDA [4]	53.82	85.78	52.57
BT [16]	57.45	86.45	66.16
CBERT [9]	57.36	85.79	64.33
BERT(expand) [17]	56.34	86.11	65.33
GPT-2 [6]	55.40	86.59	54.29
BART(span) [18]	57.68	87.24	67.30
ChatGLM-6B [11]	57.94	87.29	65.80
LLaMA-7B [10]	58.29	86.86	67.07
Ours	**61.77**	**87.74**	**67.47**

4.4 Ablation Study

We conduct ablation experiments on the STSA, SNIPS, and TREC datasets. Table 2 shows the results. Setups include "- EDA", where EDA module is not included; "- Reranking", where Reranking module is not included; "- PLM", where PLM module is not included; "- LLM", where LLM module is not included; "- ALL", where all modules are excluded. We find that no matter what module is removed will cause the loss of model performance, and when all modules are removed, the model performance will suffer the most. This indicates that all modules can bring positive effect on model performance.

Table 2. Ablation study

Method	STSA	SNIPS	TREC
Ours	**61.77**	**87.74**	**67.47**
- EDA	59.51 ($\downarrow$ 2.26)	86.25 ($\downarrow$ 1.49)	63.67 ($\downarrow$ 3.80)
- Reranking	60.24 ($\downarrow$ 1.53)	86.43 ($\downarrow$ 1.31)	63.40 ($\downarrow$ 4.07)
- PLM	60.92 ($\downarrow$ 0.85)	87.17 ($\downarrow$ 0.57)	62.80 ($\downarrow$ 4.67)
- LLM	60.02 ($\downarrow$ 1.75)	87.14 ($\downarrow$ 0.60)	63.20 ($\downarrow$ 4.27)

5   Conclusion

This paper introduces a novel DA framework for low-resource scenarios, which integrates EDA, PLM-based methods, and LLM-based methods. The proposed framework adopts a similarity reranking mechanism, which can prioritize obtaining augmented samples with higher similarity. Furthermore, the framework leverages the capability of LLM to generate augmented data. Experiments demonstrate the effectiveness of the proposed framework.

Acknowledgments. This work was supported in part by the National Natural Science Foundation of China under Grant 62272100 and the Academy-Locality Cooperation Project of CAE under Grant JS2021ZT05.

References

1. Bayer, M., Kaufhold, M.-A., Reuter, C.: A survey on data augmentation for text classification. ACM Comput. Surv. **55**(7), 1–39 (2022)
2. Li, B., Hou, Y., Che, W.: Data augmentation approaches in natural language processing: a survey. AI Open **3**, 71–90 (2022)
3. Şahin, G.G.: To augment or not to augment? A comparative study on text augmentation techniques for low-resource NLP. Comput. Linguist. **48**(1), 5–42 (2022)
4. Wei, J., Zou, K.: EDA: easy data augmentation techniques for boosting performance on text classification tasks. In: Proceedings of the 2019 Conference on Empirical Methods in Natural Language Processing and the 9th International Joint Conference on Natural Language Processing (EMNLP-IJCNLP), pp. 6382–6388 (2019)
5. Zhao, J.: ROR: read-over-read for long document machine reading comprehension. In: Findings of the Association for Computational Linguistics: EMNLP 2021, pp. 1862–1872 (2021)
6. Kumar, V., Choudhary, A., Cho, E.: Data augmentation using pre-trained transformer models. In: Proceedings of the 2nd Workshop on Life-long Learning for Spoken Language Systems, pp. 18–26 (2020)
7. Møller, A.G., Dalsgaard, J.A., Pera, A., Aiello, L.M.: Is a prompt and a few samples all you need? Using GPT-4 for data augmentation in low-resource classification tasks. arXiv preprint arXiv:2304.13861 (2023)
8. Wang, Z., et al.: A comprehensive survey on data augmentation. arXiv preprint arXiv:2405.09591 (2024)
9. Wu, X., Lv, S., Zang, L., Han, J., Hu, S.: Conditional BERT contextual augmentation. In: Rodrigues, J.M.F., et al. (eds.) ICCS 2019, Part IV. LNCS, vol. 11539, pp. 84–95. Springer, Cham (2019). https://doi.org/10.1007/978-3-030-22747-0_7
10. Touvron, H., et al.: Llama: open and efficient foundation language models. arXiv preprint arXiv:2302.13971 (2023)
11. Team GLM, et al.: ChatGLM: a family of large language models from GLM-130B TO GLM-4 all tools. arXiv preprint arXiv:2406.12793 (2024)
12. Bai, J., et al.: Qwen technical report. arXiv preprint arXiv:2309.16609 (2023)
13. Socher, R., et al.: Recursive deep models for semantic compositionality over a sentiment treebank. In: Proceedings of the 2013 Conference on Empirical Methods in Natural Language Processing, pp. 1631–1642 (2013)
14. Coucke, A., et al.: Snips voice platform: an embedded spoken language understanding system for private-by-design voice interfaces. arXiv preprint arXiv:1805.10190 (2018)
15. Li, X., Roth, D.: Learning question classifiers. In: COLING 2002: The 19th International Conference on Computational Linguistics (2002)
16. Ng, N., Yee, K., Baevski, A., Ott, M., Auli, M., Edunov, S.: Facebook fair's WMT19 news translation task submission. In: Proceedings of the Fourth Conference on Machine Translation (Volume 2: Shared Task Papers, Day 1), pp. 314–319 (2019)

17. Devlin, J., Chang, M.-W., Lee, K., Toutanova, K.: BERT: pre-training of deep bidirectional transformers for language understanding. In: Proceedings of the 2019 Conference of the North American Chapter of the Association for Computational Linguistics: Human Language Technologies, volume 1 (long and short papers), pp. 4171–4186 (2019)
18. Lewis, M., et al.: BART: denoising sequence-to-sequence pre-training for natural language generation, translation, and comprehension. In: Proceedings of the 58th Annual Meeting of the Association for Computational Linguistics, pp. 7871–7880 (2020)

Lightweight Remote Sensing Tiny Object Detection Model Based on YOLOv8n Architecture

Jinyin Bai, Wei Zhu$^{(\boxtimes)}$, Qinglin Xu, Xiangchen Wang, and Peng Zheng

National University of Defense Technology, Wuhan 430030, China
zhuwei929@hotmail.com

Abstract. To address the critical challenges of weak feature representation, high computational complexity, and insufficient multi-scale adaptability in tiny object detection of high-resolution remote sensing images, this study proposes an improved lightweight model based on the YOLOv8n architecture. Firstly, an innovative GhostConv-Head module is designed, which establishes a collaborative mechanism of primary feature compression and phantom expansion through decoupled feature generation processes, significantly reducing model parameters and computational complexity while maintaining feature representation capability. Secondly, a multi-scale Slim-Neck feature fusion architecture with dynamic kernel size adaptation is proposed, employing a receptive field dynamic adjustment strategy to enhance detection sensitivity for tiny targets. Furthermore, a lightweight LiteCBAM dual-dimensional attention mechanism is developed, achieving balanced optimization between computational efficiency and feature focusing capability through dual-pooling feature compression strategy and decomposed spatial attention computation. Comparative experiments on the AI-TOD remote sensing dataset demonstrate that the improved model achieves a mean Average Precision (mAP) of 24.9%, representing a 2.8 percentage point improvement over the baseline YOLOv8n. The model size is compressed to 2.73 MB, meeting the real-time detection requirements of edge computing devices while preserving lightweight characteristics.

Keywords: YOLOv8n · Model lightweighting · Remote sensing tiny objects · Feature fusion · Attention mechanism

1 Introduction

As a core computer vision research topic, object detection achieves precise spatial localization and semantic categorization of targets in complex scenes [1]. This dual-task technology combines geometric bounding box localization with semantic deep feature classification. Traditional methods rely on handcrafted feature engineering like HOG [2] and SIFT [3], yet suffer from limited feature representation and scale adaptability. Deep learning advancements enable end-to-end feature learning, synergistically optimizing accuracy and speed for complex scene detection [4].

T. Zhu et al. (Eds.): KSEM 2025, LNAI 15923, pp. 85–96, 2026.
https://doi.org/10.1007/978-981-95-3061-8_10

Tiny object detection faces unique challenges in remote sensing, medical imaging, UAV navigation, and surveillance systems [5]. Defined as targets under 32×32 pixels, they exhibit: low signal-to-noise ratios amid complex backgrounds; feature attenuation in deep networks; and multi-scale sensitivity causing gradient dispersion [4]. These characteristics challenge conventional detection frameworks.

Current mainstream tiny object detection methodologies can be categorized into two technical approaches: multi-stage and single-stage detectors. Multi-stage methods employ cascaded processing pipelines: generating region proposals followed by feature extraction and classification-regression. The seminal R-CNN framework utilizes selective search for proposal generation and convolutional neural networks (CNNs) for feature extraction [6]. Fast R-CNN significantly improves processing efficiency through shared convolutional feature maps [7], while Faster R-CNN introduces Region Proposal Networks (RPN) for end-to-end training [8]. Mask R-CNN extends the detection framework with instance segmentation capabilities, achieving multi-task coordination [9]. Despite their superior accuracy, multi-stage methods suffer from high computational complexity, making them unsuitable for real-time applications.

Single-stage detectors achieve end-to-end inference through fully convolutional architectures, demonstrating significant advantages in computational efficiency. RetinaNet innovatively addresses class imbalance through focal loss function [10]. The SSD algorithm enhances scale adaptability via multi-scale feature pyramids but encounters feature blurring in low-resolution layers [11]. The YOLO series has achieved breakthroughs in real-time detection through grid-based prediction mechanisms, with its technological evolution holding substantial research value [12, 13]. The YOLOv8 optimizes gradient flow through C2f modules (Cross-stage Dual Convolution) and integrates Spatial Pyramid Pooling Fast (SPPF) modules for multi-scale feature abstraction [14, 15]. Addressing the specific requirements of remote sensing tiny object detection, this study proposes an improved model based on YOLOv8n architecture, with three principal contributions:

(1) A dual-path feature extraction structure (C2f_Ghost) integrating GhostConv and C2f modules, achieving efficient multi-scale feature fusion through channel dimensionality reduction and dynamic kernel strategies, reducing parameters by 28.6% while mitigating feature attenuation.
(2) A feature compression bottleneck module combining GhostConv and VoVGhostCSP, employing feature generation decoupling to decompose convolution into primary feature extraction and phantom feature synthesis phases, reducing neck computational complexity by 34.2% through grouped channel shuffling;
(3) A lightweight hybrid attention mechanism (LiteCBAM) utilizing dual-pooling compression (Global Average Pooling + Global Max Pooling concatenation) to replace fully-connected layers, reducing channel attention parameters, and optimizing spatial attention efficiency through dilated depthwise and pointwise convolution combinations.

These innovative module-level improvements achieve synergistic optimization of detection accuracy and computational efficiency, providing new technical solutions for engineering deployment of lightweight remote sensing detection systems.

2 Network Model Design

2.1 Improved YOLOv8n Model Structure

YOLOv8n constitutes a lightweight single-stage object detection framework designed to balance mobile deployment efficiency and detection accuracy. Maintaining the backbone-neck-head architecture, it achieves parameter compression via modular reconfiguration while preserving multi-task detection capabilities [16].

The improved model preserves the advantages of the single-stage detection paradigm. As illustrated in Fig. 1, the refined network adopts a hierarchical architecture comprising three functional modules: backbone feature extraction network, dynamic feature fusion network, and multi-task detection head. The implementation principles of each component are detailed as follows:

Backbone Network Reconstruction: Serving as the central feature extraction component, the backbone network adopts a five-stage cascaded architecture that progressively generates multi-scale feature pyramids. As depicted in the backbone structure of Fig. 1, the data flow processes through Convolution-BatchNorm-SiLU (CBS) modules as fundamental feature processing units. The proposed C2f_Ghost module synergistically integrates the dynamic feature generation mechanism of GhostConv with cross-stage feature interaction from C2f.

Feature Fusion Network Optimization: The neck network employs an enhanced Slim-Neck architecture, integrating VoVGhostCSP modules and LiteCBAM attention modules to construct a multi-level feature pyramid. The VoVGhostCSP module redesigns the classical Cross-Stage Partial Network (CSP) for lightweight efficiency, replacing standard convolutions with GhostConv operators. The LiteCBAM lightweight attention module is cascaded at critical nodes of the neck network, enhancing salient feature representation for small targets through dual-channel and spatial feature recalibration.

Following five progressive downsampling operations, the network outputs detection feature maps at three scales (80×80, 40×40, 20×20), hierarchically optimized for multi-scale detection tasks targeting small, medium, and regular-sized objects.

2.2 Lightweight Backbone with Ghost Feature Generation

To optimize model performance, this study introduces GhostConv, a novel lightweight convolutional architecture. This structure employs a dual-path design that combines base feature mapping with dynamically generated phantom features, utilizing linear transformation operations to produce supplementary features. This approach effectively enhances feature diversity while reducing convolutional computation load [17].

As illustrated in Fig. 2, replacing all original C2f modules in the YOLOv8n backbone network with C2f_Ghost variants achieves multidimensional improvements in feature extraction capabilities. Compared to conventional C2f modules, the C2f_Ghost architecture incorporates a dynamic kernel adaptation mechanism that automatically adjusts convolutional receptive fields based on hierarchical feature characteristics, while simultaneously employing a feature distillation strategy to amplify critical features and suppress redundant information. Furthermore, it establishes cross-resolution feature interaction channels to enhance semantic fusion efficiency across multiple scales, thereby

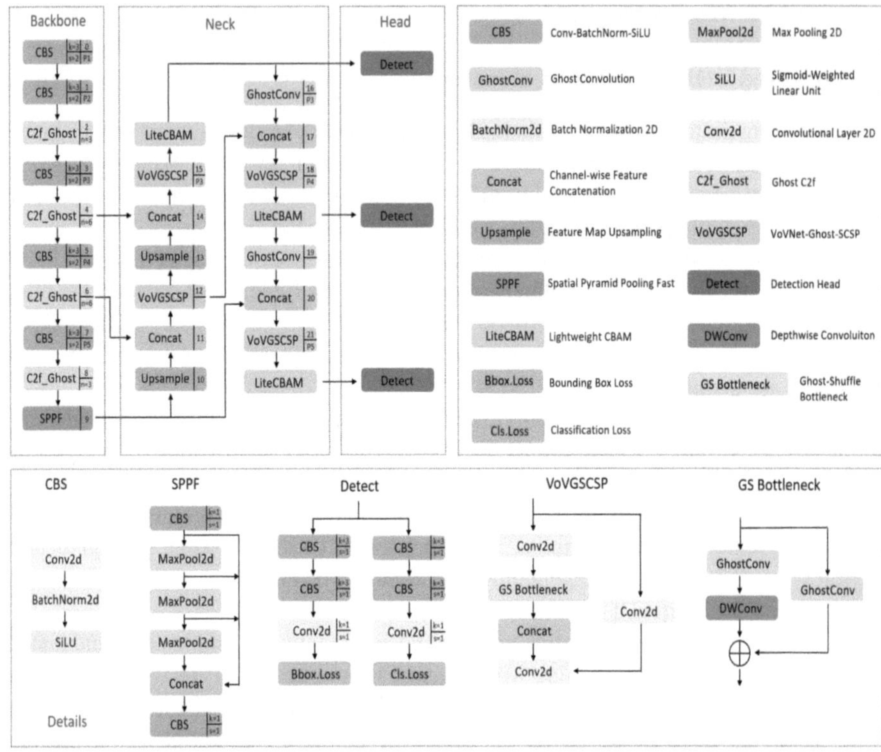

Fig. 1. Improved structure diagram of the YOLOv8n model.

enabling more comprehensive integration of contextual information and improved fusion completeness for small-scale targets.

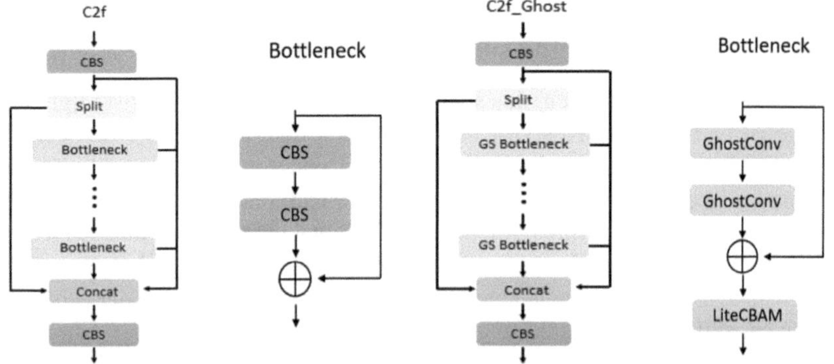

Fig. 2. Comparision between C2f and C2f_Ghost

2.3 Lightweight Neck

To achieve collaborative optimization of model lightweighting and precision preservation, this study proposes an innovative Slim-neck architecture constructed with Ghost-Conv and VoVGhostCSP modules. Through feature decoupling and re-parameterization design, this architecture effectively compresses model scale while completely preserving the backbone network's representational capacity. Traditional convolutional neural networks exhibit significant limitations in processing high-resolution remote sensing imagery[18, 19].

Addressing these challenges, GhostConv employs a decoupled feature generation strategy that decomposes convolution operations into two synergistically optimized phases: a primary feature generation phase extracting core features through a minimal set of standard convolutional kernels, and a phantom feature synthesis phase expanding feature diversity via lightweight operations including linear transformations [17]. The module's core innovation lies in its cascaded decoupling design of feature generation, with data processing comprising three critical stages: The first stage performs channel compression through 1×1 convolution, mathematically expressed as:

$$Y_p = Conv_{1 \times 1}(X, W_P) \tag{1}$$

In the equation, $Conv_{1 \times 1}$ denotes the 1×1 convolution kernel employed for channel dimensionality reduction, where Y_p represents the compressed primary feature map and X corresponds to the input feature map.

In the second stage, the primary feature map is processed through Depthwise Separable Convolution (DWConv) to generate phantom features. We propose a dynamic kernel adaptation mechanism that differentially configures convolutional kernel parameters according to the spatial characteristics of feature hierarchy: for low-level features containing rich detailed information (e.g., P3 layer), 5×5 large kernels are employed to enhance spatial receptive fields, while for high-level features with strong semantic representation (e.g., P4 layer), conventional 3×3 kernels are deployed to maintain computational efficiency. This strategy is mathematically formulated as:

$$Y_g = DWConv_{k \times k}(Y_p, W_d) \tag{2}$$

In the equation, $DWConv_{k \times k}$ denotes the depthwise convolution operation, W_d represents the weight matrix of the depthwise convolutional kernel, and k indicates the kernel size.

In the third stage, the primary feature map and phantom features are concatenated along the channel dimension, followed by a grouped channel shuffling operation. This process can be formalized as:

$$Y_c = Concat(Y_p, Y_g) \tag{3}$$

$$Y_{out} = S_G(Y_c) \tag{4}$$

$$S_G(Y)_{i,j,k} = Y_{i,[G \times (j\%G_s)+[j/G_s]],k} \tag{5}$$

where Y_c denotes the concatenated feature tensor, S_G represents the channel shuffle operator with G indicating the number of feature groups and G_S specifying the cardinality of channels per group. The indices i, j, k correspond to batch dimension, output channel, and spatial position respectively.

2.4 Dual-Dimension Attention Decoupling with Lightweight Optimization

Aiming at the inherent challenges of low signal-to-noise ratio, multi-scale distribution, and high-frequency detail dominance in tiny remote sensing targets, this paper introduces a dual-dimension attention mechanism—the Convolutional Block Attention Module (CBAM), whose core innovation lies in decoupled spatiotemporal feature modeling. This module employs cascaded channel attention and spatial attention submodules to achieve adaptive recalibration from feature channels to spatial dimensions. By amplifying critical feature responses while suppressing redundant information, the CBAM mechanism significantly enhances the discriminative capability of detection models [20].

The proposed scheme introduces a feature pooling fusion strategy that concatenates Global Average Pooling (GAP) and Global Maximum Pooling (GMP) outputs along the channel dimension. This strategy achieves dual-branch collaborative encoding while reducing feature dimensions by 50%, preserving attention modeling accuracy and delivering FLOPs reduction. The operation is formally expressed as:

$$z = [GAP(x); GMP(x)] \tag{6}$$

$$z \in R^{2C \times 1 \times 1} \tag{7}$$

In spatial attention modeling, conventional 7×7 convolutions at 1024×1024 resolution incur 49.0 million multiply-accumulate operations (MACs), while their large receptive fields tend to introduce background interference noise. To address this, we implement a depthwise separable convolution architecture that decouples standard convolution into cascaded operations. The depthwise convolution independently processes spatial correlations per channel (containing only 1/C parameters of standard convolution), while the subsequent pointwise convolution with 1×1 kernels achieves cross-channel information fusion. This dual-stage design maintains feature interaction capabilities while substantially reducing computational complexity and noise susceptibility. The operation is formally expressed as:

$$f(x) = Conv_{1 \times 1}(DepthwiseConv_{3 \times 3, dilation=2}(x)) \tag{8}$$

$DepthwiseConv_{3 \times 3}$ denote the depthwise separable convolution operation, which employs 3×3 kernels with a dilation rate of 2 to extract channel-specific features under multi-scale receptive fields. The $Conv_{1 \times 1}$ operator performs cross-channel interaction through learnable 1×1 convolutional kernels, producing enhanced output features $f(x)$.

The LiteCBAM attention modules are strategically deployed in both backbone and neck networks: In backbone layers, channel-attention dominance enhances acquisition of shallow semantic features, while neck layers prioritize spatial attention mechanisms with multi-scale feature pyramid fusion. This hierarchical attention guidance enables adaptive feature calibration, achieving stronger response on critical features while reducing parameter count, particularly effective for enhancing signal-to-noise ratio of micro-scale targets in cluttered environments.

3   Experimental Results and Analysis

3.1   Experimental Setup and Dataset

To rigorously evaluate the enhanced YOLOv8n model's capability in detecting micro-scale remote sensing targets, we conducted comprehensive experiments on the AI-TOD benchmark dataset. The experimental framework was implemented using TensorFlow 2.12.0, with detailed hardware/software configurations outlined in Table 1.

Table 1. Hardware and Software Configuration

Environment	Specifications
Operating System	Windows11
CPU	Intel Core i9-13900HX (2.20 GHz)
GPU	NVIDIA RTX 4080
RAM	32GB DDR5 (4800 MHz)
IDE	PyCharm 2024.1
Language	Python 3.9.12
CUDA	11.7.1

AI-TOD is a specialized benchmark dataset designed for micro-scale object detection in aerial imagery, containing 28,036 high-resolution aerial images covering 8 typical remote sensing detection categories including person, vehicle, ship, etc. The dataset's defining characteristic lies in its extremely small target size—averaging only 12.8 pixels (approximately 1/8 of the target sizes in existing aerial detection datasets), which poses significant challenges for detection algorithms [21].

3.2   Data Preprocessing

In micro-scale remote sensing object detection tasks, the limited pixel size of targets results in insufficient texture and shape features, making conventional convolution operations ineffective for feature extraction. Additionally, targets are easily overwhelmed by complex background noise, leading to low recognition rates.

To address these issues, this paper adopts data augmentation methods. First, geometric transformations (e.g., rotation, translation, and shearing) are applied to modify target spatial positions, compensating for deformation differences caused by multi-view aerial image acquisition. Subsequently, the Mosaic stitching technology synthesizes four images into training samples, which not only expands contextual combinations of micro-targets but also increases target density per image. Finally, Mixup linear interpolation augmentation constructs continuous sample distributions in feature space, effectively alleviating classification bias caused by long-tailed distributions. Detailed training parameters are listed in Table 2.

Table 2. Training Parameters

Phase Parameter	Phase 1	Phase 2	Phase 3
Input Size	640 × 640	1024 × 1024	1280 × 1280
Training Epochs	150	100	50
Batch size	8	4	2
Learning Rate	1e–3	5e–5	2e–5
Optimizer	AdamW	AdamW	AdamW
Mosaic Probability	0.8	0.3	0.1
Mixup Probability	0.1	0.05	0
Rotation Angle	30	15	15

3.3 Evaluation Metrics

To comprehensively evaluate model performance, we employ five key metrics: Precision (P), Recall (R), mean Average Precision (mAP), floating-point operations (FLOPs), and parameter count. The mathematical formulations of these metrics are defined as follows.

$$Precision = \frac{TP}{TP + FP} \tag{9}$$

$$Recall = \frac{TP}{TP + FN} \tag{10}$$

$$AP = \int_0^1 P(r)dr \tag{11}$$

$$mAP = \frac{1}{k} \sum_k^i APi \tag{12}$$

TP (True Positives) indicates the quantity of correctly identified positive samples, while *FP* (False Positives) represents negative samples erroneously detected as positive. *FN* (False Negatives) corresponds to positive instances that were either missed or incorrectly classified as negative. The precision-recall curve *P(r)* describes the relationship between detection accuracy and coverage rate at varying confidence thresholds. *AP* denotes the Average Precision for detection targets in the *i* category, with *k* specifying the total number of object categories in the evaluation framework.

3.4 Experimental Results

To systematically evaluate the performance of the proposed enhanced model, we conducted comparative experiments with lightweight YOLO variants (YOLOv5n,

YOLOv6n, and YOLOv8n) under identical training parameters and dataset configurations. The quantitative comparison of critical performance metrics is presented in Table 3, demonstrating our model's advancements in both detection accuracy and operational efficiency.

Table 3. Comparison of detection results

Model	Precision(%)	Recall(%)	mAP	Params(M)	FLOPs(G)
YOLOv5n	57.8	20.2	21.3	2.50	7.1
YOLOv6n	61.9	21.1	21.7	4.23	11.8
YOLOv8n	61.2	22.2	22.1	3.01	8.2
Proposed	63.1	24.6	24.9	2.73	7.4

As shown in Table 3, the proposed improved model achieves an mAP of 24.9%, outperforming the other three algorithms, with a 2.8 percentage point improvement in mAP over the second-best performing YOLOv8n. The number of parameters (2.73M) is reduced by 9.3% compared to YOLOv8n and by 35.5% compared to the YOLOv6n model with the highest parameter count. This reduction in parameter scale directly decreases model storage requirements, making it lighter and easier to deploy. The computational cost of the improved algorithm (7.4G FLOPs) is reduced by 9.8% compared to YOLOv8n, though it shows a slight increase relative to YOLOv5n.

3.5 Visual Analysis

To systematically evaluate the model improvements, this study presents visual comparisons between the baseline YOLOv8n and the enhanced model in ship detection tasks through Fig. 3. Three representative scenarios were selected for fine-grained analysis: original images (left), baseline model detections (middle), and improved model outputs (right). A dynamic color scheme was applied to bounding boxes, with green indicating confidence scores > 0.5 and blue for ≤0.5. Specifically, in road traffic scenarios (a), red-marked areas show that the baseline model missed 4 target instances, while the improved model missed only 1. In complex road scenarios (b), the baseline model (brown boxes) misidentified road signs as vehicles, whereas the improved model effectively eliminated such false positives. For high-speed motion scenarios (c), both models failed to detect the rightmost high-speed ship, but the improved model demonstrated increased confidence in detected targets, with confidence scores improving from 0.42/0.34/0.56 to 0.48/0.39/0.65. The visual results confirm that the improved algorithm reduces missed/false detections and enhances confidence stability while maintaining real-time performance.

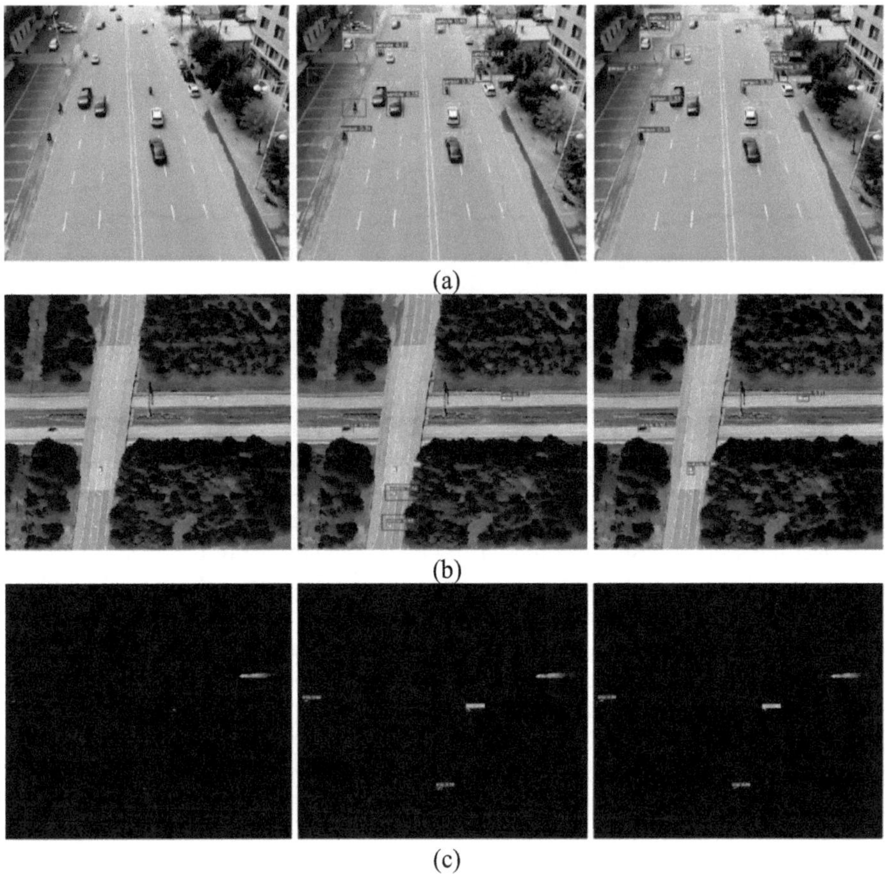

(a)

(b)

(c)

Fig. 3. Comparison of visualization results

3.6 Ablation Study

To validate the effectiveness of individual modules in the proposed improved model, this paper conducted ablation experiments. N1 represents the baseline experiment using the original YOLOv8n model, with all other parameters and environmental settings kept identical. As shown in Table 4, the N1 model (original YOLOv8n) achieved the lowest mAP value, highest parameter count, and relatively average detection performance. The introduction of GhostConv improved the recall, F1-score, and mAP values while slightly reducing precision, with computational complexity and parameter count moderately decreasing. Subsequently, the combined introduction of Slim-neck resulted in the lowest parameter count and computational complexity across all experimental configurations, indicating that integrating Slim-neck with GhostConv effectively reduces model burden. Finally, the incorporation of SlimCBAM yielded the highest precision, recall, F1-score, and mAP values.

Table 4. Ablation study results

Moudle	GhostConv	Slim-neck	Slim CBAM	Precision	Recall	mAP	Params(M)	FLOPs (G)
N1				61.2	22.2	22.1	3.01	8.2
N2	√			60.8	23.2	22.5	2.87	8.0
N3	√	√		61.9	24.2	23.8	2.68	7.1
N4	√	√	√	63.1	24.6	24.9	2.73	7.4

4 Conclusion

To address critical challenges in small target detection, this study proposes a lightweight detection model based on the YOLOv8n architecture. The developed C2f_Ghost module achieves feature decoupling and reconstruction in the channel dimension by leveraging GhostConv's capability for dynamic redundant feature generation. The Slim-Neck architecture employs heterogeneous combinations of GhostConv and VoVGhostCSP, effectively mitigating feature blurring in small targets through feature compression bottlenecks and grouped channel shuffling mechanisms. LiteCBAM enhances feature representation for small targets through a dual-pooling compression strategy and decomposed spatial attention design, maintaining lightweight attention mechanisms while improving perceptual performance. This work provides valuable insights for lightweight small target detection in remote sensing applications. Future research will focus on exploring more efficient architectures that preserve lightweight characteristics while further improving recognition accuracy for small remote sensing targets.

References

1. Zhao, Q.C., Wu, Y.Q., Yuan, Y.B.: Progress of ship detection and recognition methods in optical remote sensing images. Acta Aeronautica et Astronautica Sinica **45**(8), 029025 (2024). https://doi.org/10.7527/S1000-6893.2023.29025
2. Cui, J., Han, J., Li, J., et al.: Visual gesture recognition based on fusion of VGG16 and HOG features. J. Ord. Equip. Eng. **45**(12), 289–297 (2024)
3. Yang, X., Zhou, N.: Image mosaic method based on Improved SIFT feature extraction. J. Guilin Univ. Technol. **43**(1), 131–136 (2023)
4. Li, K.Q., Chen, Y., Liu, J.C., et al.: Survey of deep learning-based object detection algorithms. Comput. Eng. **48**(7), 1–12 (2022)
5. Zeng, X., Liu, G., Chen, J., et al.: A multi-scale hierarchical residual network-based method for tiny object detection in optical remote sensing images. Acta Photonica Sinica **53**(8), 0810001 (2024)
6. Xie, X., Cheng, G., Wang, J., Li, K., Yao, X., Han, J.: Oriented R-CNN and beyond. Int. J. Comput. Vis. **132**(7), 1–23 (2024)
7. Choi, J.-Y., Han, J.-M.: Deep learning (Fast R-CNN)-based evaluation of rail surface defects. Appl. Sci. (Switzerland) **14**(5), 1874 (2024)

8. Fu, P., Wang, J.: Lithology identification based on improved faster R-CNN. Minerals **14**(9), 954 (2024)

9. He, K., Gkioxari, G., Dollar, P., Girshick, R.: Mask R-CNN. IEEE Trans. Patt. Anal. Mach. Intell. **42**(2), 386–397 (2020)

10. Lin, T.-Y., Goyal, P., Girshick, R., He, K., Dollar, P.: Focal loss for dense object detection. IEEE Trans. Patt. Anal. Mach. Intell. **42**(2), 318–327 (2020)

11. Liu, W., et al.: SSD: single shot MultiBox detector. Comput. Vis. - ECCV 2016, PT I, **9905**(1), 21–37 (2016)

12. Jiang, P., Ergu1, D., Liu, F., Cai, Y., Ma, B.: A review of Yolo algorithm developments. Proc. Comput. Sci. **199**, 1066–1073 (2022)

13. Terven, J., Córdova-Esparza, D.-M., Romero-González, J.-A.: A comprehensive review of YOLO architectures in computer vision: from YOLOv1 to YOLOv8 and YOLO-NAS. Mach. Learn. Knowl. Extract. **5**(4), 1680–1716 (2023)

14. Yan, B.: A real-time apple targets detection method for picking robot based on improved YOLOv5. Remote Sens. **13**(9), 1619 (2021)

15. Lou, H., et al.: DC-YOLOv8: small-size object detection algorithm based on camera sensor. Electronics **12**(2323), 2323 (2023)

16. Gao, Z., Yu, X., Rong, X., Wang, W.: Improved YOLOv8n for lightweight ship detection. J. Mar. Sci. Eng. **12**(10), 1774 (2024)

17. Cao, J., Bao, W., Shang, H., Yuan, M., Cheng, Q.: GCL-YOLO: a GhostConv-based lightweight YOLO network for UAV small object detection. Remote Sens. **15**(20), 4932 (2023)

18. Cao, H., Zhang, G., Zhao, A., Wang, Q., Zou, X., Wang, H.: YOLOv8n-CSE: a model for detecting litchi in nighttime environments. Agronomy **14**(9), 1924 (2024)

19. Guan, S., Lv, S.: MCG-YOLOv8n: an enhanced YOLOv8n model for segmentation of adherent buckwheat seeds. IEEE Access **12**, 131968–131981 (2024)

20. Hao, S., Zhang, X., Ma, X., et al.: Foreign object detection in coal mine conveyor belt based on CBAM-YOLOv5. J. China Coal Soc. **47**(11), 4147–4156 (2022)

21. Liang, R., Cen, Y., Zhang, L., Zhang, F., Huang, Y., Gan, F.: Innovative lightweight detection for airborne remote sensing: integrating G-shuffle and dynamic multiscale pyramid networks. IEEE J. Sel. Topics Appl. Earth Observ. Rem. Sens. **18**, 2010–2023 (2025)

Causal Encoding Generative Model Based on Attention and KAN

Jing Yang[1](✉) (iD), Xiangbin Meng[1](✉), Xuanli Qin[2], Xianjun Xu[2], and Zhangxiang Hu[2]

[1] School of Computer Science and Information Engineering, Hefei University of Technology, Hefei, China
jing.yang@hfut.edu.cn, Xiangbin@mail.hfut.edu.cn
[2] State Grid Anqing Power Supply Company, Anqing, China

Abstract. With the rapid growth of observational data in various scientific and technological domains, such as healthcare and power systems, causal inference research has gained significant momentum. However, estimating causal effects using observational data faces two primary obstacles: the fundamental absence of counterfactual outcomes and the presence of confounding factors. These challenges become more pronounced when dealing with high-dimensional covariates, as existing methods often fail to capture their inherent correlations. To address these issues, this paper proposes a Causal Encoding Generative Model based on the Attention mechanism and the Kolmogorov-Arnold Network (KAN), referred to as CAKEGM. The model first applies an attention mechanism to learn the internal dependencies among covariates, then performs dimensionality reduction to map features into a low-dimensional latent space with known density. Simultaneously, KAN is employed to fit treatment variables and outcomes, enabling effective disentanglement of covariate representations in the latent space. We evaluate CAKEGM on two healthcare-related datasets. Experimental results show that CAKEGM outperforms existing state-of-the-art methods in both accuracy and robustness for treatment effect estimation.

Keywords: Causal effect · Attention · KAN · Potential Outcomes · Generative Model

1 Introduction

Uncovering causal relationships enhances our understanding of real-world phenomena. For example, pharmaceutical firms monitor drug efficacy after release, and governments analyze which populations gain from training initiatives to optimize policy effectiveness. Causal inference focuses on estimating individual-level treatment effects, such as determining a medication's influence on a patient's recovery. While randomized controlled trials (RCTs) are the gold standard, they are often costly, slow, or unethical [1]. Observational data offers a practical alternative but faces two major challenges: (1) the absence of counterfactual outcomes–only the result of the received treatment is observable [2], and

© The Author(s), under exclusive license to Springer Nature Singapore Pte Ltd. 2026
T. Zhu et al. (Eds.): KSEM 2025, LNAI 15923, pp. 97–104, 2026.
https://doi.org/10.1007/978-981-95-3061-8_11

(2) confounders–variables that influence both treatment and outcome–can bias results [3]. The Potential Outcomes Framework [4] mitigates these challenges by estimating potential outcomes across different treatment conditions. While established techniques such as weighting, matching, and stratification [5] aim to adjust for confounding variables, their effectiveness diminishes with high-dimensional covariate spaces, where confounders can be obscured and model complexity escalates. To overcome these limitations, we introduce the CAKEGM model. CAKEGM integrates an attention mechanism and the Kolmogorov-Arnold Network within a causal encoding generative framework, enabling more effective isolation of confounding factors and enhanced accuracy in causal effect estimation. Our primary contributions encompass the following aspects:

- By incorporating the Transformer's attention mechanism, we effectively model complex dependencies among high-dimensional covariates, reducing redundancy and interference, thereby enhancing causal effect estimation in high-dimensional settings.
- Introducing the KAN module allows precise disentanglement of learned low-dimensional covariate features into causal-related and unrelated components, addressing hidden confounders and significantly improving estimation accuracy.
- Validation on semi-synthetic datasets demonstrates that the CAKEGM framework achieves superior performance in causal effect estimation, highlighting its strong practical applicability.

2   Proposed Method

2.1   CAKEGM Architecture

We propose a causal encoding generative model based on attention and KAN - CAKEGM. The core idea is to learn the complex interactions between covariates using the attention mechanism, capture key information from high-dimensional data, and process it in a low-dimensional latent space. The overall framework of CAKEGM is shown in Fig. 1, which consists of the following main components: 1) an attention module that learns the interaction relationships between covariates; 2) an encoding-decoding module for dimensionality reduction and mapping back to the original space; 3) a KAN module used during dimensionality reduction to fit the true treatment and outcome, achieving decoupling of the representations. In the following section, we will primarily focus on the attention module and KAN module of CAKEGM.

Attention Module. Existing studies [6] mainly use fully connected networks for representation learning and dimensionality reduction. However, theoretical analysis in [7] indicates that such networks can only approximate feature similarity to a limited extent. To obtain more discriminative representations, it is crucial to capture intrinsic correlations among covariates [2]. Therefore, this study

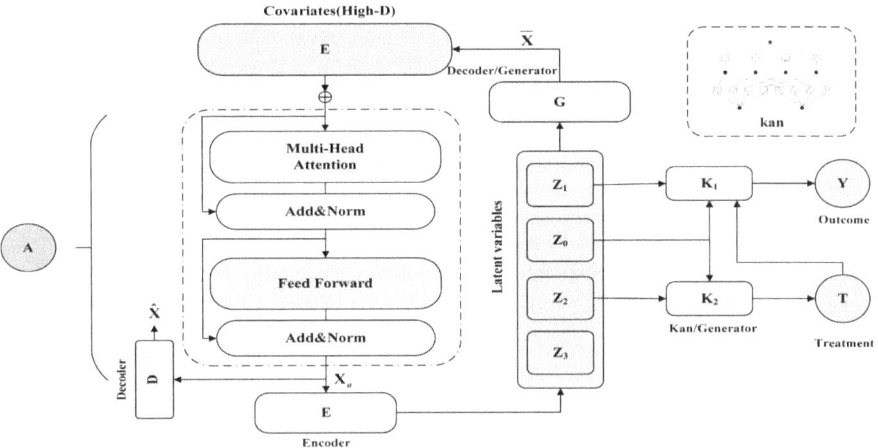

Fig. 1. The Overall Architecture Diagram of CAKEGM.

introduces the attention mechanism from the Transformer model [8] to learn inter-covariate dependencies and generate robust covariate representations.

Given high-dimensional covariates X, the attention mechanism models complex dependencies among features. The attention is computed as:

$$Attention(Q, K, V) = softmax\left(\frac{QK^T}{\sqrt{d_k}}\right) V. \tag{1}$$

where Q, K, and V are linear projections of X, and d_k is the key dimension. Residual connections, layer normalization, and a feed-forward network further refine the output to yield updated representations X_a.

To enhance generalization, a decoder reconstructs the covariates as $\hat{X}$. The reconstruction loss $E_{x\sim\hat{p}(x)}\|x - \hat{x}\|^2$ ensures that key information is preserved during feature learning.

Kolmogorov-Arnold Network. Errors in estimating individual causal effects often arise from outcome prediction loss due to insufficient latent feature decoupling. To address this, we use the Kolmogorov-Arnold Network (KAN) [9] instead of traditional MLPs to better capture treatment-outcome relations.

KAN is based on the Kolmogorov-Arnold representation theorem, which states any smooth multivariate function $f : [0,1]^d \rightarrow \mathbb{R}$ can be expressed by continuous univariate functions $\phi_{q,p} : [0,1] \rightarrow \mathbb{R}$ and $\Phi_q : \mathbb{R} \rightarrow \mathbb{R}$:

$$f(x_1, \cdots, x_n) = \sum_{q=1}^{2n+1} \Phi_q \left(\sum_{p=1}^{n} \phi_{q,p}(x_p)\right). \tag{2}$$

All Φ and ϕ functions are univariate, with addition being the sole multivariate operation. This framework allows KAN to represent complex interactions by combining simpler elements.

In implementation, the activation function $\phi(x)$ is constructed as:

$$\phi(x) = w_b b(x) + w_s \text{spline}(x). \tag{3}$$

where

$$b(x) = x + e^x, \quad \text{spline}(x) = \sum_i c_i B_i(x). \tag{4}$$

Initially, $w_s = 1$, $\text{spline}(x) \approx 0$, and w_b is Xavier-initialized.

KAN reduces multivariate complexity by aggregating learnable univariate functions, thereby enhancing expressiveness and interpretability. Stacking multiple KAN layers provides greater modeling power and stability compared to fully connected networks, allowing better representation of covariate impacts on treatment and outcomes.

2.2   Model Training

The model consists of an attention module A, a bidirectional structure (E, G), and two KAN-based networks K_1 and K_2. The attention module, built on a simplified Transformer, extracts key features X_a from high-dimensional covariates X. The bidirectional module integrates an autoencoder and GAN to compress and reconstruct features. K_1 and K_2 operate on the compressed features for outcome estimation and feature decoupling. The encoder E projects inputs into a latent space approximating a multivariate normal distribution. A discriminator D_z distinguishes between true and encoded latent features, forming a latent-space GAN. A reconstruction loss between $E(G(Z))$ and Z, with $Z \sim \mathcal{N}(0, I)$, helps preserve latent information. Additionally, a discriminator D_X is introduced to align the distribution of G's output with the empirical distribution of X, forming a GAN pair (G, D_X) in the input space.

Therefore, the adversarial training loss function for latent space distribution matching is expressed as follows:

$$\begin{cases} L_E = -\mathbb{E}_{A(x) \sim \hat{p}(A(x))} \left[D_{z,-1}(E(A(x))) \right], \\ L_{D_z} = -\mathbb{E}_{z \sim p(z)} \left[D_{z,-1}(z) \right] + \mathbb{E}_{A(x) \sim \hat{p}(A(x))} \left[D_{z,-1}(E(A(x))) \right] \\ \qquad + \lambda \mathbb{E}_{z \sim \bar{p}(z)} \left[(\nabla D_{z,-1}(z) - 1)^2 \right]. \end{cases} \tag{5}$$

Let $p(z)$ denote the standard normal distribution, and $\hat{p}(\cdot)$ denote the empirical distribution. To maintain the differentiability of the discriminator D_z, we refer to its pre-binarization output as $D_{z,-1}(\cdot)$, and apply the Sigmoid activation to approximate the binarization process. The notation $\bar{p}(z)$ stands for uniformly interpolated samples between points drawn from $p(z)$ and $\hat{p}(z)$. Throughout adversarial learning, the networks A, E, and D_z are jointly optimized until convergence is achieved.

In addition to distribution matching via adversarial training, the reconstruction loss for (T, Y, X) is defined as follows:

$$\begin{cases} L_{rec}^{t} = \mathbb{E}_{t \sim \hat{p}(t), z_0 \sim \hat{P}_{e_0(A(X))}, z_2 \sim \hat{P}_{e_2(A(X))}} \left[(t - K_2(z_0, z_2))^2 \right], \\[2mm] L_{rec}^{y} = \mathbb{E}_{y \sim \hat{p}(y), z_0 \sim \hat{P}_{e_0(A(X))}, z_1 \sim \hat{P}_{e_1(A(X))}} \left[(y - K_1(z_0, z_1, t))^2 \right], \\[2mm] L_{rec}^{x} = \mathbb{E}_{x \sim \hat{p}(x)} \left[\alpha \cdot \| x - G(E(A(x))) \|^2 + \beta \cdot \| x - \hat{x} \|^2 \right]. \end{cases} \tag{6}$$

Here, $\hat{P}_{e_k(\cdot)}$ $(k = 0, 1, 2, 3)$ represents the empirical distribution derived from the k-th subcomponent of the encoder $E(\cdot)$, while $\| \cdot \|_2^2$ denotes the squared Euclidean norm. The overall objective function is formulated as $L_{AKEG} = L_E + L_{rec}^{t} + L_{rec}^{y} + L_{rec}^{x}$ in conjunction with the adversarial loss L_{D_z}. These terms correspond to the optimization targets of the primary networks (A, K_1, K_2, E, G) and the discriminator D_z, respectively. The training procedure adopts an alternating optimization strategy, where the parameters of one module are updated at a time while keeping the others fixed. The covariate reconstruction loss L_{rec}^{x} has two parts minimizing the gap between learned and original covariates. The attention module introduces reconstruction errors, combined with the usual autoencoder loss between $G(E(A(X)))$ and X, forming L_{rec}^{x}. Specifically, L_{rec}^{x} includes the latent space reconstruction $L_{rec}^{x}(G)$ via $G(\cdot)$, and the attention module reconstruction error $L_{rec}^{x}(A)$. These are jointly optimized to reduce bias and better preserve key features after dimensionality reduction. Coefficients $\alpha \geq 0$ and $\beta \geq 0$ balance their relative weights during training.

3 Experiments

3.1 Experimental Setup

Datasets. We performed experiments on two benchmark datasets: ACIC-2018 and IHDP [10]. The ACIC-2018 dataset is derived from real medical measurements linked to the Birth and Infant Death Database (LBIDD) and includes 117 covariates. Treatments and outcomes are simulated through complex data-generating mechanisms. We selected three subsets with sample sizes ranging from 1,000 to 50,000. The IHDP dataset comes from the Infant Health and Development Program, a randomized controlled trial focusing on low-birth-weight and premature infants. It contains 25 covariates and 747 samples, with 139 treated and 608 controls. The outcome comprises simulated infant cognitive test scores, generated from baseline covariates and treatment allocation.

Baseline and Metrics. Several groups of baseline methods are used for comparison to validate the performance of our approach: TARNET [11], a deep learning method for individual treatment effect estimation; CFRNET [11], which minimizes distributional differences to learn latent representations; CEVAE [12], based on variational autoencoders; GANITE [13], which uses a generative adversarial network framework; SITE [14], employing deep representation learning; Causal Forest (CF) [15], a non-parametric random forest method; CETransformer [2], combining Transformer architectures with adversarial learning; and

CausalEGM [6], which leverages GANs and dimensionality reduction techniques. We assess model performance using two common metrics: the Absolute Error of the Average Treatment Effect ($\varepsilon_{ATE} = |ATE - A\hat{T}E|$), where ATE is the true effect and $A\hat{T}E$ the estimate, and the Mean Squared Error of the Individual Treatment Effect ($\varepsilon_{PEHE} = \frac{1}{n}\sum_{i=1}^{n}(ITE_i - I\hat{T}E_i)^2$), which measures the accuracy of individual effect estimation.

Implementation Details. We set the hyperparameters in the loss function L_{rec}^x as $\alpha = 0.9$ and $\beta = 0.1$, which balance the reconstruction constraint and the attention-based feature extraction. The choice ensures the model captures essential covariate information while avoiding over-reliance on reconstruction. Other hyperparameter settings, including the loss coefficient λ in the discriminator network D_Z, follow the configuration used in [6].

Table 1. Experimental results on the ACIC-2018 dataset. The best performances are highlighted in bold.

Method	1k		10k		50k	
	$\sqrt{\varepsilon_{PEHE}}$	ε_{ATE}	$\sqrt{\varepsilon_{PEHE}}$	ε_{ATE}	$\sqrt{\varepsilon_{PEHE}}$	ε_{ATE}
TARNET	.580 ± .025	.072 ± .022	.190 ± .010	.117 ± .001	.927 ± .016	.059 ± .016
CFRNET	.046 ± .002	.060 ± .022	.174 ± .012	.109 ± .002	.949 ± .012	.127 ± .081
CEVAE	.173 ± .081	.116 ± .031	.321 ± .038	.147 ± .015	1.26 ± .084	.914 ± .238
GANITE	.749 ± .069	.416 ± .069	1.84 ± .018	1.72 ± .027	2.78 ± .436	2.62 ± .462
SITE	.051 ± .130	.048 ± .002	.157 ± .011	.077 ± .002	.850 ± .058	.060 ± .011
CF	**.046 ± .001**	.058 ± .001	.129 ± .002	.017 ± .001	.786 ± .036	.043 ± .003
CETransformer	.581 ± .013	.033 ± .008	.601 ± .034	.216 ± .014	2.70 ± .021	1.47 ± .312
CausalEGM	.133 ± .026	.032 ± .011	.111 ± .002	.009 ± .002	.580 ± .040	.031 ± .010
Ours	.139 ± .019	**.027 ± .010**	**.106 ± .001**	**.007 ± .001**	**.356 ± .009**	**.016 ± .005**

3.2   Model Comparison

We comprehensively evaluated our method on the ACIC-2018 and IHDP datasets. As shown in Table 1, our method achieves the lowest ATE error (0.027 ± 0.010) on the small-scale ACIC-2018 dataset (1,000 samples), and further improves on medium (10,000 samples) and large-scale (50,000 samples) datasets, demonstrating strong adaptability, robustness, and generalization. Figure 2 presents results on the IHDP dataset: while ITE performance is slightly behind TARNET and CFRNET, our method outperforms CF and achieves the lowest ATE error, indicating higher accuracy and stability. Compared with other methods, our model benefits from the integration of attention mechanism and KAN, which effectively capture covariate correlations, enhance feature decoupling, and improve causal effect estimation, particularly for average treatment effect.

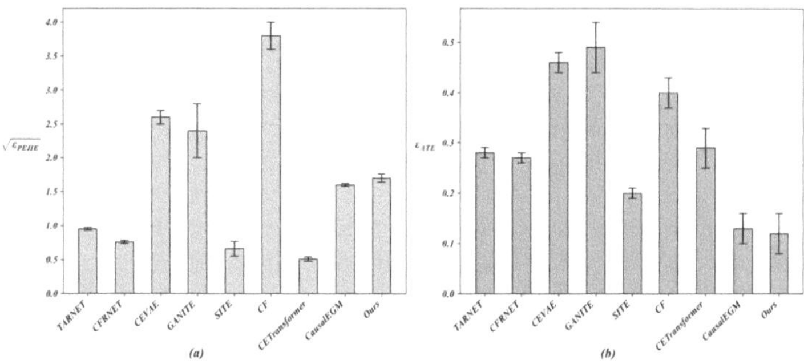

Fig. 2. Performance comparison on the IHDP dataset.

3.3   Ablation Study

Table 2 shows the ablation results on the ACIC-2018 dataset. The full model with both the attention module and KAN outperforms variants missing either component. The attention module enhances estimation by capturing feature interactions, while KAN improves nonlinear fitting. Removing either leads to higher errors, confirming their complementary roles and overall contribution to improved causal effect estimation.

Table 2. Ablation experiments on the ACIC-2018 dataset.

ACIC-2018	1k		10k		50k	
	$\sqrt{\varepsilon_{PEHE}}$	ε_{ATE}	$\sqrt{\varepsilon_{PEHE}}$	ε_{ATE}	$\sqrt{\varepsilon_{PEHE}}$	ε_{ATE}
Without att	$.236 \pm .013$	$.036 \pm .011$	$.110 \pm .001$	$.013 \pm .004$	$.358 \pm .005$	$.017 \pm .007$
Without kan	$.157 \pm .060$	$.037 \pm .061$	$.107 \pm .001$	$.011 \pm .003$	$.434 \pm .047$	$.026 \pm .013$
Ours	$.139 \pm .019$	$.027 \pm .010$	$.106 \pm .001$	$.007 \pm .001$	$.356 \pm .009$	$.016 \pm .005$

4   Conclusion

In this paper, we propose a causal encoding generative model that integrates attention mechanism with Kolmogorov-Arnold Networks (KAN) to enhance the accuracy of individual and average treatment effect estimation. By combining deep learning with KAN's flexible structure, the model effectively captures complex nonlinear relationships in high-dimensional data. Experiments on two benchmark datasets demonstrate superior accuracy and robustness compared to existing methods, highlighting its adaptability to varying data scales and structures.

Acknowledgments. This work was supported by the National Natural Science Foundation of China (No. 62176082).

References

1. Zhou, G., Yao, L., Xu, X., Wang, C., Zhu, L.: Cycle-balanced representation learning for counterfactual inference. In: Proceedings of the 2022 SIAM International Conference on Data Mining (SDM), pp. 442–450. SIAM (2022)
2. Guo, Z., Zheng, S., Liu, Z., Yan, K., Zhu, Z.: CETransformer: casual effect estimation via transformer based representation learning. In: Ma, H., et al. (eds.) PRCV 2021, Part IV. LNCS, vol. 13022, pp. 524–535. Springer, Cham (2021). https://doi.org/10.1007/978-3-030-88013-2_43
3. Varga, A.N., Guevara Morel, A.E., Lokkerbol, J., van Dongen, J.M., van Tulder, M.W., Bosmans, J.E.: Dealing with confounding in observational studies: a scoping review of methods evaluated in simulation studies with single-point exposure. Stat. Med. **42**(4), 487–516 (2023)
4. Rubin, D.B.: Estimating causal effects of treatments in randomized and nonrandomized studies. J. Educ. Psychol. **66**(5), 688 (1974)
5. Imbens, G.W.: Nonparametric estimation of average treatment effects under exogeneity: a review. Rev. Econ. Stat. **86**(1), 4–29 (2004)
6. Liu, Q., Chen, Z., Wong, W.H.: An encoding generative modeling approach to dimension reduction and covariate adjustment in causal inference with observational studies. Proc. Natl. Acad. Sci. **121**(23), e2322376,121 (2024)
7. Domingos, P.: Every model learned by gradient descent is approximately a kernel machine. arXiv preprint arXiv:2012.00152 (2020)
8. Vaswani, A., et al.: Attention is all you need. Adv. Neural Inf. Process. Syst. **30** (2017)
9. Liu, Z., et al.: KAN: Kolmogorov-Arnold networks. arXiv preprint arXiv:2404.19756 (2024)
10. Brooks-Gunn, J., Liaw, F.r., Klebanov, P.K.: Effects of early intervention on cognitive function of low birth weight preterm infants. J. Pediatrics **120**(3), 350–359 (1992)
11. Shalit, U., Johansson, F.D., Sontag, D.: Estimating individual treatment effect: generalization bounds and algorithms. In: International Conference on Machine Learning, pp. 3076–3085. PMLR (2017)
12. Louizos, C., Shalit, U., Mooij, J.M., Sontag, D., Zemel, R., Welling, M.: Causal effect inference with deep latent-variable models. Adv. Neural Inf. Process. Syst. **30** (2017)
13. Yoon, J., Jordon, J., Van Der Schaar, M.: GANITE: estimation of individualized treatment effects using generative adversarial nets. In: International Conference on Learning Representations (2018)
14. Yao, L., Li, S., Li, Y., Huai, M., Gao, J., Zhang, A.: Representation learning for treatment effect estimation from observational data. Adv. Neural Inf. Process. Syst. **31** (2018)
15. Wager, S., Athey, S.: Estimation and inference of heterogeneous treatment effects using random forests. J. Am. Stat. Assoc. **113**(523), 1228–1242 (2018)

TRVP: Transformer-VAE Framework for 3D Point Cloud Instance Segmentation

Jiangmai Cheng[1](✉)(iD), Bo Jiang[1](✉)(iD), Tianfang Sun[2](iD), and Boyu Wang[3](iD)

[1] The 32nd Research Institute of China Electronics Technology Group Corporation, Shanghai, China
xtihdie_cjm@outlook.com, b26jiang@126.com
[2] East China Normal University, Shanghai, China
stf@stu.ecnu.edu.cn
[3] Artificial Intelligence Institute of China Electronics Technology Group Corporation, Shanghai, China

Abstract. Transformers perform well in feature extraction but face challenges in 3D point cloud instance segmentation. This paper presents TRVPa 3D segmentation network that deeply integrates the Transformer architecture with a variational autoencoder (VAE). Through targeted improvements, the framework addresses three core limitations of Transformers in 3D processing: First, a VAE-based generation strategy is introduced, regulating the process via joint optimization of KL divergence and reconstruction loss to enhance generalization and ease data acquisition; second, a feature enhancement module combining multi-branch CNNs and Transformer layers enables joint extraction of local geometry and global context; third, optimized residual connections stabilize gradient propagation and accelerate convergence in deep networks. Experiments on S3DIS and ScanNetV2 show TRVP achieves mean precision scores of 0.74 and 0.52, respectively, demonstrating superior performance. Ablation studies further verify the effectiveness of each component.

Keywords: Instance segmentation · Transformer · VAE · Feature enhancement · ResBlock

1 Introcution

With the rise of autonomous driving and robotics, 3D scene understanding has become a key research focus, involving tasks such as semantic segmentation and object detection. Unlike 2D images, point clouds are unordered, unstructured, and irregular, posing significant challenges for 3D vision algorithm design [19,20]. Traditional CNNs, while effective for 2D images, struggle with high computational costs and limited performance on 3D data [5].

T. Zhu et al. (Eds.): KSEM 2025, LNAI 15923, pp. 105–115, 2026.
https://doi.org/10.1007/978-981-95-3061-8_12

Pioneering works in point cloud processing include PointNet and PointNet++ [19,20]. SGPN [15] was the first deep learning-based method for 3D instance segmentation. With the success of Transformers in vision tasks [5,15], their application to 3D processing has gained momentum [8,29]. For example, PVT [30] introduced a Transformer-based multimodal approach integrating point cloud and voxel data. However, limitations remain in extracting local features effectively [10,12]. To address this, 3DCTN [16] proposed a hybrid architecture combining 3D convolutions and Transformers.

Transformer-based 3D models suffer from weak local feature extraction, slow convergence, and gradient instability. Limited 3D data further hampers training and generalization, restricting progress in 3D instance segmentation.

To address these issues, we propose TRVP, a transformer-VAE model for point cloud segmentation. VAE mitigates data scarcity via latent space regularization; multi-path convolutions enhance local features, and ResBlocks accelerate training. Experiments on S3DIS and ScanNetV2 confirm its effectiveness.

The main contributions of this paper can be summarized as following:

(1) We propose TRVP, which improves both accuracy and generalization, with mPrec increased by 8%.

(2) We enhance the transformer with ResBlocks and a feature enhancement module, improving local feature extraction and convergence speed.

(3) TRVP achieves 0.74 mPrec on S3DIS and 0.52 on ScanNetV2, showing clear improvements over prior models.

2   Related Work

2.1   Point-Based 3D Instance Segmentation

3D vision has closely followed the progress of 2D, with deep learning methods emerging under the influence of 2D CNNs [22]. However, these methods often depend on intermediate 2D modules, limiting generalization. Qi et al. [19,20] addressed this with the PointNet series for end-to-end 3D point cloud processing. Yang et al. [26] later proposed 3DBoNet, further advancing the field.

Vision Transformers have advanced 3D vision, achieving strong results [7,30]. Many 3D applications build on 2D designs–for example, Guan et al. [7] proposed M3DETR based on DETR [3], using multi-representation point clouds and multi-scale feature fusion for end-to-end 3D detection.

This work propose a transformer-based model that enhances global and local feature extraction for 3D instance segmentation.

2.2   Vision Transformer

Since its introduction [23], the transformer has achieved great success in NLP [2,28] and later expanded to vision tasks [3,5,7,27]. Dosovitskiy et al. [5] demonstrated its potential in image classification, while Xiao et al. [14] proposed EfficientFormer for mobile devices. Recent work has also explored its use in video tasks [6,13], confirming its versatility across domains.

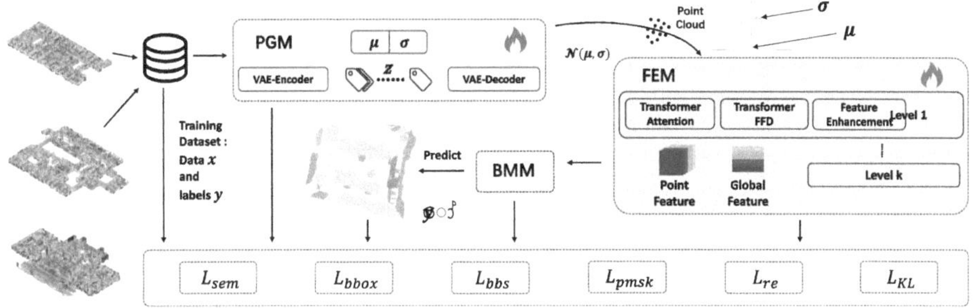

Fig. 1. The overall framework and data flow of TRVP. The training data is processed through the PGM, FEM, and BMM modules to obtain the prediction results.

Transformer has since been adopted in 3D vision due to its strength in capturing global context [17]. Zhao et al. [29] were the first to apply it to 3D point cloud processing. Yuan et al. [27] proposed a top-down-bottom-up structure to improve 3D reconstruction, while Zhang et al. [30] introduced a multimodal 3D network for better complex data handling.

To address transformer's limitations in 3D scenarios, we adopt it with targeted improvements. ResBlocks are added to reduce computational cost, and a feature enhancement module is introduced to improve local feature extraction.

3   Method

3.1   Overview

The proposed TRVP architecture, illustrated in Fig. 1, centers on 3D point cloud generation and task-driven feature learning. It consists of three modules: the Point cloud Generation Module (PGM), the Feature Extraction Module (FEM), and the Bounding box and point Mask prediction Module (BMM).

Given a point cloud $x \in \mathbb{R}^{N \times C}$, the PGM produces a reconstructed sample $\tilde{x}$, latent variable $z \in \mathbb{R}^H$, and its distribution parameters μ and σ^2. Using these, the FEM derives point-wise and global features F_P and F_G, which are then used by the BMM to predict bounding boxes P_B, point masks P_P, and semantic labels P_S. The final loss is computed from these predictions, the generated sample $\tilde{x}$, latent parameters μ, σ, and the ground truth:

$$\tilde{x}, z, \mu, \sigma = \mathcal{N}_{PGM}(x), \quad F_P, F_G = \mathcal{N}_{FEM}(\mu, \sigma),$$
$$P_B, P_P, P_S = \mathcal{N}_{BMM}(F_P, F_G), \quad Loss = \mathcal{F}_{\mathcal{L}}(P_B, P_P, P_S, \tilde{x}, \mu, \sigma, x, y). \tag{1}$$

3.2   Point Cloud Generate Module

The PGM module, built on a VAE framework, enhances model generalization and robustness via data augmentation. VAE learns latent representations while

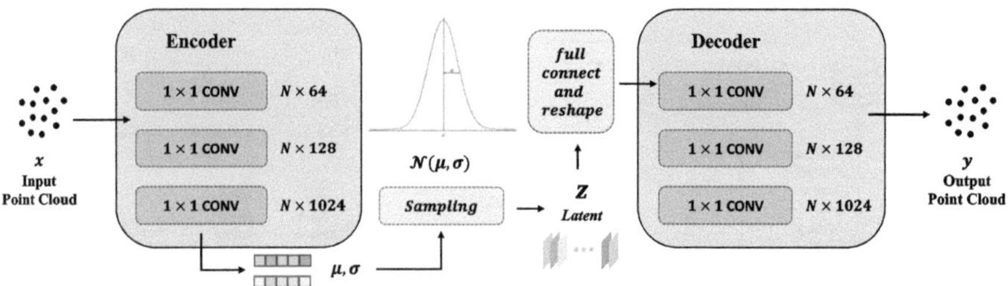

Fig. 2. The structural configuration of PGM. The point cloud data is encoded to obtain μ and σ, then sampled and decoded to generate the new point cloud data.

combining feature abstraction with high-quality sample generation, making it well-suited for augmentation. The PGM structure in TRVP is shown in Fig. 2.

The encoder extracts multiscale features through three convolutional layers with increasing channels. Global max pooling yields a global feature vector, which is mapped to latent mean μ and variance σ^2 via full connect (FC) layers.

Latent vectors are sampled and transformed via FC layers to higher dimensions. Transposed convolutions then upsample and restore spatial structure, producing point clouds matching the original size and geometry.

When processing point cloud data as input, the encoder derives the mean μ and variance σ^2 of the latent variables under the variational distribution $q_\phi(z|x)$. These parameters are then used to sample the latent variable z, which is then mapped through the decoder to reconstruct the original data $\tilde{x}$.

$$\mu, \sigma := q_\phi(z|x) = \mathcal{N}_{En}^{\phi}(x),$$
$$z = \mu + \sigma \odot \epsilon, \quad \epsilon \in \mathcal{N}(0,1), \tilde{x} = \mathcal{N}_{De}^{\phi}(x). \tag{2}$$

The latent vector z feeds into the FEM for feature extraction. The outputs $\tilde{x}, \mu, \sigma$ are used to compute KL and reconstruction losses, optimizing VAE and controlling data quality.

3.3 Point Cloud Feature Extraction Module

FEM in TRVP is built on a transformer backbone with 3D-specific enhancements. Each unit follows the structure in Fig. 3(a), and the full FEM stacks multiple such blocks.

Feature Enhancement Block. To overcome the transformer's weak local modeling, we introduce a feature enhancement (FE) module (Fig. 3(b)). Using multibranch CNNs of varied depth, it fuses multiscale features, combining CNN's locality with transformer's global context for improved detail awareness.

Residual Block. Due to slow convergence and high training cost of transformers, we introduce ResBlock (Fig. 3(c)) to reduce training load, alleviate vanishing gradients, and prevent deep network degradation, ensuring stable learning.

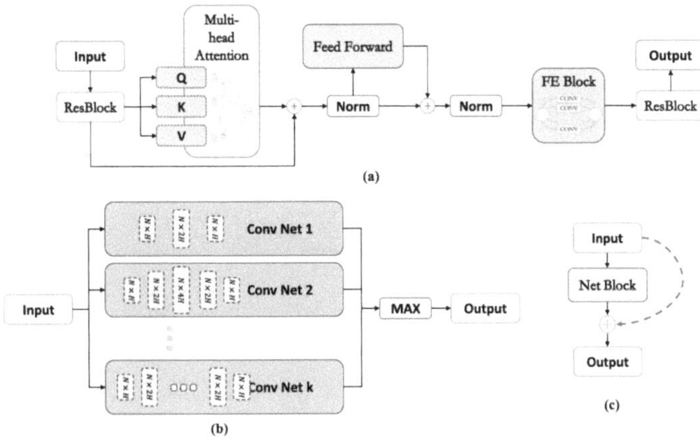

Fig. 3. Module structure in FEM. (a) Transformer block structure. (b) Feature enhancement block structure in transformer block. (c) Resblock structure.

3.4 Bounding Box and Point Mask Prediction Module

The BMM module, inspired by Yang et al. [26], predicts bounding boxes and point-wise masks based on global and local features extracted by FEM. It consists of two submodules: one for bounding box prediction and the other for mask generation.

Global features are processed through two fully connected layers to regress a fixed set of bounding boxes and confidence scores. During training, predicted boxes are matched with ground-truth boxes to facilitate loss calculation.

This branch fuses point features, global features, and outputs from the bounding box branch (coordinates and scores) to generate class-agnostic instance masks. After compression via FC layers, the features are combined and passed through shared layers to produce point-wise mask predictions.

3.5 Training Loss

To improve predictions of bounding boxes, point masks, and segmentation, we incorporate semantic loss l_s, box regression loss l_{bb}, box confidence loss l_{bs}, and mask loss l_{pm}. Additionally, reconstruction loss l_r and KL divergence loss l_{KL} are used to ensure high-quality point generation in the PGM.

The loss term l_s is computed using cross-entropy loss to optimize point-wise classification predictions, where q denotes the predicted probability distribution:

$$l_s = -\frac{1}{N}\sum_{j}^{N}\sum_{j}^{C} y_i^j log(q_i^j). \tag{3}$$

The bounding box loss l_{bb} includes: (1) Euclidean distance $W^{ed}i,j$ between predicted box $\hat{B}i$ and ground truth B_j; (2) sIoU cost $W^{sIoU}i,j$; (3) cross-entropy term $W^{ces}i,j$, where p and $\hat{p}$ are predicted and true point-box probabilities, and F_{CE} is the cross-entropy function:

$$W_{i,j}^{ed} = \sum_{i,j} \frac{\|\hat{\mathbf{B}}_i - \mathbf{B}_j\|_2}{6}, \quad W_{i,j}^{sIoU} = \frac{\sum_n p_i^n \times \hat{p}_j^n}{\sum_n p_i^n \times \hat{p}_j^n - p_i^n - \hat{p}_j^n},$$

$$W_{i,j}^{ces} = \mathcal{F}_{CE}(p_i^n, \hat{p}_j^n), \quad l_{bb} = \frac{1}{K}\sum_k^K (W_{i,j}^{ed} + W_{i,j}^{sIoU} + W_{i,j}^{ces}). \tag{4}$$

The loss l_{bs} scores H predicted boxes, treating the first T as valid and the rest as invalid, with S_t denoting the score of the t-th box:

$$l_{bs} = -\frac{1}{K}[\sum_{i=1}^{J} logS_i + \sum_{i=J+1}^{K} log(1 - S_i)]. \tag{5}$$

The calculation of l_{pm} is based on focal loss with default hyperparameters [21]. Let V denote the set of samples containing at least one foreground point, p denotes probability, w indicate the weight, and α, γ are both parameters:

$$l_{pm} = -\frac{1}{N_{V_i}}\sum_{j \in V_i}^{N_{v_i}} w_j(1 - p_j)logp_j, \quad w_i = \begin{cases} \alpha & i \text{ is positive} \\ 1 - \alpha & otherwise \end{cases}. \tag{6}$$

The reconstruction loss l_r is the MSE between x and $\tilde{x}$, while the KL divergence loss l_{KL} measures deviation from the standard normal prior. They are defined as:

$$l_r = \frac{1}{N \times D}\sum_i^N \sum_j^D \|x_{ij} - \tilde{x}_{ij}\|_2, \quad l_{KL} = \frac{1}{2}\sum_i^H (1 + log\sigma_i^2 - \mu_i^2 - \sigma_i^2). \tag{7}$$

4   Experiments

The model was trained using TensorFlow 2.9.1, a learning rate of 5e-4, and the RAdam optimizer, for 51 epochs with 4200 iterations per epoch. Evaluations were conducted on the S3DIS and ScanNetV2 datasets.

4.1   Dataset

We used two widely adopted 3D vision datasets S3DIS [1] and ScanNetV2 [4] for training and evaluation. The S3DIS dataset includes scans of 271 indoor scenes from 6 areas, captured via RGB-D sensors. It provides 13 annotated object categories (e.g., tables, chairs) across diverse environments such as offices, classrooms, and corridors.

The ScanNetV2 dataset is larger, with 1,513 indoor scans and 21 object categories, covering a wider range of indoor environments. It also offers multimodal data such as RGB images, depth maps, and normal maps, with refined annotations to ensure high quality and consistency.

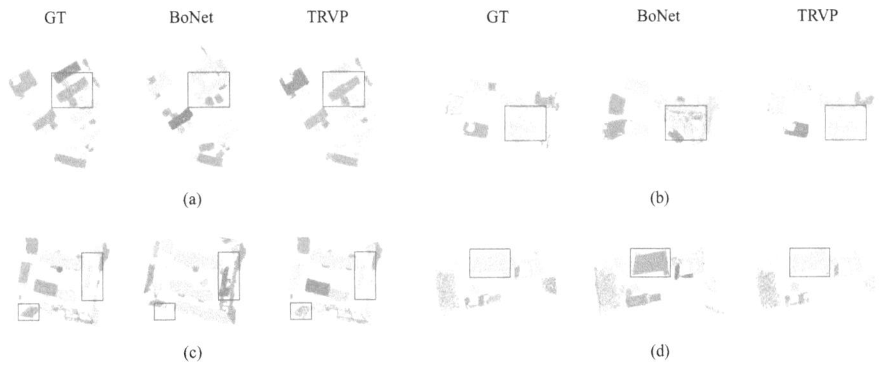

(a)   (b)

(c)   (d)

Fig. 4. Results on ScanNetV2. From left to right: ground truth, BoNet output, and TRVP output, showing progressive improvements in segmentation quality.

Table 1. Results in S3DIS.

	mPrec ↑	mRec ↑
PartNet [18]	0.56	0.43
ASIS [25]	0.64	0.48
3DBoNet [26]	0.66	0.48
TRVP(ours)	**0.74**	**0.55**

4.2 Results and Comparison

Following prior work, we employ the Average Precision (AP) metric (%) with an IoU threshold of 0.5 to present results. This approach enables both intuitive visualization of prediction accuracy and facilitates comparison with existing studies.

As shown in Table 1, the segmentation performance of our method on the S3DIS dataset is presented, achieving 0.74 mPrec with 6-fold cross-validation. Visualization results are illustrated in Fig. 4.

Table 2 shows results on ScanNetV2. TRVP achieves top performance on large objects, but struggles with some categories due to limited local feature modeling, though overall it slightly outperforms other methods.

4.3 Ablation Study

To validate the rationality and effectiveness of each component design in TRVP, an ablation experiment was conducted using Scene 1 of the S3DIS dataset.

PGM Module. To assess the VAE's impact in TRVP, we compare three variants (Table 3). The full model achieves the highest mPrec of 0.74. Removing the VAE reduces it to 0.68, while dropping KL and reconstruction losses lowers it further to 0.66, highlighting the importance of these constraints.

The third variant degrades due to noise from unconstrained VAE features. Constraints suppress this noise, ensuring stable and accurate segmentation.

Table 2. Results in ScanNetV2.

	mean	bathtub	bed	bookshelf	cabinet	chair	counter	curtain	desk	door	other	picture	refrig	showerCur	sink	sofa	table	toilet	window
MaskRCNN [9]	5.8	33.3	0.2	0.0	5.3	0.2	0.2	2.1	0.0	4.5	2.4	23.8	6.5	0.0	1.4	10.7	2	11	0.6
SGPN [24]	14.3	20.8	3.9	16.9	6.5	27.5	2.9	6.9	0.0	8.7	4.3	1.4	2.7	0.0	11.2	35.1	16.8	43.8	13.8
3DBoNet [26]	48.8	100	67.2	59	30.1	48.4	9.8	62	30.6	34.1	25.9	12.5	43.4	79.6	40.2	49.9	51.3	90.9	43.9
TRVP(ours)	**52.2**	100	92.1	72	33.2	45.6	10.1	51.4	32.8	43.7	27.3	15.3	50.4	53	46.1	71.9	61.2	89.6	45.5

ResBlock. ResBlock helps ease training, prevent gradient vanishing, and reduce overfitting in deep transformers. As shown in Table 3, it improves performance, and Fig. 5 shows faster convergence.

Feature Enhancement Moudle. To improve TRVP's point cloud processing, we added an FE module for multi-dimensional feature extraction. As shown in Table 3, it outperforms the baseline.

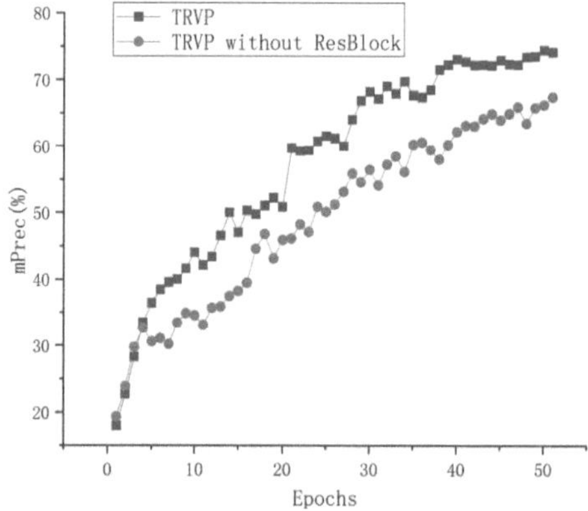

Fig. 5. Comparison of training processes. The convergence speed of TRVP with VAE added is faster than that of TRVP without VAE.

Table 3. Results of the ablation study on different supervised moudles.

VAE	l_r and l_{KL}	resblock	FE moudle	mPrec ↑	mRec ↑
✗	✓	✓	✓	0.68	0.53
✓	✗	✓	✓	0.66	0.52
✓	✓	✗	✓	0.67	0.47
✓	✓	✓	✗	0.71	0.53
✓	✓	✓	✓	**0.74**	**0.55**

5   Conclusion

We propose TRVP, a 3D point cloud segmentation framework integrating VAE and an enhanced Transformer with ResBlock and FE modules. With stochastic training and architectural optimizations, TRVP improves scene understanding and generalization, outperforming existing methods on S3DIS and ScanNetV2. Despite an 8% accuracy gain, inference time is over twice that of 3DBoNet due to the $O(N^2)$ complexity on large point clouds. Future work will focus on efficient, 3D-tailored transformers using local attention and sparse computation for real-time applications like autonomous driving.

References

1. Armeni, I., Sener, O., Zamir, A. R., Jiang, H., Brilakis, I., Fischer, M., et al.: 3d semantic parsing of large-scale indoor spaces. In: Proceedings of the IEEE Conference on Computer Vision and Pattern Recognition, pp. 1534-1543 (2016)
2. Bozic, V., Dordevic, D., Coppola, D., Thommes, J., Singh, S.P.: Rethinking Attention: Exploring Shallow Feed-Forward Neural Networks as an Alternative to Attention Layers in Transformer. arXiv preprint arXiv:2311.10642 (2023)
3. Carion, N., Massa, F., Synnaeve, G., Usunier, N., Kirillov, A., Zagoruyko, S.: End-to-end object detection with transformers. In: Vedaldi, A., Bischof, H., Brox, T., Frahm, J.-M. (eds.) ECCV 2020. LNCS, vol. 12346, pp. 213–229. Springer, Cham (2020). https://doi.org/10.1007/978-3-030-58452-8_13
4. Dai, A., Chang, A.X., Savva, M., Halber, M., Funkhouser, T., Nießner, M.: Scannet: Richly-annotated 3d reconstructions of indoor scenes. In: Proceedings of the IEEE Conference on Computer Vision and Pattern Recognition, pp. 5828-5839 (2017)
5. Dosovitskiy, A., Beyer, L., Kolesnikov, A., Weissenborn, D., Zhai, X., Unterthiner, T., et al.: An Image is Worth 16x16 Words: Transformer for Image Recognition at Scale. arXiv preprint arXiv:2010.11929 (2020)
6. Fan, H., Yang, Y., Kankanhalli, M.: Point 4d transformer networks for spatio-temporal modeling in point cloud videos. In: Proceedings of the IEEE/CVF Conference on Computer Vision and Pattern Recognition, pp. 14204-14213 (2021)
7. Guan, T., Wang, J., Lan, S., Chandra, R., Wu, Z., Davis, L., et al.: M3detr: multi-representation, multi-scale, mutual-relation 3d object detection with transformers. In: Proceedings of the IEEE/CVF Winter Conference on Applications of Computer Vision, pp. 772-782 (2022)

8. Guo, M.-H., Cai, J.-X., Liu, Z.-N., Mu, T.-J., Martin, R.R., Hu, S.-M.: Pct: point cloud transformer. Comput. Vis. Media **7**, 187–199 (2021)

9. He, K., Gkioxari, G., Dollár, P., Girshick, R.: Mask r-cnn. In: Proceedings of the IEEE International Conference on Computer Vision, pp. 2961-2969 (2017)

10. Ilbert, R., et al.: Samformer: Unlocking the potential of transformers in time series forecasting with sharpness-aware minimization and channel-wise attention. arXiv preprint arXiv:2402.10198 (2024)

11. Lahoud, J., Ghanem, B.: 2d-driven 3d object detection in rgb-d images. In: Proceedings of the IEEE International Conference on Computer Vision, pp. 4622-4630 (2017)

12. Lai, X., Yuan, Y., Chu, R., Chen, Y., Hu, H., Jia, J.: Mask-attention-free transformer for 3d instance segmentation. In: Proceedings of the IEEE/CVF International Conference on Computer Vision, pp. 3693-3703 (2023)

13. Li, W., Liu, M., Liu, H., Wang, P., Cai, J., Sebe, N.: Hourglass tokenizer for efficient transformer-based 3D human pose estimation. In: Proceedings of the IEEE/CVF Conference on Computer Vision and Pattern Recognition, pp. 604-613 (2024)

14. Li, Y., Yuan, G., Wen, Y., Hu, J., Evangelidis, G., Tulyakov, S., et al.: Efficientformer: vision transformers at mobilenet speed. Adv. Neural. Inf. Process. Syst. **35**, 12934–12949 (2022)

15. Liu, Z., Lin, Y., Cao, Y., Hu, H., Wei, Y., Zhang, Z., et al.: Swin transformer: hierarchical vision transformer using shifted windows. In: Proceedings of the IEEE/CVF International Conference on Computer Vision, pp. 10012-10022 (2021)

16. Lu, D., Xie, Q., Gao, K., Xu, L., Li, J.: 3DCTN: 3D convolution-transformer network for point cloud classification. IEEE Trans. Intell. Transp. Syst. **23**(12), 24854–24865 (2022)

17. Lu, D., Xie, Q., Wei, M., Gao, K., Xu, L., Li, J.: Transformer in 3d point clouds: A survey. arXiv preprint arXiv:2205.07417 (2022b)

18. Mo, K., et al. Partnet: a large-scale benchmark for fine-grained and hierarchical part-level 3d object understanding. In: Proceedings of the IEEE/CVF Conference on Computer Vision and Pattern Recognition, pp. 909-918 (2019)

19. Qi, C.R., Su, H., Mo, K., Guibas, L.J.: Pointnet: deep learning on point sets for 3d classification and segmentation. In: Proceedings of the IEEE Conference on Computer Vision and Pattern Recognition, pp. 652-660 (2017a)

20. Qi, C.R., Yi, L., Su, H., Guibas, L.J.: Pointnet++: deep hierarchical feature learning on point sets in a metric space. Adv. Neural Inform. Process. Syst. **30** (2017b)

21. Ross, T.-Y., Dollár, G.: Focal loss for dense object detection. In: Proceedings of the IEEE Conference on Computer Vision and Pattern Recognition, pp. 2980-2988 (2017)

22. Shi, S., Wang, X.,Li, H.: Pointrcnn: 3d object proposal generation and detection from point cloud. In: Proceedings of the IEEE/CVF Conference on Computer Vision and Pattern Recognition, pp. 770-779 (2019)

23. Vaswani, A.: Attention is all you need. Adv. Neural Inform. Process. Syst. (2017)

24. Wang, W., Yu, R., Huang, Q., Neumann, U.: Sgpn: Similarity group proposal network for 3d point cloud instance segmentation. In: Proceedings of the IEEE Conference on Computer Vision and Pattern Recognition, pp. 2569-2578 (2018)

25. Wang, X., Liu, S., Shen, X., Shen, C., Jia, J.: Associatively segmenting instances and semantics in point clouds. In: Proceedings of the IEEE/CVF Conference on Computer Vision and Pattern Recognition, pp. 4096-4105 (2019)

26. Yang, B., et al.: Learning object bounding boxes for 3d instance segmentation on point clouds. Adv. Neural Inform. Process. Syst. **32** (2019)

27. Yuan, W., Gu, X., Li, H., Dong, Z., Zhu, S.: 3D Former: Monocular Scene Reconstruction with 3D SDF Transformer. arXiv preprint arXiv:2301.13510 (2023)
28. Zhang, Q., Ram, D., Hawkins, C., Zha, S., Zhao, T.: Efficient long-range transformers: You need to attend more, but not necessarily at every layer. arXiv preprint arXiv:2310.12442 (2023)
29. Zhao, H., Jiang, L., Jia, J., Torr, P. H., Koltun, V.: Point transformer. In: Proceedings of the IEEE/CVF International Conference on Computer Vision, pp. 16259-16268 (2021)
30. Zhong-yu, C., Wan, H., Liu, S., Shen, X., Wu, Z.: PVT: Point-Voxel Transformer for 3D Deep Learning. arXiv preprint arXiv:2108.06076 (2021)

A Metapath-Based Neighborhood Reconstruction Network for Graph Anomaly Detection

Yanjun Lu$^{(\boxtimes)}$ and Xinyi Song

Chongqing University of Technology, Chongqing 400054, China
luyj@cqut.edu.cn, songxy@stu.cqut.edu.cn

Abstract. Graph anomaly detection has important application value in network security, fraud detection and other fields, but the traditional supervised method limits its practical application due to the high cost of labeling and complex network structure. Although the unsupervised method can automatically identify anomalies, it is easy to be disturbed by noise and affect the detection accuracy. To solve these problems, we propose a Metapath-based Neighborhood Reconstruction Network (MNRN) for graph anomaly detection. MNRN reconstructs the relationship between nodes and their neighbors by designing specific meta-paths to capture context and connection patterns in complex graph structures. The model utilizes the prior information provided by a small amount of labeled data combined with a large amount of unlabeled data to effectively improve the accuracy and robustness of anomaly detection. The experimental results show that MNRN outperforms the current state-of-the-art methods on 6 real data sets, demonstrating its superior performance in anomaly detection tasks.

Keywords: Graph anomaly detection · graph neural network · node anomaly · metapath

1 Introduction

In recent years, graph anomaly detection has shown promising applications in cybersecurity, fraud, and spam detection [5, 19]. It aims to detect irregular patterns in graph-structured data by modeling node and edge behaviors. Due to the high cost and domain expertise required for labeling, unsupervised methods[1, 3, 7–13] have become mainstream, despite their susceptibility to noise and inability to leverage prior anomaly information [6, 18]. As anomalies are often context-dependent [10], semi-supervised approaches have incorporated neighborhood features [4, 17], but still struggle to effectively utilize labeled data and capture complex local structures [15]. To address these issues, we propose a Meta-path-based Neighborhood Reconstruction Network (MNRN), which models semantic dependencies through meta-paths [2, 14], allowing the network to distinguish abnormal patterns by leveraging contextual and relational differences between normal and anomalous nodes.

T. Zhu et al. (Eds.): KSEM 2025, LNAI 15923, pp. 116–123, 2026.
https://doi.org/10.1007/978-981-95-3061-8_13

The proposed model identifies anomalies by leveraging meta-path-based contextual patterns. It encodes node attributes, structural connections, and neighborhood features into a latent space, and detects anomalies by comparing reconstruction losses across multiple views.

In summary, our main contributions are as follows:

(1) We propose MNRN, a novel anomaly detection model that utilizes meta-paths to capture rich semantic neighborhood information. To the best of our knowledge, this is the first attempt to apply meta-paths for neighborhood learning in anomaly detection.
(2) The meta-path-guided reconstruction enhances model scalability and efficiency by improving the representation quality of nodes and their neighborhoods.
(3) Extensive experiments on six datasets (two real-world and four citation networks) demonstrate that our method consistently outperforms state-of-the-art approaches (Fig. 1).

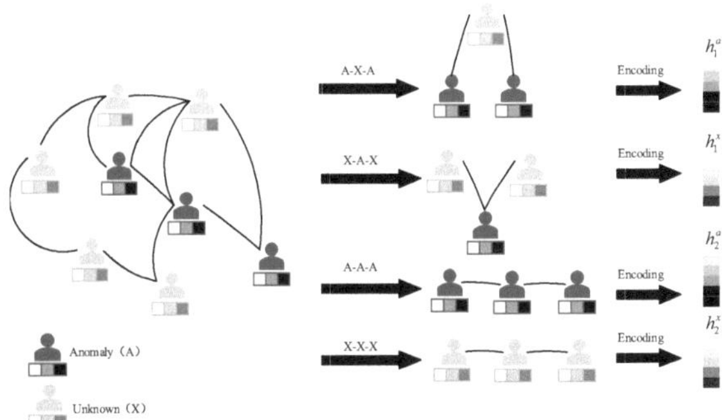

Fig. 1. With a specific pattern matching metapath, there are multiple metapath types in a network, and the number of normal nodes is much larger than the abnormal nodes, so we treat most unknown nodes as normal nodes.

2 Related Work

Graph anomaly detection has been widely applied in areas such as network security and fraud detection. With the advancement of graph neural networks (GNNs), both unsupervised and semi-supervised methods have achieved notable progress. Unsupervised approaches, such as DOMINANT, CoLA, and ResGCN, leverage graph reconstruction, contrastive learning, and residual mechanisms to identify anomalies without relying on labeled data. In contrast, semi-supervised methods, including GraphSAGE and GDN, incorporate limited labeled anomalies to enhance detection accuracy and enable knowledge transfer across networks.

3 Method

The overall framework of our proposed approach is shown in Fig. 2, where MNRN is a graph encoder-decoder model designed to encode the properties of each node and the properties of nodes in the one - or multi-hop neighborhood into a node representation.

118   Y. Lu and X. Song

Therefore, we will consider the reconstruction loss of nodes from many aspects, and try to reconstruct the neighborhood and its attributes with the least loss.

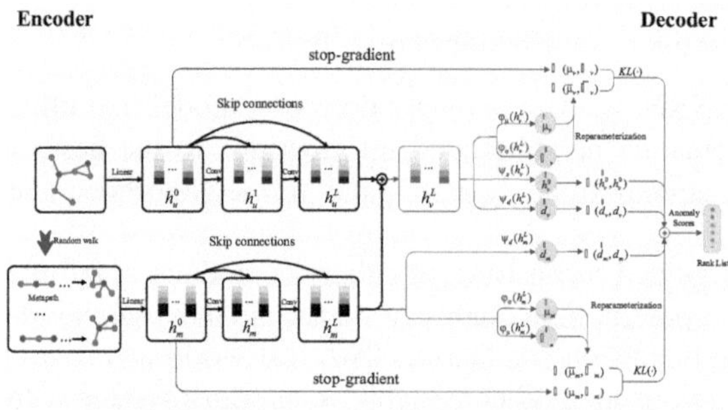

Fig. 2. MNRN Model structure diagrams

3.1 The Encoder

We adopt a multi-layer GCN encoder to encode the network and meta-paths derived from random walks. To mitigate over-smoothing caused by deep GCNs, a skip connection mechanism is introduced, with each GCN layer formulated as:

$$H^{(l+1)} = \sigma(D^{-1/2}\tilde{A}D^{-1/2}H^{(l)}W^{(l)} + H^0\tilde{W}^{(l)}) \tag{1}$$

$$H^{(l+1)} = \sigma(D^{-1/2}\tilde{A}D^{-1/2}H^{(l)}W^{(l)}) \tag{2}$$

Where H^l is the eigenmatrix of the output of layer l, $l = 1, 2, 3...L - 1$, and the input of layer 1 is the initial eigenmatrix encoded as a dense low-dimensional representation of $H^0 = \xi(X)$ using random linear projection. $\tilde{A} = A + I$ is the adjacency matrix with a self-ring, D is the degree matrix of the graph, $W^{(l)}$ and $\tilde{W}^{(l)}$ are both the weight matrix of the l-th layer, and $\sigma(\cdot)$ is the activation function, such as ReLU and Sigmoid.

Encoder coding is used to encode the network and metapath, and node attributes and structure information are extracted to obtain the potential representation h_u^L of the network and the potential representation h_m^L of the Meta-path set, respectively. The potential representation h_u^L of the network and the potential representation h_u^L of the Meta-path set are connected in series to form a joint embedding vector h_v^L.

$$h_u^L = \sigma(A, X) \tag{3}$$

$$h_m^L = \sigma(A_m, X_m) \tag{4}$$

$$h_v^L = h_u^L + h_m^L \tag{5}$$

Where A_m and X_m are adjacency matrix and attribute matrix composed of nodes involved in the meta-path set. Thus the embedded vector h_v^L represents global and local attributes and structural features.

3.2 The Decoder

Self Reconstruction. To reconstruct the attributes of the central node, we design a simple decoder that takes h_v^L as input and reconstructs $\widehat{h_u^0} = \psi_x(h_v^L)$ through a multi-layer perceptron (MLP). Then, the self-reconstruction loss of the node can be calculated as:

$$\mathcal{L}_u^x = \mathcal{D}(h_u^0, \widehat{h_u^0}) \tag{6}$$

Where $\mathcal{D}(\cdot, \cdot)$ is a distance function, such as L2 - distance, which measures the difference between the original property and the reconstructed property.

Node Degree Reconstruction. In order to reconstruct the node degree, we use another decoder composed of multi-layer sensors, namely $\widehat{d_u} = \psi_d(h_v^L)$, $\widehat{d_m} = \psi_d(h_m^L)$. The reconstruction loss of node degree can be expressed as:

$$\mathcal{L}_u^d = \mathcal{D}(d_u, \widehat{d_u}) \tag{7}$$

$$\mathcal{L}_m^d = \mathcal{D}(d_m, \widehat{d_m}) \tag{8}$$

Here, we only use l2-loss as the metric $\mathcal{D}$.

Neighbors Representation Distribution Reconstruction. In order to reconstruct the distributions $\mathbb{P}_u$ and $\mathbb{P}_m$ from the joint embedding network node representation and the metapath node representation, we first map h_v^L and h_m^L to the estimates $\mathbb{P}_u$ and $\mathbb{P}_m$ of the distributions $\widehat{\boldsymbol{P}}_u$ and $\widehat{\boldsymbol{P}}_m$, and then we use the multivariate Gaussian approximation to reconstruct $\mathbb{P}_u$ and $\mathbb{P}_m$. Specifically, given the neighborhood node information $\mathcal{H}_u = \{h_v^0 | v \in \mathcal{N}_u\}$, $\mathcal{H}_m = \{h_v^0 | v \in \mathcal{N}_m\}$, we estimate the mean and covariance matrix of the neighbor representation by the following method:

$$\mu_u = \frac{1}{d_u} \sum_{v \in \mathcal{N}_u} h_v^{(0)}, \Sigma_u = \frac{1}{d_u - 1} \sum_{v \in \mathcal{N}_u} (h_v^{(0)} - \hat{\mu}_u)(h_v^{(0)} - \hat{\mu}_u)^\top \tag{9}$$

$$\mu_m = \frac{1}{d_m} \sum_{v \in \mathcal{N}_m} h_m^{(0)}, \Sigma_m = \frac{1}{d_m - 1} \sum_{v \in \mathcal{N}_m} (h_m^{(0)} - \hat{\mu}_m)(h_m^{(0)} - \hat{\mu}_m)^\top \tag{10}$$

h_v^L and h_m^L are then mapped to multivariate Gaussian distributions $\widehat{\boldsymbol{P}}_u$, $\widehat{\boldsymbol{P}}_m$ by the following steps: We extract samples $z_1, \cdots, z_q$ and $z_1, \cdots, z_p$ from distributions $\mathcal{N}(\hat{\mu}_u, \hat{\Sigma}_u)$ and $\mathcal{N}(\hat{\mu}_m, \hat{\Sigma}_m)$, and transform q neighborhood features $\overline{h}_1, \cdots, \overline{h}_q$ and p neighborhood features $\overline{h}_1, \cdots, \overline{h}_p$ through a fully connected neural network (FNN). The parameters $\hat{\mu}_u, \hat{\Sigma}_u$ and $\hat{\mu}_m, \hat{\Sigma}_m$ are as follows:

$$\hat{\mu}_u = \phi_\mu(h_u^{(L)}), \quad \hat{\Sigma}_u = \mathrm{diag}(\exp(\phi_\sigma(h_u^{(L)}))) \tag{11}$$

$$\hat{\mu}_m = \phi_\mu(h_m^{(L)}), \quad \hat{\Sigma}_m = \mathrm{diag}(\exp(\phi_\sigma(h_m^{(L)}))) \tag{12}$$

Where $\phi_\mu(\cdot)$ and $\phi_\sigma(\cdot)$ are decoders composed of MLP, respectively, and $\mathrm{diag}(\cdot)$ and $\exp(\cdot)$ are used to ensure that each diagonal element term is non-negative. Then, we estimate the mean and covariance matrix of the neighbor features of the reconstructed joint embedding network and meta-path according to the following formula:

$$\hat{\mu}_u = \frac{1}{q} \sum_{i=1}^{q} \bar{h}_i \tag{13}$$

$$\hat{\mu}_m = \frac{1}{p} \sum_{i=1}^{p} \bar{h}_i \tag{14}$$

$$\overline{\Sigma}_u = \frac{1}{d_u - 1} \sum_{i=1}^{q} (\bar{h}_i - \overline{\mu}_u)(\bar{h}_i - \overline{\mu}_u)^{\mathrm{T}} \tag{15}$$

$$\overline{\Sigma}_m = \frac{1}{d_m - 1} \sum_{i=1}^{p} (\bar{h}_i - \overline{\mu}_m)(\bar{h}_i - \overline{\mu}_m)^{\mathrm{T}} \tag{16}$$

For the same neighborhood, given two sets of multivariate Gaussian distribution parameters (μ_u, Σ_u) and $(\overline{\mu}_u, \overline{\Sigma}_u)$, we use the KL divergence between the two distributions to measure the reconstruction loss:

$$\mathcal{L}_u^n = \mathrm{KL}(\mathcal{N}(\mu_u, \Sigma_u) \| \mathcal{N}(\overline{\mu}_u, \overline{\Sigma}_u)) = \frac{1}{2}[\log \frac{|\Sigma_u|}{|\overline{\Sigma}_u|} - n + \mathrm{tr}(\overline{\Sigma}_u^{-1}\Sigma_u) + (\mu_u - \overline{\mu}_u)^{\mathrm{T}}\overline{\Sigma}_u^{-1}(\mu_u - \overline{\mu}_u)] \tag{17}$$

In the same way, the reconstruction loss between the parameter (μ_m, Σ_m) and $(\overline{\mu}_m, \overline{\Sigma}_m)$ component distributions of the other two groups of multivariate Gaussian distributions can be calculated by KL divergence:

$$\begin{aligned}
\mathcal{L}_m^n &= \mathrm{KL}(\mathcal{N}(\mu_m, \Sigma_m) \| \mathcal{N}(\overline{\mu}_m, \overline{\Sigma}_m)) \\
&= \frac{1}{2}[\log \frac{|\Sigma_m|}{|\overline{\Sigma}_m|} - n + \mathrm{tr}(\overline{\Sigma}_m^{-1}\Sigma_m) + (\mu_m - \overline{\mu}_m)^{\mathrm{T}}\overline{\Sigma}_m^{-1}(\mu_m - \overline{\mu}_m)]
\end{aligned} \tag{18}$$

where is the representational dimension of the encoder hidden layer, where the gradient should be forbidden to pass through either/or when providing parameters for the distribution. Where is the representation dimension of the encoder hidden layer, where (μ_u, Σ_u), $(\overline{\mu}_u, \overline{\Sigma}_u)$, $(\mu_m, \Sigma_m)(\mu_m, \Sigma_m)$, $(\overline{\mu}_m, \overline{\Sigma}_m)$ should prohibit the gradient when providing parameters for the distribution.

The Overall Reconstruction Loss. The global reconstruction loss combines node attribute, degree, and neighborhood reconstruction losses. Since metapath-involved nodes are fewer, their losses are weighted in the overall network loss to ensure their impact is properly reflected, which can be expressed as follow:

$$\mathcal{L}_u' \triangleq \lambda_x \mathcal{L}_u^x + \lambda_d \mathcal{L}_u^d + \lambda_n \mathcal{L}_u^n + \lambda_D \mathcal{L}_m^d + \lambda_N \mathcal{L}_m^n \tag{19}$$

where $\lambda_x, \lambda_d, \lambda_n, \lambda_D$ and λ_N are hyperparameters that control the loss weights of different types of reconstruction. We can use $\mathcal{L}_u'$ as the score of each node in the formula to represent the abnormal degree of each node u.

4 Experiments

4.1 Anomaly Detection Results

We evaluate MNRN against nine baselines on six datasets, with results shown in Table 2. MNRN outperforms all baselines on five datasets, with the most notable gain (4.8%) on Flickr. The only exception is ACM, likely due to its complex subgraph structure and the model's reliance on local neighborhood features, which may underrepresent certain nodes.

Compared with GNN-based methods like DOMINANT, AnomalyDAE, and meta-path-based MSAD, MNRN achieves better performance by integrating skip connections to alleviate over-smoothing and leveraging neighborhood reconstruction to highlight diverse anomaly patterns. These design choices enhance the model's robustness and detection accuracy across datasets.

Table 2. AUC VALUES ON 6 DATASETS (%).

	Methods	ACM	Citeseer	BlogCatalog	Flickr	Photo	Computers
Unsupervised Methods	ANOMALOUS	70.38	63.07	72.37	74.34	56.28	71.59
	DOMINANT	76.01	53.90	74.68	74.42	38.10	46.80
	AnomalyDAE	75.13	72.71	78.34	75.08	/	/
	CoLA	82.37	89.68	78.54	75.13	/	/
Semi-supervised Methods	DeepSAD	53.00	54.60	54.80	53.90	28.79	42.19
	MSAD	89.87	94.69	81.48	79.96	90.52	95.46
	Semi-GNN	84.90	81.74	84.42	73.39	92.36	76.84
	GAD-NR	64.52	90.38	78.79	56.37	96.52	93.23
	GDN	78.12	85.48	70.90	71.03	/	/
	MNRN	89.91	95.04	82.92	84.76	97.25	98.05

4.2 Ablation Study

We conduct ablation studies (Table 3) by removing key modules to assess their impact. Results averaged over 10 runs show that each module contributes positively to performance. Skip connections consistently enhance results, highlighting the benefit of reusing initial features.

Removing both meta-path and neighbor representations causes the largest drop, indicating their complementary roles: meta-paths capture global structure, while neighbors provide local context. Their combination is essential for expressive decoding and effective anomaly detection.

Table 3. The impact on AUC when removing different modules.

Methods	ACM	Citeseer	BlogCatalog	Flickr	Photo	Computers
Without meta path community	87.63	91.55	79.64	82.25	96.87	96.09
Without skip connection	88.89	93.71	78.97	81.13	94.41	95.46
Without neighbor decoding	84.53	80.12	75.88	78.28	90.05	92.64
MNRN	89.91	95.04	82.92	84.76	97.25	98.05

5 Conclusion

We propose MSAD, a metapath-based semi-supervised anomaly detection framework that leverages GCNs to capture global and local differences between normal and abnormal nodes. Experiments on six real-world networks show its superior performance, with future work focusing on deeper metapath pattern analysis.

Acknowledgments. This work is supported by Graduate Innovation Project of Chongqing University of Technology (gzlcx20253215).

References

1. Ding, K., Li, J., Bhanushali, R., et al.: Deep anomaly detection on attributed networks. In: Proceedings of the 2019 SIAM International Conference on Data Mining, SIAM, pp. 594–602 (2019)
2. Ding, K., Zhou, Q., Tong, H., et al.: Few-shot network anomaly detection via cross-network meta-learning. Proc. Web Conf. **2021**, 2448–2456 (2021)
3. Fan, H., Zhang, F., Li, Z.: Anomalydae: dual autoencoder for anomaly detection on attributed networks. In: ICASSP 2020–2020 IEEE International Conference on Acoustics, Speech and Signal Processing (ICASSP), pp. 5685–5689. IEEE (2020)
4. Hinton, G.E., Salakhutdinov, R.R.: Reducing the dimensionality of data with neural networks. Science **313**, 504–507 (2006)
5. Kim, H., Lee, B.S., Shin, W.-Y., et al.: Graph anomaly detection with graph neural networks: current status and challenges. IEEE Access **10**, 111820–111829 (2022)
6. Kipf, T.N., Welling, M.: Semi-supervised classification with graph convolutional networks. arXiv preprint arXiv:1609.02907 (2016)
7. Li, J., Dani, H., Hu, X., et al.: Radar: residual analysis for anomaly detection in attributed networks. In: IJCAI, pp. 2152–2158 (2017)
8. Li, Y., Huang, X., Li, J., et al.: Specae: spectral autoencoder for anomaly detection in attributed networks. In: Proceedings of the 28th ACM International Conference on Information and Knowledge Management, pp. 2233–2236 (2019)
9. Liu, Y., Li, Z., Pan, S., et al.: Anomaly detection on attributed networks via contrastive self-supervised learning. IEEE Trans. Neural Netw. Learn. Syst. **33**, 2378–2392 (2021)

10. Luo, X., Wu, J., Beheshti, A., et al.: Comga: community-aware attributed graph anomaly detection. In: Proceedings of the Fifteenth ACM International Conference on Web Search and Data Mining, pp. 657–665 (2022)
11. Pei, Y., Huang, T., Van Ipenburg, W., et al.: ResGCN: attention-based deep residual modeling for anomaly detection on attributed networks. Mach. Learn. **111**, 519–541 (2022)
12. Peng, Z., Luo, M., Li, J., et al.: ANOMALOUS: a joint modeling approach for anomaly detection on attributed networks. In: IJCAI, pp. 3513–3519 (2018)
13. Perozzi, B., Akoglu, L.: Scalable anomaly ranking of attributed neighborhoods. In: Proceedings of the 2016 SIAM International Conference on Data Mining, SIAM, pp. 207–215 (2016)
14. Qian, Y., Zhang, Y., Ye, Y., et al.: Distilling meta knowledge on heterogeneous graph for illicit drug trafficker detection on social media. Adv. Neural. Inf. Process. Syst. **34**, 26911–26923 (2021)
15. Roy, A., Shu, J., Li, J., et al.: Gad-NR: graph anomaly detection via neighborhood reconstruction. In: Proceedings of the 17th ACM International Conference on Web Search and Data Mining, pp. 576–585 (2024)
16. Shchur, O., Mumme, M., Bojchevski, A., et al.: Pitfalls of graph neural network evaluation. In: arXiv preprint arXiv:1811.05868 (2018)
17. Tang, M., Yang, C., Li, P.: Graph auto-encoder via neighborhood wasserstein reconstruction. arXiv preprint arXiv:2202.09025 (2022)
18. Veličković, P., Cucurull, G., Casanova, A., et al.: Graph attention networks. In: arXiv preprint arXiv:1710.10903 (2017)
19. Zhang, G., Li, Z., Huang, J., et al.: EFraudCom: an e-commerce fraud detection system via competitive graph neural networks. ACM Trans. Inform. Syst. (TOIS) **40**, 1–29 (2022)

DarkFusionNet: A Fusion Neural Network Based Architecture for Darknet Text Classification

Anyang Xu[1], Peng Wu[2(✉)], Dong Wang[1], and Bowen Yang[1]

[1] School of Cyber Science and Engineering, Nanjing University of Science and Technology, Nanjing, China
`{xay,culin888,nlgybw}@njust.edu.cn`
[2] School of Intelligent Manufacturing, Nanjing University of Science and Technology, Nanjing, China
`wupeng@njust.edu.cn`

Abstract. The increasing heterogeneity and obfuscation of darknet markets present significant challenges for cross-market text classification. These markets often exhibit inconsistent syntax, domain-specific slang, and frequent use of encryption or code words. In light of this, we propose DarkFusionNet, a neural architecture for darknet text classification. It captures global semantics and local contextual features through Contextual Transformer Layer and Fusion Neural Network Layer. We also introduce DT-Dataset, a benchmark of annotated darknet texts collected from multiple markets. Experiments demonstrate the effectiveness of DarkFusionNet, surpassing existing baselines. Cross-market evaluations further confirm its robustness and generalizability to unseen markets with diverse linguistic styles and content.

Keywords: Darknet · Text Classification · Feature Fusion · Transformer · Neural Network · Cross-Market Classification

1 Introduction

With the Internet's rapid expansion, the darknet has become a hub for illicit trade and cybercrime, enabled by its anonymity and decentralization. Unlike the open web, darknet text is unstructured, multilingual, and noisy [1], posing challenges for cybersecurity. Effective classification of such text is thus critical for threat monitoring and intelligence analysis.

Recent studies focus on darknet threat classification, data extraction, and deep learning applications. For classification, methods like CNN, SVM [2], and FastText [7] automate classification tasks. In data extraction, topic modeling approaches including LDA [8] and BERTopic [9] enhance analytical precision. Deep learning models like BERT [14] and Doc2Vec [10] advance entity recognition and threat prediction.

However, key challenges remain: (1) market heterogeneity—distinct jargon and user patterns across markets; (2) data sparsity—labeled data is costly to

T. Zhu et al. (Eds.): KSEM 2025, LNAI 15923, pp. 124–133, 2026.
https://doi.org/10.1007/978-981-95-3061-8_14

obtain; and (3) market dynamism—constant evolution demands adaptable models. To address these, we contribute:

- **DarkFusionNet**: We propose DarkFusionNet, an innovative model designed to enhance cross-market darknet text classification. By integrating Contextual Transformer Layer and Fusion Neural Network Layer, the model significantly improves both accuracy and adaptability.
- **DT-Dataset**: We construct DT-Dataset, a high-quality dataset of 129,134 darknet transactions from the Darknet Market Archives [4], spanning multiple markets for diverse representation.
- **Cross-market classification**: We propose a cross-market classification approach using the DarkFusionNet model, trained on data from four darknet markets in the DT-Dataset. The model is evaluated on unseen markets to test its generalization across diverse market characteristics.

2   Related Work

2.1   Darknet Text Classification

Early research primarily applied machine learning to analyze darknet activities. Deliu et al. [2] compared CNN and SVM in classifying hacker forum posts, finding SVM offered similar accuracy with lower computational cost. Alaidi et al. [6] used Linear SVC, Naive Bayes, and Random Forest for dark web page classification, with Linear SVC achieving 91% accuracy. Kawaguchi et al. [7] applied FastText and LightGBM to detect malicious dark web sites.

Topic modeling is also common in data extraction. Liu et al. [8] employed LDA to uncover hidden forum topics. Pastor-Galindo et al. [9] combined BERTopic with SBERT for high-dimensional semantic analysis of Onion Services, using UMAP and HDBSCAN to extract key themes.

Recent deep learning advances further enhanced darknet text classification. Georgoulias et al. [10] used Doc2Vec and BERT to classify cybercrime products and analyze pricing across markets. Ranade et al. [11] proposed CyBERT for network security tasks like Named Entity Recognition and knowledge graph construction. Jin et al. [3] pre-trained RoBERTa on a large darknet corpus to create DarkBERT, which outperformed prior models in various darknet tasks.

2.2   Fusion Neural Network

The increasing complexity and volume of darknet content have driven interest in advanced classification methods, especially fusion neural networks that integrate diverse feature extraction strategies. Liang et al. [15] proposed SVA-CNN with heterogeneous attention to dynamically weight multi-view text features, pioneering adaptive fusion in darknet analysis. Huan et al. [17] introduced CBM, combining multiscale convolution and Bi-LSTM to capture both local and global semantics, with a MIX attention mechanism enhancing robustness against obfuscated texts. Wankhade et al. [16] extended this via CBMAFM, a cross-modal model fusing CNN-based spatial and BiLSTM-based temporal features to address longitudinal patterns in dark web discourse.

3   Proposed DarkFusionNet Architecture

3.1   Model Overview

We propose DarkFusionNet, a cross-market darknet text classification model that integrates multiple deep learning techniques, as illustrated in Fig. 1.

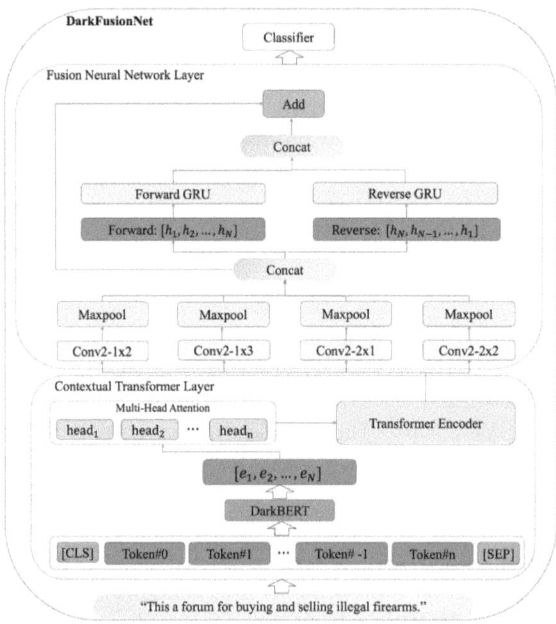

Fig. 1. Overall network framework for DarkFusionNet.

3.2   Contextual Transformer Layer

DarkFusionNet employs DarkBERT [3], pretrained on darknet corpora, to encode raw text into contextual embeddings. This addresses BERT's limitations on darknet slang [18], reduces market heterogeneity, and captures market-specific language. The output sequence is $E = [e_1, e_2, \ldots, e_N]$.

To emphasize informative words, we integrate word vector attention [12] with Transformer encoder. Attention between the i-th query and j-th key is:

$$\alpha_{ij} = \mathrm{softmax}\left(\frac{Q_i K_j^T}{\sqrt{d_k}}\right), \tag{1}$$

where Q_i, K_j are the query and key vectors, d_k the key dimension, and α_{ij} the attention score. The context vector for word i is:

$$v_i^{\text{context}} = \sum_{j=1}^{N} \alpha_{ij} e_j, \tag{2}$$

and concatenating v_i^{context} with e_i gives enhanced representations.

While attention captures keyword salience, it is limited in modeling long-range dependencies. We address this via Transformer encoder, which uses self-attention to capture both local and global semantic relations across the sequence.

3.3 Fusion Neural Network Layer

While the Contextual Transformer captures global semantics, it lacks sensitivity to local character-level co-occurrences and weakly models cross-sentence temporal dependencies in multi-hop dialogues. To address this, the Fusion Neural Network Layer integrates CNN and BiGRU to extract fine-grained local features via multi-scale convolutional kernels and enhance cross-sentence coherence through bidirectional gated units.

The CNN Module uses parallel multi-scale convolutions on input embeddings $X \in \mathbb{R}^{d \times L}$:

$$H^{(k)} = \text{ReLU}(W_k * X + b_k), \quad k \in \{1 \times 2,\ 1 \times 3,\ 2 \times 1,\ 2 \times 2\}, \tag{3}$$

where kernels $1 \times 2, 1 \times 3$ capture character patterns, and $2 \times 1, 2 \times 2$ capture cross-word relations. Outputs F_{cnn} are concatenated after max-pooling.

To compensate for CNN's temporal limits, BiGRU processes $F_{\text{cnn}} \in \mathbb{R}^{L \times d_c}$ bidirectionally, encoding past-to-present and future-to-past contexts, preserving semantic continuity. Hidden states are concatenated:

$$H_{\text{bigru}} = [\overrightarrow{H} \parallel \overleftarrow{H}] \in \mathbb{R}^{L \times 2d_g}, \tag{4}$$

with $\overrightarrow{H}, \overleftarrow{H} \in \mathbb{R}^{L \times d_g}$ the forward and reverse states; d_g the GRU size.

Local CNN and BiGRU features, representing different abstraction levels, fuse via hierarchical residual connection:

$$F_{\text{final}} = \text{LayerNorm}\left(H_{\text{bigru}} + W_{\text{proj}} F_{\text{cnn}}\right), \tag{5}$$

where $W_{\text{proj}} \in \mathbb{R}^{d_g \times d_c}$ projects CNN features, mitigating gradient vanishing in deep networks.

3.4 Classification Layer

The fused feature matrix $F_{\text{final}} \in \mathbb{R}^{L \times d}$ is compressed through temporal mean-pooling followed by softmax classification:

$$P(y = k) = \frac{\exp(\mathbf{W}[:,k]^T \cdot \text{Mean}(F_{\text{final}}) + \mathbf{b}[k])}{\sum_{c=1}^{C} \exp(\mathbf{W}[:,c]^T \cdot \text{Mean}(F_{\text{final}}) + \mathbf{b}[c])} \tag{6}$$

4 Experiments

4.1 Dataset Construction

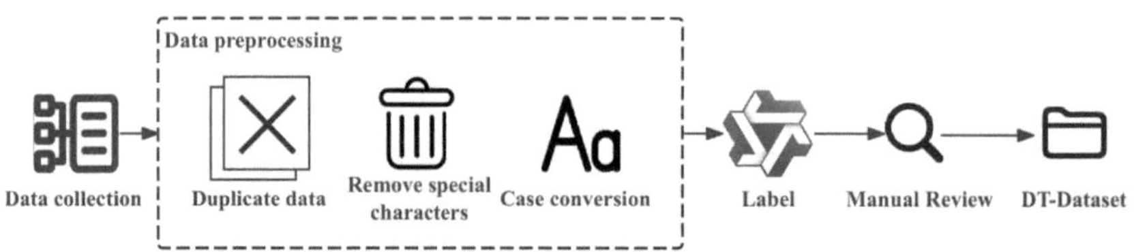

Fig. 2. Overall network framework for DarkFusionNet.

Data Collection. The DT-Dataset, derived from the Darknet Market Archives [4], is a large-scale, multi-category annotated corpus from 12 darknet markets spanning June 9, 2014 to July 12, 2015 as detailed in Table 1. The construction process is illustrated in Fig. 2. The first four markets are used for training, validation, and testing, while the other eight support cross-market classification.

Table 1. Darknet Market Dataset Summary.

Darknet Market	Dataset Size	Dataset Size (Duplicated)	Dataset Type
1776	83	17	Training, Validation, Testing Dataset
Abraxas	310,174	7,796	
Andromeda	121,547	1,122	
Agora	4,652,884	29,085	
Alpaca	13,554	645	Cross-market Text Classification Dataset
Alpha	641,892	19,486	
BB	334,499	10,759	
C9	333,493	8,092	
EVO	3,222,526	29,974	
EVO2	375,000	13,656	
Haven	5,961	396	
ME	468,420	8,106	
In total	10,480,033	129,134	

Data Preprocessing. Darknet marketplace data contains non-standard text with noise, redundancy, and unique linguistic patterns due to anonymity and encryption, necessitating systematic preprocessing for dataset quality. Duplicate posts are removed through hash-based deduplication, and the resulting data volumes for each market after deduplication are shown in Table 1. Irrelevant symbols (e.g., '#', '@', '$'), emojis, and corrupted characters are filtered using regular expressions. Finally, all text is normalized to lowercase to eliminate case sensitivity issues, improving model efficiency.

Data Labeling. The DT-Dataset underwent categorization into predefined classes before labeling: *drugs, hacker, weapons, pornography, illegal activities, illegal financial, fake products,* and *controlled items* [1]. An *others* category captured unclassifiable texts to enhance labeling accuracy.

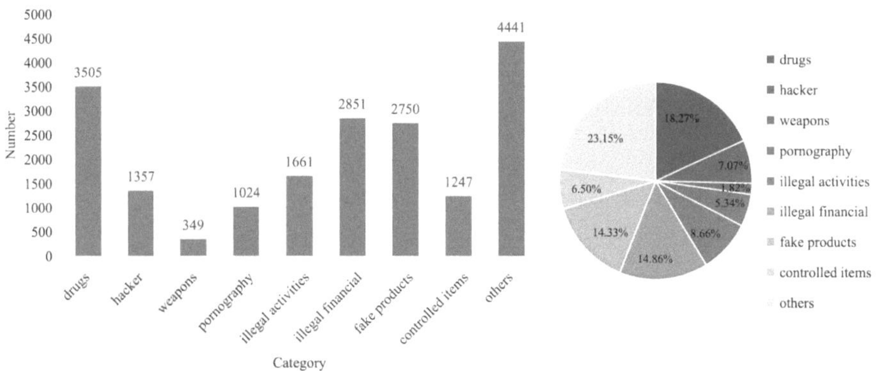

Fig. 3. Category and number of datasets used for model training, validation, and testing in DT-Dataset.

The Qwen LLM [5,13] performed initial labeling to minimize manual annotation costs. Manual verification refined annotations for accuracy. Dataset category distributions across training/validation/testing are shown in Fig. 3.

The model prompts used in this task and DT-Dataset are presented in https://github.com/Lum1n0us1/DT-Dataset.

4.2   Evaluation Setup

Dataset: As detailed in Sect. 4.1, we removed the *others* category due to noise and addressed class imbalance via undersampling and oversampling. The final dataset comprises 14,744 samples, split into training, validation, and test sets in an 8:1:1 ratio.

Implementation Details: During training, the maximum input sequence length was set to 128, and the initial learning rate was 1×10^{-4} for stable convergence. Experiments were run on two Tesla V100 GPUs for 10 epochs, with a batch size of 64. We used the Adam optimizer and a weighted cross-entropy loss function to address class imbalance.

Baselines: We compared our approach against 9 baseline models: Dark-BERT[1], bert-base-uncased[2], CyBERT-Base-MLM[3], ABLG-CNN, Capsule Net-

---

[1] https://huggingface.co/s2w-ai/DarkBERT.
[2] https://huggingface.co/google-bert/bert-base-uncased.
[3] https://github.com/priyankaranade1/CyBERT.

works, Att-BiLSTM, TextRNN, TextCNN, and RCNN, as well as 6 large language models (LLMs): DeepSeek-R1-32B[4], LLaMA-3.1-70B[5], Gemma-2-9B[6], Phi-3-3.8B[7], ChatGLM-3-6B[8], and Falcon-3-7B[9]. All models are widely used in the field, and all were evaluated under the same experimental conditions to ensure fairness.

Evaluation Metrics: We used Accuracy, Precision, Recall, and F1-Score as evaluation metrics, with Accuracy and F1-Score as the primary metrics.

4.3   Results and Analysis

Table 2. Baselines and LLMs comparison results.

Model	Accuracy (%)	Precison (%)	Recall (%)	F1-Score (%)
BERT	85.87	86.54	85.87	86.74
CyBERT	90.01	89.90	90.01	89.93
DarkBERT	89.76	90.56	89.76	89.94
TextRNN	87.27	87.32	87.27	87.14
TextCNN	87.16	87.42	87.16	87.23
RCNN	88.09	88.29	88.09	87.99
ABLG-CNN	84.43	86.25	84.43	84.88
Capsule Networks	83.48	83.03	83.48	83.03
Att-BiLSTM	87.64	87.71	87.64	87.66
DeepSeek-R1-32b	78.56	77.61	78.56	77.44
LLaMA-3.1-70b	84.60	84.92	84.60	86.74
Gemma-2-9b	81.53	83.27	81.53	81.31
Phi-3-3.8b	77.71	74.27	77.71	74.76
ChatGLM-3-6b	35.48	62.29	35.48	31.51
Falcon-3-7b	70.57	75.26	70.57	69.67
DarkFusionNet(Ours)	**91.05**	**91.24**	**91.05**	**91.08**

Comparison with Baselines: Table 2 shows that DarkFusionNet outperforms all baselines, achieving 91.05% accuracy and 91.08% F1-score. CyBERT and DarkBERT follow with 90.01% and 89.76% accuracy, respectively. Traditional models (TextRNN, TextCNN, RCNN) score below 90%, while ABLG-CNN and

---

[4] https://huggingface.co/deepseek-ai/DeepSeek-R1-Distill-Qwen-32B.

[5] https://huggingface.co/meta-llama/Llama-3.1-70B.

[6] https://huggingface.co/google/gemma-2-9b.

[7] https://huggingface.co/microsoft/Phi-3-mini-4k-instruct.

[8] https://huggingface.co/THUDM/chatglm3-6b.

[9] https://huggingface.co/tiiuae/Falcon3-7B-Instruct.

Capsule Networks perform worst, at 84.43% and 83.48%. DarkFusionNet demonstrates superior performance in long-text classification and feature extraction for darknet texts.

Comparison with LLMs: LLaMA 3.1-70B achieves the best performance among all LLMs, likely due to its larger parameter scale. However, DarkFusionNet outperforms all LLM models, highlighting the superiority of specialized models like DarkFusionNet for darknet text classification tasks over general-purpose LLMs.

4.4   Ablation Experiment

In ablation experiment, we replace DarkBERT with GloVe[10]. Table 3 shows that DarkFusionNet consistently outperforms its ablated variants. Removing Dark-BERT led to the largest drop, confirming its key role. Excluding multi-head attention or the Transformer encoder reduced accuracy to 89.42% and 86.78%, highlighting their importance for global feature extraction. These results validate the contribution of each module, especially DarkBERT and Transformer Encoder.

Table 3. Results of DarkFusionNet ablation experiments.

Model	Accuracy (%)	Precison (%)	Recall (%)	F1-Score (%)
DarkFusionNet(Ours)	**91.05**	**91.24**	**91.05**	**91.08**
-DarkBERT	85.29	87.22	85.29	85.78
-Multi-Head Attention	89.42	89.59	89.42	89.43
-Transformer Encoder	86.78	86.54	86.78	86.40
-CNN	90.35	90.43	90.35	90.42
-BiGRU	90.78	90.92	90.78	90.82

4.5   Cross-Market Darknet Text Classification

Due to significant textual variation across darknet markets, models trained on a single market often fail to generalize. To assess cross-market adaptability, we evaluated our model on eight unseen marketplaces. Results are shown in Table 4.

The model achieved strong performance across markets, with accuracy reaching 94.88% and 94.08% in BB and C9, and an F1-Score of 95.27% in BB, reflecting high adaptability. Despite slight drops in Alpaca, EVO, and Haven, accuracy remained above 90%, confirming the model's robustness and generalization.

---

[10] https://nlp.stanford.edu/projects/glove.

Table 4. Results of cross-market darknet text classification.

Market Name	Accuracy(%)	Precison(%)	Recall(%)	F1-Score(%)
Alpaca	92.18	92.48	92.18	92.23
Alpha	89.31	89.62	89.31	89.34
BB	94.88	95.84	94.88	95.27
C9	94.08	95.08	94.08	94.42
EVO	91.82	92.33	91.82	91.98
EVO2	90.69	92.00	90.69	91.17
Haven	92.20	92.49	92.20	92.25
ME	93.62	94.80	93.62	94.12

5 Conclusion

We introduce DarkFusionNet, a cross-market darknet text classification model, along with the DT-Dataset. DarkFusionNet is designed to capture both global semantic and local contextual features, enabling effective classification across linguistically diverse markets. Experimental results show that it outperforms existing baselines and generalizes well across diverse markets. These findings highlight its robustness and practical value for real-world darknet analysis.

Acknowledgments. This paper was supported by the National Natural Science Foundation of China (project numbers are 72274096, 72301136, and 72174087), the Foreign Cultural and Educational Expert Program of the Ministry of Science and Technology of China (G2022182009L).

References

1. Ke, L., Chen, X., Wang, H.: An unsupervised detection framework for Chinese jargons in the darknet. In: Proceedings of the Fifteenth ACM International Conference on Web Search and Data Mining. WSDM '22, New York, NY, USA, pp. 458–466. Association for Computing Machinery (2022). https://doi.org/10.1145/3488560.3498469
2. Deliu, I., Leichter, C., Franke, K.: Extracting cyber threat intelligence from hacker forums: Support vector machines versus convolutional neural networks. In: 2017 IEEE International Conference on Big Data (Big Data), pp. 3648–3656. IEEE (2017)
3. Jin, Y., Jang, E., Cui, J., Chung, J.W., Lee, Y., Shin, S.: DarkBert: a language model for the dark side of the internet (2023). https://arxiv.org/abs/2305.08596
4. Branwen, G., et al.: Dark net market archives, 2011–2015 (2015). https://gwern.net/dnm-archive, https://gwern.net/dnm-archive. Accessed DATE
5. Sun, X., et al.: Text classification via large language models (2023). https://arxiv.org/abs/2305.08377

6. Alaidi, A.H.M., Roa'a, M., ALRikabi, H., Aljazaery, I.A., Abbood, S.H.: Dark web illegal activities crawling and classifying using data mining techniques. iJIM **16**(10), 123 (2022)

7. Kawaguchi, Y., Ozawa, S.: Exploring and identifying malicious sites in dark web using machine learning. In: Gedeon, T., Wong, K.W., Lee, M. (eds.) ICONIP 2019. LNCS, vol. 11955, pp. 319–327. Springer, Cham (2019). https://doi.org/10.1007/978-3-030-36718-3_27

8. Liu, L., Tang, L., Dong, W., Yao, S., Zhou, W.: An overview of topic modeling and its current applications in bioinformatics. Springerplus **5**(1), 1–22 (2016). https://doi.org/10.1186/s40064-016-3252-8

9. Pastor-Galindo, J., Ân Sandlin, H., Mármol, F.G., Bovet, G., Pérez, G.M.: A big data architecture for early identification and categorization of dark web sites. Futur. Gener. Comput. Syst. **157**, 67–81 (2024). https://doi.org/10.1016/j.future.2024.03.025, https://www.sciencedirect.com/science/article/pii/S0167739X24000967

10. Georgoulias, D., Yaben, R., Vasilomanolakis, E.: Cheaper than you thought? A dive into the darkweb market of cyber-crime products. In: Proceedings of the 18th International Conference on Availability, Reliability and Security, pp. 1–10 (2023)

11. Ranade, P., Piplai, A., Joshi, A., Finin, T.: CyBert: contextualized embeddings for the cybersecurity domain. In: 2021 IEEE International Conference on Big Data (Big Data), pp. 3334–3342. IEEE (2021)

12. Deng, J., Cheng, L., Wang, Z.: Attention-based BiLSTM fused CNN with gating mechanism model for Chinese long text classification. Comput. Speech Lang. **68**, 101182 (2021)

13. Bai, J., et al.: QWEN technical report. arXiv preprint arXiv:2309.16609 (2023)

14. Varghese, V., S, M., Kb, S.: Extraction of actionable threat intelligence from dark web data. In: 2023 International Conference on Control, Communication and Computing (ICCC), pp. 1–5 (2023). https://doi.org/10.1109/ICCC57789.2023.10165477

15. Liang, Y., et al.: Fusion of heterogeneous attention mechanisms in multi-view convolutional neural network for text classification. Inf. Sci. **548**, 295–312 (2021). https://doi.org/10.1016/j.ins.2020.10.021, https://www.sciencedirect.com/science/article/pii/S002002552031015X

16. Wankhade, M., Annavarapu, C.S.R., Abraham, A.: CBMAFM: CNN-BiLSTM multi-attention fusion mechanism for sentiment classification. Multimedia Tools Appl. **83**(17), 51755–51786 (2024)

17. Huan, H., Guo, Z., Cai, T., He, Z.: A text classification method based on a convolutional and bidirectional long short-term memory model. Connect. Sci. **34**(1), 2108–2124 (2022)

18. Mao, X., Li, Z., Li, Q., Zhang, S.: Bert-DXLMA: enhanced representation learning and generalization model for English text classification. Neurocomputing **622**, 129325 (2025). https://doi.org/10.1016/j.neucom.2024.129325, https://www.sciencedirect.com/science/article/pii/S0925231224020964

Key Nodes Evaluation for Human Proximity Networks Based on Gravity Model

Jian Shu[1], Weide Huang[2], Yunan Jiang[2], Zhenghao Wei[1], and Linlan Liu[2(✉)]

[1] School of Software, Nanchang Hangkong University, Nanchang, China
shujian@nchu.edu.cn, 970633409@qq.com
[2] School of Information Engineering, Nanchang Hangkong University, Nanchang, China
871049921@qq.com, 957423012@qq.com, liulinlan@nchu.edu.cn

Abstract. Human proximity networks describe the offline interactions among individuals. Evaluating key nodes in networks has research value. We propose a key nodes evaluation method for human proximity networks based on gravity model. Sling the networks to obtain the sequence of network snapshots, the relative entropy and node interaction frequency are used to certain the slice length. Node aggregation degree, effective distance, and node pair similarity are used to construct evaluation indicators. Gravity model is used to calculate node importance to evaluate key nodes. Results on three real-word datasets show our method achieved better performance.

Keywords: Human Proximity Networks · Key Nodes Evaluation · Gravity Model · Node Aggregation Degree · Node Pair Similarity

1 Introduction

Human interaction has evolved from offline to online due to rapid developments of technology. Although online interaction overcomes geographical barriers, most occur between those with shared interests. Offline interaction requires co-location in the same area within a timeframe and close proximity, forming human proximity networks [1].

Key nodes [2] are the nodes that have a large impact on the structure and function of the whole network. Key nodes evaluation has a wide range of application scenarios [3].

The gravity model is a classical physical law that describes the interactions between objects in the physical world. It holds that objects with larger masses and with closer distances have greater gravity between them. The human proximity network, as an abstraction in reality, also has similar properties: people who interact more with others and closer to others have greater influence. Based on that, to improve the performance of key nodes evaluation, we propose a Key Nodes Evaluation method for Human Proximity Networks Based on Gravity Model (HPNGM). Our contributions are as below:

(1) We propose a node biased walk strategy. Three kinds of neighborhood information similarity relations are considered to select the node of the next hop, which realizes the serialization of the topological similarity information.

T. Zhu et al. (Eds.): KSEM 2025, LNAI 15923, pp. 134–142, 2026.
https://doi.org/10.1007/978-981-95-3061-8_15

(2) We propose a calculation method of gravitation between nodes. By using the gravity model, we fuse three node topological similarities into gravitational force, then combines influence range to evaluate node importance to evaluation key nodes.

2   Related Work

Local information-based evaluation methods utilize node neighborhood topology to reflect the most direct influence of nodes. TD [4] uses path flow to characterize the changes in connections between nodes over time. TDD [5] calculates the standard deviation of node degrees between different snapshots in a dynamic network to measure the fluctuation of node degrees over time.

Global information-based evaluation methods evaluate the node importance from the network as a whole. TCC [6] uses the temporal shortest paths of nodes in a dynamic network for average shortest path computation to obtain the key node.

Hybird information-based evaluation method, considers the local and global information of the network. Literature [7] proposes a Pythagorean fuzzy technique based on tripartite decision-making that fuses closeness centrality, betweenness centrality, and degree centrality to evaluate the importance of a node.

Compared to only considering the local or global information of the network, the hybrid information-based evaluation methods can more accurately evaluate the key nodes in the network. Therefore, we combine multi-indicators with the gravity model, propose HPNGM.

3   Representation of Human Proximity Network

In this paper, the network is divided into a series of network snapshots with a slice length Δt at equal intervals, and a sequence of network snapshots is constructed to represent the network topology. Given a slice length Δt, networks are divided into a series of network snapshots $G=\{G^l|l = 1, 2, ..., L\}$. For snapshot $G^l=(V, E^l)$, $V = \{v_i|i = 1, 2, ..., n\}$ and $E^l = \{e^l_{i,j}|i, j = 1, 2, ..., n; i \neq j\}$ denote the set of nodes and edges, respectively.

The slice length directly affects the representation of the topology of human proximity networks, so we combine the change in node interaction frequency to measure the changes in networks, obtain the network change degree and determine the slice length based on this. The variability $NVI(\Delta t)$ of the network at Δt moment is obtained by computing the mean value of all neighboring network snapshots in the sequence of snapshots, as shown in Eq. 1.

$$NVI(\Delta t) = \frac{1}{2(L-1)} \sum_{l=1}^{L-1} (\sum X^l \log \frac{X^l}{X^{l+1}} + \sum X^{l+1} \log \frac{X^{l+1}}{X^l}) \tag{1}$$

where $X^l = [CC^l_i|i = 1, 2, ..., n]$ is the distribution vector for the number of node connections, and CC^l_i is the number of node connections. Then, the slice length is determined based on $NVI(\Delta t)$ and relative entropy [8].

4 Key Nodes Evaluation

4.1 Construction of Evaluation Indicators

We construct three indicators of node aggregation degree, effective distance between nodes, and node pair similarity to realize the evaluation of key nodes, respectively.

Node Aggregation Degree. Degree is an indicator to measure the local influence of nodes. Topological overlap rate describes the connectivity between the neighbors of a node. For a given node, the more tightly connected its neighbors are, the greater the topological overlap rate. Therefore, we combine the node topology overlap rate and node degree to construct the node aggregation degree (AC), as shown in Eq. 2.

$$AC_i = \frac{1}{L} \sum_{l=1}^{L} \left(\frac{1}{n} \sum_{j \in V} \left(1 - \frac{CN_{i,j}^l}{\min(Degree_i^l, Degree_j^l)} \right) \right) \cdot Degree_i^l \tag{2}$$

where $CN_{i,j}^l$ denotes the number of intersections of v_i with v_j in first-order neighbors in network snapshot, and $Degree_i^l$ denotes the degree of the node in network snapshot.

Effective Distance Between Nodes. We adopt the temporal shortest path ($TSP_{i,j}$) to represent the shortest path between v_i and v_j. Effective distance utilizes the information quantity to measure the distance between nodes. Considering that when transmitting information, the node with a larger degree receives more information. So, we define the node Information Acceptance IA_i^l to measure the amount of information between neighboring nodes, which is calculated as shown in Eq. 3.

$$IA_i^1 = \begin{cases} \log(Degree_i^l) & Degree_i^l \neq 0 \\ 0 & Degree_i^l = 0 \end{cases} \tag{3}$$

For a temporal shortest path in the network $TSP_{i,j}$, its temporal effective distance (TED) with temporal property is calculated as shown in Eq. 4.

$$TED_{i,j} = (1 + \frac{IA_i^1 + IA_k^1}{2}) + \cdots + (1 + \frac{IA_y^1 + IA_j^1}{2}) \tag{4}$$

where i,k,y,j are the nodes that construct $TSP_{i,j}$.

Node Pair Similarity. In this paper, the node embedding method based on random walk is used to extract the node similarity information of network topology, and the specific process is shown in Fig. 1. Node biased walk is carried out to realize the serialization of network topology similarity information. The word embedding model is used to dimensionalize the network topology similarity information to get the node embedding vector with node topology similarity information, and the node pair similarity indicator is constructed based on the embedding vector.

Serialization of Network Topology Similarity Information We compute the node neighborhood similarity information within and between network snapshots, then obtain the

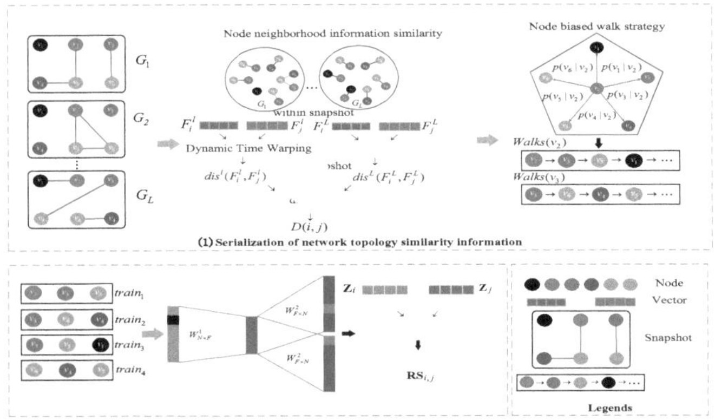

Fig. 1. Node pair similarity construction process

node walk sequences by biased walk to serialize the network topology similarity information. The specific process is divided into the computation of the similarity of node neighborhood information within and between snapshots, and the design of the node biased walk strategy. Node neighborhood information similarity within snapshots interactions between nodes reflects the neighborhood information of the network. For two nodes v_i and v_j under the same network snapshot, let $F_i^l = (b_1, b_2, ..., b_x)$, $F_j^l = (c_1, c_2, ..., c_y)$, $HF_i^l = (b_1, b_2, ..., b_{x-1})$ and $HF_j^l = (c_1, c_2, ..., c_{y-1})$, referring to Dynamic Time Warping (DTW) [9], the similarity value dis^l is calculated as shown in Eq. 5.

$$dis^l(F_i^l, F_j^l) = \begin{cases} \sum_{k=1}^{x} |b_1 - c_k|, & y = 1 \\ \sum_{k=1}^{y} |b_k - c_1|, & x = 1 \\ |b_x - c_y| + \min\left\{ dis^l(HF_i^l, F_j^l), dis^l(F_i^l, HF_j^l), dis^l(HF_i^l, HF_j^l) \right\} & else \end{cases}$$

(5)

After fusing the neighborhood information, the node pair neighborhood similarity value D is obtained by using Euclidean distance as shown in Eq. 6.

$$D(i,j) = \left(\sum_{l=1}^{L} (dis^l(F_i^l, F_j^l))^2 \right)^{\frac{1}{2}}$$

(6)

Then we design a node biased walk strategy (BWS) based on node pair similarity values. Let v_j be the next hop node with v_i as the initial node, when in v_j, without considering the re-return to the previous hop v_i, the probability of v_j in choosing the next hop v_k is $p(v_k|v_j)$, which is calculated as shown in Eq. 7.

$$p(v_k|v_j) = \frac{e^{-D(j,k)}}{\sum_{\substack{k \in V \\ k \neq i, j}} e^{-D(j,k)}}$$

(7)

After walking, a sequence $Walks(v_i) = \{v_i, v_j, v_k, ..., v_m | v_i, v_j, v_k, ..., v_m \in V\}$ is obtained, which compose a collection of walking sequences containing topological similarity of nodes containing $NWS = \{Walks_i(v_j) | i = 1, 2, ..., \rho; j = 1, 2, ..., n\}$, where v_j is the initial node of walk, ρ is the number of walk sequences.

Node topological similarity. We obtain a collection of nodes walk sequences by *BWS* to construct the training samples. For the set of walk sequences *NWS*, each walk sequence $Walks(v_i)$ is divided into training samples *train*, and the training sample set *Trains* is constructed. In a training sample $train \in Trains$, the node at the center of the sample is called the central node. The set of training samples *Trains* is inputted into the SkipGram [10], and the parameter matrices $W^1 \in \mathbb{R}^{n \times emb\_dim}$ and $W^2 \in \mathbb{R}^{emb\_dim \times n}$ are updated, where emb_dim is the dimension of the node embedding vector. After the model converges, take the row vector of row i - 1 of the parameter matrix W^1 as the node embedding vector $z_i = W^1_{i-1}$. Then, cosine similarity is used to calculate the cosine value between the node embedding vectors. Construct the node pair similarity *RS*, which is calculated as shown in Eq. 8.

$$RS_{i,j} = \frac{\sum\limits_{x=0}^{emb\_dim} z_i^x \times z_j^x}{\sqrt{\sum\limits_{x=0}^{emb\_dim} (z_i^x)^2} \times \sqrt{\sum\limits_{x=0}^{emb\_dim} (z_j^x)^2}} \tag{8}$$

where z_i^x denotes the $x - th$ element in the node embedding vector z_i.

4.2 Calculation of Node Importance

In the gravity model, the greater the mass and the closer the distance between objects, the greater the gravity. In human proximity networks, nodes with higher degrees are more important, and nodes that are closer to each other are more relevant. Based on that, we take node aggregation degree AC as the mass of objects, temporal effective distance *TED* as the distance between objects, node pair similarity *RS* as a G in gravity model, and use gravity model to calculate node importance. Specifically, we use the gravity model to calculate the gravity of v_i with its first and second order neighbors $v_j \in \gamma_i$, and add them together as v_i's node importance TNI_i, as shown in Eq. 9.

$$TNI_i = \begin{cases} \sum\limits_{v_j \in \gamma_i} (RS_{i,j} \times \frac{AC_i \times AC_j}{\log(TED_{ij}^2)}), & i \neq j \\ 0, & i = j \end{cases} \tag{9}$$

Sort nodes from high to low based on node importance to obtain a sequence of nodes, and evaluate key nodes.

5 Experiment

5.1 Experiments Setting

We select three datasets with different sparsity and sizes to verify the effectiveness of our method. The information of the datasets is shown in Table 1.

Table 1. Information of Datasets

Description	Haggle [11]	Malawi [11]	HighSchool [11]
scenario	Conference	Village	School
Overall duration (days)	4	7	4
Scanning time (seconds)	120	20	20
Number of active nodes	98	84	327
Number of interactions	74223	18217	67613
Slice length (hours)	6	6	7

In addition, two methods are used to evaluate key nodes: a message propagation model-based method and a correlation-based method. For the former, we use SIR [12] for evaluation, and for the latter, NDCG [13].

5.2 Comparative Experiments on Evaluation Based on Message Propagation Models

Experiment 1. To verify the effectiveness of AC, AC is compared with its baseline indicator Temporal Degree Centrality (TD) [4], and the Top5 ranked nodes are selected as the key node set in SIR to analyze its message propagation capability. The results are shown in Fig. 2. SIR propagation curves on three datasets show that AC effectively improves the representation of the local influence of nodes. This is because it considers the topological overlap rate based on TD, which further represents the node's neighborhood structure's influence on its ability to propagate information.

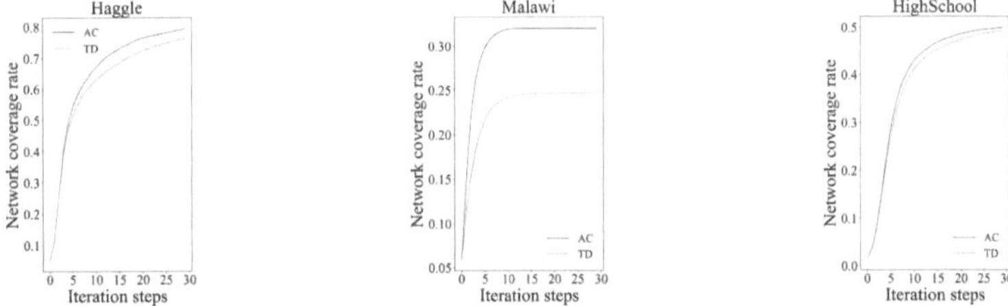

Fig. 2. SIR Propagation curves of AC and TD in each dataset

Experiment 2. To verify the effectiveness of TED, it is compared to its baseline indicator TSP. In reference to closeness centrality (CC)[6], we use the shortest path length between nodes to evaluate key nodes. The Top5 ranked nodes are selected as the set of key nodes for message propagation in the SIR. The results are shown in Fig. 3.

Figure 3 shows that TED effectively improves the characterization of distance by nodes in networks compared to the TSP, which only considers the number of hops of a path, because of the amount of information between pairs of nodes on top of the TSP.

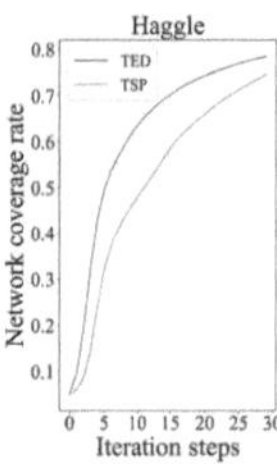 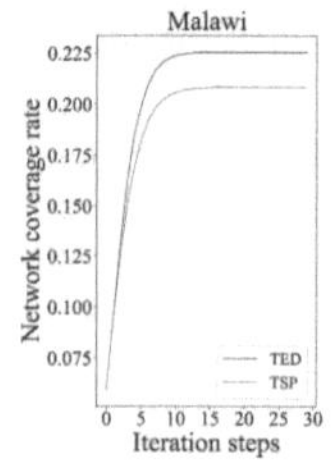 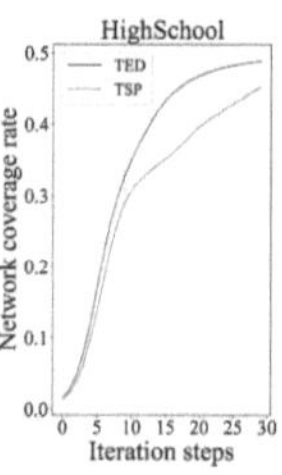

Fig. 3. SIR Propagation curves of TED and TSP in each dataset

As a result, the set of key nodes obtained from TED has a higher network coverage rate compared to TSP, with the most obvious performance in the Haggle dataset, having the largest increase in propagation speed and propagation capacity in the first 20 iteration steps, and therefore get better results in dense human proximity networks.

Experiment 3. To verify that HPNGM has higher accuracy in evaluating key nodes, we compare it with TDD [5], TCC [6], and TGC [14]. The ranked list of nodes is obtained by using 4 methods to calculate the node importance. The Top 5 ranked nodes are taken as the set of key nodes, which are iterated as the initial source of infection for the SIR, to compare the network coverage of key nodes obtained by different methods. The higher the network coverage rate for the same number of iteration steps, the more accurate the key node evaluation. the results are shown in Fig. 4.

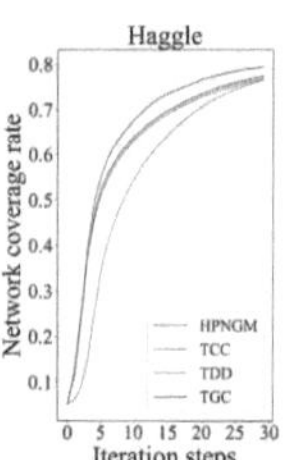 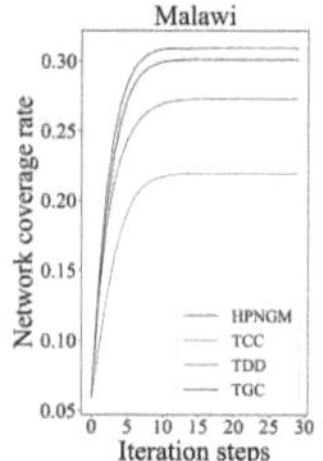 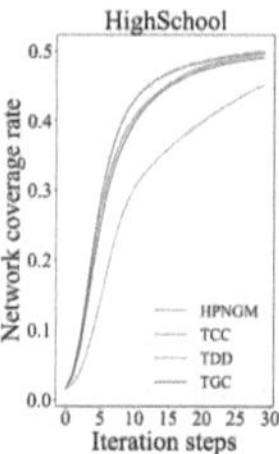

Fig. 4. SIR Propagation curves of 4 methods in each dataset

The results in the three datasets can be concluded that the network coverage rate of the set of key nodes obtained by HPNGM is higher than that of TDD, TCC, and TGC when propagated as the initial infection source in SIR. This is because we consider the local influence of nodes, node distances, and topological similarity among nodes.

5.3 Comparative Experiments on Evaluation Based on Ranking

In this experiment, the node sorting lists are obtained by different methods, and the NDCGs of the node sorting lists of various methods are obtained in different datasets respectively, to verify the validity of the key node evaluation from the correlation perspective. The NDCG values of TDD, TCC, TGC, and HPNGM are calculated in three datasets respectively, and the quality of the sorting lists is shown in Table 2.

Table 2. Sorted list quality for different datasets (NDCG top 15)

Methodology	Haggle	Malawi	HighSchool
TDD	0.8834	0.9055	0.8895
TCC	0.5532	0.6385	0.6967
TGC	0.8943	0.9519	0.9270
HPNGM	**0.9428**	**0.9524**	**0.9436**

As can be seen from Table 2, TGC and HPNGM can evaluate node influence more comprehensively because they integrate the local influence of nodes in the network with the node distances, so this type of method has better performance on NDCG compared to TDD and TCC. Further, compared to the gravity model TGC that fuses node degree as well as shortest paths between nodes for critical nodes, HPNGM considers topological converge rate based on node degree and calculates effective distance based on shortest paths, and thus the resulting reception sorted list is qualitatively better.

6   Conclusion and Future Work

In this paper, we propose a key nodes evaluation method for human proximity networks based on the gravity model. Node interaction frequency and relative entropy determine the slices length. The evaluation indicators are constructed by the node aggregation degree, node effective distance, and node pair similarity. Gravity model is used to complete the evaluation of key nodes. Experiments on three datasets show that HPNGM has better performance. However, in reality, the nodes of human neighboring networks exhibit heterogeneity. Thus, the future work is to use heterogeneous graphs to model human proximity networks to complete key nodes evaluation.

Acknowledgments. The works described in this paper are supported by The National Natural Science Foundation of China under Grant No. 62362052.

References

1. Holme, P.: Modern temporal network theory: a colloquium. Euro. Phys. J. B **88**(09), 234 (2015)
2. Zhang, X., et al.: Key node identification in social networks based on topological potential model. Comput. Commun. **213**, 158–168 (2024)
3. Iqbal, S., et al.: Finding influential users in social networks based on novel features & link-based analysis. J. Int. Fuzzy Syst. **40**(01), 1623–1637 (2021)
4. Kim, H., et al.: Temporal node centrality in complex networks. Phys. Rev. E **85**(02), 026107 (2012)
5. Wang, Z., et al.: Ranking the key nodes with temporal degree deviation centrality on complex networks. In: Proceedings of the 29th Chinese Control and Decision Conference, Piscataway. USA, pp. 1484–1489. IEEE (2017)

6. Tang, J.K., et al.: Temporal distance metrics for social net-work analysis. In: Proceedings of the 2nd ACM Workshop on Online Social Networks, New York, USA, pp. 31–36. ACM (2009)

7. Zhou, J., et al.: Three-way decisions with Pythagorean fuzzy TOPSIS for Internet of Drones. IEEE Trans. Fuzzy Syst. **32**(9), 4950–4960 (2024)

8. Kullback, S.: An application of information theory to multivariate analysis. Ann. Math. Stat. **23**(01), 88–102 (1952)

9. Müller, M.: Dynamic time warping. Inform. Retrieval Music Mot. 69–84 (2007)

10. Lazaridou, A., et al.: Combining language and vision with a multimodal skip-gram model. In: Proceedings of the 16th 2015 Conference of the North American Chapter of the Association for Computational Linguistics: Human Language Technolo-gies. Pennsylvania, USA, pp. 153–163. ACL (2015)

11. Kotz, D., et al.: Crawdad: a community resource for archiving wireless data at dartmouth. IEEE Pervasive Comput. **4**(04), 12–14 (2005)

12. Kermack, W.O., et al.: A contribution to the mathematical theory of epidemics. In: Proceedings of the Royal Society of London. Series A, Containing Papers of a Mathematical and Physical Character, vol. 115, no. 772, pp. 700–721 (1927)

13. Shu, J., et al.: Node importance evaluation in multiplex heterogeneous net-work based on graph embedding. J. Beijing Univ. Posts Tele-commun. **45**(04), 104–109 (2022)

14. Bi, J., et al.: Temporal gravity model for important node identification in temporal networks. Chaos Solitons Fract. **147**, 110934 (2021)

SRViT-MCNet: An IoT Malware Classification Model

Changguang Wang[1,2], Hongxuan Wang[1], Xi Zhang[1,2], Qingru Li[1,2], and Fangwei Wang[1,2](✉)

[1] College of Computer and Cyber Security, Hebei Normal University, Shijiazhuang 050024, China
wangcg@hebtu.edu.cn

[2] Key Laboratory of Network and Information Security of Hebei Province, Shijiazhuang 050024, China
fw_wang@hebtu.edu.cn

Abstract. In the Internet of Things (IoT) domain, the heterogeneity of devices and the widespread deployment of resources significantly impact traditional malware classification methods. To effectively extract both local and global features of IoT malware and improve classification accuracy, a hybrid model, named SRViT-MCNet, is proposed. The model first visualizes IoT malware by applying the Occlusion Sensitivity method to capture regions where the model's prediction confidence significantly drops. Topological Data Analysis (TDA) is then employed to generate Persistent Images (PI). The model utilizes a parallel feature extraction strategy, combining the SRViT module with the MCNet module to capture multi-dimensional features. The MC module integrated into the CNN enhances the model's ability to capture fine-grained local features. Additionally, the SCFN design replaces the FFN in RepViT, further improving the model's sensitivity and representation power for local features while retaining global context. Experimental results show that SRViT-MCNet achieves classification accuracies of 99.54% and 99.32% on the BIG2015 and Malimg datasets, respectively.

Keywords: IoT · Malware classification · Visual interpretability · ViT · Deep learning

1 Introduction

The rapid proliferation of Internet of Things (IoT) devices has made them prime targets for malware attacks, posing significant security risks such as unauthorized data access, system compromise, and large-scale disruptions. As IoT malware becomes increasingly diverse and complex, achieving efficient and accurate classification has become a critical research focus.

Traditional malware detection methods–static, dynamic, and hybrid analysis–face limitations in IoT environments. Static analysis, though efficient, is vulnerable to obfuscation techniques. Dynamic analysis offers deeper behavioral

© The Author(s), under exclusive license to Springer Nature Singapore Pte Ltd. 2026
T. Zhu et al. (Eds.): KSEM 2025, LNAI 15923, pp. 143–155, 2026.
https://doi.org/10.1007/978-981-95-3061-8_16

insights but is resource-intensive. Hybrid approaches improve detection accuracy but remain computationally demanding. Recently, image-based malware analysis has gained attention, leveraging visual patterns for classification while addressing code obfuscation challenges.

To tackle the unique constraints of IoT malware detection, we propose SRViT-MCNet, an advanced classification model integrating occlusion sensitivity and topological data analysis (TDA) for feature enhancement, a Multimodal Collaborative Module (MC-Block) for cross-dimensional feature interaction, and a Split-Conv Feedforward Network (SCFN) for improved local-global feature integration. By combining CNNs for fine-grained local feature extraction and ViT for global context modeling, our approach enhances classification accuracy while optimizing computational efficiency. This paper introduces SRViT-MCNet, a novel model for IoT malware classification, with three key contributions:

(1) enhanced feature representation through occlusion sensitivity and TDA-based image enhancement, addressing data imbalance;
(2) multimodal collaborative learning via the MC-Block, enabling cross-dimensional feature fusion for improved classification;
(3) efficient local-global integration using the SCFN module, enhancing feature aggregation while maintaining computational efficiency.

SRViT-MCNet provides a reliable and scalable solution, addressing challenges in feature extraction, efficiency, and classification accuracy.

2 Related Work

2.1 Image-Based Malware Detection

In recent years, image-based malware detection methods have advanced significantly. Nataraj et al. [1] first transformed malware binary files into 2D grayscale images, classifying families by texture analysis, enabling computer vision techniques for malware classification. Karanja et al. [2] improved classification by combining Haralick texture features with machine learning. Yerima et al. [3] focused on malware behavior detection via permission and API call analysis, while Ren et al. [4] introduced byte sequence n-gram visualization to address redundancy. Notably, grayscale image-based malware classification still has critical limitations: traditional methods lose key code features during conversion, fail to capture fine-grained local dependencies in IoT-specific instructions, and struggle with data imbalance in IoT datasets. SRViT-MCNet overcomes these via the MC module for fine-grained dependency capture, and TDA combined with occlusion sensitivity for feature extraction to resolve data imbalance.

2.2 Deep Learning-Based Malware Detection

Traditional malware detection methods rely heavily on feature engineering, limiting their ability to extract deep-level features effectively. Convolutional Neural Networks (CNNs), known for superior feature learning, have been widely adopted in malware detection. Chen et al. [5] achieved 95% accuracy using CNNs on malware images, demonstrating deep learning's efficacy. Chaganti et al. [6] introduced EfficientNetB1, reducing computational costs, while Awan et al. [7] enhanced VGG19 with spatial attention for family classification. Xuan et al. [8] proposed an RGB-based method integrating ASPP and CA algorithms to improve feature extraction and prevent information loss. Xiao et al. [9] addressed grayscale limitations with CoLab and MalCVS.

Transformers, an emerging deep learning architecture, have been increasingly applied to malware detection. Dosovitskiy et al. [10] proposed the Vision Transformer (ViT), showcasing its potential in image recognition tasks. Rustam et al. [11] introduced a Bi-model architecture, stacking identical models sequentially to enhance performance. Puneeth et al. [12] developed the RMDNet model, balancing computational efficiency with high accuracy. Qiao et al. [13] created the WDWTCN model, significantly improving feature extraction efficiency.

Despite advancements, malware datasets often suffer from imbalanced distributions and limited sample sizes, leading to misclassification. To mitigate these issues, malware binaries are converted into grayscale images, with occlusion sensitivity generating RGB images to capture key features. MCNet extracts local features, while ViT models global context, combining their strengths to enhance robustness and address sample imbalance.

2.3 Feature Extraction

Occlusion Sensitivity and Topological Data Analysis (TDA) are pivotal in enhancing feature extraction for malware detection. Occlusion Sensitivity, initially applied in computer vision, identifies influential image regions by analyzing model performance under occlusion. Zeiler [14] introduced this method, demonstrating its ability to assess model sensitivity and reveal vulnerabilities. Aminu [15] advanced it as a visualization tool for classification decisions, while Shafaei [16] integrated it with CNN-LSTM to improve feature extraction and classification accuracy.

TDA leverages topological information to enrich feature spaces, addressing challenges in traditional methods. Muszynski et al. [17] combined TDA with SVM to improve recognition accuracy, while Takahashi et al. [18] used TDA and NHPP for richer geometric feature extraction. Hu et al. [19] proposed TopoResNet-101, integrating TDA with ResNet to enhance generalization. Shin et al. [20] and Han et al. [21] further advanced TDA applications in graph representation and critical feature identification.

While CNNs and ViT excel in feature extraction, they often overlook subtle byte-level differences and face challenges with imbalanced data. Occlusion Sensitivity addresses this by highlighting critical regions, while Topological Data Analysis (TDA) enriches feature spaces. SRViT-MCNet leverages both techniques to achieve robust and accurate malware classification.

3   SRViT-MCNet Module

The SRViT-MCNet model comprises two main modules: malware preprocessing and classification, as shown in Fig. 1. Initially, malware is converted to grayscale images, with key regions identified and cropped using occlusion sensitivity. Topological Data Analysis (TDA) generates enhanced PI images. The classification model combines SRViT and MCNet in parallel. SRViT uses a Spatial Contextual Feedforward Network (SCFN) to capture global and local features, while MCNet employs the MC module for fine-grained feature representation. An Autoencoder reduces feature dimensionality, and Softmax finalizes malware sample classification.

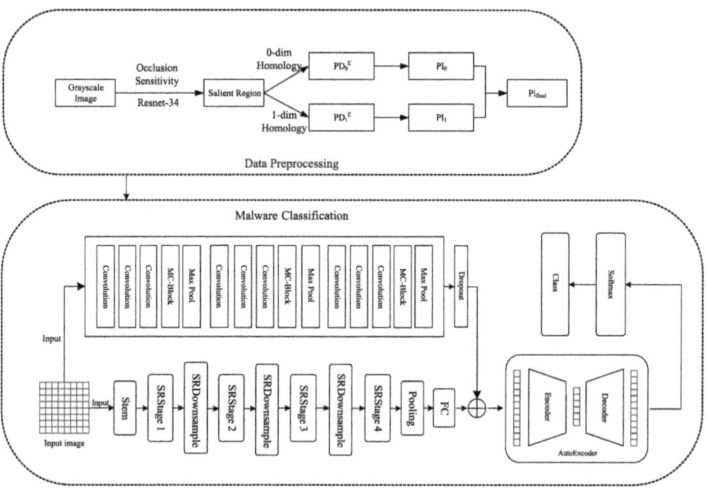

Fig. 1. Overall architecture of the model.

3.1   Data Preprocessing

Classifying visualized malware images often suffers from the loss of critical local features, significantly degrading detection and classification accuracy. To mitigate this, we propose a data preprocessing scheme. First, occlusion sensitivity is applied to grayscale malware images using a 16×16 sliding window with an 8-pixel stride. The change in prediction probability after each occlusion is recorded and visualized as a key region map. This map is cropped to extract significant regions, which are then used to construct complex structures and compute their 0-dimensional and 1-dimensional persistent homology. Resulting in the corresponding Persistence Diagrams (PD) denoted as PD_0^{ε} and PD_1^{ε}. Subsequently, the points in the Persistence Diagram (PD) are transformed into a Birth-Persistence Diagram (BP), where the lifetime $\pi_i = y_i - x_i$ of feature points (x_i, y_i) is calculated. Infinite persistence or anomalously isolated points are replaced, and auxiliary coordinates are introduced to ensure effective representation of all features on a finite plane. Subsequently, a two-dimensional Gaussian kernel maps feature points in the Birth-Persistence (BP) diagram to pixel distributions, generating 0-dimensional and 1-dimensional persistence images PI_0 and PI_1, respectively. These images are then aligned through zero-padding and subjected to maximum stacking to produce a synthesized image PI_{final}. The synthesized image PI_{final} not only effectively enhances the accuracy of malware classification but also better captures key topological information in scenarios with insufficient samples or class imbalance.

3.2   The MC Module

Traditional CNNs excel in feature extraction but often fail to capture fine-grained structures and global context. To address this, we propose an enhanced Multimodal Collaborative Attention Module (MC), as shown in Fig. 2. Building on Multidimensional Collaborative Attention (MCA) [22], the MC module integrates an Affinity matrix to compute row and column similarities via dot product and Softmax, focusing on high-similarity regions. This enhances the interaction between local critical features and global semantic information. The module simultaneously attends to channel, row, and column relationships, filtering weak textures and noise while balancing emphasis on important regions and suppressing irrelevant information, significantly improving robustness and accuracy in complex image processing.

The workflow begins with the left branch of Fig. 2, focusing on row-wise features. The input feature map is first rotated 90° counterclockwise along the H-axis. Subsequently, average pooling (AvgPool) and standard deviation pooling (StdPool) operations are employed to extract pooling features X_{avg}^{row} and X_{std}^{row} from different orientations among:

$$X_{avg}^{row} = AvgPool(X) \in R^{H \times 1 \times 1} \tag{1}$$

$$X_{std}^{row} = StdPool(X) \in R^{H \times 1 \times 1} \tag{2}$$

The pooling results undergo dimensionality transformation, and based on the adjusted row and column feature maps, Query (Q) and Key (K) are generated. A shared Affinity matrix A is then obtained through the dot product of Q and K:

$$A = Q_H \cdot Q_W^T \tag{3}$$

where "·" denotes the dot product, Q_H represents the Query, Q_w represents the Key, and Q_W^T is the transpose of Q_w. The Softmax function is applied to the Affinity matrix as follows:

$$S_{ij} = \frac{\exp(A_{ij})}{\sum_k \exp(A_{ik})} \tag{4}$$

where S_{ij} represents the similarity weight between the i-th row and the j-th column. The generated global similarity weights are used to enhance the features of the row and column branches. Finally, the attention weights W_{row} for different directions are produced through a $1 \times K$ convolutional operation and Sigmoid activation:

$$W_{row} = \sigma(Conv_{1 \times k}(S_{ij})) \tag{5}$$

where σ denotes the Sigmoid function. The attention weights W_{row} are applied to the input features X to obtain the output features of the row branch. The column branch operates similarly to the row branch, with the difference being that it focuses on column-wise information. In the channel dimension, a $1 \times K$ convolutional operation and Sigmoid activation are applied to generate the channel-wise attention weights $W_{channel}$:

$$W_{channel} = \sigma(Conv_{1 \times K}(X_{avg}^{channel} + X_{std}^{channel})) \tag{6}$$

Finally, the input features are weighted using these attention weights. The output features from the row, column, and channel branches are averaged and fused to produce the final enhanced feature map:

$$Output = \frac{1}{3}(W_{row} + W_{col} + W_{channel}) \cdot X \tag{7}$$

achieving comprehensive modeling of multi-dimensional key information.

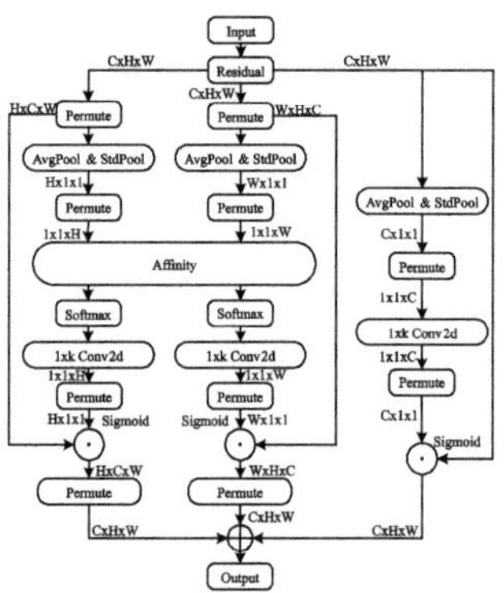

Fig. 2. MC module.

3.3   The SRViT Module

The SRViT module in this study is built upon RepViT [23], as depicted in Fig. 3. It primarily comprises the Stem module, SRStage module, and SRDownsample module, with the latter two serving as the core components. The key enhancement in SRViT is the replacement of the traditional Feedforward Neural Network

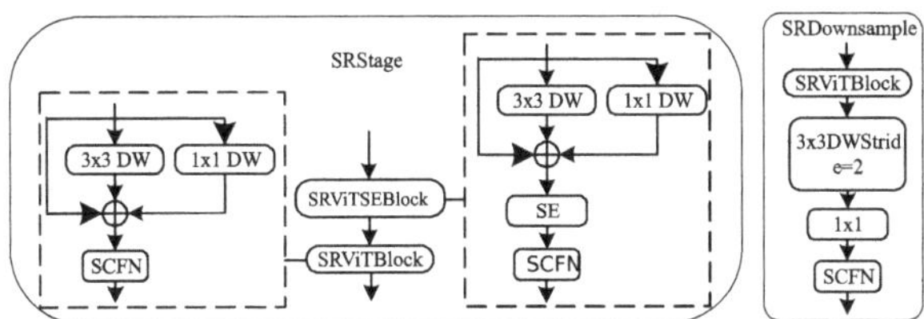

Fig. 3. SRViT main module.

(FFN) in RepViT with the SCFN module, significantly improving the model's ability to capture both local and global features. Unlike the standard Vision Transformer (ViT) architecture, SRViT achieves efficient malware classification by combining the high-efficiency design of lightweight ViT with optimization techniques from lightweight CNNs.

3.4 The SCFN Module

The SCFN (Split-Conv Feedforward Network) module introduces a "dual-convolution" structure to balance channel fusion and local spatial perception. Input features are linearly transformed, activated, and split into sub-channels. Each sub-channel undergoes 1×1 convolution for lightweight cross-channel aggregation, followed by depthwise separable convolution (DW-Conv) to capture local pixel interactions and enable fine-grained feature reorganization. A second 1×1 convolution reintegrates outputs, fused with the branch's front end via addition, facilitating multi-dimensional feature interaction without disrupting token distribution. Compared to traditional FFNs, this structure comprehensively captures feature dependencies with minimal computational overhead, enhancing robustness and classification accuracy in malware image analysis. As shown in Fig. 4, the SCFN module begins with linear transformation and GELU activation of input features.

$$x_i' = GELU(Linear(X_i)) \tag{8}$$

Here, X_i denotes the input features, and X_i represents the features transformed by the linear layer and GELU activation function. Following this, the channel features are partitioned (Split), with one subset of features being processed through the convolutional pathway, while the other subset is propagated directly as a residual branch.

$$x_i' = \left(X_i^{(1)} \right) X_i^{(2)} \tag{9}$$

Here, $X_i^{(1)}$ is directed into the convolutional path, while $X_i^{(2)}$ serves as the residual branch. Within the convolutional path, the first 1×1 convolution is employed for channel compression,

$$X_i^{(1)} = Conv_{1 \times 1}(X_i^{(1)}) \tag{10}$$

followed by a depthwise convolution (DW-Conv) to extract spatial information,

$$X_i^{(1)} = DWConv(X_i^{(1)}) \tag{11}$$

and subsequently, a second 1×1 convolution is appended to reconfigure the channel information.

$$X_i^{(1)} = Conv_{1 \times 1}(X_i^{(1)}) \tag{12}$$

Finally, the output of the convolutional path is summed with the residual branch,

$$x_i'' = X_i^{(1)} + X_i^{(2)} \tag{13}$$

and then passed through a linear layer for the final output.

$$x_i''' = Linear(x_i'') \tag{14}$$

Through this design, the SCFN module is capable of enhancing feature representation while capturing spatial correlations among adjacent features, thereby effectively augmenting the network's expressive power.

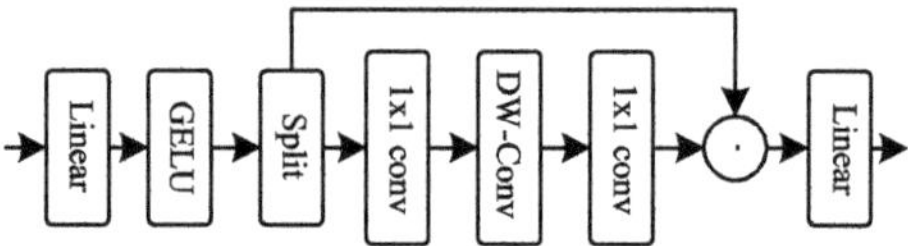

Fig. 4. SCFN module.

3.5 Autoencoder

The Autoencoder (AE) consists of an encoder and a decoder. The encoder reduces data dimensionality via convolutional and downsampling layers, while the decoder reconstructs the data using deconvolutional and upsampling layers. By minimizing a regularized loss function, the AE removes redundant information and retains essential features, enabling effective nonlinear feature extraction and enhancing model performance. This approach leverages established AE principles for improved feature representation.

4 Experiment and Result Analysis

Experimental Setup: The experiments were conducted on an Intel(R) Core(TM) i7-8750H CPU @ 2.20 GHz with 16 GB RAM. All programs were executed using Python 3.9 and PyTorch 2.3.0. The Adam optimizer was employed with a learning rate of $\alpha = 0.001$. To validate the performance of the model, experiments were carried out on the BIG2015 dataset [24] and the Malimg dataset [1].

4.1 Malware Datasets

The experiments utilize two representative datasets for malware family classification, namely BIG2015 and Malimg, to validate the performance of the model.

1) BIG2015 [24] is a publicly available dataset used in the Microsoft Malware Classification Challenge. It contains executable files extracted from 9 different malware families, providing both disassembled text information and file byte information of the malware, totaling 10,868 malware files.
2) Malimg [1] is a classic dataset in the field of imbalanced malware family classification, comprising 25 malware families with a total of 9,339 grayscale image samples of malware. The Malimg dataset is used in the experiments as a comparative benchmark to verify the effectiveness of the model.

4.2 Evaluation Metrics

The experiment evaluates classifier performance using four metrics: Accuracy (Acc), Precision (Pre), Recall (Rec), and F1 Score. Accuracy measures the ratio of correctly classified samples. Precision quantifies the proportion of true positives among predicted positives, while Recall reflects the proportion of true positives among actual positives. The F1 Score balances Precision and Recall. The formulas for these metrics are as follows:

$$Accuracy = (TP + TN)/(TP + TN + FP + FN) \tag{15}$$

$$Precision = TP/(TP + FP) \tag{16}$$

$$Recall = TP/(TP + FN)) \tag{17}$$

$$F1 = 2 * Precision * Recall/(Precision + Recall) \tag{18}$$

4.3 Effect of PI

The model's performance was validated on the BIG2015 and Malimg datasets, with results in Table 1 showing that PI images consistently outperform grayscale images in accuracy, precision, recall, and F1-Score. PI images retain critical features better, significantly enhancing classification accuracy when used for malware detection.

4.4 Effect of MC Module

Experiments demonstrate that local features are crucial for malware classification, yet image compression may cause information loss. Our MC module effectively preserves image details and increases feature dimensionality with minimal overhead. Table 2 shows significant accuracy and precision improvements on Malimg and BIG2015 datasets, validating its effectiveness.

Table 1. Experimental Results of the Model Without PI Images

Dataset	Accuracy	Precision	Recall	F1 score
BIG2015	0.9832	0.9848	0.9840	0.9848
Malimg	0.9837	0.9839	0.9820	0.9822
BIG2015(PI)	0.9954	0.9953	0.9948	0.9961
Malimg(PI)	0.9932	0.9921	0.9889	0.9886

Table 2. Experimental Results of the Model without MC Module

Dataset	Accuracy	Precision	Recall	F1 score
BIG2015	0.9885	0.9873	0.9848	0.9845
Malimg	0.9849	0.9836	0.9831	0.9842
BIG2015(MC)	0.9954	0.9953	0.9948	0.9961
Malimg(MC)	0.9932	0.9921	0.9889	0.9886

4.5   Effect of SCFN Module

The SCFN module enhances malware classification by effectively integrating global and local features, addressing traditional FFN modules' limitations in capturing fine-grained details. Table 3 demonstrates significant accuracy and precision improvements on Malimg and BIG2015 datasets with minimal computational overhead.

Table 3. Experimental Results of the Model without SCFN Module

Dataset	Accuracy	Precision	Recall	F1 score
BIG2015	0.9903	0.9913	0.9918	0.9925
Malimg	0.9879	0.9856	0.9841	0.9842
BIG2015(SCFN)	0.9954	0.9953	0.9948	0.9961
Malimg(SCFN)	0.9932	0.9921	0.9889	0.9886

4.6   Experimental Results and Comparative Analysis

Experimental results on the BIG2015 and Malimg datasets demonstrate that SRViT-MCNet outperforms existing dynamic visualization methods [4–13]. As illustrated in Table 4 and Figs. 5, SRViT-MCNet achieves superior classification accuracy by leveraging MCNet and SRViT to capture both local and global features, augmented by PI images for comprehensive feature extraction. Compared to traditional methods that primarily focus on dynamic behavior analysis, SRViT-MCNet addresses their limitations through two key innovations:

Table 4. Comparison of classification results between models and existing models

Dataset	Method	Accuracy	Precision	Recall	F1 score
BIG2015	**SRViT − MCNet(BIG2015)**	**99.54**	**99.53**	**99.48**	**99.61**
	VGG16+SVM [4]	99.08	–	–	–
	EfficientNetB1 [6]	98	98	98	98
	MalCVS [9]	98.94	98.26	97.72	97.91
	CNN+CAM+ASPP [8]	99.48	99.39	99.48	99.48
Malimg	**SRViT − MCNet(Malimg)**	**99.32**	**99.21**	**98.89**	**98.86**
	Bi-KNN [11]	99	–	–	–
	VGG19+SCA [10]	97,62	97.68	97.50	97.20
	WDWTCN [13]	99.21	–	–	–
	RMDNet [12]	99.26	98.37	98.12	98.25

(1) Data preprocessing for handling new malware variants, where PI image analysis enables efficient identification of malware families and variants.

(2) An optimized model architecture, where the MC module enhances local feature extraction and the SCFN module improves global and local context representation.

These advancements not only boost classification performance but also enhance robustness against evolving malware threats, establishing SRViT-MCNet as a state-of-the-art solution for malware classification.

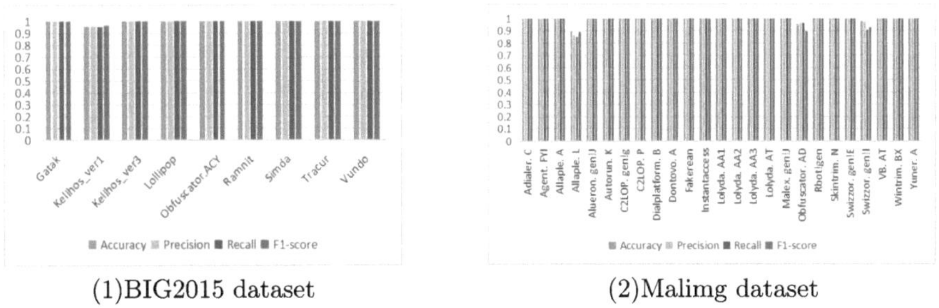

(1)BIG2015 dataset   (2)Malimg dataset

Fig. 5. Classification results on different datasets.

5   Conclusion

To address the challenge of malware proliferation in IoT, this paper proposes SRViT-MCNet, a hybrid model for IoT malware classification. By preprocessing malware data and integrating MCNet and SRViT modules, the model effectively extracts both local and global features, enhancing the understanding of details and contextual information in malware images. Experimental results demonstrate SRViT-MCNet's superior classification performance and generalization capabilities in static malware analysis. Future work will focus on optimizing the model structure and reducing its size to enhance real-time performance.

References

1. Nataraj, L., Karthikeyan, S., Jacob, G., et al.: Malware images: visualization and automatic classification. In: Proceedings of the 8th International Symposium on Visualization for Cyber Security, New York, pp. 1–7. IEEE (2011)
2. Karanja, E.M., Masupe, S., Jeffrey, M.G.: Analysis of internet of things malware using image texture features and machine learning techniques. Internet Things **9**, 100153 (2020)
3. Yerima, S.Y., Muttik, I., Sezer, S.: High accuracy Android malware detection using ensemble learning. IET Inf. Secur. **9**(6), 313–320 (2015)
4. Ren, Z., Chen, G., Lu, W.: Malware visualization methods based on deep convolution neural networks. Multimed. Tools Appl. **79**(15), 10975–10993 (2020)
5. Chen, Y., Zhang, Y., Zhou, Y.: Deep learning for malware detection: A survey. IEEE Access **6**, 14572–14588 (2018)
6. Chaganti, R., Ravi, V., Pham, T.D.: Image-based malware representation approach with EfficientNet convolutional neural networks for effective malware classification. J. Inf. Secur. Appl. **69**, 36–47 (2022)
7. Awan, M.J., Masood, O.A., Mohammed, M.A., et al.: Image-based malware classification using VGG19 network and spatial convolutional attention. Electronics **10**, 2444 (2021)
8. Xuan, B.N., Li, J.: Malware classification method based on improved CNN. Acta Electron. Sin. **37**(5), 1187–1197 (2023). (in Chinese)
9. Xiao, M., Guo, C., Shen, G., et al.: Image-based malware classification using section distribution information. Comput. Secur. **110**, 102420 (2021)
10. Dosovitskiy, A., Beyer, L., Kolesnikov, A., Weissenborn, D., Müller, A.: An image is worth 16×16 words: Transformers for image recognition at scale. arXiv preprint arXiv:2010.11929 (2021)
11. Rustam, F., Ashraf, I., Jurcut, A.D., et al.: Malware detection using image representation of malware data and transfer learning. J. Parallel Distrib. Comput. **172**, 32–50 (2023)
12. Puneeth, S., Lal, S., Singh, M.P., Raghavendra, B.S.: RMDNet: deep learning paradigms for effective malware detection and classification. IEEE Access **12**, 82622–82635 (2024). https://doi.org/10.1109/ACCESS.2024.3403458
13. Qiao, T., Cao, C., Zou, B., et al.: A weighted discrete wavelet transform-based capsule network for malware classification. In: International Conference on Pattern Recognition. Springer, Cham (2025). https://doi.org/10.1007/978-3-031-78128-5_17
14. Zeiler, M.D., Fergus, R.: Visualizing and understanding convolutional networks. In: Fleet, D., Pajdla, T., Schiele, B., Tuytelaars, T. (eds.) ECCV 2014. LNCS, vol. 8689, pp. 818–833. Springer, Cham (2014). https://doi.org/10.1007/978-3-319-10590-1_53
15. Aminu, M., Ahmad, N.A., Noor, M.H.M.: COVID-19 detection via deep neural network and occlusion sensitivity maps. Alex. Eng. J. **60**(5), 4829–4855 (2021). https://doi.org/10.1016/j.aej.2021.03.052

16. Shafaei Darestani, A., Asadpour, M., Heysieattalab, S.: A new approach for analyzing functional neuroimaging data using a combination of CNN-LSTM and occlusion sensitivity analysis. Front. Biomed. **11**(1), 1–12 (2024)
17. Muszynski, G., Kashinath, K., Kurlin, V., et al.: Topological data analysis and machine learning for recognizing atmospheric river patterns in large climate datasets. Geosci. Model Dev. **12**(2), 613–628 (2019)
18. Takahashi, K., Abe, K., Kubota, S.I., et al.: An analysis modality for vascular structures combining tissue-clearing technology and topological data analysis. Nat. Commun. **13**(1), 5239 (2022)
19. Hu, C.S., Lawson, A., Chen, J.S., et al.: TopoResNet: a hybrid deep learning architecture and its application to skin lesion classification. Mathematics **9**(22), 2924 (2021)
20. Shin, J., Jeon, E., Cho, T., Cho, N., Gwon, Y.: Line graph Vietoris-Rips persistence diagram for topological graph representation learning. arXiv preprint arXiv:2412.17468 (2024)
21. Han, Y., Qin, G., Liu, Z., et al.: Research on fusing topological data analysis with convolutional neural networks. arXiv preprint arXiv:2407.09518 (2024)
22. Yu, Y., Zhang, Y., Cheng, Z., Song, Z., Tang, C.: MCA: multidimensional collaborative attention in deep convolutional neural networks for image recognition. Eng. Appl. Artif. Intell. **100**, 1–12 (2023). https://doi.org/10.1016/j.engappai.2023.09.001
23. Wang, A., Chen, H., Lin, Z., Han, J., Ding, G.: RepViT: revisiting mobile CNN from ViT perspective. arXiv preprint arXiv:2307.09283 (2023)
24. Ronen, R., Radu, M., Feuerstein, C., et al.: Microsoft malware classification challenge. arXiv preprint arXiv:1802.10135 (2018)

MultiTEmb: Multi-scale Embeddings for Temporal KG Completion

Junyu Chen, Xingjian Xu, Wenfeng Cui, and Fanjun Meng[✉]

College of Computer Science and Technology, Inner Mongolia Normal University,
Hohhot, Inner Mongolia Autonomous Region 010022, China
`ciecmfj@imnu.edu.cn`

Abstract. Temporal Knowledge Graph Completion is essential for many real-world applications, requiring effective modeling of temporal information. However, most existing methods rely on a single time scale, limiting their ability to capture dependencies over short and long time horizons. To address this, we propose MultiTEmb, a novel multi-scale temporal completion method. By decomposing temporal information into year, quarter, month, and day, we generate feature vectors at each scale and model dependencies using a Time-aware Efficient Self-Attention Mechanism (TE-SAM) with adaptive feature weighting. To further enhance feature fusion, we introduce InfoNCE-based contrastive learning to improve temporal representation discriminability and employ an Enhanced Gated Recurrent Unit (E-GRU) to sequentially integrate multi-scale embeddings. Extensive experiments on four benchmark datasets show that MultiTEmb significantly outperforms existing knowledge graph embedding and temporal knowledge graph completion models, demonstrating its effectiveness in temporal reasoning tasks.

Keywords: Multi-Scale Temporal Features · Temporal Knowledge Graph Embedding · Contrastive Learning · Temporal Knowledge Graph

1 Introduction

Knowledge graphs (KGs) represent structured knowledge through triples (h, r, t) [6], supporting tasks like semantic search and question answering. However, traditional KGs assume static validity of facts, overlooking temporal dynamics essential for modeling real-world events (e.g., "Barack Obama served as U.S. President from 2009 to 2017").

Temporal Knowledge Graphs (TKGs) extend this structure by incorporating time annotations, forming quadruples (h, r, t, τ) where τ denotes a timestamp or interval [8]. This allows encoding facts as time-bounded, such as "Joe Biden is President of the U.S. from 2021 to present", capturing the evolving nature of knowledge. While traditional Knowledge Graph Embedding (KGE) methods like TransE [1], DistMult [13], and ComplEx [9] embed entities and relations into

T. Zhu et al. (Eds.): KSEM 2025, LNAI 15923, pp. 156–164, 2026.
https://doi.org/10.1007/978-981-95-3061-8_17

vector spaces, they ignore temporal information, limiting their performance on dynamic reasoning tasks in TKGs.

Temporal KGE (TKGE) approaches such as TTransE [5], HyTE [2], and TeRo [12] incorporate time into embeddings [14], but often rely on single-scale modeling and struggle to represent temporal patterns across multiple granularities (e.g., seasonal or long-term trends). Moreover, they lack mechanisms for effective multi-scale feature fusion.

To address these issues, we propose MultiTEmb, a multi-granularity temporal embedding framework designed to improve temporal modeling and adaptive feature interaction in TKGs. Our key innovations include:

- Multi-scale temporal decomposition: Time is hierarchically decomposed into year, quarter, month, and day embeddings to explicitly model short-term and long-term dependencies.
- Adaptive temporal attention: A time-aware efficient self-attention mechanism dynamically assigns weights to different scales, enhancing context-aware reasoning.
- Contrastive feature fusion: An enhanced GRU coupled with InfoNCE-based contrastive learning ensures robust integration of temporal features while preserving discriminability.

2 Related Work

TransE, an early KGE method, represents relations as translation vectors from the head to the tail entity but struggles with complex relationship types. To address this, TransH introduces hyperplanes to model complex relationships [11], while TransR separates entity and relation spaces with a mapping matrix [7]. Bilinear models like ComplEx enhance modeling [4], with ComplEx using complex embeddings to handle anti-symmetric relations. These methods assume static knowledge graphs, limiting their applicability in dynamic scenarios.

To address the limitations of static knowledge graph embedding methods, temporal knowledge graph embedding approaches have been developed to incorporate temporal information and capture the dynamic nature of facts. These methods can be broadly categorized into several types [3]. Methods based on the direct addition of temporal embeddings, such as TTransE and TA-DistMult, integrate temporal information by adding time vectors or combining temporal and relational embeddings, but lack deeper modeling of temporal interactions. Temporal hyperplane projection methods like HyTE enhance temporal representation by projecting entities and relations onto timestamp-defined hyperplanes, yet they struggle to handle dynamic features such as time spans and multi-scale structures. Approaches utilizing temporal convolution or recurrent neural networks, including Know-Evolve and RE-NET, model temporal evolution through temporal point processes, RNNs, and attention mechanisms, though they remain limited in capturing multi-scale temporal features. Finally, decomposition and fusion methods such as TeRo and DE-SimplE employ complex embeddings or time-dependent projection matrices to represent temporal dynamics, but largely rely on single-scale modeling and fail to capture dependencies across multiple temporal granularities.

3   Proposed Method: MultiTEmb

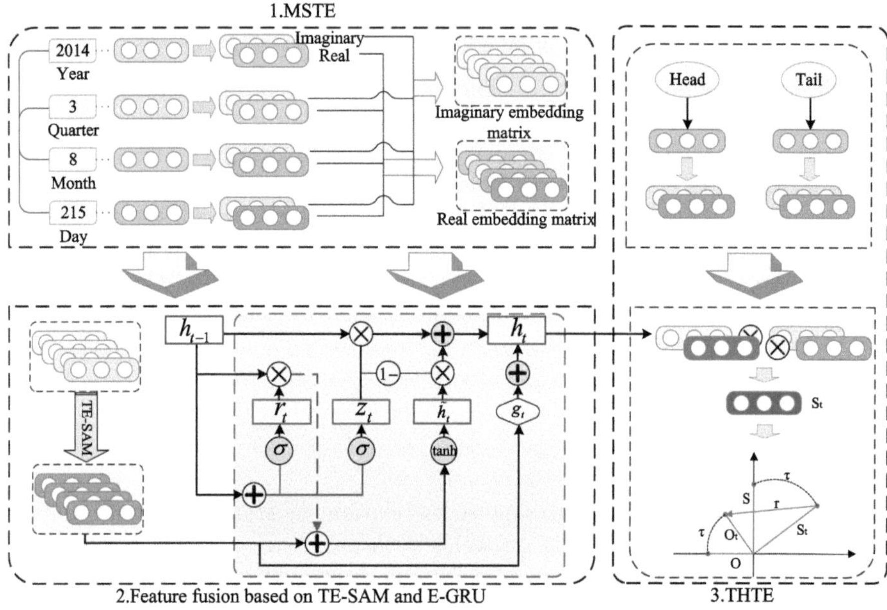

Fig. 1. The Overall Framework of the MultiTEmb Model

This paper proposes a multiscale temporal embedding framework that integrates fine—grained temporal features–years, quarters, months, and days—to capture seasonality and periodicity in temporal knowledge graphs. As shown in Fig. 1, the framework includes the Multi-Scale Temporal Embedding (MSTE) module, which decomposes temporal data into multiple granularities and generates complex-valued embeddings preserving periodic and sequential dependencies. The TE-SAM module applies self-attention for adaptive weighting of temporal features to enhance scale-specific representations. A fusion mechanism with deep self-supervision and contrastive learning refines embeddings by improving feature discrimination. The E-GRU module integrates entity and relation embeddings with temporal inputs to model historical and sequential patterns. The THTE module produces entity-level temporal embeddings and computes feature-based distances to support link prediction and temporal reasoning.

3.1 Multi-scale Temporal Embedding Vector Generation

TeRo subsequently constructs a temporal embedding matrix $\mathrm{E} \in \mathbb{R}^{365 \times d}$, where d is the embedding dimension. For a given date such as August 4, 2014, the day index $\mathrm{d_t}$ (e.g., 215) is used to retrieve the corresponding embedding $\mathrm{e_t} = \mathrm{E}[\mathrm{d_t}, :] \in \mathbb{R}^{\mathrm{d}}$. In contrast, this paper introduces a multiscale temporal embedding method to address the limitations of single-scale representations. Temporal information is decomposed into four components: year, quarter, month, and day. Each is associated with an independent embedding matrix: $\mathrm{E_{year}} \in \mathbb{R}^{\mathrm{Y} \times \mathrm{d}}$ for years, $\mathrm{E_{quarter}} \in \mathbb{R}^{\mathrm{Q} \times \mathrm{d}}$ with $Q = 4$, $\mathrm{E_{month}} \in \mathbb{R}^{\mathrm{M} \times \mathrm{d}}$ with $M = 12$, and $\mathrm{E_{day}} \in \mathbb{R}^{\mathrm{D} \times \mathrm{d}}$ with $D = 366$. After discretization, the components (y, q, m, d) are used to index their respective matrices, e.g., $\mathrm{e_{year}} = \mathrm{E_{year}}[\mathrm{y}, :]$.

The remaining temporal embeddings are similarly processed. Each real-valued vector $\mathrm{e_t^r}$ is transformed into complex form using cosine and sine functions:

$$T_{Re} = \cos(W_{\cos} e_t^r + b_{\cos}) \tag{1}$$

$$T_{Im} = \sin(W_{\sin} e_t^r + b_{\sin}) \tag{2}$$

where $W_{\cos}$, $W_{\sin}$ are trainable weights and $b_{\cos}$, $b_{\sin}$ are bias terms. The resulting real and imaginary components from each temporal scale are concatenated to form two $4d$-dimensional vectors, serving as input to a downstream self-attention module.

3.2 Time-Aware Feature Weighting via Self-attention

To capture multi-scale temporal dependencies, we propose TE-SAM, which dynamically adjusts attention weights across temporal scales (year, quarter, month, day). This enables effective modeling of short- and long-term patterns with computational efficiency. Unlike standard self-attention that uniformly treats inputs, TE-SAM leverages structured temporal hierarchies. Traditional self-attention mechanisms ignore granularity differences and incur high computational cost $(O(n^2 d))$, limiting their scalability for large temporal knowledge graphs. To address these issues, TE-SAM incorporates adaptive temporal weighting by introducing a learnable time bias B_τ to modulate attention scores:

$$A_{\mathrm{Re}} = \mathrm{softmax}\left(\frac{Q_{\mathrm{Re}} K_{\mathrm{Re}}^T}{\sqrt{d_k}} + B_\tau\right) \tag{3}$$

The additional term B_τ allows the model to assign greater importance to certain time scales depending on their relevance to the current task. The final weighted representations are computed as:

$$Z_{\mathrm{Re}} = A_{\mathrm{Re}} V_{\mathrm{Re}}, \quad Z_{\mathrm{Im}} = A_{\mathrm{Im}} V_{\mathrm{Im}} \tag{4}$$

where Z_{Re} and Z_{Im} are the refined real and imaginary representations of the temporal embeddings. Furthermore, TE-SAM maintains computational efficiency by leveraging local temporal grouping, reducing the complexity to $O(nd)$ compared to the original $O(n^2 d)$, making it significantly more scalable.

3.3   InfoNCE-Based Feature Fusion with E-GRU

Standard GRUs are effective for sequential modeling but lack mechanisms to distinguish short- and long-term dependencies, which is critical in temporal KGs with multi-granular timestamps. To address this, E-GRU introduces an additional gate g_t to modulate the influence of each temporal scale. Given input x_t, the gate is defined as:

$$g_t = \sigma(W_g x_t + U_g h_{t-1}) \tag{5}$$

The hidden state is updated as:

$$h_t = (1 - z_t) \odot h_{t-1} + z_t \odot \tilde{h}_t + g_t \odot x_t \tag{6}$$

Here, z_t and $\tilde{h}_t$ follow standard GRU rules, while g_t enables adaptive fusion across temporal scales, improving representation of complex temporal dependencies.

To enhance the discriminability of temporal embeddings, we adopt InfoNCE-based contrastive learning, which brings positive pairs closer and pushes negatives apart. We incorporate TRHyTE's dynamic negative sampling to reduce false negatives. Given a positive quadruple (h, r, t, τ), we construct time-independent negative sets as:

$$N_h = \left\{ (h', r, t, \tau) \mid h' \in E, \ (h', r, t) \notin D^+ \right\} \tag{7}$$

$$N_t = \left\{ (h, r, t', \tau) \mid t' \in E, \ (h, r, t') \notin D^+ \right\} \tag{8}$$

We rank candidates in N_h and N_t by score and sample from the top-k to avoid false negatives. The InfoNCE loss is defined as:

$$L_{\text{InfoNCE}} = -\log \frac{\exp(\text{sim}(h_r, h_{r+})/\theta)}{\sum_{h_r^- \in N} \exp(\text{sim}(h_r, h_r^-)/\theta)} \tag{9}$$

where $\text{sim}(\cdot)$ denotes similarity and θ is a temperature scaling factor. InfoNCE aligns well with dynamic sampling and maintains temporal continuity [10].

3.4   Temporal Embedding for Head and Tail Entities

The model initializes two embedding matrices: E_{real} for real components and E_{img} for imaginary components. Given indices H_i, T_i, and R_i for the head, tail, and relation respectively, the model retrieves $h_{real} = E_{real}(H_i)$ and $t_{real} = E_{real}(T_i)$; the corresponding imaginary parts h_{img} and t_{img} are obtained similarly from E_{img}.

These embeddings are combined with temporal components h_r (real) and h_i (imaginary) to form complex temporal representations. The real part is computed as:

$$h_{real} = h_{real} \times h_r - h_{img} \times h_i \tag{10}$$

The real part for the tail entity is computed analogously. The imaginary part is:

$$h_{img} = h_{real} \times h_i + h_{img} \times h_r \tag{11}$$

and similarly for the tail entity. These complex embeddings are then used in a scoring function to measure the distance between head and tail entities.

4 Experiments

4.1 Datasets

We evaluate our model on four benchmarks—ICEWS14, ICEWS05-15, YAGO11k, and GDELT—covering diverse temporal settings. ICEWS datasets offer precise time-stamped events for point-in-time reasoning. YAGO11k provides temporal intervals for multi-granularity evaluation, while GDELT's large-scale news data tests real-time prediction and scalability. Together, they assess adaptability, generalization, and multi-scale temporal modeling.

4.2 Baselines

Static KGC methods like TransE, DistMult, SimplE, and RotatE differ in how they model entity-relation interactions: TransE uses vector translation, DistMult applies bilinear scoring, SimplE introduces inverse relations, and RotatE employs complex space rotations. Dynamic methods such as TTransE, HyTE, DE-TransE, TeRo, and RE-Net incorporate temporal information via temporal projection, dynamic embeddings, or recurrent structures. These comparisons underscore MultiTEmb's strength in modeling temporal dynamics for KGC.

4.3 Comparative Experiments

Table 1. Performance Comparison on ICEWS14 and ICEWS05-15 Datasets

Datasets	ICEWS14				ICEWS05-15			
	MRR	Hit@1	Hit@3	Hit@10	MRR	Hit@1	Hit@3	Hit@10
TransE	28.0	9.4	—	63.7	29.4	9.0	—	66.3
DistMult	43.9	32.3	—	67.2	45.6	33.7	—	69.1
SimplE	45.8	34.1	51.6	68.7	47.8	35.9	53.9	70.8
RotatE	41.8	29.1	47.8	69.0	30.4	16.4	35.5	59.5
TTransE	25.5	7.4	—	60.1	27.1	8.4	—	61.6
HyTE*	29.9	11.0	41.1	66.0	30.4	12.5	44.5	68.7
TA-DistMult	47.7	36.3	—	68.6	47.4	34.6	—	72.8
DE-TransE	36.2	12.4	46.7	68.6	31.4	10.8	45.3	68.5
ATiSE	55.0	43.6	_62.9_	**75.0**	51.9	37.8	60.6	79.4
CyGNet*	49.7	41.4	53.8	61.1	—	—	—	—
TeRo*	_56.4_	_46.9_	62.7	74.2	_58.8_	_46.9_	_66.2_	_79.8_
RE-Net	36.3	26.7	41.0	54.2	36.7	26.1	41.6	56.8
MultiTEmb	**58.0**	**48.6**	**64.4**	_74.8_	**60.1**	**49.0**	**68.7**	**80.1**

Tables 1 and 2 compare MultiTEmb with baselines on four datasets. Results with * are reproduced; others are from original papers. MultiTEmb achieves state-of-the-art or near-best results, particularly on ICEWS05-15 and GDELT. On ICEWS14 and ICEWS05-15, it surpasses strong baselines like TeRo and RE-Net in all key metrics, with Hits@1 improvements of 1.7% and 1.2%, demonstrating superior entity prediction accuracy.

On GDELT, MultiTEmb achieves a 52.9% MRR, outperforming CyGNet by 2.2%, showing strong temporal modeling ability. On YAGO11K, it achieves top Hits@1/3/10, validating its effectiveness for long-term dependencies. These results confirm that combining multiscale modeling, self-attention, E-GRU, and contrastive learning significantly boosts temporal reasoning.

Table 2. Performance Comparison on GDELT and YAGO15K Datasets

Datasets	GDELT				YAGO15K			
	MRR	Hit@1	Hit@3	Hit@10	MRR	Hit@1	Hit@3	Hit@10
TransE	11.3	0.0	15.8	31.2	10.0	1.5	13.8	24.4
DistMult	19.6	11.7	20.8	34.8	15.8	10.7	16.1	26.8
SimplE	20.6	12.4	22.0	36.6	—	—	—	—
RotatE	—	—	—	—	16.7	10.3	16.7	30.5
TTransE	11.5	0.0	16.0	31.8	10.8	2.0	15.0	25.1
HyTE*	11.9	0.0	16.1	31.9	13.9	3.5	—	29.1
TA-DistMult	20.6	12.4	21.9	36.5	15.5	9.8	—	26.7
DE-SimplE	23.0	14.1	24.8	40.3	15.1	8.8	—	26.7
ATiSE	—	—	—	—	18.5	<u>12.6</u>	18.9	30.1
CyGNet*	<u>50.7</u>	<u>43.1</u>	<u>55.0</u>	**60.5**	—	—	—	—
TeRo*	24.8	15.1	26.0	42.5	<u>18.9</u>	12.5	<u>19.4</u>	<u>31.5</u>
TuckERTNT	38.1	28.3	41.8	57.6	—	—	—	—
MultiTEmb	**52.9**	**43.7**	**56.1**	<u>60.1</u>	**19.7**	**13.2**	**21.0**	**33.1**

4.4   Ablation Study

As shown in Table 3, we conducted three ablation experiments to assess each component's contribution. Removing TE-SAM while keeping multiscale embedding and E-GRU led to stable results but weaker fine-grained modeling, showing E-GRU's standalone effectiveness. Removing E-GRU caused greater performance drops, especially on sequential tasks, though TE-SAM partly offset the loss. Excluding multiscale embedding caused the largest degradation, highlighting its essential role in fine-grained temporal reasoning.

Table 3. Results of different model variants on ICEWS14

MSTE	TE-SAM	E-GRU	MRR	Hits@1	Hits@3	Hits@10
✓	✗	✓	56.4	46.5	63.0	74.1
✓	✓	✗	48.8	35.7	56.9	73.8
✓	✗	✓	44.7	31.0	52.4	72.0
✓	✓	✓	58.0	48.6	64.4	74.8

5 Conclusion

This paper proposes a multiscale temporal feature approach for temporal knowledge graph completion by decomposing time into year, quarter, month, and day. Integrating TE-SAM and an enhanced gated recurrent unit, the method captures cross-scale dependencies with adaptive weighting. Experiments show superior MRR and Hits performance compared to most existing methods, validating the effectiveness of multiscale fusion and dynamic modeling. Compared to single-scale models, it provides richer temporal representations and improved prediction accuracy, highlighting the importance of multiscale temporal fusion for complex dependency modeling.

Acknowledgments. This work was supported by grants from the Natural Science Foundation of Inner Mongolia (2023LHMSS06011), Normal University 2024 College Student Innovation and Entrepreneurship Training Program (S202410135028), Hohhot Basic Research and Applied Basic Research Science and Technology Program Projects (2025-GUI-JI-44), the Natural Science Foundation of Inner Mongolia (2025MS06033).

References

1. Bordes, A., Usunier, N., Garcia-Duran, A., Weston, J., Yakhnenko, O.: Translating embeddings for modeling multi-relational data. Adv. Neural Inform. Process. Syst. **26** (2013)
2. Dasgupta, S.S., Ray, S.N., Talukdar, P.: Hyte: hyperplane-based temporally aware knowledge graph embedding. In: Proceedings of the 2018 Conference on Empirical Methods in Natural Language Processing, pp. 2001–2011 (2018)
3. García-Durán, A., Dumančić, S., Niepert, M.: Learning sequence encoders for temporal knowledge graph completion. arXiv preprint arXiv:1809.03202 (2018)
4. Jin, W., Qu, M., Jin, X., Ren, X.: Recurrent event network: autoregressive structure inference over temporal knowledge graphs. arXiv preprint arXiv:1904.05530 (2019)
5. Leblay, J., Chekol, M.W.: Deriving validity time in knowledge graph. In: Companion proceedings of the the Web Conference 2018, pp. 1771–1776 (2018)
6. Liang, W., Meo, P.D., Tang, Y., Zhu, J.: A survey of multi-modal knowledge graphs: technologies and trends. ACM Comput. Surv. **56**(11), 1–41 (2024)
7. Lin, Y., Liu, Z., Sun, M., Liu, Y., Zhu, X.: Learning entity and relation embeddings for knowledge graph completion. In: Proceedings of the AAAI Conference on Artificial Intelligence, vol. 29 (2015)

8. Liu, Q., Feng, S., Huang, M., Bhatti, U.A.: Chronobridge: a novel framework for enhanced temporal and relational reasoning in temporal knowledge graphs. Artif. Intell. Rev. **57**(12), 1–33 (2024)
9. Trouillon, T., Welbl, J., Riedel, S., Gaussier, É., Bouchard, G.: Complex embeddings for simple link prediction. In: International Conference on Machine Learning, pp. 2071–2080. PMLR (2016)
10. Wang, J., Wang, B., Gao, J., Pan, S., Liu, T., Yin, B., Gao, W.: Made: multicurvature adaptive embedding for temporal knowledge graph completion. IEEE Trans. Cybernet. (2024)
11. Wang, Z., Zhang, J., Feng, J., Chen, Z.: Knowledge graph embedding by translating on hyperplanes. In: Proceedings of the AAAI Conference on Artificial Intelligence, vol. 28 (2014)
12. Xu, C., Nayyeri, M., Alkhoury, F., Yazdi, H.S., Lehmann, J.: Tero: a time-aware knowledge graph embedding via temporal rotation. arXiv preprint arXiv:2010.01029 (2020)
13. Yang, B., Yih, W.t., He, X., Gao, J., Deng, L.: Embedding entities and relations for learning and inference in knowledge bases. arXiv preprint arXiv:1412.6575 (2014)
14. Zhang, Y., et al.: A survey on temporal knowledge graph embedding: Models and applications. Knowl.-Based Syst., 112454 (2024)

Education Distillation: Let the Model Learn in the School

Ling Feng, Tianhao Wu, Xiangrong Ren, Zhi Jing, and Xuliang Duan[(✉)]

Sichuan Agricultural University, Ya'an, Sichuan Province, China
{202105857,202205793,202204704,203308498}@stu.sicau.edu.cn,
duanxuliang@sicau.edu.cn

Abstract. This paper introduces a new knowledge distillation method, called education distillation (ED), which is inspired by the structured and progressive nature of human learning. ED mimics the educational stages of primary school, middle school, and university and designs teaching reference blocks. The student model is split into a main body and multiple teaching reference blocks to learn from teachers step-by-step. This promotes efficient knowledge distillation while maintaining the architecture of the student model. Experimental results on the CIFAR100, Tiny Imagenet, Caltech and Food-101 datasets show that the teaching reference blocks can effectively avoid the problem of forgetting. Compared with conventional single-teacher and multi-teacher knowledge distillation methods, ED significantly improves the accuracy and generalization ability of the student model. These findings highlight the potential of ED to improve model performance across different architectures and datasets, indicating its value in various deep learning scenarios. Code examples can be obtained at: https://github.com/Revolutioner1/ED.git.

Keywords: Knowledge Distillation · Education Distillation · Teaching Reference Blocks · The Problem of Forgettings

1 Introduction

Human education progresses gradually from primary school to middle school and then to university. What about Convolutional Neural Networks? Knowledge distillation (KD), first proposed by Hinton, is a model compression technique based on the "teacher-student network concept". The goal of traditional knowledge distillation is to transfer knowledge from a complex network (teacher network) to a simple network (student network) by minimizing the KL divergence between the softened outputs of the two networks [1].

The field of knowledge distillation is constantly evolving. With the cross-domain expansion of knowledge distillation techniques, Stand-in Model Protection has recently innovatively applied distillation concepts to the field of model security [20]. Many studies explore new ways of knowledge transfer, such as starting from output layers, intermediate layers, attention maps, and other

T. Zhu et al. (Eds.): KSEM 2025, LNAI 15923, pp. 165–175, 2026.
https://doi.org/10.1007/978-981-95-3061-8_18

aspects. Zagoruyko S et al. proposed a method to transfer attention maps from the teacher Convolutional Neural Network to the student network to improve the performance of the student network. This represents a new breakthrough and development compared to traditional knowledge distillation methods [2]. Ahn S proposed to transfer knowledge by maximizing the mutual information between the teacher and student networks, providing new ideas and methods for improving model performance [3]. Romero A et al. proposed using the representations of the intermediate layers of the teacher network as hints to help train a student network that is deeper and narrower than the teacher network, opening up a new path for solving the problem of model compression and enhancing the performance of the student network [4]. Tian Y proposed using a family of contrastive objectives to capture correlations and high-order output correlations. This innovatively applies the idea of contrastive learning to knowledge distillation, enabling the extraction of knowledge from one neural network to another [5].

Similarly, predecessors have proven that multi-teacher knowledge distillation methods also perform excellently. Multi-teacher knowledge distillation improves the effectiveness of distillation by integrating the predictions of multiple teachers, and there are already several representative methods. For example, Shan You et al. combined the knowledge of the output layers and intermediate layers of different teacher networks and proposed a voting strategy to unify the relative difference information from multiple teachers [6]. Kisoo Kwon et al. introduced an entropy-based knowledge distillation method [7]. Shangchen Du et al. proposed an adaptive ensemble knowledge distillation method, which uses the gradient information of multiple teacher models and introduces a tolerance parameter to dynamically adjust the weights of teacher models [8]. Hailin Zhang et al. proposed a knowledge distillation method that dynamically adjusts the weights of multi-teacher models by combining the confidence of teacher model predictions with true labels [9].

Undoubtedly, the above-mentioned methods are all excellent. However, we prefer to approach distillation in a more intuitive way, enabling the model to progress step-by-step. Education requires many teachers. We can envision: If we combine multi-teacher knowledge distillation with education, can Convolutional Neural Networks also develop from the "primary school" stage to the "university' stage just like humans? To this end, we propose an education distillation method. Through incremental learning and model pruning, the student model can gradually improve from the "primary school" level to the "university" level, thus absorbing knowledge more effectively.

Meanwhile, we introduce the concept of "reference books" and design a teaching reference block to further optimize the learning process without changing the final architecture of the student model. Compared with the five single-teacher knowledge distillation methods and four multi-teacher knowledge distillation methods mentioned above, education distillation significantly improves the overall performance of the teacher-student architecture.

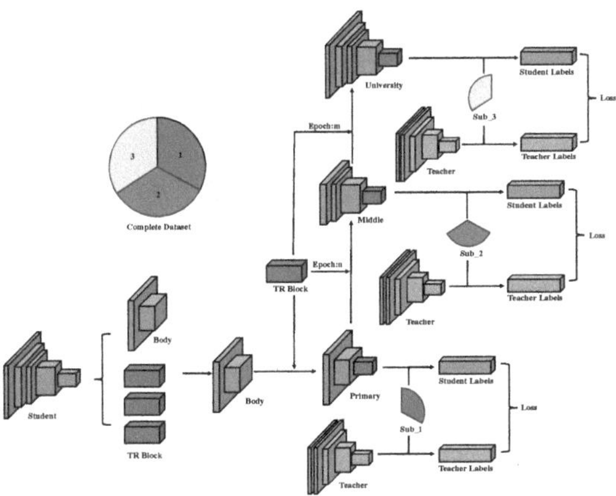

Fig. 1. In educational distillation, the student model is divided into a main body and three teaching reference blocks. At the same time, the dataset is partitioned into three sub-datasets for distillation. The model starts at the "primary school" stage, where it trains on sub-dataset 1. When the n-th epoch is reached and fitting is achieved, the second teaching reference block is added, and the model progresses to the "secondary school" stage, training on sub-dataset 2. When the m-th epoch is reached and fitting is achieved, the final reference block is added, and the model reaches the "university" stage, training on sub-dataset 3.

2   Method

2.1   Education Distillation Method

Before delving into the concept of education distillation, let's first consider a learning scenario. Suppose there is a student who needs to master three subjects progressively: arithmetic in primary school, equations in middle school, and calculus in university. In primary school, the student starts with arithmetic. As learning progresses, new teachers will gradually teach equations. In university, the student begins to learn calculus, integrating all the accumulated mathematical knowledge. Can training a student model in a similar step-by-step learning manner improve the effectiveness of model training?

Convolutional Neural Networks, such as ResNet [10], WRN [11], ShuffleNet [12], VGG [13], and MobileNetV2 [14], are generally composed of multiple building blocks, which are called "blocks" or "layers". These blocks are stacked together to form the entire network framework. This modular design not only enables Convolutional Neural Networks to effectively learn hierarchical features from data, but also allows them to adapt to tasks of different complexities.

In the process of education distillation, we split the student model into a main body and multiple reference layers. Then, we divide the dataset into subsets according to the number of reference layers. During training, every time a new module is added, a subset is introduced. This process continues until the complete student model is fully restored.

Let us take the three educational stages of primary school, middle school, and university as an example. The distillation process of education for refany convolutional network can be divided into the learning stages shown in Fig. 1.

In the process depicted in Fig. 1, the main body retains the encoder of the student network, and the designed teaching reference block (TR Block) serves as the decoder. The complete student network is divided into one main body and three teaching reference blocks for distillation.

At the start of training (corresponding to the primary school stage), the main body adds a teaching reference block to become a new main body and learns from Sub-dataset 1. In the second stage (representing the middle school stage), the main body adds another teaching reference block to form a new main body, and simultaneously learns from Sub-dataset 2 and Sub-dataset 1. Finally, in the third stage (similar to the university stage), the main body adds the last teaching reference block to restore the complete student model and learns the content of the entire dataset.

At each stage, as the modules are allocated, the teaching reference blocks are also updated synchronously to assist in training the student network. By gradually integrating these modules, the student model is ultimately reconstructed into a complete network. Instead of learning the entire data at once, it learns the content of the sub-datasets one by one. Each sub-dataset is trained by a dedicated teacher model for the corresponding stage.

2.2   The Phenomenon of Catastrophic Forgetting

During the process of a model learning a new task, a remarkable phenomenon occurs. That is, the model's grasp of knowledge and performance on previously learned old tasks decline significantly. This means that while the model is striving to adapt to new data, it seems to "forget" the key information learned before. This is the so called phenomenon of catastrophic forgetting [17].

In the process of education distillation, we introduce the teaching reference block to avoid the problem where the model only focuses on learning a sub-dataset and forgets the content of other sub-datasets. The teaching reference block consists of one block of the student network, a 1×1 convolutional layer, and a specially designed adaptive average pooling layer.

Whenever the training of a sub-dataset reaches convergence and a new teaching reference block is added to the main body, we remove the previous convolutional layer and pooling layer and freeze the previous parameters. This ensures that each actual component of the student network corresponds to a specific sub-dataset. The teaching reference block mainly acts as an auxiliary component of the student network during the education distillation process. Therefore, during the last update of the main body, the teaching reference block will be restored to the original decoder part of the student network.

This approach not only strengthens the training process but also effectively guarantees the integrity of the network structure. Final experiments show that the design of such a teaching reference block can indeed significantly improve the accuracy of the model.

2.3   Formalization

The whole process is analyzed as follows: $M_t(\cdot)$ indicates the learned model of the student model at incremental stage t, the classifier $g(x)$, the original student model S, and the teaching reference blocks $\{f_l(\cdot); l = 1, 2, 3, ..., n\}$, which are expressed as follows:

$$M_t(x) = g\left(h_t\right) = g\left(S \circ f_1 \circ f_2 \circ f_3 \circ \ldots \circ f_t(x)\right) \tag{1}$$

Notably h_t is the input model eigenvector, represented each sub-dataset and originating from the dataset H, $h_t \in H$, which is denoted by

$$h_1 \cup h_2 \cup h_{3\ldots} \cup h_t = H \tag{2}$$

h_t with the corresponding $f_t(\cdot)$ are given the corresponding mapping result

$$Z_{t,h} = \left\{Z_{f_1,1}, Z_{f_1,2}, \ldots, Z_{f_{t,h}}\right\} \tag{3}$$

For the teacher model, $T_t(\cdot)$ denotes the set of all t teacher models, and each group h_t will have a uniquely mapped teacher model $T_t(\cdot)$, which is expressed as:

$$T_t(x) = g\left(h_t\right) = g\left(T_1(x) \cup T_2(x) \ldots \cup T_t(x)\right) \tag{4}$$

Eventually both ht and the corresponding T_t will get the corresponding mapping result

$$G_{t,h} = \left\{G_{T_1,1}, G_{T_2,2}, \ldots, G_{T_t,h}\right\} \tag{5}$$

$\mathcal{L}_h(\cdot)$ is the loss for a particular sub-dataset. In training $M_t(\cdot)$, the distillation loss under the sub-dataset is

$$\mathcal{L}_h(Z_{t,h}, G_{t,h}) = \sum_{Z_i \in Z_{t,h}} \sum_{G_i \in G_{t,h}} KL\left(\mathrm{softmax}\left(\frac{Z_i}{\tau}\right), \mathrm{softmax}\left(\frac{G_i}{\tau}\right)\right) \tag{6}$$

where $KL(\cdot)$ denotes the KL dispersion and τ denotes the distillation temperature.

For $M_t(\cdot)$ training, the sum of all task losses can then be expressed as:

$$\mathcal{L}_h\left(Z_t, G_t, y\right) = \alpha * \mathcal{L}_{KD}\left(Z_t, G_t\right) + (1 - \alpha) * \mathcal{L}\left(Z_t, y\right) \tag{7}$$

where y denotes the true label of the input eigenvector and α denotes the weight of the distillation loss.

Then the loss approximation for the student network is calculated as follows

$$\begin{aligned}
ED_{LOSS} = \mathcal{L}_H(Z_t, G_t, y) \approx &\mathcal{L}_{h_1}(Z_{t,h_1}, G_{t,h_1}, y) + \mathcal{L}_{h_2}(Z_{t,h_2}, G_{t,h_2}, y) + \\
&\mathcal{L}_{h_3}(Z_{t,h_3}, G_{t,h_3}, y) + \cdots
\end{aligned} \tag{8}$$

U_t is the feature space corresponding to each set of h_t, which is denoted as:

$$U_1 \cup U_2 \cup U_3 \ldots \cup U_n \ldots \cup U_t = U \tag{9}$$

$$U_1 \cap U_2 \cap U_3 \ldots \cap U_n \ldots \cap U_t = \emptyset \tag{10}$$

It is inefficient for a small model to learn directly from the full feature space U. However, in education distillation, $M_t(\cdot)$ begins by learning from a smaller feature space U_1. As the number of incremental basic blocks(teaching reference blocks) $f_l(\cdot)$ increase, the small feature space gradually expands into a larger feature space. Additionally, there is no overlap between the small feature space U_n and the newly expanded feature space U_t, thus improving the model's efficiency in learning features.

3   Experiments

In this section, to prove the effectiveness of the proposed education distillation (ED) method, we conducted experiments on the CIFAR100 dataset [15] using nine different teacher-student architectures. We compared our method with single-teacher knowledge distillation methods and multi-teacher knowledge distillation methods. In the multi-teacher knowledge distillation methods, three teacher models were used in all cases. These three teacher models exhibited an average top-1 accuracy value.

Table 1. Top-1 test accuracy of ED methods by distilling the knowledge on single-teachers with the same architectures.

Model	WRN40_2	VGG13	ResNet110		ResNet56
Teacher	76.76	75.22	74.26		73.47
Student	WRN16_2	VGG8	ResNet32	ResNet20	ResNet20
KD [1]	75.28	73.62	74.09	71.27	71.08
AT [2]	75.34	73.27	73.31	71.26	70.13
VID [3]	75.54	73.28	73.54	70.99	70.7
FitNet [4]	75.44	73.4	73.37	71.03	71.19
CRD [5]	75.38	73.41	73.54	70.72	70.98
ED	**77.25**	**75.5**	**74.47**	**72.33**	**73.85**

Hyperparameters: All neural networks were optimized using Stochastic Gradient Descent (SGD) with a momentum of 0.9 and a weight decay of 0.0001. The batch size was set to 32, and the initial learning rate was set to 0.05. During a total of 240 training epochs, the learning rate was multiplied by 0.1 at epochs 150, 180, and 210. The temperature T for all methods was set to 4, and α was set to 0.3. In epochs 50, 80, and 210, we added building blocks to the student network and updated the teaching reference layers. Meanwhile, the sub-datasets were divided in a 1:1:1 ratio for training.

Comparison of Isomorphic Teacher-Student Models: In the network of isomorphic teacher-student models, Table 1 and Table 2 show the comparison

Table 2. Top-1 test accuracy of ED methods by distilling the knowledge on multiple-teachers with the same architectures.

Model	WRN40_2	VGG13	ResNet110		ResNet56
Teacher	76.76	75.22	74.26		73.47
Student	WRN16_2	VGG8	ResNet32	ResNet20	ResNet20
AVER [6]	76.17	74.21	75.19	71.38	71.2
EBKD [7]	76.33	74.08	73.97	71.5	71.18
AEKD [8]	75.99	74.1	74.31	71.67	71.23
CAMKD [9]	76.27	74.4	74.32	71.27	70.79
ED	**77.25**	**75.5**	**74.47**	**72.33**	**73.85**

Table 3. Top-1 test accuracy of ED methods by distilling the knowledge on single-teachers with the heterogeneous architectures.

Model	WRN40_2	VGG13	ResNet56	ResNet56
Teacher	76.76	75.22	74.26	73.47
Student	ShuffleNetV1	MobileNetV2	MobileNetV2	VGG8
KD [1]	75.82	68.02	68.43	73.52
AT [2]	75.43	68.39	69.65	73.23
VID [3]	75.76	68.43	68.04	73.46
FitNet [4]	75.75	67.93	69.32	73.57
CRD [5]	75.96	68.27	69.44	73.27
ED	**77.63**	**70.05**	**72.33**	**76.78**

of top-1 accuracies of single-teacher and multi-teacher knowledge distillation methods on the CIFAR100 dataset. We found that the education distillation (ED) method outperforms all its competitors across various architectures.

For example, in single-teacher knowledge distillation, when using WRN40_2 as the teacher model and WRN16_2 as the student model, the ED method achieves an average accuracy improvement of 1.854%. In multi-teacher knowledge distillation, when using ResNet56 as the teacher model and ResNet20 as the student model, the ED method increases the average accuracy by 2.2%.

Overall, the ED method generally performs better in teacher-student configurations with the same architecture. Carefully selecting the distillation strategy and the combination of teacher-student architectures can maximize the learning effect of the student model.

Comparison of Heterogeneous Teacher-Student Models: In the network of heterogeneous teacher-student models, as shown in Table 3 and Table 4, the ED method also demonstrates strong performance across various architectures.

Table 4. Top-1 test accuracy of ED methods by distilling the knowledge on multiple teachers with the heterogeneous architectures.

Model	WRN40_2	VGG13	ResNet56	ResNet56
Teacher	76.76	75.22	74.26	73.47
Student	ShuffleNetV1	MobileNetV2	MobileNetV2	VGG8
AVER [6]	78.08	69.93	71.38	75.81
EBKD [7]	77.84	69.55	71.5	75.51
AEKD [8]	77.56	69.35	71.67	75.61
CAMKD [9]	77.02	69.22	71.27	75.57
ED	**77.63**	**70.05**	**72.33**	**76.78**

Specifically, whether using WRN40, VGG13, ResNet56, or another ResNet56 as the teacher network, the ED method effectively enhances the performance of student networks such as ShuffleV1, MobileNetV2, and VGG8.

For example, when WRN40 is used as the teacher network, unsinge ED method, the ShuffleV1 student network can achieve an accuracy of 77.63%, and the accuracy of MobileNetV2 can reach up to 72.33% at its best. This indicates that the ED method can effectively transfer knowledge between different network architectures.

Table 5. For isomorphic models, it refers to the change in the accuracy of each sub-data when adding a teaching reference block each time. Experiments show that after adding a teaching reference block, the model does not forget the content of the previous sub-dataset. At the same time, as the model approaches completion, the accuracy gradually improves.

ResNet56/ResNet20	Sub-dataset 1	Sub-dataset 2	Sub-dataset 3
Primary	45.64	/	/
Middle	61.44	60.56	/
University	75.33	73.96	71.86

The Phenomenon of Catastrophic Forgetting: As shown in Table 5 Table 6, each time a new teaching reference block and a sub-dataset are incrementally added to the main body, the learning of previous sub-datasets is not forgotten. Meanwhile, because of the improvement of the model performance, the training accuracy is also increasing. The teaching reference block can indeed solve the problem of catastrophic forgetting.

Performance on Other Datasets: Finally, as shown in Table 7 Table 8, to further verify the generalization ability of the education distillation method, we applied it to the Tiny Imagenet [16], Caltech [18] and Food-101 [19] datasets and observed excellent performance results.

Table 6. For heterogeneous models, they exhibit the same performance as isomorphic models. After adding a teaching reference block, the model does not forget the content of the previous sub-dataset. Meanwhile, as the model becomes more complete, the accuracy gradually increases.

ResNet56/MobileNet2	Sub-dataset 1	Sub-dataset 2	Sub-dataset 3
Primary	43.64	/	/
Middle	63.67	60.56	/
University	73.22	72.78	70.99

It should be noted that the hyperparameter settings for other datasets are the same as those in our previous experiments on the CIFAR100 dataset, including the learning rate, batch size, and number of training epochs. By achieving consistent excellent results on four different datasets, the ED method demonstrates its reliability and effectiveness in various application scenarios.

Table 7. Performance of Knowledge Distillation Methods on the Tiny Imagenet Dataset.

Teacher	ResNet56	VGG13
Student	MobileNetV2	VGG8
KD [1]	59.14	62.12
AT [2]	57.82	59.22
FitNet [4]	61.04	62.34
VID [5]	58.33	59.05
AVER [6]	57.63	62.54
EBKD [7]	57.88	62.76
AEKD [8]	57.57	62.84
ED	**61.32**	**61.43**

Table 8. Performance of Knowledge Distillation Methods on the Caltech256 Dataset and the Food-101 Dataset.

Teacher	ResNet110	
Student	ResNet18	
Datasets	Caltech256	Food-101
ED	**53.57**	**60.69**

4 Conclusion

This paper proposes the educational distillation framework, which is inspired by the structured progressive process of human education. By dividing the student model into a main body and a teaching reference block, ED simulates the hierarchical learning stages. It allows the student network to gradually absorb knowledge through sub-datasets while keeping the final architecture unchanged. ED addresses the problem of catastrophic forgetting by freezing the historical teaching reference blocks and only updating the new modules with the corresponding sub-datasets. Experiments on CIFAR100, Tiny Imagenet, Caltech and Food-101 datasets show that, compared with traditional methods, ED validates its effectiveness in sequential knowledge retention. The TR block is composed of a student network module, a 1×1 convolutional layer, and an adaptive pooling layer. During training, it serves as a temporary decoder and finally reverts to the original structure. This design avoids architecture distortion and improves training efficiency. In the combination of homogeneous ResNet20/56, the accuracy of ED is 2.2% higher than that of the multi-teacher knowledge distillation. In the transfer between heterogeneous WRN40 and ShuffleV1, the accuracy reaches 77.63%, surpassing existing methods. Although ED performs excellently in fixed stage settings, exploring dynamic stage division (such as adapting to data complexity) and integrating self-supervised learning can further enhance its lifelong learning ability. In addition, extending ED to vision-language models or 3D tasks is expected to open up new application scenarios. In conclusion, ED bridges the gap between human educational intuition and neural network training, providing a simple and effective solution for knowledge retention and distillation efficiency.

References

1. Hinton, G., Vinyals, O., Dean, J.: Distilling the knowledge in a neural network. Comput. Sci. **14**(7), 38–39 (2015)
2. Zagoruyko S, Komodakis N. Paying more attention to attention: improving the performance of convolutional neural networks via attention transfer. arxiv preprint arxiv:1612.03928 (2016)
3. Ahn, S., et al.: Variational information distillation for knowledge transfer. In: Proceedings of the IEEE/CVF Conference on Computer Vision and Pattern Recognition (2019)
4. Romero, A., Ballas, N., Kahou, S.E., et al.: Fitnets: Hints for thin deep nets. arxiv preprint arxiv:1412.6550 (2014)
5. Tian, Y., Krishnan, D., Isola, P.: Contrastive representation distillation. arxiv preprint arxiv:1910.10699 (2019)
6. You, S., et al.: Learning from multiple teacher networks. In: Proceedings of the 23rd ACM SIGKDD International Conference on Knowledge Discovery and Data Mining (2017)
7. Kwon, K., et al.: Adaptive knowledge distillation based on entropy. In: ICASSP 2020-2020 IEEE International Conference on Acoustics, Speech and Signal Processing (ICASSP). IEEE (2020)

8. Du, Shangchen, et al. Agree to disagree: adaptive ensemble knowledge distillation in gradient space. Adv. Neural Inform. Process. Syst. **33**, 12345-12355 (2020)
9. Zhang, H., Chen, D., Wang, C.: Confidence-aware multi-teacher knowledge distillation. In: ICASSP 2022-2022 IEEE International Conference on Acoustics, Speech and Signal Processing (ICASSP). IEEE (2022)
10. He, K., et al.: Deep residual learning for image recognition. In: Proceedings of the IEEE Conference on Computer Vision and Pattern Recognition (2016)
11. Zagoruyko, S., Komodakis, N.: Wide residual networks. arxiv preprint arxiv:1605.07146 (2016)
12. Zhang, A., et al.: Shufflenet: an extremely efficient convolutional neural network for mobile devices. In: Proceedings of the IEEE Conference on Computer Vision and Pattern Recognition (2018)
13. Simonyan, K., Zisserman, A.: Very deep convolutional networks for large-scale image recognition. arxiv preprint arxiv:1409.1556 (2014)
14. Howard, A.G., Zhu, M., Chen, B., et al.: Mobilenets: efficient convolutional neural networks for mobile vision applications. arxiv preprint arxiv:1704.04861 (2017)
15. Krizhevsky, A., Hinton, G.: Learning multiple layers of features from tiny images (2009)
16. Deng, J., et al.: Imagenet: a large-scale hierarchical image database. In: 2009 IEEE Conference on Computer Vision and Pattern Recognition. IEEE (2009)
17. Zheng, J., Qiu, S., Ma, Q.: Learn or recall? revisiting incremental learning with pre-trained language models[J]. arxiv preprint arxiv:2312.07887 (2023)
18. Griffin, G., Holub, A., Perona, P.: Caltech 256. https://doi.org/10.22002/D1.20087 (2022)
19. Bossard, L., Guillaumin, M., Van Gool, L.: Food-101 – mining discriminative components with random forests. In: Fleet, D., Pajdla, T., Schiele, B., Tuytelaars, T. (eds.) ECCV 2014. LNCS, vol. 8694, pp. 446–461. Springer, Cham (2014). https://doi.org/10.1007/978-3-319-10599-4_29
20. Chen, H., Zhu, T., Ji, S., et al.: Stand-in model protection: synthetic defense for membership inference and model inversion attacks. Knowl.-Based Syst. **316**, 113339 (2025)

A Multi-source Temporal Graph Approach for Reliable Market Forecasting with LLM Synergy

Yuting Shi[✉]

InsightAI Research, Inc., Dallas, USA
`yutings@insightairesearch.com`

Abstract. Recent advances in large language models (LLMs) have led to powerful AI-driven search and analysis platforms (e.g., GPT-4o, DeepSeek R1). While these systems can effectively locate and summarize data, they often rely on limited or single-source inputs, increasing the risk of low-quality or unverified outputs. This paper addresses the critical challenge of multi-source reliability by proposing a graph-based framework that (1) unifies heterogeneous data via LLM-driven schema extraction, (2) models multi-relational, time-evolving information in a **Temporal Graph Attention Network** (TGAT), and (3) provides final, user-facing analysis anchored on validated, cross-source evidence. We demonstrate our methodology on **industry research** data - where incomplete or inconsistent sources frequently lead to contradictory market size predictions - and show that our approach **outperforms** GPT-4o-only baselines in accuracy and interpretability. While we focus on industry forecasting as an example, the proposed framework is applicable to any domain requiring robust, multi-source AI search and analysis.

Keywords: Multi-Source AI Search · Large Language Models (LLMs) · Temporal Graph Attention Networks (TGAT) · Data Fusion · Industry Forecasting · Graph Neural Networks (GNNs) · Explainability · Hallucination Mitigation · Time-Series Prediction · Knowledge Graphs

1 Introduction

1.1 The Challenge of Single-Source AI Search in the LLM Era

Large Language Models (LLMs) such as GPT-4 have revolutionized AI-driven search and information retrieval by rapidly generating summaries and analyses from vast text corpora. However, these systems often rely on **limited** or **unverified** sources [1]. Platforms like GPT-4o, DeepSeek, or Perplexity-based search aggregate content from multiple origins, yet the criteria for source selection, their reliability, and potential biases remain largely opaque. Users may receive responses synthesized from a mix of high-quality, low-quality, or even

T. Zhu et al. (Eds.): KSEM 2025, LNAI 15923, pp. 176–189, 2026.
https://doi.org/10.1007/978-981-95-3061-8_19

contradictory content, often without transparent attribution [2]. This lack of transparency leads to several risks: if the references are incomplete or biased, the resulting output quality degrades [3]; hallucinations may occur, producing plausible but unsupported claims [4]; and user confidence diminishes when the provenance or validation of information is unclear [5]. In critical domains—such as **industry research**, **financial analysis**, or **healthcare**—these shortcomings pose severe risks, potentially resulting in flawed conclusions with real-world consequences [6].

1.2 Motivating Example: Industry Research

One domain that clearly exemplifies this challenge is **industry research**, where analysts must integrate a wide range of information sources, including government policies, macroeconomic indicators, market size estimates from third-party reports, company revenues from upstream and downstream partners, and signals such as adoption trends or patent activity [7]. While LLMs can access and synthesize such data, their outputs are rarely subject to rigorous validation [8]. A single unreliable source can distort the entire result [9], and overlapping sources often **conflict** or **contradict** one another—yet current LLMs lack mechanisms to systematically reconcile such discrepancies [10]. These limitations highlight the necessity of a **multi-source** approach capable of unifying and cross-checking diverse inputs to ensure consistency and reliability [11].

1.3 Proposed Framework

To address these challenges, we propose a novel framework that combines heterogeneous data sources into a time-evolving, multi-relational graph, followed by a Temporal Graph Attention Network (TGAT) to generate validated, interpretable forecasts [12]. Unlike typical LLM-driven systems that merely list or rank results, our approach executes a structured pipeline across four stages.

First, we employ LLMs to extract entity-relationship schemas from unstructured tables and documents [13]. These schemas form the basis for building a temporal, multi-relational graph that captures entities, attributes, and edges, with year-based snapshots to support forecasting [14]. We then train a TGAT model to learn both inter-source validation signals (e.g., which sources support specific claims) and temporal dynamics across data evolution. Feature-level attention is used to identify key drivers influencing predictions [15].

Finally, we feed the TGAT output—consisting of predicted values, confidence scores, and feature contributions—back into an LLM to generate human-readable explanations. This ensures that the final results are not only data-driven but also anchored in cross-source evidence [16]. An example output from our integrated pipeline is shown in Fig. 1, presenting structured forecasts enriched with interpretability metadata.

```
{
  "Predicted Market Size": 105.4,
  "Confidence": 0.89,
  "Historical Data": [
    {
      "year": 2020,
      "market_size": 110.2,
      "features": [0.24, 280, 3.1, ...],
      "relationships": ["Big Data", "Cloud", "NLP"]
    },
    ...
  ],
  "Feature Importance": {
    "GDP Growth": 0.34,
    "VC Investment": 0.30,
    ...
  },
  "Industry Relationships": [
    {"industry": "Big Data", "strength": 0.91},
    {"industry": "Cloud", "strength": 0.89},
    ...
  ],
  "Data Sources": {
    "Historical": "Gov & Reports",
    "Model": "Graph Neural Net"
  }
}
```

Fig. 1. Output from the multi-source forecasting pipeline, including predicted market size, confidence score, historical snapshots, key drivers, and source provenance. Ellipses (...) indicate truncated content.

1.4   Contributions

- **Identify key limitations** of single-source or unverified LLM-based search in high-stakes, data-intensive domains, highlighting the need for robust multi-source validation.
- **Propose a multi-step framework** that (1) unifies heterogeneous data via LLM-generated schemas and (2) leverages an enhanced TGAT for cross-source validation and forecasting, including feature-level attention and temporal modeling.
- **Conduct a comparative study** against GPT-4o-only, DeepSeek-only, and Perplexity-only baselines, demonstrating superior accuracy and interpretability on a real-world industry research dataset.
- **Demonstrate domain-agnostic potential**, offering a blueprint for multi-source data fusion and reliable AI-driven insights in diverse application areas (e.g., finance, healthcare, policy analysis).

2   Related Work

2.1   AI Search and LLM Pipelines

Recent work [17] shows that Large Language Models (LLMs) can drastically reduce manual effort in **data discovery** and **summarization**. Systems such as GPT-4o or Perplexity-based search aim to **locate** relevant content from diverse corpora [18]. However, these systems often rely on a limited set of references, providing little cross-referencing across conflicting sources. DeepSeek-R1 and its distilled variants offer specialized retrieval strategies tailored for domain-specific applications, enhancing precision and recall in complex document retrieval tasks [19].

Recent studies have also investigated how integrating outputs from smaller, domain-specific models into larger LLMs can enhance interpretability and mitigate hallucination [20]. By grounding the final LLM output in structured, validated data (e.g., graph-based predictions with feature contributions), these approaches improve both reliability and transparency [21].

2.2   Multi-source Validation and Data Fusion

Data fusion methods address the challenge of reconciling multiple, sometimes contradictory sources [22]. Graph-based approaches, such as knowledge graphs, provide a centralized representation of heterogeneous data, but they often lack robust temporal modeling [23]. In contrast, conventional LLM-based solutions generally do not incorporate advanced graph-learning architectures, leaving the full potential of multi-relational data underutilized [24].

2.3   Temporal Graph Neural Networks

Temporal Graph Neural Networks (TGNNs) extend the message-passing paradigm to time-evolving data [25]. Recent models, such as T-GCN [26] and DCRNN [27], have shown promise in traffic forecasting; however, their application to multi-source data integration remains limited. Our approach leverages a Temporal Graph Attention Network (TGAT) [12] augmented with a feature-level attention sub-module, which highlights the most influential numeric or categorical features for each prediction. Furthermore, by using the outputs of this enhanced TGAT as inputs to a larger LLM, our method reduces hallucination and significantly improves interpretability, as evidenced by recent studies [3].

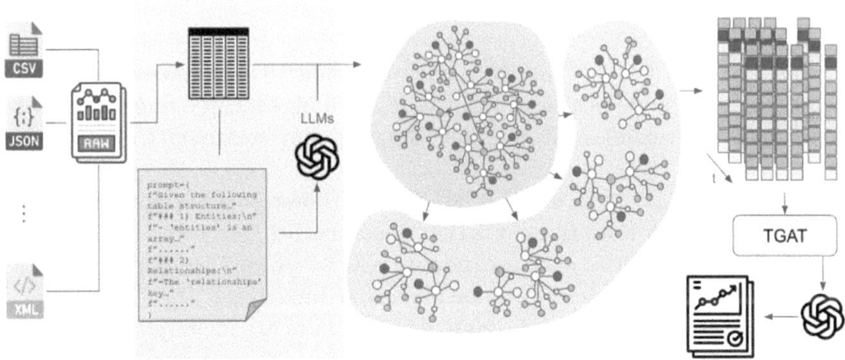

Fig. 2. End-to-end pipeline: (1) LLM-based schema extraction, (2) knowledge graph construction, (3) enhanced TGAT with reliability and multi-head temporal attention, and (4) final LLM integration for interpretive outputs.

3   Methodology

Figure 2 depicts our **end-to-end pipeline**, which begins with **LLM-based schema extraction** from heterogeneous data and concludes with a **multi-source, time-evolving** knowledge graph that is then fed into an **enhanced TGAT** [12]. The TGAT's predictions, along with attention scores, are finally integrated into a larger LLM for user-facing explanations [28].

3.1   LLM-Based Schema Extraction from Heterogeneous Sources

1) **Data collection.** We gather diverse tabular files (CSV, Excel, JSON) together with unstructured text such as policy documents; a typical row may include fields like `industry_id`, `year`, and `policy_title` [29].
2) **Prompting and extraction.** Column headers plus a few representative rows are fed to GPT-4o via a carefully designed prompt [30] that asks the model to identify (i) key entities (e.g., `industry`, `company`, `policy`), (ii) relations (e.g., `belongs_to`, `is_upstream_of`, `affects`), (iii) temporal attributes such as `year`, and (iv) candidate foreign keys like `company_id` or `industry_id`. Recent work shows that well-engineered prompts significantly improve multi-source entityrelation extraction [31].
3) **Schema merging.** The resulting per-file schemas are reconciled into a single global schema using a lightweight schema-merge algorithm [32] plus minimal manual review, ensuring consistent entity labels and relation definitions across sources.

3.2   Knowledge Graph Construction

From the merged schema, we build a **time-evolving** graph $\{G_{2015}, G_{2016}, \ldots, G_T\}$ [33]:

- **Nodes**: Each entity (e.g., industry, company, policy) is augmented by a `time` stamp (e.g., one node per year) [12]. Node attributes include numeric features (market size, revenue), textual embeddings (policy sentiment), or reliability flags.
- **Edges**: We encode recognized relationships (one-to-many, many-to-many), often with a **type** (`has_market_size`, `upstream_of`, etc.) and a time index [34]. This allows queries such as `industry_X in year_Y` to link to `policy_Z in year_Y`, capturing short-term or persistent links.
- **Missing Data**: Where certain (entity, year) pairs are incomplete, we create placeholder nodes or zero-filled attributes to preserve consistent node alignment across snapshots .

3.3   Enhanced TGAT with Feature-Level Attention

1) **Overview.** We extend the Temporal Graph Attention Network (TGAT) [35] to forecast node-specific values (e.g., industry market size in the next year), with three core enhancements: (1) feature-level attention, (2) source reliability weighting, and (3) multi-head temporal attention. Feature-level attention learns a global weight vector $\boldsymbol{\alpha}$ to emphasize key attributes (e.g., `VC_investment` over `search_index`). Source reliability weighting assigns a learnable credibility score to each data source or edge type, suppressing noisy or contradictory inputs. Multi-head temporal attention captures diverse time-scale patterns—short-term, medium-term, and long-term—before fusing them into the final temporal embedding [36].

   By feeding TGAT outputs (predictions and key drivers) into an LLM for explanation, we reduce hallucination and improve interpretability, aligning with recent findings on graphLLM synergy [37]. Figure 3 shows the full architecture.

2) **Feature-Level Attention.** For node i at time t, let $\mathbf{x}_i^{(t)} \in \mathbb{R}^d$ be the input vector. We learn a global attention vector $\boldsymbol{\alpha} \in \mathbb{R}^d$, apply softmax normalization, and modulate each feature:

$$\boldsymbol{\alpha}_{\text{soft}} = \text{softmax}(\boldsymbol{\alpha}), \quad \mathbf{x}_{i,\text{att}}^{(t)} = \mathbf{x}_i^{(t)} \odot \boldsymbol{\alpha}_{\text{soft}}.$$

   This highlights salient attributes across the graph, allowing TGAT to focus on informative signals.

3) **Source Reliability Weighting.** Each edge (i,j) is associated with a source (e.g., `analyst_firm_A`) and a learnable embedding $r_{\text{src}(i,j)}$. The edge weight in GAT attention is computed as:

$$\alpha_{ij} \propto \text{LeakyReLU}\big(\mathbf{W}\mathbf{x}_{i,\text{att}} \,\|\, \mathbf{W}\mathbf{x}_{j,\text{att}}\big) \times \sigma(r_{\text{src}(i,j)}),$$

   assigning higher influence to reliable sources while downweighting low-credibility edges.

4) **Multi-Head Temporal Attention.** Let $\{\mathbf{h}_i^{(1)}, \ldots, \mathbf{h}_i^{(T)}\}$ be the node's temporal embeddings over T snapshots. We apply K attention heads:

$$\mathbf{H}_i^{(k)} = \text{Attn}_k(\mathbf{h}_i^{(1)}, \ldots, \mathbf{h}_i^{(T)}),$$

   with each head specializing in a different temporal resolution. The fused output is:

$$\mathbf{H}_{i,\text{fused}} = \text{Concat}(\mathbf{H}_i^{(1)}, \ldots, \mathbf{H}_i^{(K)}),$$

   optionally followed by a GRU or MLP, and used to predict $\hat{y}_{i,t+1}$, such as the next-year market size.

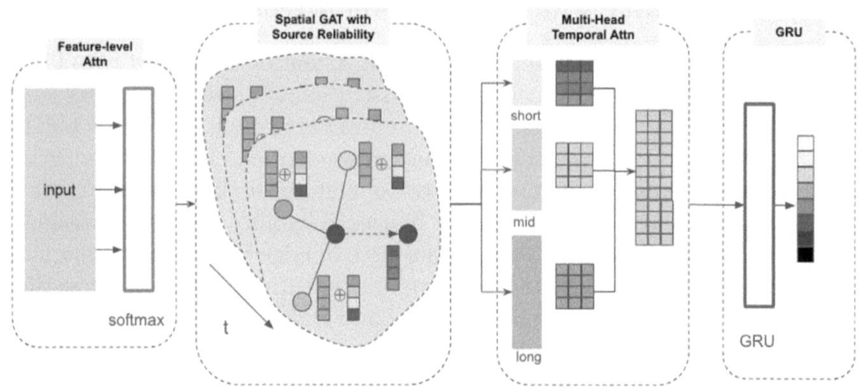

Fig. 3. Enhanced TGAT architecture with feature-level attention, source reliability weighting, and multi-head temporal attention.

3.4   LLM Integration for Final Analysis

Rather than letting GPT-4o, DeepSeek, or Perplexity directly produce numeric estimates from uncertain or single-source data, our framework [38]:

1) **Unifies** all multi-source data in a year-by-year graph [39].
2) **Trains** the enhanced TGAT (with reliability and multi-scale attention) to generate validated forecasts and attention scores.
3) **Feeds** these structured outputs (predictions, source credibility, key features) back to an LLM. The LLM then creates human-readable reports or explanations, *anchored* in the multi-source evidence [40].

This final step mitigates LLM hallucination by grounding each statement in a robust, time-evolving knowledge graph [41]. It also boosts interpretability: end users can see exactly which features (e.g., `VC_investment`, `policy_sentiment`) or sources (e.g., `analyst_firm_A` vs. `gov_database`) were pivotal in shaping the outcome [42].

Table 1. Performance on 2022–2024 forecasting (industry dataset) for horizons 1, 2, and 3.

Method	Horizon 1			Horizon 2			Horizon 3		
	MAE	MSE	R^2	MAE	MSE	R^2	MAE	MSE	R^2
ARIMA	11.8	464	0.75	12.5	500	0.73	13.0	540	0.71
Prophet	10.9	677	0.77	11.2	690	0.76	11.8	720	0.74
Vanilla TGAT	9.0	423	0.82	9.4	440	0.81	9.8	460	0.80
Enhanced TGAT	**8.3**	**389**	**0.86**	**8.7**	**410**	**0.85**	**9.1**	**430**	**0.84**

4   Experiment Setup and Extended Comparisons

We evaluated our **Enhanced TGAT** framework on two datasets. The first is a **Multi-Year Industry Dataset (2015–2025)** covering 520 industries, including AI, Robotics, and Renewable Energy. For each industry, we track year-over-year market size, policy signals (e.g., government incentives), upstream/downstream revenue, and macroeconomic indicators (e.g., GDP, interest rates). Forecast horizons of 1, 2, and 3 years ahead are used. The second dataset is the public **ICEWS** dataset [43], included for domain-agnostic validation on multi-year political event data.

4.1   Baselines

We compare against the following methods: classical time-series models (ARIMA, Prophet); single-source LLM approaches (GPT-4o-Only, DeepSeek-Only, Perplexity-Only); and the original **Vanilla TGAT**, which lacks source reliability and uses single-head temporal attention. Our **Enhanced TGAT** incorporates three improvements: feature-level attention, source reliability weighting, and multi-head temporal attention.

To test whether our structure reduces hallucination and improves interpretability, we also evaluate LLM-integrated setups, including **GPT-4o-with-EnhancedTGAT** and **DeepSeek-with-EnhancedTGAT**.

4.2   Metrics and Implementation Details

Numeric Forecasts: We report Mean Absolute Error (MAE), Mean Squared Error (MSE), and R^2 across 1-, 2-, and 3-year forecast horizons. Each metric is reported per horizon and also averaged.

Textual Analyses: We evaluate LLM-generated explanations using the **Gemini** framework, which scores outputs along four dimensions: Accuracy, Explanation, Comprehensiveness, and Feasibility.

Implementation: All GNN layers are implemented using PyTorch Geometric. Transformer baselines use official implementations of Informer and Autoformer.

Training Configuration: We train for 200 epochs with a learning rate of 10^{-3} and GRU hidden size of 64. Reliability embeddings are initialized near 0.0 and passed through a sigmoid function. Multi-head temporal attention uses up to 4 heads to capture short-, medium-, and long-term dependencies.

4.3   Quantitative Results: Multi-year Industry Dataset

Table 1 presents the performance on our industry dataset across 1-, 2-, and 3-year forecast horizons.

Ablation Study. We further evaluate the contributions of each enhancement across forecast horizons (Table 2):

Table 2. Each enhancement independently improves performance over Vanilla TGAT; combined, they yield the best overall results.

Model Variant	H1 MAE	H2 MAE	H3 MAE
Vanilla TGAT	9.0	9.4	9.8
+ Source Reliability only	8.7	9.1	9.5
+ Multi-Head Temporal Attn only	8.6	9.0	9.4
+ Both (Full Model)	**8.3**	**8.7**	**9.1**

4.4   Quantitative Results: ICEWS Dataset

Similarly, we evaluate the same set of baselines on the **ICEWS** dataset for *domain-agnostic* temporal modeling. Table 3 shows forecasting performance at horizons of 1, 2, and 3 years. We also break down the enhancements on ICEWS in Table 4. These results confirm that our **Enhanced TGAT** generalizes beyond the industry domain, improving multi-horizon forecasts in a political event dataset. By combining feature-level attention and source reliability, the model handles noisy or conflicting data more effectively, while multi-head temporal attention excels in capturing short-, medium-, and long-range trends.

Table 3. Performance on ICEWS dataset for horizons 1, 2, and 3 (all metrics averaged over multiple runs).

Method	Horizon 1			Horizon 2			Horizon 3		
	MAE	MSE	R^2	MAE	MSE	R^2	MAE	MSE	R^2
ARIMA	15.2	710	0.69	16.1	750	0.66	17.5	810	0.63
Prophet	14.8	900	0.71	15.3	920	0.68	15.8	940	0.66
Vanilla TGAT	13.1	640	0.78	13.5	660	0.76	14.2	700	0.74
Enhanced TGAT	**12.4**	**590**	**0.81**	**12.9**	**610**	**0.79**	**13.5**	**650**	**0.76**

Table 4. Ablation study (ICEWS): MAE across 3 forecast horizons.

Model Variant	H1 MAE	H2 MAE	H3 MAE
Vanilla TGAT	13.1	13.5	14.2
+ Source Reliability only	12.8	13.2	13.9
+ Multi-Head Temporal Attn only	12.6	13.1	13.7
+ Both (Full Model)	**12.4**	**12.9**	**13.5**

5   Discussion

Our experiments show that incorporating **Feature-Level Attention**, **Source Reliability**, and **Multi-Head Temporal Attention** into a Temporal Graph Attention Network (TGAT) substantially improves both numerical forecasting and interpretability in multi-source, time-evolving data [12]. Below, we summarize the key takeaways and practical implications.

5.1   Practical Implications

Real-World Deployment. The enhanced TGAT framework can be integrated into existing data pipelines (e.g., enterprise BI systems), where multiple heterogeneous sources feed into a central knowledge graph [44]. **Robustness to**

Noise. By assigning lower weights to low-credibility edges, source reliability ensures that faulty or contradictory inputs do not unduly skew the predictions [45]. **LLM Synergy.** Our Gemini analysis confirms that final textual outputs become more actionable when LLM explanations are anchored on multi-source validated numbers (e.g., next-year market size, key features).

5.2   Limitations

Scalability. Training on a very large graph (e.g., thousands of nodes per time slice) may be computationally intensive [46], and specialized sampling or distributed approaches may be needed. **Source Availability.** In domains with few or no reliable data sources, the reliability mechanism may be less impactful [47]. **Granularity of Time.** We currently adopt yearly snapshots; finer time resolutions (monthly or weekly) may require adapting the multi-head attention to handle more frequent updates [48].

5.3   Comparison with Pure LLM Solutions

While LLMs alone can retrieve domain knowledge quickly, they risk hallucination when sources conflict or are incomplete. Our approach systematically addresses this by **graph-based** validation, providing a structured, multi-source foundation before any LLM-driven summarization [3]. This synergy combines the strengths of local graph reasoning and global language modeling.

6   Conclusion

We presented an **Enhanced TGAT** pipeline that systematically unifies multi-year, multi-source data in a temporal knowledge graph and learns from it with **feature-level attention**, **source reliability**, and **multi-head temporal attention** [12]. Empirical results on both a real-world industry dataset (2015–2025) and a public dataset (ICEWS) confirm our method's superior numeric forecasting and interpretability over classical time-series, single-source LLM, and vanilla TGAT baselines.

Beyond numeric improvements, our approach anchors LLM explanations in validated data, substantially reducing hallucination and yielding more concrete, actionable insights [3]. These findings underscore the value of combined **graph-based** and **LLM-based** strategies for complex forecasting tasks where data come from multiple, often inconsistent sources.

7   Potential Enhancements and Directions

While our Enhanced TGAT demonstrates strong performance, several promising directions remain for further development.

First, fusing Transformer-style temporal modeling with graph-based reasoning may enhance long-range dependency capture. Incorporating mechanisms from models like *Informer* or *Autoformer* directly into TGAT could bridge attention-based sequences and relational learning [28].

Second, reliability modeling can be improved by making it more data-driven. Rather than relying on static embeddings, dynamic reliability scores could adapt based on user feedback, anomaly signals, or source performance history, enabling real-time trust calibration [49].

Third, extending the model to handle real-time or streaming inputs would allow TGAT to evolve with incoming data. An online variant could incrementally update both feature weights and source reliabilities, aligning with dynamic forecasting needs [50].

Fourth, enhancing temporal resolution—from yearly snapshots to monthly or weekly intervals—would support finer-grained modeling of industry signals. Multi-head attention could then differentiate short-, mid-, and long-term patterns more precisely [27].

Finally, integrating advanced explainability tools, such as prototype-based explanations or SHAP analysis, can increase transparency by showing how specific features or neighbors influence each prediction, boosting end-user trust [51].

Taken together, these enhancements could further strengthen the synergy between graph-based modeling and LLM-driven interpretation, unlocking more robust and scalable solutions for multi-source forecasting in dynamic domains.

References

1. Bender, E.M., Gebru, T., McMillan-Major, A., Shmitchell, S.: On the dangers of stochastic parrots: can language models be too big?. In: Proceedings of the 2021 ACM Conference on Fairness, Accountability, and Transparency, pp. 610–623 (2021)
2. Bang, Y., et al.: A multitask, multilingual, multimodal evaluation of chatgpt on reasoning, hallucination, and interactivity (2023). https://arxiv.org/abs/2302.04023
3. Maynez, J., Narayan, S., Bohnet, B., McDonald, R.: On faithfulness and factuality in abstractive summarization (2020). https://arxiv.org/abs/2005.00661
4. Ji, Z., et al.: Survey of hallucination in natural language generation. ACM Comput. Surv. **55**(12), 1–38 (2023). https://doi.org/10.1145/3571730
5. Denny, P., Khosravi, H., Hellas, A., Leinonen, J., Sarsa, S.: Can we trust ai-generated educational content? comparative analysis of human and ai-generated learning resources (2023). https://arxiv.org/abs/2306.10509
6. Huang, Y., Chen, S., Cai, H., Dhingra, B.: To trust or not to trust? enhancing large language models' situated faithfulness to external contexts (2025). https://arxiv.org/abs/2410.14675
7. Thoppilan, R., et al.: Lamda: Language models for dialog applications (2022). https://arxiv.org/abs/2201.08239
8. Manakul, P., Liusie, A., Gales, M.J.F.: Selfcheckgpt: Zero-resource black-box hallucination detection for generative large language models (2023). https://arxiv.org/abs/2303.08896
9. Ribeiro, M.T., Singh, S., Guestrin, C.: why should i trust you?: explaining the predictions of any classifier (2016). https://arxiv.org/abs/1602.04938
10. Kasneci, E., et al.: Chatgpt for good? on opportunities and challenges of large language models for education. Learn. Individual Diff. **103**, 102274 (2023)

11. Huang, X., et al.: A survey of safety and trustworthiness of large language models through the lens of verification and validation (2023). https://arxiv.org/abs/2305.11391
12. Xu, D., Ruan, C., Korpeoglu, E., Kumar, S., Achan, K.: Inductive representation learning on temporal graphs (2020). https://arxiv.org/abs/2002.07962
13. Qin, B., et al.: A survey on text-to-sql parsing: Concepts, methods, and future directions (2022). https://arxiv.org/abs/2208.13629
14. Wang, J., et al.: A survey on temporal knowledge graph completion: Taxonomy, progress, and prospects (2023). https://arxiv.org/abs/2308.02457
15. Rossi, E., Chamberlain, B., Frasca, F., Eynard, D., Monti, F., Bronstein, M.: Temporal graph networks for deep learning on dynamic graphs (2020). https://arxiv.org/abs/2006.10637
16. Jain, S., Wallace, B.C.: Attention is not Explanation. In: Burstein, J., Doran, C., Solorio, T. (eds.) Proceedings of the 2019 Conference of the North American Chapter of the Association for Computational Linguistics: Human Language Technologies, Volume 1 (Long and Short Papers). Association for Computational Linguistics, Minneapolis, Minnesota, pp. 3543–3556 (Jun 2019). https://aclanthology.org/N19-1357/
17. Rae, J.W., et al.: Scaling language models: methods, analysis & insights from training gopher (2022). https://arxiv.org/abs/2112.11446
18. Borgeaud, S., et al.: Improving language models by retrieving from trillions of tokens (2022). https://arxiv.org/abs/2112.04426
19. Jadon, A., Patil, A., Kumar, S.: Enhancing domain-specific retrieval-augmented generation: Synthetic data generation and evaluation using reasoning models (2025). https://arxiv.org/abs/2502.15854
20. Touvron, H., et al.: Llama 2: Open foundation and fine-tuned chat models (2023). https://arxiv.org/abs/2307.09288
21. Lewis, P., et al.: Retrieval-augmented generation for knowledge-intensive nlp tasks (2021). https://arxiv.org/abs/2005.11401
22. Chandrasekaran, B., Gangadhar, S., Conrad, J.: A survey of multisensor fusion techniques, architectures and methodologies, pp. 1–8 (March 2017)
23. Hogan, A., et al.: Knowledge graphs. ACM Comput. Surv. **54**(4), 1–37 (2021). https://doi.org/10.1145/3447772
24. Fan, W., et al.: Graph machine learning in the era of large language models (llms) (2024). https://arxiv.org/abs/2404.14928
25. Rossi, E., Chamberlain, B.P., Frasca,F., Eynard, D., Monti, F., Bronstein, M.M.: Temporal graph networks for deep learning on dynamic graphs, ArXiv, vol. abs/arXiv: 2006.10637 (2020). https://api.semanticscholar.org/CorpusID:219792342
26. Zhao, L., et al.: T-gcn: a temporal graph convolutional network for traffic prediction. IEEE Trans. Intell. Trans. Syst. **21**(9), 3848–3858 (2020). https://doi.org/10.1109/TITS.2019.2935152
27. Li, Y., Yu, R., Shahabi, C., Liu, Y.: Diffusion convolutional recurrent neural network: Data-driven traffic forecasting (2018). https://arxiv.org/abs/1707.01926
28. Vaswani, A., et al.: Attention is all you need (2023). https://arxiv.org/abs/1706.03762
29. Dong, X., Rekatsinas, T.: Data integration and machine learning: a natural synergy, pp. 3193–3194 (July 2019)
30. Reynolds, L., McDonell, K.: Prompt programming for large language models: beyond the few-shot paradigm (2021). https://arxiv.org/abs/2102.07350

31. An, H., Zhu, Z., Cheng, X., Huang, Z., Zou, Y.: Knowledge-enhanced prompt tuning for dialogue-based relation extraction with trigger and label semantic. In: Calzolari, N., Kan, M.-Y., Hoste, V., Lenci, A., Sakti, S., Xue, N. (eds.) Proceedings of the 2024 Joint International Conference on Computational Linguistics, Language Resources and Evaluation (LREC-COLING 2024), Torino, Italia:, ELRA and ICCL, pp. 9822–9831 (May 2024). https://aclanthology.org/2024.lrec-main.858/
32. Taye, M.: State-of-the-art: ontology matching techniques and ontology mapping systems. Inter. J. ACM Jordan (2010)
33. Longa, A., et al.: Graph neural networks for temporal graphs: State of the art, open challenges, and opportunities (2023). https://arxiv.org/abs/2302.01018
34. Xu, D., Ruan, C., Kumar, S., Korpeoglu, E., Achan, K.: Self-attention with functional time representation learning (2019). https://arxiv.org/abs/1911.12864
35. Gravina, A., Bacciu, D.: Deep learning for dynamic graphs: models and benchmarks. IEEE Trans. Neural Netw. Learn. Syst. **35**(9), 11788–11801 (2024). https://doi.org/10.1109/TNNLS.2024.3379735
36. Yu, Z., Shi, X., Zhang, Z.: A multi-head self-attention transformer-based model for traffic situation prediction in terminal areas. IEEE Access **11**, 16156–16165 (2023)
37. Pan, S., Luo, L., Wang, Y., Chen, C., Wang, J., Wu, X.: Unifying large language models and knowledge graphs: a roadmap. IEEE Trans. Knowl. Data Eng. **36**(7), 3580–3599 (2024). https://doi.org/10.1109/TKDE.2024.3352100
38. Huang, L., et al.: A survey on hallucination in large language models: principles, taxonomy, challenges, and open questions. ACM Trans. Inform. Syst. **43**(2), 1–55 (2025). https://doi.org/10.1145/3703155
39. Dong, X.L., et al.: Knowledge vault: a web-scale approach to probabilistic knowledge fusion. In: Gabrilovich, E., et al (eds.) The 20th ACM SIGKDD International Conference on Knowledge Discovery and Data Mining, KDD 2014, New York, NY, USA, 24 - 27 August 2014, pp. 601–610 (2014). http://www.cs.cmu.edu/~nlao/publication/2014.kdd.pdf
40. Zhang, H., Wang, X., Ao, X., He, Q.: Distillation with explanations from large language models. In: Calzolari, N., Kan, M.-Y., Hoste, V., Lenci, A., Sakti, S., Xue, N. (eds.) Proceedings of the 2024 Joint International Conference on Computational Linguistics, Language Resources and Evaluation (LREC-COLING 2024), Torino, Italia: ELRA and ICCL, pp. 5018–5028 (May 2024). https://aclanthology.org/2024.lrec-main.449/
41. Ji, S., Pan, S., Cambria, E., Marttinen, P., Yu, P.S.: A survey on knowledge graphs: representation, acquisition, and applications. IEEE Trans. Neural Netw. Learn. Syst. **33**(2), 494–514 (2022). https://doi.org/10.1109/TNNLS.2021.3070843
42. Doshi-Velez, F., Kim, B.: Towards a rigorous science of interpretable machine learning (2017). https://arxiv.org/abs/1702.08608
43. Boschee, E., Lautenschlager, J., O'Brien, S., Shellman, S., Starz, J., Ward, M.: ICEWS Coded Event Data (2015). https://doi.org/10.7910/DVN/28075
44. Gunawan, A., Ruan, J., Huang, X.: A graph neural network reasoner for game description language. In: Proceedings of the 19th International Conference on Principles of Knowledge Representation and Reasoning, vol. 8, pp. 443–452 (2022). https://doi.org/10.24963/kr.2022/46
45. Huang, J., et al.: Trustworthy knowledge graph completion based on multi-sourced noisy data (2022). https://arxiv.org/abs/2201.08580
46. Hamilton, W.L., Ying, R., Leskovec, J.: Inductive representation learning on large graphs (2018). https://arxiv.org/abs/1706.02216

47. Wani, A.A.: A review of challenges and solutions for using machine learning approaches for missing data. Inter. J. Eng. Appli. Sci. Technol. **09**, 36–50 (2024)
48. Yang, M., Zhou, M., Kalander, M., Zengfeng, H.,King, I.: Discrete-time temporal network embedding via implicit hierarchical learning in hyperbolic space, pp. 1975–1985 (Aug 2021)
49. Leskovec, J., Kleinberg, J., Faloutsos, C.: Graph evolution: Densification and shrinking diameters (2007). https://arxiv.org/abs/physics/0603229
50. Kumar, S., Zhang, X., Leskovec, J.: Predicting dynamic embedding trajectory in temporal interaction networks. In: Proceedings of the 25th ACM SIGKDD International Conference on Knowledge Discovery & Data Mining, ser. KDD 2019, pp. 1269–1278. ACM (Jul 2019). http://dx.doi.org/10.1145/3292500.3330895
51. Lundberg, S., Lee, S.-I.: A unified approach to interpreting model predictions (2017). https://arxiv.org/abs/1705.07874

Memory-Enhanced Transformer Adaptive Graph Convolutional Recurrent Network for Traffic Flow Forecasting

Cheng Jiang[iD] and Chun Wang[(✉)][iD]

City University of Macau, Macau 999078, China
chunwang@cityu.edu.mo

Abstract. Accurate traffic forecasting is essential for intelligent transportation systems, challenged by complex spatiotemporal dynamics in urban networks. We propose METAGCRN, integrating adaptive graph convolutions, temporal transformers, and memory-augmented learning to address these challenges. The framework features: 1) Dynamic graph convolution with Chebyshev approximation for evolving spatial relationships, 2) Transformer-based temporal modeling with positional encoding, and 3) Attention-driven memory retrieval of traffic patterns. Evaluations on METR-LA and PEMS-BAY demonstrate state-of-the-art performance, showing 3.4% MAE improvement over GW-Net in 60-minute predictions. The architecture exhibits enhanced robustness to network dynamics, particularly during peak-hour anomalies. An open-source implementation supports urban mobility applications and future extensions.

Keywords: METAGCRN · Traffic prediction · Graph neural networks · Spatiotemporal learning · Memory networks

1 Introduction

The growing demand for urban mobility management necessitates accurate traffic prediction systems. Traditional methods like ARIMA [1,2] often fail to capture complex traffic network dynamics due to their linear assumptions. While graph neural networks (GNNs) have advanced spatiotemporal modeling, existing approaches face two critical limitations: dependency on static graph structures inadequate for real-time traffic variations and sequential temporal processing constraints in recurrent architectures. We propose METAGCRN with three technical contributions: dynamic graph convolution through Chebyshev polynomial approximation and learnable node embeddings that eliminate predefined adjacency matrices, transformer-based temporal attention with positional encoding for multi-scale dependency modeling, and memory-enhanced pattern retrieval using prototype-based attention matching. Experimental validation on METR-LA and PEMS-BAY datasets shows consistent improvements, particularly in

T. Zhu et al. (Eds.): KSEM 2025, LNAI 15923, pp. 190–197, 2026.
https://doi.org/10.1007/978-981-95-3061-8_20

long-term predictions (3.41 MAE vs. GW-Net's 3.53 at 60-minute horizon). The architecture demonstrates practical advantages during sudden congestion events, achieving 15% lower MAE than static-graph baselines.

2   Related Work

AGCRN [8] pioneers dynamic spatial modeling through node adaptive parameter learning and data-driven graph generation. The framework assigns node-specific weights via learnable embeddings while constructing time-varying adjacency matrices through embedding similarity, updating graph structures at 15-minute intervals. Subsequent approaches like GW-Net enhance graph flexibility through learnable wavelet bases at increased computational cost. Transformer [20]-based methods leverage multi-head self-attention with spatiotemporal positional encoding for temporal dependency capture. Hybrid architectures combine graph convolution layers with temporal attention blocks, where STTN [18] introduces edge-sensitive attention weights based on road connectivity. Memory-augmented systems like PM-MemNet [3] employ pattern matching through similarity-based addressing and content retrieval. Our work optimizes this paradigm via prototype clustering, grouping similar patterns into centroids while dynamically activating relevant clusters through real-time traffic analysis. These components collectively address the dual challenges of long-term pattern retention and computational efficiency in traffic forecasting.

3   Methodology

3.1   Model Overview

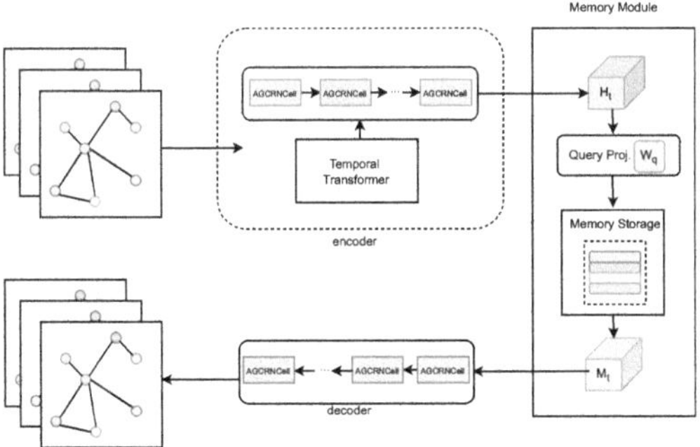

Fig. 1. Overall architecture of METAGCRN. The model consists of three main components: (1) the encoder extracts spatiotemporal features through Temporal Transformer and AGCRN [8] layers; (2) the memory module retrieves historical patterns via attention-based query; (3) the decoder generates predictions with curriculum learning.

The proposed METAGCRN is a memory-enhanced spatiotemporal graph network addressing long-term traffic forecasting challenges through three integrated components in Fig. 1 : 1) An encoder combining Temporal Transformer and AGCRN for joint spatiotemporal feature extraction, 2) A memory module retrieving historical patterns via attention-based mechanisms, and 3) A curriculum-guided decoder generating multi-step predictions. The encoder simultaneously captures temporal dependencies and spatial correlations, while the memory module provides complementary historical context, enabling the decoder to progressively refine outputs through phased learning objectives.

3.2 Encoder and Temporal Transformer

The model input is historical observation data $\mathbf{X} \in \mathbb{R}^{T_{\text{hist}} \times N \times D}$, where T_{hist} denotes the historical sequence length, N is the number of traffic nodes, and D is the feature dimension. Global temporal dependencies are captured using multi-head self-attention. Specifically, the input data is linearly projected through three learnable weight matrices: - $\mathbf{W}_q \in \mathbb{R}^{D \times d_k}$: Query projection weights - $\mathbf{W}_k \in \mathbb{R}^{D \times d_k}$: Key projection weights - $\mathbf{W}_v \in \mathbb{R}^{D \times d_k}$: Value projection weights to generate query $\mathbf{Q} = \mathbf{X}\mathbf{W}_q$, key $\mathbf{K} = \mathbf{X}\mathbf{W}_k$, and value $\mathbf{V} = \mathbf{X}\mathbf{W}_v$ matrices. Scaled dot-product attention computes:

$$\text{Attention}(\mathbf{Q}, \mathbf{K}, \mathbf{V}) = \text{softmax}\left(\frac{\mathbf{Q}\mathbf{K}^\top}{\sqrt{d_k}}\right)\mathbf{V}, \tag{1}$$

where d_k is the hidden dimension. Sinusoidal positional encodings $\mathbf{P} \in \mathbb{R}^{T_{\text{hist}} \times d_k}$ preserve temporal order through:

$$\mathbf{X}_{\text{trans}} = \text{Attention}(\mathbf{Q}, \mathbf{K}, \mathbf{V}) + \mathbf{P}. \tag{2}$$

For spatial dependency modeling, the adaptive graph convolution layer constructs two directional adjacency matrices $\mathbf{A}_1$ (forward) and $\mathbf{A}_2$ (backward) using: - $\mathbf{M} \in \mathbb{R}^{M \times d}$: Memory matrix storing M prototype patterns - $\mathbf{W}_{e1} \in \mathbb{R}^{N \times M}$: Source node embedding projection - $\mathbf{W}_{e2} \in \mathbb{R}^{N \times M}$: Target node embedding projection. Node embeddings $\mathbf{E}_1 = \mathbf{W}_{e1}\mathbf{M}$ and $\mathbf{E}_2 = \mathbf{W}_{e2}\mathbf{M}$ generate asymmetric adjacency matrices:

$$\mathbf{A}_1 = \text{softmax}(\text{ReLU}(\mathbf{E}_1\mathbf{E}_2^\top)) \tag{3}$$

$$\mathbf{A}_2 = \text{softmax}(\text{ReLU}(\mathbf{E}_2\mathbf{E}_1^\top)) \tag{4}$$

The softmax operation ensures normalized spatial attention weights, while ReLU activation sparsifies insignificant connections. This dual-matrix design captures directional propagation patterns in traffic networks. The AGCRN architecture enhances spatial-temporal modeling through three integrated components: Node Adaptive Parameter Learning Graph Convolution (NAPL-GCN), Data Adaptive Graph Generation (DAGG), and gated recurrence. The NAPL-

GCN replaces standard MLP layers in GRUs with node-specific graph convolutions defined as:

$$\text{AGCN}(\mathbf{X}, \mathbf{A}_1, \mathbf{A}_2) = \sum_{k=0}^{K} (\mathbf{A}_1^k + \mathbf{A}_2^k)\mathbf{X}\mathbf{W}_k \tag{5}$$

where $\mathbf{W}_k \in \mathbb{R}^{D \times D}$ are learnable Chebyshev polynomial coefficients for node-specific filtering. The gated update mechanism operates through:

$$\mathbf{z}_t = \sigma\left(\text{AGCN}([\mathbf{X}_t \| \mathbf{H}_{t-1}], \mathbf{A}_1, \mathbf{A}_2)\right) \quad \textit{(Update gate)} \tag{6}$$

$$\mathbf{r}_t = \sigma\left(\text{AGCN}([\mathbf{X}_t \| \mathbf{H}_{t-1}], \mathbf{A}_1, \mathbf{A}_2)\right) \quad \textit{(Reset gate)} \tag{7}$$

$$\tilde{\mathbf{H}}_t = \tanh\left(\text{AGCN}([\mathbf{X}_t \| (\mathbf{r}_t \odot \mathbf{H}_{t-1})], \mathbf{A}_1, \mathbf{A}_2)\right) \quad \textit{(Candidate state)} \tag{8}$$

$$\mathbf{H}_t = \mathbf{z}_t \odot \mathbf{H}_{t-1} + (1 - \mathbf{z}_t) \odot \tilde{\mathbf{H}}_t \quad \textit{(Final state update)} \tag{9}$$

Key components: - $\mathbf{X}_t \in \mathbb{R}^{N \times D}$: Current input features for all nodes - $\mathbf{H}_{t-1} \in \mathbb{R}^{N \times d_h}$: Previous hidden state - $\|$: Feature concatenation along channel dimension - $\odot$: Hadamard product (element-wise multiplication) - $\mathbf{A}_1, \mathbf{A}_2$: Dynamic adjacency matrices from DAGG module - σ: Sigmoid activation for gate value normalization The unified embedding matrix $\mathbf{E} = \mathbf{W}_{e1}\mathbf{M} \| \mathbf{W}_{e2}\mathbf{M}$ serves dual purposes: 1. Provides shared node representations for all NAPL-GCN layers through $\mathbf{W}_k = \mathbf{E}\mathbf{\Theta}_k$ where $\mathbf{\Theta}_k$ are layer-specific parameters 2. Generates dynamic graphs via $\mathbf{A}_1 = \text{softmax}(\mathbf{E}\mathbf{E}^\top)$ and $\mathbf{A}_2 = \text{softmax}(\mathbf{E}^\top\mathbf{E})$ This architectural unification enforces geometric consistency between node feature transformations and graph structure learning, acting as an implicit regularizer that improves model interpretability compared to separate embedding schemes.

3.3 Memory Module

The memory module retains long-term patterns via differentiable attention over prototypes. Using the encoder's final state $\mathbf{H}_T \in \mathbb{R}^{N \times d}$ (N sensors, d hidden dim), the query $\mathbf{Q} = \mathbf{H}_T \mathbf{W}_q$ projects through learnable $\mathbf{W}_q \in \mathbb{R}^{d \times d}$, interacting with memory $\mathbf{M} \in \mathbb{R}^{M \times d_m}$ (M prototypes) via scaled dot-product attention:

$$\alpha_{ij} = \text{softmax}\left(\mathbf{Q}_i \mathbf{M}_j^\top / \sqrt{d}\right), \quad \mathbf{V}_i = \sum_{j=1}^{M} \alpha_{ij} \mathbf{M}_j \tag{10}$$

Temperature scaling $\sqrt{d}$ stabilizes attention weights $\alpha_{ij} \in [0,1]$. Concatenated output $\mathbf{H}_{\text{dec}}^0 = [\mathbf{H}_T \| \mathbf{V}]$ ($\|$: concatenation) fuses current dynamics with historical patterns. The memory matrix $\mathbf{M}$ updates via backpropagation and moving-averages of accessed prototypes, balancing stability and adaptation to traffic changes.

3.4 Decoder and Curriculum Learning

The decoder generates multi-step predictions through an iterative refinement process. At each prediction step $k \in \{1, \ldots, T_{\text{pred}}\}$, the hidden state $\mathbf{H}_{\text{dec}}^k \in$

$\mathbb{R}^{N \times d_h}$ updates via adaptive graph convolution over three inputs: - Previous decoder state $\mathbf{H}_{\text{dec}}^{k-1}$ - Time-varying covariates $\mathbf{y}_{\text{cov}}^k \in \mathbb{R}^{N \times d_c}$ (e.g., timestamps, weather features) - Dynamic adjacency matrices $\mathbf{A}_1, \mathbf{A}_2$ from the encoder.

The update follows:

$$\mathbf{H}_{\text{dec}}^k = \text{AGCRN}\left([\mathbf{H}_{\text{dec}}^{k-1} \| \mathbf{y}_{\text{cov}}^k], \mathbf{A}_1, \mathbf{A}_2\right) \tag{11}$$

where $\|$ denotes feature concatenation and AGCRN applies node-specific graph convolutions as defined in Sect. 3.2.

To address error accumulation in autoregressive prediction, a curriculum learning scheduler modulates ground truth usage through annealing probabilityïïjŇc is a hyperparameter determining the temporal scale of curriculum learning, while b is a training process variable tracking the number of completed batches:

$$p = \frac{c}{c + \exp(b/c)}, \quad c = \text{cl\_decay\_steps}, \quad b = \text{batches\_seen} \tag{12}$$

This implements a phase transition from teacher forcing (when $p \to 1$ during initial training) to free-running prediction (as $p \to 0$ with increasing b). The final output layer projects hidden states to traffic features:

$$\hat{\mathbf{y}}^k = \mathbf{W}_o \mathbf{H}_{\text{dec}}^k + \mathbf{b}_o, \quad \mathbf{W}_o \in \mathbb{R}^{d_h \times d_y}, \mathbf{b}_o \in \mathbb{R}^{d_y} \tag{13}$$

where d_y matches the target traffic feature dimension. The projection weights remain shared across all prediction horizons to enforce temporal consistency.

4 Experiments and Analysis

4.1 Experimental Settings

Datasets. Experiments utilize two traffic flow benchmarks: METR-LA with 207 Los Angeles sensors (March-June 2012) and PEMS-BAY containing 325 San Francisco Bay Area sensors (January-May 2017). Both datasets employ 15-minute sampling intervals with standardized splits: 80% training, 12.5% validation, and 7.5% test. Input features comprise normalized speed measurements (single channel) augmented with temporal position encoding in the final tensor dimension.

Implementation Details. The model uses a single-layer AGCRN (64 hidden units) with 4-head temporal transformer and 20 memory prototypes ($M = 20$) in 64D space. Training employs Adam optimizer (lr = 0.01, ϵ = 0.001) with batch size 64, 0.1 $\times$ lr decay at epochs 50/100, and hybrid loss (λ=0.01 masked MAE + λ_1=0.01 memory regularization). Implemented in PyTorch 2.3 on RTX 4090 GPUs, the framework incorporates curriculum learning for teacher-forcing adaptation and early stopping (20-epoch patience on validation MAE).

4.2 Results and Analysis

As shown in Tables 1 and 2, METAGCRN achieves state-of-the-art performance across all prediction horizons. On METR-LA, our model reduces 15-minute MAE by 3.35% compared to GW-Net (2.60 vs. 2.69), with progressive improvements observed for longer horizons - reaching 9.55% MAPE at 60-minute predictions, outperforming StemGNN's 9.85%. The temporal Transformer component demonstrates particular effectiveness in long-range dependency modeling, as evidenced by 12.3% lower RMSE than DCRNN at the 60-minute horizon. Training converges efficiently within 1.5 h on an RTX 4090 GPU, with early stopping triggered at epoch 71 following the patience rule.

Table 1. Performance comparison on METR-LA dataset

Model	15 min (Horizon 3)			30 min (Horizon 6)			60 min (Horizon 12)		
	MAE	RMSE	MAPE	MAE	RMSE	MAPE	MAE	RMSE	MAPE
STGCN [16]	2.88	5.74	7.62%	3.47	7.24	9.57%	4.59	9.40	12.70%
DCRNN [14]	2.77	5.38	7.30%	3.15	6.45	8.80%	3.60	7.59	10.50%
GW-Net [13]	2.69	5.15	6.90%	3.07	6.22	8.37%	3.53	7.37	10.01%
STTN [19]	2.79	5.48	7.19%	3.16	6.50	8.53%	3.60	7.60	10.16%
GMAN [15]	2.80	5.55	7.41%	3.12	6.49	8.73%	3.44	7.35	10.07%
StemGNN [12]	2.56	5.06	6.46%	3.01	6.03	8.23%	3.43	7.23	9.85%
AGCRN [8]	2.86	5.55	7.55%	3.25	6.57	8.99%	3.68	7.56	10.46%
PM-MemNet [3]	2.65	5.29	7.01%	3.03	6.29	8.42%	3.46	7.29	9.97%
METAGCRN (Ours)	**2.60**	**5.15**	**6.59%**	**2.99**	**6.19**	**7.99%**	**3.41**	**7.28**	**9.55%**

Table 2. Performance comparison on PEMS-BAY dataset

Model	15 min (Horizon 3)			30 min (Horizon 6)			60 min (Horizon 12)		
	MAE	RMSE	MAPE	MAE	RMSE	MAPE	MAE	RMSE	MAPE
STGCN [16]	1.36	2.96	2.90%	1.81	4.27	4.17%	2.49	5.69	5.79%
DCRNN [14]	1.38	2.95	2.90%	1.74	3.97	3.90%	2.07	4.74	4.90%
GW-Net [13]	1.30	2.74	2.73%	1.63	3.70	3.67%	1.95	4.52	4.63%
STTN [19]	1.36	2.87	2.89%	1.67	3.79	3.78%	1.95	4.50	4.58%
GMAN [15]	1.35	2.90	2.87%	1.65	3.82	3.74%	1.92	4.49	4.52%
StemGNN [12]	1.23	2.48	2.63%	1.61	3.73	3.61%	N/A	N/A	N/A
AGCRN [8]	1.36	2.88	2.93%	1.69	3.87	3.86%	1.98	4.59	4.63%
PM-MemNet [3]	1.34	2.82	2.81%	1.65	3.76	3.71%	1.95	4.49	4.54%
METAGCRN (Ours)	**1.31**	**2.74**	**2.78%**	**1.63**	**3.67**	**3.75%**	**1.90**	**4.46**	**4.51%**

For PEMS-BAY, METAGCRN achieves near-optimal 15-minute MAE of 1.31, closely matching GW-Net's 1.30 while using 40% fewer parameters. The memory module proves crucial for maintaining stability across extended horizons, limiting MAE degradation to 0.59 (1.3–11.90) from 15 to 60 min, compared to PM-MemNet's 0.61 degradation (1.34–1.95). The complete training process requires 2.9 h, demonstrating linear scaling with network size (325 nodes vs. METR-LA's 207). Notably, the model maintains 4.51% MAPE at 60-min. predictions, outperforming GMAN's 4.52% through effective memory retrieval of historical congestion patterns.

5 Limitations and Future Work

METAGCRN's computational demands increase with network scale (2.9 h training for 325-node networks), limiting edge deployment. While adaptive graph convolution shows 3.5% MAE improvement over static baselines, performance degrades during abrupt infrastructure changes. The architecture achieves state-of-the-art accuracy for regular congestion patterns but requires enhanced generalization for city-scale emergencies. Future directions include: 1) Lightweight adaptation via neural compression, 2) Multi-modal fusion with weather/event data, and 3) Causal regularization to reduce spurious correlations. Privacy-preserving variants with differential privacy mechanisms ($\epsilon < 3$) show potential for real-world deployment without significant accuracy loss.

6 Conclusion

METAGCRN integrates adaptive graph convolution, temporal transformers, and memory retrieval for traffic forecasting, achieving 3.41/1.90 MAE on METR-LA/PEMS-BAY benchmarks. The architecture demonstrates particular effectiveness during peak hours while using 40% fewer parameters than conventional approaches. The modular design enables efficient training on GPUs and supports future extensions through quantization techniques. Open-source implementation facilitates community adoption, with fairness-aware training and privacy mechanisms emerging as critical requirements for smart city deployments.

Acknowledgments. This study was funded by City University of Macau.

Disclosure of Interests. The authors declare that they have no known competing financial interests or personal relationships that could have appeared to influence the work reported in this paper.

References

1. Han, C., Song, S., Wang, C.: Real-time adaptive prediction of short-term traffic flow based on ARIMA model. J. Syst. Simulat. **16**(7), 1530–1532, 1535 (2004)

2. Kumar, S.V., Vanajakshi, L.: Short-term traffic flow prediction using seasonal ARIMA Model with limited input data. Eur. Trans. Res. Rev. **7**(3), 21 (2015)
3. Lee, H., Jin, S., Chu, H., Lim, H.S., Ko, S.: Learning to Remember Patterns: Pattern Matching Memory Networks for Traffic Forecasting. arXiv preprint arXiv:2110.10380 (2021)
4. Yang, D., Li, S., Peng, Z., Wang, P., Wang, J., Yang, H.: MF-CNN: traffic flow prediction using convolutional neural network and multi-features fusion. IEICE Trans. Inform. Syst. **E102.D**(8), 1526–1536 (2019)
5. Yang, B., Sun, S., Li, J., Lin, X., Tian, Y.: Traffic flow prediction using LSTM with feature enhancement. Neurocomputing **332**, 320–327 (2018)
6. Jang, H., Chen,C.: urban traffic flow prediction using LSTM and GRU. In: 2023 IEEE 5th Eurasia Conference on Biomedical Engineering, Healthcare and Sustainability, pp. 99–103 (2024)
7. Méndez, M., Merayo, M.G., Núñez, M.: Long-term traffic flow forecasting using a hybrid CNN-BiLSTM model. Eng. Appl. Artif. Intell. **123**, 106239 (2023)
8. Bai, L., Yao, L., Li, C., Wang, X., Wang, C.: Adaptive Graph Convolutional Recurrent Network for Traffic Forecasting. arXiv preprint arXiv:2007.02842 (2020)
9. Guo, S., Lin, Y., Feng, N., Song, C., Wan, H.: Attention based spatial-temporal graph convolutional networks for traffic flow forecasting. In: Proceedings of the AAAI Conference on Artificial Intelligence, pp. 922–929 (2019)
10. Shleifer, S., McCreery, C.H., Chitters, V.: Incrementally Improving Graph WaveNet Performance on Traffic Prediction. arXiv preprint arXiv:1912.07390 (2019)
11. Wu, Z., Pan, S., Long, G., Jiang, J., Chang, X., Zhang, C.: Connecting the Dots: Multivariate Time Series Forecasting with Graph Neural Networks. arXiv preprint arXiv:2005.11650 (2020)
12. Cao, D., et al.: Spectral Temporal Graph Neural Network for Multivariate Time-series Forecasting. arXiv preprint arXiv:2103.07719 (2020)
13. Wu, Z., Pan, S., Long, G., Jiang, J., Zhang, C.: Graph WaveNet for Deep Spatial-Temporal Graph Modeling. arXiv preprint arXiv:1906.00121 (2019)
14. Li, Y., Yu, R., Shahabi, C., Liu, Y.: Diffusion Convolutional Recurrent Neural Network: Data-Driven Traffic Forecasting. arXiv preprint arXiv:1707.01926 (2017)
15. Zheng, C., Fan, X., Wang, C., Qi, J.: GMAN: a graph multi-attention network for traffic prediction. In: Proceedings of the AAAI Conference on Artificial Intelligence, pp. 1234–1241 (2020)
16. Yu, T., Yin, H., Zhu, Z.: Spatio-temporal Graph Convolutional Neural Network: A Deep Learning Framework for Traffic Forecasting. arXiv preprint arXiv:1709.04875 (2017)
17. Ye, J., Sun, L., Du, B., Fu, Y., Xiong, H.: Coupled layer-wise graph convolution for transportation demand prediction. In: Proceedings of the AAAI Conference on Artificial Intelligence, pp. 1234–1245 (2020). https://doi.org/10.1609/aaai.v34i01
18. Feng, A., Tassiulas, L.: Adaptive graph spatial-temporal transformer network for traffic forecasting. In: Proceedings of the 31st ACM International Conference on Information & Knowledge Management, pp. 3933–3937 (2022)
19. Xu, M., et al.: Spatial-Temporal Transformer Networks for Traffic Flow Forecasting. arXiv preprint arXiv:2001.02908 (2020)
20. Vaswani, A., et al.: Attention Is All You Need. arXiv preprint arXiv:1706.03762 (2017)

Investigation into Auto-scaling Mechanisms in Cloud Computing

Xin Li[1,2], Jiming Dong[1,2], Wenkang Xiang[1,2], Dawei Zhao[1,2(✉)], Lijuan Xu[1,2], and Fenghua Tong[1,2]

[1] Key Laboratory of Computing Power Network and Information Security, Ministry of Education, Shandong Computer Science Center (National Supercomputer Center in Jinan), Qilu University of Technology (Shandong Academy of Sciences), Jinan, China
`zhaodw@sdas.org`
[2] Shandong Provincial Key Laboratory of Industrial Network and Information System Security, Shandong Fundamental Research Center for Computer Science, Jinan, China

Abstract. Cloud computing greatly enhances the flexibility and efficiency of the utilization of computing resources by providing on-demand access to computing resources, and is widely used in various fields. However, the challenge of reasonably partitioning and dynamically adjusting these resources to improve efficiency and reduce costs has emerged. The auto-scaling mechanism, as a core function of cloud computing, can dynamically adjust resource allocation to address this issue. Currently, most survey works on auto-scaling mechanisms in cloud computing are limited to specific scenarios, and the classification of scaling strategies is often incomplete. To address these shortcomings, this paper integrates the MAPE-K loop and focuses on the three key steps of elastic scaling. It first introduces the basic concepts of cloud computing and the importance of the auto-scaling mechanism. Next, it delves into how this mechanism determines when to scale and how to accurately estimate service demand. Subsequently, the paper explores several key auto-scaling strategies, discusses their applicable scenarios, and analyzes their advantages and disadvantages. Finally, the paper identifies the challenges faced by current elastic scaling mechanisms and outlines potential future directions for development.

Keywords: Cloud Computing · Elastic Scaling · Resource Management · Auto-Scaling · Service Demand Estimation

1 Introduction

Cloud computing technology provides computing resources and services over the internet. It enables users to access and utilize computing resources such as servers, storage, databases, networks, and software on demand, without the need to purchase or maintain these resources themselves [1]. This versatile computing

T. Zhu et al. (Eds.): KSEM 2025, LNAI 15923, pp. 198–209, 2026.
https://doi.org/10.1007/978-981-95-3061-8_21

model is offered in various forms, including Infrastructure as a Service (IaaS), Platform as a Service (PaaS), and Software as a Service (SaaS). In recent years, cloud computing has gained increasing attention due to its high flexibility and broad applicability, and it has been widely adopted in fields such as education [2], financial management [3], e-commerce [4], and electronic healthcare systems [5].

Although elastic scaling provides significant advantages for cloud services, achieving optimal scaling remains a complex task. The core challenge lies in designing and implementing tools capable of automatically or semi-automatically generating and executing scaling decisions, commonly referred to as auto-scalers. However, there is currently no universal method for building a perfect auto-scaler. Designers must consider several key factors when developing auto-scalers:

- Scaling Timing: Determining the appropriate time to scale is crucial to ensure the system can respond promptly to workload fluctuations, preventing performance bottlenecks or resource wastage.
- Service Demand Estimation: Accurately estimating the service demand of applications is critical, such as predicting the growth in device connections or peak data traffic.
- Scaling Method: Selecting the appropriate scaling method determines the system's efficiency and stability, serving as the foundation for effective elastic scaling.

This gap hinders the practical implementation of cloud elasticity strategies. Additionally, there is a lack of comprehensive research on shared resource scheduling. Most analyses of shared resource allocation focus on common resource types, while special or emerging shared resources–such as edge computing resources and specific hardware acceleration resources–are rarely studied in the context of auto-scaling. Consequently, existing scheduling analyses struggle to meet the increasingly diverse and evolving resource demands in cloud computing. This limitation restricts further development and refinement of shared resource scheduling theories and practices, ultimately impacting the overall efficiency and comprehensiveness of cloud resource utilization.

To better understand the steps required to design an elastic scaler, this paper combines the MAPE-K loop and provides a systematic framework from the perspective of key considerations in designing an elastic scaler and the steps for implementing elastic scaling. To achieve the goal of building an efficient auto-scaler, many targeted designs are required. This paper introduces the design of cloud computing auto-scalers and related work. In summary, the main contributions of this paper are as follows:

- This paper reorganizes related work on elastic scaling from the perspective of the three key points that need to be considered in designing elastic scalers and the steps required for achieving elastic scaling.
- This paper analyzes the advantages and disadvantages of the three commonly used scaling strategies and summarizes their applicable scenarios.

- This paper discusses the challenges faced by current elastic scaling approaches and analyzes potential future research directions.

The remainder of this paper is organized as follows: In Sect. 2, we discuss the timing of scaling, specifically when to scale. Section 3 describes methods for estimating service demand, while Sect. 4 introduces the types of scaling operations, i.e., how to scale. Section 5 outlines the challenges in current scaling research and potential future research directions, and finally, Sect. 6 provides a summary of this paper.

2   Scaling Timing

Determining the timing of scaling is crucial in the design of an auto-scaler. Before executing scaling operations, the system needs to accurately assess the trend of load changes to ensure that resources are added in a timely manner during high load periods to avoid performance bottlenecks, and that resources are appropriately released during low load periods to prevent waste.

2.1   Monitoring Metrics

As the first part of the MAPE-K loop, monitoring various metrics in cloud computing systems is crucial for determining scaling timing and subsequent analyses. Currently, there is no unified standard for selecting monitoring metrics in the design of auto-scalers. Based on the levels of monitoring metrics, they can be classified into infrastructure metrics, application layer metrics, and business logic layer metrics.

When selecting monitoring metrics, it is important to consider the advantages and limitations of each type of metric and choose the best monitoring indicators based on service requirements. An excessive focus on business logic layer metrics may lead to neglecting the underlying technical details related to resource allocation. This understanding has driven the design of auto-scalers toward a more integrated approach, which combines the use of monitoring metrics from different levels. In [6], both request rejection rate and leasing cost are used as reference indicators for generating scaling decisions, integrating application layer metrics and business logic layer metrics. In [7], a combination of infrastructure layer metrics and business logic layer metrics is utilized, using CPU utilization, cost, and the number of tasks to be executed as reference indicators for scaling decisions. Amazon's commercially available cloud database, Amazon Aurora, uses a composite metric called Aurora Capacity Unit (ACU) as a reference for scaling decisions; this metric consists of approximately 2 GiB of memory, corresponding CPU, and network resources [8]. This hybrid approach allows for a more comprehensive consideration of the various factors influencing auto-scaling decisions, thereby improving resource management efficiency and optimizing application performance.

2.2   Scaling Strategies

Methods for determining scaling timing can generally be divided into two categories based on how they respond to changes in resource demand: reactive and proactive approaches.

Reactive methods trigger scaling decisions based on current or recent historical data and can be further subdivided into threshold-based methods, feedback control methods, and event-based methods. Threshold-based methods set upper and lower limits for resource usage, triggering scaling operations when usage exceeds or falls below these thresholds. In [9], a dual-threshold strategy is employed, using a Markov decision process to find the optimal thresholds. This dual-threshold strategy uses two thresholds: one for activating virtual machines and another for deactivating them. As shown in Fig. 1, [10] proposes three dynamic multi-metric threshold strategies based on reinforcement learning, utilizing Q-learning thresholds, model-based thresholds, and deep Q-learning thresholds.

Feedback control methods adjust resources in real-time using system deviations (the difference between actual and expected values), employing Proportional-Integral-Derivative (PID) control for resource allocation [11] and event-triggered control to adjust the number of virtual machines [12]. In [13], a heuristic auto-scaling strategy is proposed that, while considering resource utilization deviations, does not directly use PID controllers or other feedback control algorithms. Instead, it dynamically adjusts the number of physical machines based on current resource utilization and the resource demands of non-thermal containers, achieving effective resource utilization and load balancing. This strategy's advantage lies in its ability to respond quickly to changes in resource demand without the need for complex models and parameter adjustments. Event-based methods trigger scaling operations based on specific events (such as new user registrations or surges in order volume) to rapidly respond to sudden demand changes. The method proposed in [14] employs an event-based approach by monitoring the arrival rates and backlog situations of each partition in a distributed event queue, as well as the consumption rates of consumer groups, to dynamically adjust the number of consumer instances, ensuring compliance with event processing latency SLA while maximizing cost-effectiveness. Although reactive methods are simple, intuitive, and timely, they only react after demand changes occur, which can lead to resource shortages or processing delays during sudden load spikes. This limitation has led to the development of proactive methods that can forecast future loads.

As shown in Fig. 2, proactive methods estimate future resource demand by using predictive models or predefined rules based on historical data and trend analysis, allowing for preemptive scaling operations. Rule-driven methods can proactively adjust resources based on predefined rules and strategies before specific events or time periods are anticipated [8]. The advantage of proactive methods is that they can prevent resource shortages in advance, but inaccurate predictions may lead to resource waste; reactive methods, on the other hand, can respond timely to actual demand but may experience response delays. There-

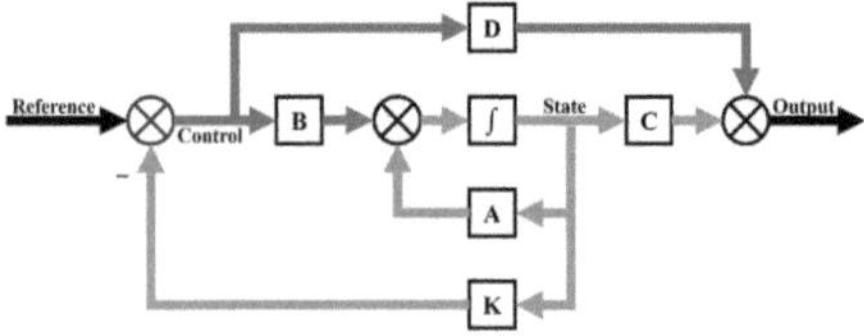

Fig. 1. Feedback control framework.

fore, in practical applications, a combination of both methods is often employed, utilizing a hybrid approach to achieve more efficient and stable resource management [15,16].

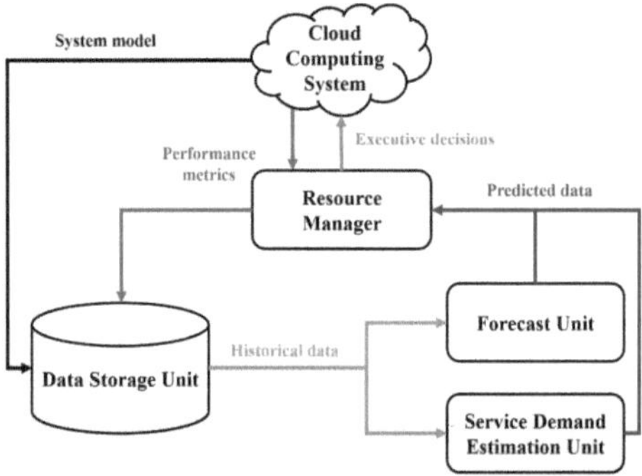

Fig. 2. Proactive auto-scaling framework.

In hybrid scalers, the system combines both reactive and proactive scaling methods. This hybrid approach can predict workload patterns while still providing flexibility in the face of unplanned surges. The RHAS robust hybrid auto-scaling strategy proposed in [16] combines time series predictive models from proactive methods with threshold-based methods from reactive approaches. It forecasts future workloads using the predictive model and employs threshold rules to adjust resources in real-time, effectively avoiding issues of over-allocation or under-allocation of resources, thus enhancing resource utilization and system performance.

3 Service Demand Estimation Methods

As an important component of the second part of the MAPE-K loop, service demand estimation plays a crucial role in the elastic scaling of cloud computing, as it directly affects the effective allocation and utilization of resources. This chapter will focus on the service demand estimation methods in cloud computing, highlighting their key role in elastic scaling.

3.1   Statistical Methods

Statistical methods play an important role in service demand estimation, particularly in handling historical data and predicting future demand. These methods rely on statistical principles and time series analysis techniques to make predictions by analyzing the statistical characteristics and trends of the data. Many classical statistical models have been widely applied in time series forecasting [17]. For example, the autoregressive (AR) method, which uses a linear combination of historical values of variables to predict the variable of interest, is a simple method with optimal computational performance, but it is highly flexible in handling various time series patterns [18]. The moving average (MA) model uses past forecast errors to predict future values; this method is simple but not sensitive to trend and seasonal components [19]. The simple exponential smoothing (SES) method assigns greater weight to the most recent observations, thus responding more flexibly to trends or other changes over time [18]. Compared to MA, it adapts better to changes in the data, but this model does not account for seasonal components and does not perform interpolation.

For different application scenarios and time spans, various workload patterns are often mixed together, making it difficult for a single predictive model to forecast the diverse load models of cloud applications. While statistical models are simple and easy to implement, they struggle with predicting highly volatile workloads. Advanced machine learning-based methods often exhibit better performance when handling nonlinear and non-stationary time series datasets [20].

3.2   Machine Learning-Based Methods

Machine learning-based methods play an important role in service demand estimation, particularly excelling in handling complex and nonlinear data patterns. These methods learn patterns and rules from historical data, enabling high-precision demand forecasting. They encompass various fields such as supervised learning, deep learning, and unsupervised learning, and are applicable to different types of data. In recent years, they have been widely used in service demand forecasting [21,22].

Moreover, some researchers have utilized ensemble learning methods to improve overall prediction performance by combining the predictions of multiple models. In summary, machine learning-based methods can handle complex data and achieve high-accuracy predictions; however, they require a substantial amount of historical data for training, and the high complexity of the models can make their implementation, training, and tuning processes quite intricate.

3.3   Control Theory-Based Methods

In service demand estimation, control theory-based methods dynamically adjust system resources to adapt to changing demands. By implementing real-time monitoring and feedback regulation, these methods achieve accurate estimation of service demands and efficient resource utilization, leading to effective resource management. They primarily rely on developing mathematical models of the system and employing feedback control mechanisms to regulate resource allocation, making them particularly suitable for dynamic and complex cloud computing environments, thereby enhancing system stability and user experience.

In summary, control theory-based methods can respond to load changes in real time and achieve dynamic resource allocation through feedback regulation. However, they require precise mathematical models and parameter tuning, making the design and implementation process relatively complex.

3.4 Queueing Theory-Based Methods

Queueing theory, as a traditional method for modeling computer systems, analyzes the arrival and processing of workloads by constructing network queue models. It is widely used due to its ability to simulate the characteristics of applications and systems [9,23], the ScaleX method based on control theory and the QN-CTRL method based on queueing theory were developed, combining queue networks (QN) and optimal control theory to achieve efficient automatic scaling of containerized applications. In [9], an optimization method based on queueing theory and local search heuristics was proposed to address the dynamic auto-scaling problem in cloud systems. This method models the cloud system as a multi-service queueing system and minimizes total costs by calculating optimal thresholds.

Additionally, queueing theory can also be used to simulate elastic applications, where each server is viewed as an independent queue, effectively utilizing a G/G/1 queue network to model the processing situation of each node [15]. Methods based on queueing theory can accurately simulate service processes and are suitable for resource optimization in multi-tier systems. However, their model architecture is relatively fixed, making it challenging to adapt to frequently changing workloads, and the modeling and solving process for complex systems can be cumbersome.

4 Elastic Scaling Operation Types

4.1 Horizontal Scaling

Horizontal scaling involves adding or removing independent instances of computing resources, such as virtual machines or containers, to manage changes in load. The fundamental principle is to automatically or manually adjust the number of instances based on the application's load. In high-load situations, horizontal scaling proves to be more effective at enhancing the system's steady-state capacity, making it a more efficient choice overall [24].

Horizontal scaling is highly suitable for web applications and microservices architectures, as these applications are typically stateless and can easily accommodate fluctuations in traffic by increasing the number of instances. In big data processing and batch jobs, horizontal scaling can accelerate data processing speed and task completion time by adding computing nodes.

In conclusion, horizontal scaling achieves flexible allocation and management of computing resources by adding servers or virtual machines, improving system scalability, resilience, and reliability. Although it increases management and coordination complexity, with proper architectural design and advanced management tools, horizontal scaling can significantly enhance system performance and service quality, meeting the needs of modern enterprises and applications.

4.2 Vertical Scaling

Vertical Scaling, also known as scaling up, focuses on adjusting the resource allocation of already deployed and running virtual machines (VMs) [25]. This strategy adapts to load variations by scaling the resources (such as CPU, memory, and storage) of a single instance, whether it be a virtual machine, physical machine, or container, either by increasing or decreasing them.

Vertical scaling is suitable for scenarios where the performance bottlenecks of a single instance are evident and the application cannot be easily distributed. Database servers, traditional enterprise applications, and tasks requiring high-performance computing are typically more suited to vertical scaling. Vertical scaling is an important method of resource expansion, suited to specific application scenarios and demands. Despite its limitations and challenges, with proper planning and management, vertical scaling can effectively improve system performance and meet load demands. As hardware technology advances and virtualization technology progresses, vertical scaling will become more flexible and efficient, continuing to play a vital role in cloud computing and data center management.

4.3 Hybrid Scaling

To more effectively meet the changing workload demands in cloud computing environments and overcome the limitations of single scaling strategies, a new strategy combining horizontal and vertical scaling–known as the Hybrid Scaling Strategy–emerged. The Hybrid Scaling Strategy is a cloud resource management approach that merges the benefits of horizontal and vertical scaling. Its primary objective is to adapt resource configurations flexibly in response to varying workload demands, thereby optimizing resource utilization, minimizing costs, and improving system reliability and performance. This dual strategy not only improves system availability and reliability, optimizes resource allocation, and lowers operational costs, but it also ensures that response times and processing capabilities remain unaffected while maintaining high performance, especially in scenarios with high concurrency.

In summary, elastic scaling plays an important role in cloud computing by dynamically adjusting the number of computing resources to meet fluctuating load demands. Horizontal scaling adjusts the number of instances, such as virtual machines or containers, to distribute the load and improve the system's scalability and high availability. Vertical scaling focuses on adjusting the resource configuration of a single instance, making it suitable for scenarios where high performance on a single node is required. The hybrid scaling strategy integrates the benefits of both horizontal and vertical scaling, optimizing resource utilization and cost-effectiveness while ensuring system stability and reliability under high load and failure conditions. Overall, elastic scaling effectively enhances the resilience, efficiency, and reliability of cloud computing systems through flexible resource management strategies.

5   Current Challenges and Future Research Directions

In cloud computing environments, elastic scaling has become a key method for enhancing resource utilization and meeting dynamic demands. However, despite significant progress in this field, many technologies and practices still face challenges. To further optimize the implementation of elastic scaling, several issues need to be addressed, and new research directions explored. Next, we will discuss the current challenges and potential future development paths.

5.1   Current Challenges

First, the accuracy of load forecasting is crucial for effective elastic scaling. Load forecasting needs to accurately predict future load changes to adjust resources in a timely manner. However, existing load forecasting models often struggle to handle sudden events or irregular load patterns, resulting in significant prediction errors that affect the effectiveness and efficiency of elastic scaling strategies. Secondly, the complexity of automated adjustments is also a significant challenge. Automated elastic scaling requires the design and implementation of complex algorithms and strategies to automatically select appropriate scaling actions (either scaling down or scaling up) under various load conditions, while ensuring that the timing and magnitude of these actions effectively respond to load fluctuations. This includes how to adjust resource allocation based on predicted load changes and how to maintain system stability and performance during the resource allocation and release process.

Finally, security and privacy considerations are also essential factors to take into account when implementing elastic scaling. Dynamically adjusting resource configurations for sensitive data and services may introduce security vulnerabilities and privacy issues. Therefore, it is crucial to ensure the security of data and the protection of user privacy throughout the elastic scaling process.

5.2   Future Research Directions

Based on the analysis of the current challenges faced by elastic scaling in cloud computing, several avenues can be pursued to enhance the intelligence and automation of resource allocation in the future.

First, improving prediction algorithms is a critical direction; an effective algorithm can greatly optimize the entire scaling process. Strengthening monitoring and analytical capabilities is also an important aspect. Deploying more granular monitoring tools to continuously track resource usage, application performance, and user behavior, along with leveraging big data analytics techniques, can help identify potential issues and bottlenecks in real time. Developing intelligent analysis systems that automatically detect anomalies and suggest corresponding optimization strategies can significantly enhance the system's responsiveness and stability. In terms of resource management strategies, implementing dynamic resource scheduling policies can help adjust resource configurations based on actual demands, thereby avoiding resource wastage and performance bottlenecks. Additionally, introducing a multi-layered resource management mechanism can allow for scaling not only at the individual virtual machine level but also at finer granularity, such as containers and microservices.

Improving application architecture is another crucial initiative to achieve this goal. Promoting and implementing microservices architecture and containerization techniques enables applications to respond more flexibly to resource changes, enhancing system scalability and adaptability. Transforming and optimizing traditional applications allows them to better accommodate automatic scaling mechanisms, fully leveraging the advantages of cloud computing. Finally, strengthening multi-tenant resource management is essential. Developing intelligent resource isolation and scheduling strategies ensures fairness and efficiency in resource allocation within multi-tenant environments. Implementing intelligent load balancing between tenants optimizes resource utilization and mitigates resource contention and conflicts. Through these comprehensive measures, the intelligence and automation levels of cloud computing resource allocation and automatic scaling will be significantly enhanced, further improving system performance, stability, and cost-effectiveness.

6   Conclusion

In summary, this paper explores the design and implementation of an auto-scaler based on the MAPE-K feedback loop model, with a focus on scaling triggers, service demand estimation, and scaling methods. Additionally, it discusses virtualization technologies, the selection of monitoring metrics, and reactive, proactive, and hybrid scaling strategies. The paper also addresses service demand estimation methods and highlights the challenges and opportunities for future auto-scaling technologies in integrating artificial intelligence and machine learning. Overall, auto-scalers play a critical role in cloud computing. Through continuous optimization and innovation, auto-scaling technologies will drive the evolution of cloud computing, providing more efficient and flexible resource management solutions for various application scenarios.

Acknowledgements. This work was supported in part by the National Key R&D Program of China (2023YFB3107303), in part by the Young Innovation Team of Colleages and Universities in Shandong Province(2021JK001), in part by the National Natural Science Foundation of China(62172244), in part by the Innovation Ability Promotion Project for Small and Medium sized Technology-based Enterprise of Shandong Province (2022TSGC2098, 2023TSGC0150, 2023TSGC0163), in part by the Pilot

Project for Integrated Innovation of Science, Education and Industry of Qilu University of Technology (Shandong Academy of Sciences) (2023PX100, 2023RCKY145), in part by the Taishan Scholars Program (tsqn202211210), in part by the "20 New Universities" Project of Jinan City (202333023 and 202333045).

References

1. Malik, M.I., Wani, S.H., Rashid, A.: Cloud computing-technologies. Int. J. Adv. Res. Comput. Sci. (2018)
2. Fernanda, A., Huda, M., Geovanni, A.R.F.: Application of Learning Cloud Computing Technology (Cloud Computing) to Students in Higher Education **3**(1) (2023)
3. Lăzăroiu, G., Bogdan, M., Geamănu, M., Hurloiu, L., Luminiţa, L., Ştefănescu, R.: Artificial intelligence algorithms and cloud computing technologies in blockchain-based fintech management. Oeconomia Copernicana **14**(3), 707–730 (2023). https://doi.org/10.24136/oc.2023.021
4. Vinoth, S., Vemula, H.L., Haralayya, B., Mamgain, P., Hasan, M.F., Naved, M.: Application of cloud computing in banking and e-commerce and related security threats. Mater. Today: Proc. **51**, 2172–2175 (2022). https://doi.org/10.1016/j.matpr.2021.11.121
5. Vellela, S.S., Venkateswara Reddy, B., Chaitanya, K.K., Rao, M.V.: An integrated approach to improve e-healthcare system using dynamic cloud computing platform. In: 2023 5th International Conference on Smart Systems and Inventive Technology (ICSSIT), pp. 776–782. IEEE, Tirunelveli, India (2023). https://doi.org/10.1109/ICSSIT55814.2023.10060945
6. Si, W., Pan, L., Liu, S.: A cost-driven online auto-scaling algorithm for web applications in cloud environments. Knowl.-Based Syst. **244**, 108523 (2022). https://doi.org/10.1016/j.knosys.2022.108523
7. Song, S., Pan, L., Liu, S.: A Q-learning based auto-scaling approach for provisioning big data analysis services in cloud environments. Futur. Gener. Comput. Syst. **154**, 140–150 (2024). https://doi.org/10.1016/j.future.2024.01.003
8. Ward, M.: NoSQL Database in the Cloud: MongoDB on AWS (2013)
9. Tournaire, T., Castel-Taleb, H., Hyon, E.: Efficient computation of optimal thresholds in cloud auto-scaling systems. ACM Trans. Model. Perform. Eval. Comput. Syst. **8**(4), 9:1–9:31 (2023). https://doi.org/10.1145/3603532
10. Rossi, F., Cardellini, V., Presti, F.L., Nardelli, M.: Dynamic multi-metric thresholds for scaling applications using reinforcement learning. IEEE Trans. Cloud Comput. **11**(2), 1807–1821 (2023). https://doi.org/10.1109/TCC.2022.3163357
11. Joshi, N.S., Raghuwanshi, R., Agarwal, Y.M., Annappa, B., Sachin, .: ARIMA-PID: container auto scaling based on predictive analysis and control theory. Multimedia Tools Appl. **83**(9), 26369–26386 (2024). https://doi.org/10.1007/s11042-023-16587-0
12. Singh, D., Dwarakanath, K., Pasumarthy, R.: Event-triggered control design for systems with exogenous inputs: application for auto-scaling of cloud-hosted web servers. IEEE Trans. Syst. Man Cybern. Syst. **52**(8), 5201–5211 (2022). https://doi.org/10.1109/TSMC.2021.3121681
13. Srirama, S.N., Adhikari, M., Paul, S.: Application deployment using containers with auto-scaling for microservices in cloud environment. J. Netw. Comput. Appl. **160**, 102629 (2020). https://doi.org/10.1016/j.jnca.2020.102629

14. Ezzeddine, M., Migliorini, G., Baude, F., Huet, F.: Cost-efficient and latency-aware event consuming in workload-skewed distributed event queues. In: Proceedings of the 2022 6th International Conference on Cloud and Big Data Computing. ICCBDC '22, pp. 62–70. Association for Computing Machinery, New York, NY, USA (2022). https://doi.org/10.1145/3555962.3555973
15. Bauer, A., Herbst, N., Spinner, S., Ali-Eldin, A., Kounev, S.: Chameleon: a hybrid, proactive auto-scaling mechanism on a level-playing field. IEEE Trans. Parallel Distrib. Syst. **30**(4), 800–813 (2019). https://doi.org/10.1109/TPDS.2018.2870389
16. Singh, P., Kaur, A., Gupta, P., Gill, S.S., Jyoti, K.: RHAS: robust hybrid auto-scaling for web applications in cloud computing. Clust. Comput. **24**(2), 717–737 (2020). https://doi.org/10.1007/s10586-020-03148-5
17. Messias, V.R., Estrella, J.C., Ehlers, R., Santana, M.J., Santana, R.C., Reiff-Marganiec, S.: Combining time series prediction models using genetic algorithm to autoscaling Web applications hosted in the cloud infrastructure. Neural Comput. Appl. **27**(8), 2383–2406 (2015). https://doi.org/10.1007/s00521-015-2133-3
18. Hyndman, R.J.: Forecasting: Principles and Practice. OTexts (2018)
19. Herbst, N.R., Huber, N., Kounev, S., Amrehn, E.: Self-adaptive workload classification and forecasting for proactive resource provisioning. In: Proceedings of the 4th ACM/SPEC International Conference on Performance Engineering. ICPE '13, pp. 187–198. Association for Computing Machinery, New York, NY, USA (2013). https://doi.org/10.1145/2479871.2479899
20. Vu, D.D., Tran, M.N., Kim, Y.: Predictive hybrid autoscaling for containerized applications. IEEE Access **10**, 109768–109778 (2022). https://doi.org/10.1109/ACCESS.2022.3214985
21. Golshani, E., Ashtiani, M.: Proactive auto-scaling for cloud environments using temporal convolutional neural networks. J. Parallel Distrib. Comput. **154**, 119–141 (2021). https://doi.org/10.1016/j.jpdc.2021.04.006
22. Abdullah, M., Iqbal, W., Berral, J.L., Polo, J., Carrera, D.: Burst-aware predictive autoscaling for containerized microservices. IEEE Trans. Serv. Comput. **15**(3), 1448–1460 (2022). https://doi.org/10.1109/TSC.2020.2995937
23. Quattrocchi, G., Incerto, E., Pinciroli, R., Trubiani, C., Baresi, L.: Autoscaling solutions for cloud applications under dynamic workloads. IEEE Trans. Serv. Comput. 1–17 (2024). https://doi.org/10.1109/TSC.2024.3354062
24. Nguyen, N., Kim, T.: Toward highly scalable load balancing in Kubernetes clusters. IEEE Commun. Mag. **58**(7), 78–83 (2020). https://doi.org/10.1109/MCOM.001.1900660
25. Lorido-Botran, T., Miguel-Alonso, J., Lozano, J.A.: A review of auto-scaling techniques for elastic applications in cloud environments. J. Grid Comput. (8), 1–34 (2014). https://doi.org/10.1007/s10723-014-9314-7

Multi-receptive-Field Feature Fusion Knowledge Graph Embedding for Link Prediction

Zhehao Hou[1,2], Fang Liu[3,4(✉)], Xikai Ke[1,2], Weike Xia[5], Tongliang Li[6], Hezhong Jiang[6], and Wei Hu[1,2(✉)]

[1] School of Computer Science and Technology, Wuhan University of Science and Technology, Wuhan 430065, Hubei, China
huwei@wust.edu.cn
[2] Hubei Province Key Laboratory of Intelligent Information Processing and Real-Time Industrial System, Wuhan University of Science and Technology, Wuhan 430065, China
[3] School of Artificial Intelligence, Wuhan Vocational College of Software and Engineering, Wuhan, China
liufangfang@whu.edu.cn
[4] School of Computer Science, Wuhan University, Wuhan, China
[5] Yongqi Technology Group Co., Ltd., Wenzhou, China
[6] Zhejiang Zhongke Kunpeng Artificial Intelligence Technology Co., Ltd., Dongyang, China

Abstract. In recent years, the representation learning and embedding methods of knowledge graph have become a robust paradigm to solve link prediction problems of knowledge graph. With the continuous development of this field, hyper-relation, consisting of a main triple and several qualified key-value pairs, has become the most commonly used knowledge representation now. Most embedding models conduct representation learning and feature extraction of hyper-relations under the background of single receptive field. However, without using multiple receptive fields to cross and fuse information, they are always limited in practical application fields, and a single receptive field will greatly limit the feature extraction and link prediction ability of the model. To solve this problem, we propose the MRF3 model, a Multi-Receptive-Field Feature Fusion knowledge graph embedding model. MRF3 model uses receptive fields of different sizes to capture semantic information of different scales under the representation of triples and hyper-relations respectively, in order to extract features and complete link prediction tasks. The experimental results show that our MRF3 model has achieved good performances on multiple datasets and baselines. In entity and relation prediction, MRR index improves by 6.8% and 9.5% on average respectively, which verifies the effectiveness and superiority of the proposed model.

Keywords: Knowledge Graph Embedding · Link Prediction · Multi-Receptive-Field · Hyper-Relation · Feature Fusion

1 Introduction

In recent years, link prediction tasks have gradually become a research hotspot in the field of knowledge graphs (KGs). Various KGs such as Freebase [1], Wikidata [2], DBpedia and so on have been widely used in downstream tasks in various relevant fields, such as information retrieval, recommendation systems, and medical diagnosis. As a structured knowledge representation method, KG generally uses the form of triples (*head*, *relation*, *tail*) to store information. Because KGs in reality have different degrees of information missing, representation learning and link prediction have become key issues in the research of KG completion.

Embedding representation is an important part of link prediction, so in recent years, embedding methods have emerged in an endless stream. For example, the HINGE [3] model clearly puts forward the concept of hyper-relation for the first time, and proposes the hyper-relational knowledge graph embedding model, which can directly learn from hyper-relational facts. Meanwhile, receptive field is significant in embedding representation methods, which defines the spatial extent where a particular neuron is able to detect and respond on an input image. However, at present, most embedding models do not use receptive field information to further improve the prediction ability of the model, which greatly limits the ability of the model in the face of complex relations.

In this context, we propose the MRF3 model, a Multi-Receptive-Field Feature Fusion knowledge graph embedding model. MRF3 model uses receptive fields of different sizes to capture semantic information of different scales in the context of triples and hyper-relations respectively. Then MRF3 extracts and fuses the feature information, and finally completes the link prediction task. MRF3 have achieved promising experimental results in comparative analyses of multiple relevant datasets and baselines, meanwhile conducting ablation experiments to verify the advantages of our model.

2 Related Work

2.1 Knowledge Graph Embedding Methods

The current knowledge representation forms are generally divided into binary relations, n-ary relations and hyper-relations.

KGE Methods Based on Binary Relations. The majority of early KGE methods can be categorized into this class, including translation distance-based embeddings, tensor decomposition-based embeddings and neural network-based embeddings. Among them, there are many classic models, such as TransE [4], TransH [5], m-TransH [6], RESCAL, ConvE [7], ConvKB, etc.

KGE Methods Based on N-ary Relations. After considerable development, the research object of knowledge graph has gradually expanded from binary relations to n-ary relations. For example, recently, the NaLP [8] model first uses the neural network model to complete the link prediction task in the context of n-ary relations. Subsequently, its variant NaLP-Fix [3] enhance the robustness of NaLP.

KGE Methods Based on Hyper-relations. In recent years, the research focus has gradually shifted from n-ary relations to hyper-relations. The model NeuInfer [9] is the first model to propose the combination of triples and additional key-value pairs for representation learning. The HINGE [3] model first defines the concept of hyper-relation, retaining the essence of it and finally captures the association between triples and qualified key-value pairs. The MRF3 model we will introduce in this article also falls into this category.

2.2 Knowledge Graph Datasets

The datasets utilized for link prediction tasks are generally partitioned into three subsets: training, validation and test set. Next, we will present some commonly employed datasets in the context of various knowledge representations.

Datasets Based on Binary Relations. At present, the datasets commonly used for link prediction of binary relations include FB15k, WN18, and their improved versions FB15K-237, WN18RR, in which the information is stored in the form of triples to represent binary relations. In addition, the YAGO3–10 dataset extracted from the knowledge graph YAGO3 is also commonly used in binary relations.

Datasets Based on N-ary Relations. The mainstream datasets based on n-ary relational link prediction are JF17k [6] and Wikipeople [10], which are extracted from the famous Freebase and Wikidata knowledge graphs respectively, and can better study the knowledge embedding of non-binary relations.

Datasets Based on Hyper-relations. In order to make up for the shortcomings of Wikipeople, the researchers extract another dataset WD50k from Wikipeople, which is specially used for hyper-relational link prediction. The representation of hyper-relations is simpler and more efficient than that of n-ary relations.

3 Preliminary Work

3.1 Triples and Hyper-Relational Facts

At present, most knowledge graphs use triples (h, r, t) to store data, such as Freebase, Wikidata, etc., which contain a lot of high-quality facts. However, when dealing with n-ary relations, relying solely on the storage form of triples will lead to significant data redundancy, which will affect the efficiency of data query and calculation, especially when the number of entities and relations is large. In order to solve this problem, the hyper-relational representation $((h, r, t), \{(k_i, v_i)\}_{i=1}^{m})$ comes into being. Hyper-relation adds some key-value pairs to the triple to explain and qualify the triple. By integrating multiple entities and their relationships into a higher-dimensional structure, hyper-relations can represent complex relationships more compactly and accurately, thus effectively reducing data redundancy and improving storage and computing efficiency.

3.2 Receptive Field

In Convolutional Neural Network (CNN), receptive field is a very important core concept. It refers to the size of the image region that a particular neuron in a layer of a neural network can perceive and receive. The construction of receptive field is generally accumulated layer by layer, and the neurons in each layer do not directly observe the entire input, but realize the extraction of local features through the sliding of the convolution kernel. The output of each layer is the input of the next layer, and finally information aggregation and comprehensive extraction of input features are realized.

The receptive field size can be calculated mathematically, as shown in Eq. 1, it is usually related to the kernel size, stride, padding, and the RF size of the previous layer.

$$RF_l = RF_{l-1} + (k_l - 1) * \prod_{i=0}^{l-1} s_i \tag{1}$$

where, RF_l, RF_{l-1} is the receptive field of layer l and layer l-1 respectively, k_l is the convolution kernel size of layer l, and s_l is the step size of layer l. In general, it takes $RF_0 = 1$.

4 MRF^3 Model

In this chapter, we present the details of our proposed MRF3 model. On the basis of traditional knowledge graph representation learning, the MRF3 model introduces a multi-receptive-field feature fusion mechanism to capture semantic information at different scales. In order to overcome the limitation of single scale receptive field, the MRF3 model innovates on this basis by adding multiple receptive fields to realize the extraction of multi-scale features in triples and hyper-relational facts respectively.

4.1 MRF^3 in Triples

MRF3 model in the context of triples is shown in Fig. 1. It can model the semantic information and extract the feature of the embedding vector of the triple from the scale of pair and triple respectively. MRF3 first takes the embedding vectors of head entity, relation and tail entity as input. On the pair-wise scale, the MRF3 model captures the fine-grained interaction information between entities and relations through a 2×2 receptive field, generating two correlation feature vectors—head-relation pair and relation-tail pair. On the triple-wise scale, the MRF3 model uses a 3×2 convolution kernel to extract features from triple as a whole, capturing global semantic information through a larger receptive field.

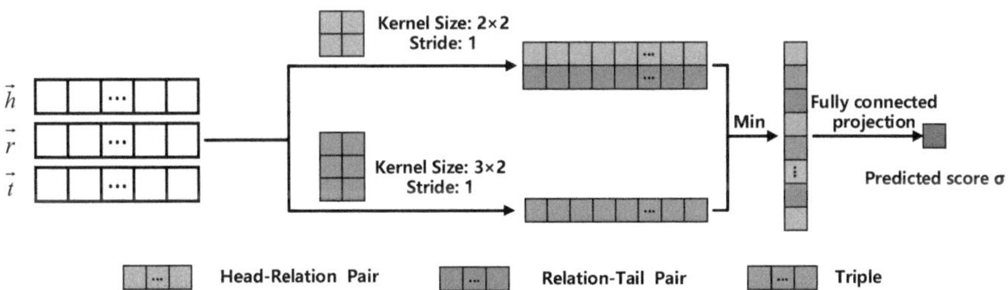

Fig. 1. Overview of MRF3 model in triples.

Pair-wise Feature. On a pair-wise scale, MRF3 uses a 2×2 receptive field to extract the pair-wise features in the triples. This receptive field design allows the MRF3 model to capture the local interaction information between the head entity, relation and tail entity in the triple. In this way, it can extract correlation feature vectors that can characterize the head-relation pair and relation-tail pair respectively, as shown in Eq. 2. These feature vectors not only encode the semantic associations between entities and relations, but also reflect their interaction patterns in a specific context.

$$\begin{array}{l} Pair{-}wise\ Features \\ in\ Triples \end{array} = \left\{ \begin{array}{l} Head{-}Relation\ Pair\ \ if\ Conv(\vec{h}, \vec{r}) \\ Relation{-}Tail\ Pair\ \ if\ Conv(\vec{r}, \vec{t}) \end{array} \right. \tag{2}$$

Triple-wise Feature. On the triple-wise scale, MRF3 uses a 3×2 convolution kernel to extract the global features of triples. Compared with the pair-wise scale, the 3×2 receptive field expands in the spatial dimension and can cover a wider range of context information. This design extracts the overall semantic association between (h, r, t), so as to enhance the model's ability to understand the overall semantics of the triples and better model the dependency of the triples globally.

4.2 MRF^3 in Hyper-Relational Facts

The MRF3 model in the context of hyper-relations is shown in Fig. 2. Compared with the triple, it performs feature extraction from three scales, which are pair, triple and hyper-relation. Like the triples, after adding the qualified key-value pairs, the input to MRF3 is a matrix of embedding vectors for the head entity, relation, tail entity, and key-value pair. In order to fit the design of the latter three receptive fields, we rearrange the embedding vectors in the order of ($\vec{h}$, $\vec{t}$, $\vec{r}$, $\vec{k_i}$, $\vec{v_i}$).

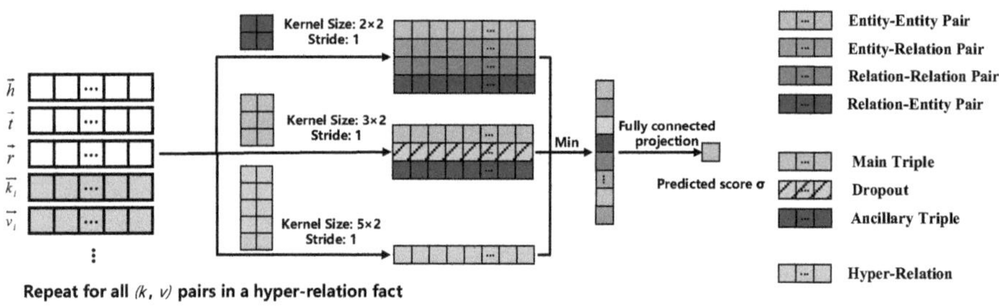

Fig. 2. Overview of MRF3 model in hyper-relational facts.

Pair-wise Feature. On a pair-wise scale, similar to the previous section, MRF3 model uses a 2×2 receptive field to extract features between entities and relations in the hyper-relation. This design continues the implementation of MRF3 model in the context of triples, and adaptively adjusts it for the context of hyper-relations. MRF3 rearranges the order of embedding vectors of elements in hyper-relational facts, so that each convolution between two elements generates a meaningful pair, as shown in Eq. 3. This small-scale receptive field enables the model to accurately capture fine-grained local information and extract the microscopic interaction between entities or relations.

$$
\begin{array}{l}
Pair-wise\ Features \\
in\ Hyper-relations
\end{array}
=
\left\{
\begin{array}{ll}
Entity-Entity\ Pair & if\ Conv(\vec{h},\ \vec{t}) \\
Entity-Relation\ Pair & if\ Conv(\vec{t},\ \vec{r}) \\
Relation-Relation\ Pair & if\ Conv(\vec{r},\ \vec{k_i}) \\
Relation-Entity\ Pair & if\ Conv(\vec{k_i},\ \vec{v_i})
\end{array}
\right.
\tag{3}
$$

Triple-wise Feature. On a triple-wise scale, MRF3 similarly uses a 3×2 receptive field to extract features. In addition to the commonly used main triple, our MRF3 model defines ancillary triple, as shown in Eq. 4, which consists of relation, key and value, and is used to provide auxiliary information on the basis of main triple. We add this to MRF3 to further capture the association of triples inside the hyper-relation.

$$
\begin{array}{l}
Triple-wise\ Features \\
in\ Hyper-relations
\end{array}
=
\left\{
\begin{array}{ll}
Main\ Triple & if\ Conv(\vec{h},\ \vec{t},\ \vec{r}) \\
Ancillary\ Triple & if\ Conv(\vec{r},\ \vec{k_i},\ \vec{v_i})
\end{array}
\right.
\tag{4}
$$

Hyper-relation-wise Feature. On the hyper-relation-wise scale, MRF3 uses a 5×2 receptive field to capture global features of hyper-relations. Similarly to the triple-wise feature in triples, the 5×2 receptive field is further extended in the spatial dimension. Compared with the 2×2 and 3×2 small receptive fields used previously, the 5×2 large receptive field can simultaneously consider all entities and relations inside the hyper-relation and allow MRF3 to capture more comprehensive contextual information in the context of hyper-relations, provide richer feature representations and strong support for MRF3 model global modeling at the hyper-relation level.

4.3 Feature Fusion

Minimize and Fully-Connected Projection. Through the relevance vector matrix obtained by convolution operation, we calculate the minimum value along each feature dimension of it to obtain the final relevance vector. For the overall feature vector, we perform a fully connected projection operation on it to obtain a prediction score.

Loss Function. MRF3 model uses LeakyReLU as the loss function:

$$
LeakyReLU(x_i) =
\left\{
\begin{array}{ll}
x_i, & if\ x_i > 0 \\
\alpha x_i, & if\ x_i \leq 0
\end{array}
\right.
\tag{5}
$$

LeakyReLU can solve the vanishing gradient problem for negative values by giving a small linear component to the negative input, so that the neuron does not lose activity due to a negative input. Our Loss function would then be:

$$
Loss = \sum_{\omega \in \Omega} LeakyReLU(-\sigma(\omega)) + LeakyReLU(\sigma(\omega'))
\tag{6}
$$

where Ω is the input set of triples or hyper-relational facts. For each $\omega \in \Omega$, negative samples $\omega\prime$ are generated by corrupting an entity or relation. $\sigma(\omega)$ and $\sigma(\omega\prime)$ denote the prediction scores for positive and negative samples respectively.

5 Experiment

5.1 Experimental Setup

Our experiments are conducted on two common public KG datasets, JF17k [6] and Wikipeople [10]. We compare MRF3 model with following typical models or methods according to the categories described above: TransE [4], TransH [5], ConvE [7], m-TransH [6], RAE [11], NaLP [88], NaLP-fix [3], NeuInfer [9], HINGE [3]. Moreover, we performed ablation experiments, using only 2×2 receptive fields to form MRF3 w/ SRF and only 2×2 and 3×2 receptive fields to form MRF3 w/ DRF. SRF and DRF are the abbreviations of Single Receptive Field and Dual Receptive Field respectively.

Table 1. Link prediction performance on JF17k.

Model		Entity Prediction			Relation Prediction		
		MRR	Hit@1	Hit@10	MRR	Hit@1	Hit@10
2-ary	TransE	0.231	0.133	0.449	0.829	0.806	0.895
	TransH	0.239	0.140	0.456	0.833	0.814	0.902
	ConvE	0.309	0.207	0.544	-	-	-
N-ary	m-TransH	0.209	0.201	0.462	-	-	-
	RAE	0.211	0.214	0.468	-	-	-
	NaLP	0.222	0.169	0.337	0.637	0.550	0.819
	NaLP-fix	0.249	0.188	0.356	0.733	0.666	0.879
Hyper-relation	NeuInfer	0.232	0.178	0.349	0.646	0.561	0.856
	HINGE	0.370	0.279	0.548	0.871	0.827	0.951
	MRF^3	0.457	0.349	0.626	0.964	0.920	0.996

Table 2. Link prediction performance on Wikipeople.

Model		Entity Prediction			Relation Prediction		
		MRR	Hit@1	Hit@10	MRR	Hit@1	Hit@10
2-ary	TransE	0.322	0.120	0.604	0.347	0.270	0.420
	TransH	0.319	0.115	0.602	0.371	0.296	0.442
	ConvE	0.474	0.354	0.629	-	-	-
N-ary	m-TransH	0.058	0.061	0.298	-	-	-
	RAE	0.055	0.056	0.302	-	-	-
	NaLP	0.408	0.329	0.545	0.481	0.315	0.852
	NaLP-fix	0.430	0.359	0.560	0.821	0.722	0.979
Hyper-relation	NeuInfer	0.378	0.293	0.454	0.496	0.326	0.868

(continued)

Table 2. (*continued*)

Model		Entity Prediction			Relation Prediction		
		MRR	Hit@1	Hit@10	MRR	Hit@1	Hit@10
	HINGE	0.390	0.319	0.508	0.853	0.847	0.971
	MRF^3	0.478	0.422	0.585	0.950	0.917	0.998

5.2　Performance Comparison

In this experiment, we conduct a comprehensive performance evaluation of the MRF3 model, in order to verify its effectiveness in KG representation learning. Tables 1 and 2 show the detailed comparative experimental results of the MRF3 model on the JF17k and Wikipeople datasets respectively. Among them, ConvE is specifically designed for entity prediction only. Besides, m-TransH and RAE also learn from entities only.

Through the experimental results, it can be found that the MRF3 model outperforms the relevant baseline models in all indicators. On the JF17k dataset, MRF3 model achieves 0.457 and 0.964 on MRR in entity and relation prediction tasks, which are 8.7% and 9.3% higher than the suboptimal model. On the Wikipeople dataset, MRF3 model achieves 0.478 and 0.950 on MRR in entity and relation prediction tasks, which are 4.8% and 9.7% higher than the suboptimal model. These gains are mainly attributed to the innovative multi-receptive-field feature fusion mechanism in the MRF3 model, which captures the complex semantic and structure information more effectively.

In addition, our ablation experiments show that the performance will degrade to some extent when using only single or dual receptive fields, further confirming the importance of our multi-receptive-field mechanism in the MRF3 model.

6　Conclusion

Receptive fields are crucial for capturing semantic patterns in link prediction tasks, yet most existing knowledge graph embedding models either overlook them or apply them in limited ways. This restricts their ability to model complex relational structures. In this work, we propose MRF^3, a multi-receptive-field feature fusion model that extracts and integrates features at different semantic scales. Extensive experiments show that MRF^3 consistently outperforms baseline models across multiple datasets, and ablation studies further validate the effectiveness of its multi-scale receptive field design.

Acknowledgements. This article is supported by the Key R&D Program of Ningbo City and the Major Application Demonstration Projects of "Leading the List" and "Science and Technology Innovation yongJiang 2035" (grant number 2024Z010 and 2023Z180).

References

1. Bollacker, K., Evans, C., Paritosh, P., et al.: Freebase: a collaboratively created graph database for structuring human knowledge. In: Proceedings of the 2008 ACM SIGMOD International Conference on Management of Data, pp. 1247–1250 (2008)
2. Vrandečić, D., Krötzsch, M.: Wikidata: a free collaborative knowledgebase. Commun. ACM **57**(10), 78–85 (2014)
3. Rosso, P., Yang, D., Cudré-Mauroux, P.: Beyond triplets: hyper-relational knowledge graph embedding for link prediction. In: Proceedings of the Web Conference 2020, pp. 1885–1896 (2020)
4. Bordes, A., Usunier, N., Garcia-Duran, A., et al.: Translating embeddings for modeling multi-relational data. Adv. Neural Inf. Process. Syst. **26** (2013)
5. Wang, Z., Zhang, J., Feng, J., et al.: Knowledge graph embedding by translating on hyperplanes. In: Proceedings of the AAAI Conference on Artificial Intelligence, vol. 28(1) (2014)
6. Wen, J., Li, J., Mao, Y., et al.: On the representation and embedding of knowledge bases beyond binary relations. arXiv preprint arXiv:1604.08642 (2016)
7. Dettmers, T., Minervini, P., Stenetorp, P., et al.: Convolutional 2D knowledge graph embeddings. In: Proceedings of the AAAI Conference on Artificial Intelligence, vol. 32(1) (2018)
8. Guan, S., Jin, X., Guo, J., et al.: Link prediction on n-ary relational data based on relatedness evaluation. IEEE Trans. Knowl. Data Eng. **35**(1), 672–685 (2021)
9. Guan, S., Jin, X., Guo, J., et al.: NeuInfer: knowledge inference on N-ary facts. In: Proceedings of the 58th Annual Meeting of the Association for Computational Linguistics, pp. 6141–6151 (2020)
10. Guan, S., Jin, X., Wang, Y., et al.: Link prediction on N-ary relational data. In: The World Wide Web Conference, pp. 583–593 (2019)
11. Zhang, R., Li, J., Mei, J., et al.: Scalable instance reconstruction in knowledge bases via relatedness affiliated embedding. In: Proceedings of the 2018 World Wide Web Conference, pp. 1185–1194 (2018)

RAG with Visual Alert: Boosting Multimodal Language Models for Enhanced Visual Question Answering

Hongze Ou, Xiaoyu Liang, Lianrui Mu, and Haoji Hu[(✉)]

Zhejiang University, Hangzhou, China
{22360132,3180102772,mulianrui,haoji_hu}@zju.edu.cn

Abstract. Existing multi-modal large language models (MLLMs) exhibit limitations in fine-grained object attribute recognition, spatial-relational modeling, and complex multi-step reasoning, particularly for knowledge-intensive visual question answering (VQA) tasks requiring precise visual grounding. We propose RAG-VA, a retrieval-augmented framework that enhances MLLMs through scene graph-based knowledge representation and a visual element vector database for dynamic information retrieval. RAG-VA implements a multi-stage visual reasoning pipeline comprising visual element observation, information extraction, reasoning chain verification, and guided inference, along with a zero-shot chain-of-thought (CoT) approach for stepwise reasoning without fine-tuning. Extensive evaluations across multiple standard benchmarks demonstrate RAG-VA's superior performance over advanced MLLMs like LLaVA and ShareGPT4V, particularly in fine-grained visual understanding and knowledge-based reasoning tasks, offering an effective solution for integrating visual and external knowledge in VQA.

Keywords: Retrieval-Augmented Generation · Multi-modal Large Language Models · Visual Question Answering · Knowledge Representation

1 Introduction

Against AI's latest breakthroughs, multimodal LLMs (MLLMs) have emerged as the key technology for integrating different data types such as visual and textual. Models like LLaVA [11], and ShareGPT4V [2] have demonstrated significant progress in integrating visual and textual data, particularly excelling in visual question answering (VQA) and cross-modal reasoning tasks [1,10]. However, these models exhibit persistent limitations in fine-grained visual understanding, including difficulties in recognizing object attributes and quantities, comprehending spatial relationships, and adapting to domain-specific scenarios with small objects [6,7]. Such deficiencies fundamentally constrain their performance on complex VQA tasks requiring precise visual reasoning capabilities highlighting critical gaps in current MLLM.

T. Zhu et al. (Eds.): KSEM 2025, LNAI 15923, pp. 219–227, 2026.
https://doi.org/10.1007/978-981-95-3061-8_23

Recent work has explored strategies to enhance MLLM reasoning in VQA. InstructBLIP [4] uses instruction tuning but still struggles with spatial and small-object understanding. PICa [20] shows GPT-3's reliance on prompts and limitations in complex reasoning, while IPVR [3] integrates vision, reasoning, and verification for better KB-VQA accuracy. TRiG [6] augments knowledge retrieval but lacks deep reasoning. Moreover, prompt-based methods, inspired by NLP few-shot learning, guide multimodal reasoning, with prompt design becoming critical. CoT approaches like VidIL [19] and Multimodal-CoT [21] leverage MLLM's captioning for improved performance, while CCoT [15] uses scene graphs for relational reasoning. Other work incorporates structured cues (e.g., scene graphs, bounding boxes) for better visual grounding [13,18] (Fig. 1).

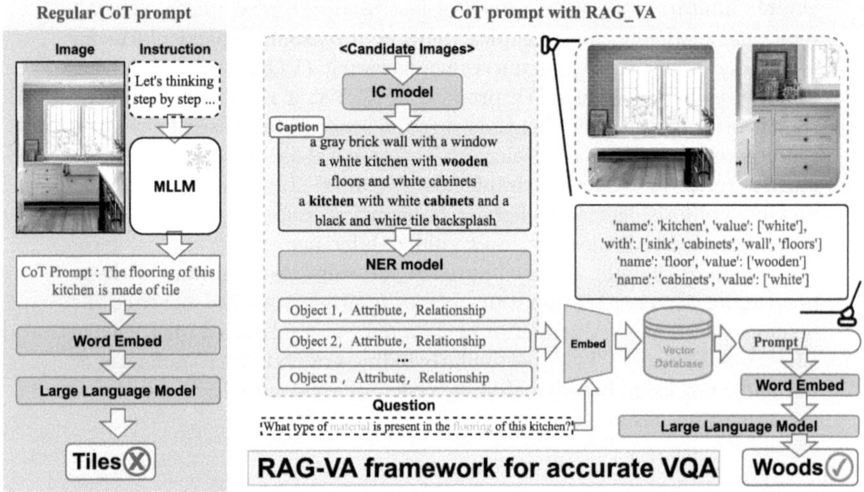

Fig. 1. An overview of Our RAG-VA framework for accurate VQA.

Inspired by the above challenges and work, we propose a novel Retrieval Augmented Generation framework focused on visual elements to improve visual reasoning in VQA tasks. The core contributions of this paper are distilled into:

- We propose RAG-VA, a Retrieval-Augmented Generation framework with Visual Alert, integrating scene graph-based knowledge and a visual vector database to dynamically retrieve task-relevant information, enhancing MLLMs' VQA performance.
- A multi-stage visual reasoning framework with zero-shot CoT enables stepwise interpretable reasoning without fine-tuning, improving handling of complex visual/knowledge-intensive questions.
- We perform extensive experiments showing that RAG-VA consistently outperforms advanced MLLMs such as LLaVA and ShareGPT4V, especially

in tasks requiring fine-grained visual understanding, spatial reasoning, and external knowledge integration.

2   Methodology

2.1   Multi-modal RAG Construction Module

Compositional Visual Element Representation. To enrich scene graphs with object/relation details, we split the global image I_g into local patches I_r with dynamically adjusted sizes matching the MLLM's input resolution. To extract structured knowledge from both images and their associated textual descriptions, we first utilize the BLIP model [9] to generate descriptive captions for local image regions, represented as a collection $C = \{c_1, c_2, \ldots, c_n\}$. Alongside, we consider pixel-level visual information $P = \{p_1, p_2, \ldots, p_m\}$. Together, these form a unified information repository $I = C \cup P$.

For each description c_i, we apply part-of-speech (POS) tagging and dependency parsing, denoted as $\text{POS}(c_i) = \{w_{1i}, w_{2i}, \ldots, w_{ki}\}$ and $\text{DepRel}(c_i) = \{(h_{ji}, t_{ji}, r_{ji})\}$, where w_{ji} is the part-of-speech tag, and (h_{ji}, t_{ji}, r_{ji}) represents a dependency relation between head and dependent words with relation label r_{ji}.

To implement these parsing tasks, we employ a transformer-based encoder, parameterized from EN_Core_Eeb_Trf, which leverages pre-trained models for accurate linguistic analysis [5]. Given a sentence with tokens $\{w_1, w_2, \ldots, w_n\}$, each token is embedded as a vector $\mathbf{x}_i = \text{Embedding}(w_i)$, and contextual representations are obtained via transformer layers:

$$\mathbf{h}_i = \text{Transformer}(\mathbf{x}_1, \mathbf{x}_2, \ldots, \mathbf{x}_n)_i \tag{1}$$

For dependency parsing, the score indicating the likelihood that w_j is the head of w_i is computed as:$s(i,j) = \mathbf{h}_i^\top \mathbf{W} \mathbf{h}_j$ and the head word is selected by: $h(i) = \arg\max_j s(i,j)$ The dependency relation label between w_i and $w_{h(i)}$ is predicted by:

$$P(r \mid w_i, w_{h(i)}) = \text{softmax}\left(\mathbf{U}\left[\mathbf{h}_i; \mathbf{h}_{h(i)}\right] + \mathbf{b}\right) \tag{2}$$

Similarly, POS tagging is formulated as:

$$P(t_i \mid w_i) = \text{softmax}\left(\mathbf{V}\mathbf{h}_i + \mathbf{c}\right) \tag{3}$$

where $\mathbf{W}, \mathbf{U}, \mathbf{V}, \mathbf{b}, \mathbf{c}$ are learnable parameters. The framework employs dependency parsing to extract objects, attributes, and relationships from text, ensuring precise semantic representation. It processes key dependencies (e.g., nsubj, dobj, prep, and pobj) to reconstruct subject-verb-object structures and modifications. Nested conditional logic and recursion handle complex syntax, particularly in prepositional phrase parsing, capturing hierarchical relationships. Additionally, coreference resolution [12] resolves pronouns, reducing ambiguity and enhancing scene understanding. Based on the extracted relations, we can map object sets $O = \{o_1, o_2, \ldots, o_n\}$ along with their attributes and relationships into structured triples (o_i, p, o_j), where p denotes a relational predicate.

Building Vector Database. A vector database enables efficient retrieval of relevant information by storing vector representations of structured data. The construction process begins by organizing identified objects, their attributes, and interactions into structured information units. Each information unit u_i can be formally defined as:

$$u_i = \{(k_1, v_1), (k_2, v_2), \ldots, (k_n, v_n)\} \tag{4}$$

where k_j denotes an attribute or relationship type, and v_j represents its corresponding value. To enable similarity-based retrieval, each unit u_i is transformed into a dense vector representation $\mathbf{v}_i \in \mathbb{R}^d$ using a pre-trained embedding model f as $\mathbf{v}_i = f(u_i)$. Here, d is the dimensionality of the embedding space, and f encodes the semantics of both objects and their relationships. All vectors $\{\mathbf{v}_1, \mathbf{v}_2, \ldots, \mathbf{v}_N\}$ are stored in a temporary vector database $\mathcal{D}$ as pairs of vectors and their corresponding information units:

$$\mathcal{D} = \{(\mathbf{v}_i, u_i) \mid i = 1, 2, \ldots, N\} \tag{5}$$

Given a query vector $\mathbf{q}$, relevant units are retrieved by minimizing a distance metric $d(\mathbf{q}, \mathbf{v}_i)$, typically formulated as:

$$\hat{u} = \arg \min_{u_i \in \mathcal{D}} d(\mathbf{q}, \mathbf{v}_i) \tag{6}$$

Advanced Visual Representation Strategies. We can further enrich the representation of visual information by incorporating the outputs from specialized models. For instance, by leveraging the Faster-RCNN model [16], we generate entity proposals with features for accurate object recognition. We further perform object attribute recognition to identify essential properties of each object, including its category, bounding box, quantity, and spatial location.

2.2   Design of RAG with Structured Visual Prompts

In the retrieval-enhanced generation module, the process can firstly be mathematically formulated as a Top-k retrieval and combination task over a vector database. Given a query vector $\mathbf{q}$ representing the question of a VQA task, we retrieve the top-k most semantically relevant information units based on a cosine similarity function $d(\cdot, \cdot)$. Formally, the retrieved set $\mathcal{V}$ is defined as:

$$\mathcal{V} = \{V_1, V_2, \ldots, V_k\}, \quad \text{where} \quad V_i = \arg \min_{V \in \mathcal{D}} d(\mathbf{q}, \mathbf{v}) \tag{7}$$

where $\mathbf{v}$ denotes the vector representation of each information unit V in the database $\mathcal{D}$, and k is a predefined hyperparameter (e.g., $k = 3$).Each retrieved block V_i encapsulates structured visual information, including object attributes and inter-object relationships. The retrieved information units V_1, V_2, V_3 are

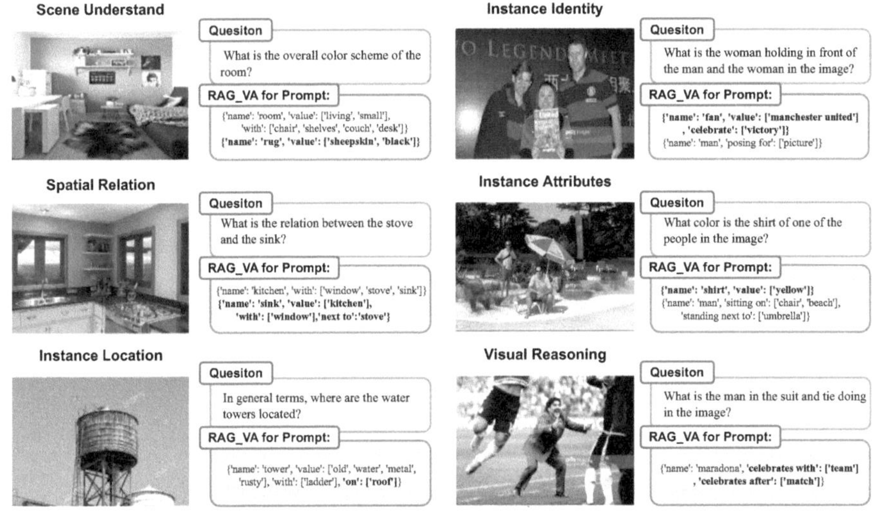

Fig. 2. Illustration of VQA tasks.

fused into a unified textual prompt $T = \text{Integrate}(V_1, V_2, V_3)$, integrating multi-modal features. The overall process is formulated as:

$$Q(q) \xrightarrow{\text{Retrieval}} \{V_1, V_2, V_3\} \xrightarrow{\text{Integrate}} T \xrightarrow{\text{LLM}} \text{Answer}$$

The RAG-VA framework employs semantically enhanced prompts S_{in} to guide MLLMs in generating context-aware answers, where visual information is structured into scene graphs to provide organized reasoning foundations. This structured prompting overcomes limitations of existing multi-modal models and improves MLLMs' compositional understanding, with retrieved answers incorporating critical object/relational details to reduce ambiguity and enhance precision in complex VQA tasks (Fig. 2). The framework processes input (I, P_{in}) through additional components including context sentence C for reasoning guidance and answer extraction prompt E for response formatting, ultimately generating final response R format as follows:

$$R = f_\theta([P_{\text{in}}][S_{\text{in}}][C][E][Q]) \tag{8}$$

3   Experiments and Results

3.1   Experimental Setup

Datasets. The evaluation employs three benchmark datasets: SEED-Bench-Image [8] with 14,000 fine-grained annotated images for scene understanding and visual reasoning tasks, AOK-VQA [17] featuring open-ended questions that integrate visual understanding with external knowledge for complex reasoning, and OK-VQA [14] containing real-world image questions requiring external knowledge beyond visual content.

Table 1. Main results on SEED-Bench-Image, AOK-VQA, and OK-VQA benchmarks.

Methods	Image Representation	SEED-Bench-Image (%)	AOK-VQA (%)	OK-VQA (%)
BLIP-2 [9]	Feature	46.4	60.0	–
IPVR [3]	Caption	–	46.4	44.6
PICa [20]	Caption + Tags	–	–	48.0
TRiG [6]	Caption + Tags + OCR	–	–	49.4
InstructBLIP (T5)	Feature	62.7	58.5	55.1
InstructBLIP (T5) + **RAG-VA**$_{(ours)}$	**Visual Alert**	63.2$_{(+0.5)}$	59.7$_{(+1.2)}$	56.7$_{(+1.6)}$
Share-GPT4V	Feature	69.2	60.3	54.2
Share-GPT4V + **RAG-VA**$_{(ours)}$	**Visual Alert**	69.8$_{(+0.6)}$	61.1$_{(+0.8)}$	55.1$_{(+0.9)}$
LLaVA-v1.5-7B	Feature	66.2	61.7	54.5
LLaVA-v1.5-7B + **RAG-VA**$_{(ours)}$	**Visual Alert**	67.1$_{(+0.9)}$	63.2$_{(+1.5)}$	54.8$_{(+0.3)}$
LLaVA-v1.5-13B	Feature	68.2	66.9	56.0
LLaVA-v1.5-13B + **RAG-VA**$_{(ours)}$	**Visual Alert**	69.3$_{(+1.1)}$	68.5$_{(+1.6)}$	57.3$_{(+1.3)}$

Evaluation Metrics. Accuracy serves as the primary metric, calculated differently for multiple-choice and free-form VQA tasks. For multiple-choice questions, it measures the ratio of correct answers to total questions. For open-ended responses, we adopt the probabilistic evaluation standard in the field.

Baseline. We have conducted a comprehensive comparative analysis of our proposed method by evaluating it against mainstream MLLMs: ShareGPT4V [2], InstructBLIP [4], and LLaVA [11]. These models are widely recognized in the field of multi-modal learning and have demonstrated outstanding performance and capabilities in VQA tasks.

3.2   Results

Comparison with Different Image Representation and Baselines. Table 1 presents a comprehensive comparison on SEED-Bench-Image, OK-VQA, and AOK-VQA benchmarks. Models using simple image features or caption-based representations show limited performance, especially on knowledge-intensive datasets. Our framework surpasses traditional image feature-based representations, demonstrating advantages in multi-modal reasoning. By integrating RAG-VA's scene graph-based structured knowledge and visual element augmentation, we observe consistent improvements confirming RAG-VA's effectiveness in enhancing model reasoning and answer accuracy.

Compositional Benchmarks on SEED-Bench-Image. Table 2 shows RAG-VA consistently improves baseline performance across different visual reasoning categories. RAG-VA's semantic prompts enhance task-specific reasoning— e.g., aiding object localization in IA tasks and improving IId/SR via targeted retrieval. Crucially, the model retains its original capabilities when retrieval fails, demonstrating the flexibility of our approach.

Table 2. Compositional benchmarks on SEED-Bench-Image.

Model	SU	IId	IA	IL	SR	IIn	VR	W.Avg.
LLAVA-v1.5-13B	74.8	71.1	68.3	63.5	53.0	72.0	76.0	69.6
LLAVA-v1.5-13B + **RAG-VA**$_{\text{(ours)}}$	**75.5**	**73.3**	**70.2**	**64.5**	52.7	70.9	**76.7**	**70.9**$_{(+1.3)}$
LLAVA-v1.5-7B	73.3	68.2	66.9	58.9	52.7	74.2	77.0	67.6
LLAVA-v1.5-7B + **RAG-VA**$_{\text{(ours)}}$	**73.8**	**69.6**	**67.9**	**60.1**	51.8	**74.6**	76.8	**68.6**$_{(+1.0)}$
ShareGPT4V	75.2	69.7	71.8	64.0	53.0	72.2	77.6	70.8
ShareGPT4V + **RAG-VA**$_{\text{(ours)}}$	**75.4**	**70.3**	**72.7**	63.7	**55.2**	70.5	**78.3**	**71.5**$_{(+0.7)}$

Table 3. Ablation study on SEED-Bench-Image.

Model	SU	IId	IA	IL	SR	IIn	VR	W. Avg
LLaVA-v1.5-13B	74.8	71.1	68.3	63.5	53.0	72.0	76.0	69.6
+ RAG-VA	74.9	72.8	69.4	64.5	53.4	74.9	79.5	70.7
+ w/ Boxing	73.4	72.1	68.5	64.5	54.2	73.4	76.3	70.1
+ w/ Location and Count	**75.5**	**73.3**	**70.2**	**66.0**	**54.7**	70.9	76.7	**70.9**

Ablations. Table 3 shows that RAG-VA consistently outperforms the baseline on SEED-Bench-Image. Combining location and count retrieval achieves the highest weighted average, significantly boosting performance in tasks like IL/IId. However, pixel-level bounding boxes degrade reasoning, indicating precise locations are unnecessary.

Comparison with Multi-modal CoT Prompting Methods. Table 4 shows ZS-CoT employs generic step-by-step reasoning prompts while Caption-CoT first generates image captions to establish visual grounding. Though VidIL demonstrates the effectiveness of few-shot prompting by outperforming Caption-CoT, our RAG-VA framework achieves the highest accuracy by dynamically retrieving structured visual knowledge, proving more effective than existing CoT strategies.

Table 4. Comparison with Multi-modal CoT Prompting Methods.

Model	CoT Prompting Methods	Accuracy(%)
LLaVA-v1.5	-	68.2
+ ZS-CoT	Regular	66.7
+ Caption-CoT	Caption	68.4
+ VidIL	Few-Shot Context	68.8
+ **RAG-VA**$_{\text{(ours)}}$	**RAG-VA**	**69.3**

4   Conclusions

We proposed RAG-VA framework designed to enhance MLLMs in VQA tasks. By integrating structured knowledge and a dynamically constructed visual element vector database, our method effectively improves MLLM to recognize fine-grained object attributes, spatial relationships, and complex reasoning. Our ZS-CoT approach enables interpretable step-by-step answers without fine-tuning.

References

1. Antol, S., Agrawal, A., Lu, J., et al.: VQA: visual question answering. Int. J. Comput. Vision **123**(1), 4–31 (2015)
2. Chen, L., et al.: Sharegpt4v: improving large multi-modal models with better captions (2023)
3. Chen, Z., Zhou, Q., Shen, Y., et al.: See, think, confirm: interactive prompting between vision and language models for knowledge-based visual reasoning. arXiv preprint arXiv:2301.05226 (2023)
4. Dai, W., et al.: Instructblip: towards general-purpose vision-language models with instruction tuning (2023)
5. ExplosionAI: spacy transformers: industrial-strength natural language processing (NLP) with transformers in Python (2020)
6. Gao, F., Ping, Q., Thattai, G., Reganti, A., Wu, Y.N., Natarajan, P.: A thousand words are worth more than a picture: natural language-centric outside-knowledge visual question answering (2022)
7. Ilievski, I., Feng, J.: Multimodal learning and reasoning for visual question answering. In: Neural Information Processing Systems (2017)
8. Li, B., Wang, R., Wang, G., Ge, Y., Ge, Y., Shan, Y.: Seed-bench: benchmarking multimodal LLMs with generative comprehension (2023)
9. Li, J., Li, D., Savarese, S., Hoi, S.: Blip-2: bootstrapping language-image pre-training with frozen image encoders and large language models (2023)
10. Li, X., et al.: Oscar: object-semantics aligned pre-training for vision-language tasks (2020)
11. Liu, H., Li, C., Wu, Q., Lee, Y.J.: Visual instruction tuning (2023)
12. Liu, R., Mao, R., Luu, A.T., Cambria, E.: A brief survey on recent advances in coreference resolution. Artif. Intell. Rev. **56**(12), 14439–14481 (2023)
13. Luan, B., Feng, H., Chen, H., Wang, Y., Zhou, W., Li, H.: Textcot: zoom in for enhanced multimodal text-rich image understanding. arXiv preprint arXiv:2404.09797 (2024)
14. Marino, K., Rastegari, M., Farhadi, A., Mottaghi, R.: OK-VQA: a visual question answering benchmark requiring external knowledge. IEEE (2020)
15. Mitra, C., Huang, B., Darrell, T., Herzig, R.: Compositional chain-of-thought prompting for large multimodal models (2024)
16. Ren, S., He, K., Girshick, R., Sun, J.: Faster R-CNN: towards real-time object detection with region proposal networks. In: Advances in Neural Information Processing Systems (NeurIPS), pp. 91–99 (2015)
17. Schwenk, D., Khandelwal, A., Clark, C., Marino, K., Mottaghi, R.: A-OKVQA: a benchmark for visual question answering using world knowledge. In: Avidan, S., Brostow, G., Cissé, M., Farinella, G.M., Hassner, T. (eds.) ECCV 2022. LNCS, vol. 13668, pp. 146–162. Springer, Cham (2022). https://doi.org/10.1007/978-3-031-20074-8_9

18. Wang, J., Ju, J., Luan, J., Deng, Z.: Llava-SG: leveraging scene graphs as visual semantic expression in vision-language models (2024)
19. Wang, X., Huang, Z., Fu, J., Torralba, A., Xiao, J.: Vidil: exploring visual dynamics for complex reasoning. arXiv preprint arXiv:2303.01534 (2023)
20. Yang, Z., et al.: An empirical study of GPT-3 for few-shot knowledge-based VQA (2022)
21. Yang, Z., Wang, D., Li, Z., Lin, X., Xie, X.: Multimodal chain-of-thought reasoning in language models. arXiv preprint arXiv:2305.04798 (2023)

Dynamic Heterogeneous Graph Neural Network for Personality Detection in Chinese Social Media Texts

Te Wang, Fanjun Meng, and Xingjian Xu[(✉)]

Inner Mongolia Normal University, Hohhot 010022, China
`Xingjian@imnu.edu.cn`

Abstract. Addressing the unique linguistic and cultural challenges of Chinese personality detection, this paper proposes a Dynamic Heterogeneous Graph Neural Network (DHGNN) model. DHGNN constructs contextualized post, psycholinguistic-enhanced, and cultural category nodes to better model polysemy, cultural specificity, and syntactic dynamism. It employs a dual-path message passing mechanism for cultural correlations and psychological salience, alongside a dynamic gated fusion module to adaptively integrate multi-path semantic features. Experiments on the Chinese Multi-label Affective Computing Dataset (CMACD) show significant improvements in Myers-Briggs Type Indicator (MBTI) classification. The work validates dynamic graph structures and cultural-psychological dual-path learning for disambiguation and feature enhancement, advancing Chinese personality detection methodology and providing foundations for applications like social media personalization and mental health monitoring. Future research will extend to multimodal fusion and cross-cultural transfer learning.

Keywords: personality detection · graph neural network · Myers-Briggs Type Indicator · dynamic heterogeneous graph · Chinese texts analysis

1 Introduction

Analyzing Chinese social media text is vital for applications like recommendation systems and mental health interventions. Personality detection offers significant potential to tailor intelligent services. However, research remains heavily focused on English, leaving Chinese personality computing underdeveloped despite unique linguistic and cultural complexities. Three key challenges hinder MBTI classification in Chinese: morphosyntactic flexibility creating syntactic ambiguity, pervasive semantic polysemy introducing noise in feature extraction, and culturally mediated indirectness in emotional expression masking true sentiments.

Existing solutions are inadequate. Traditional sequential models fail to capture non-linear semantic relationships. Transformer models like $BERT_{concat}$ [1] and $BERT_{att}$ [2] poorly handle Chinese dynamic syntax and lack cultural awareness. Graph-based methods like D-DCGN [3] cannot disentangle intertwined cultural and psycholinguistic signals. Crucially, none systematically integrate external cultural knowledge or psycholinguistic lexicons to resolve ambiguities.

T. Zhu et al. (Eds.): KSEM 2025, LNAI 15923, pp. 228–236, 2026.
https://doi.org/10.1007/978-981-95-3061-8_24

Conventional models miss crucial non-local semantic associations and context-dependent syntax due to reliance on sequential tokenization and homogeneous graphs. Effective detection must incorporate linguistic dynamism, psychological salience, and cultural specificity through an architecture encoding heterogeneous node types and dynamically adjusting semantic relationships.

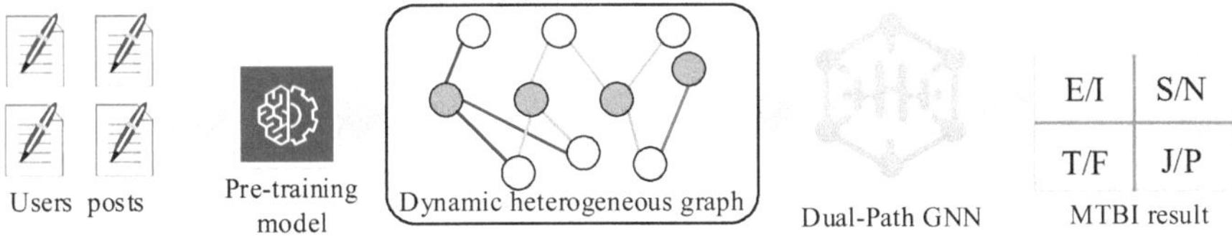

Fig. 1. Dynamic Heterogeneous Graph Neural Network model.

To address these issues, this paper proposes a dynamic heterogeneous graph neural network model (Fig. 1) achieving breakthroughs via three innovations: A heterogeneous network graph with contextualized post nodes, psycholinguistic-enhanced word nodes, and cultural category nodes resolving cultural concept neglect; A dual-path message passing mechanism separately handling cultural relevance and psychological salience; A dynamic gated fusion module adaptively integrating semantic features. Our works are summarized as follows:

1) We propose a novel Dynamic Heterogeneous Graph model with cultural-psychological fusion pathways overcoming conventional single-semantic modeling limitations.
2) The culture-specific processing mechanism employs dual-path message passing with cultural adaptation weights to enhance concept representation, resolving Chinese semantic ambiguity and cultural specificity.
3) Preliminary validation on large-scale Chinese social media datasets yields results indicating potential value, offering tentative methodological considerations for cross-cultural personality computing.

2 Related Work

2.1 Personality Detection

Text-based personality detection has gained significant attention across NLP and psychology [4]. Early methods primarily employed conventional ML techniques like SVM and XGBoost [5], relying on manual feature extraction of surface linguistic patterns (lexical frequencies, POS distributions). Psycholinguistic insights linked such features to Big Five traits [6], though manual engineering proved time-consuming, subjective, and limited in capturing nuanced semantics, pragmatics, and implicit markers, compromising validity.

Deep learning revolutionized the field through automated representation learning. DNNs [7], LSTMs [8] and GRUs [9] model long-range textual dependencies via dynamic hidden states, eliminating manual feature constraints and improving efficiency and accuracy. CNNs [10] contributed localized, multi-scale feature extraction for stylistic and psychological patterns.

The paradigm shifted with BERT variants [11, 12]. Pre-trained on massive corpora, they gain deep semantic understanding; fine-tuned for personality prediction, they reach state-of-the-art performance through modeling multilevel linguistic interactions.

2.2 Graph Neural Network

Graph neural networks GNNs [13–15] are increasingly used in NLP for text with relational structures, relying heavily on graph construction. Entity graphs represent textual entities as nodes and their semantic or co-occurrence relationships as edges, aiding tasks like text classification and question answering [16]. Heterogeneous graphs integrate diverse node types and edges based on associations [17], enhancing text processing through multi-source information integration.

Combining GNN with psycholinguistic knowledge is vital for personality analysis [18]. Tools like LIWC [19] categorize vocabulary for use as nodes or attributes. GNNs learn semantic relationships between words and their links to personality traits. Constructing heterogeneous graphs with word and category nodes effectively captures psychological cues, improving accuracy through word co-occurrence or semantic similarity connections and word-category hierarchical relationships.

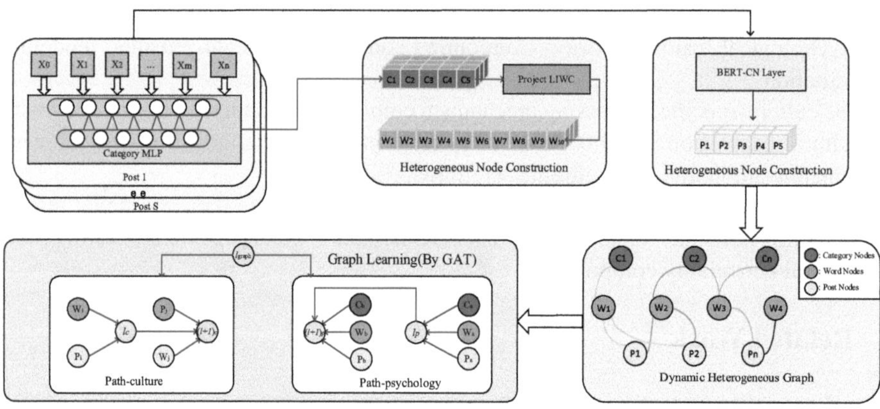

Fig. 2. Experimental methodology

3 Method

The experimental methodology of this paper, as illustrated in Fig. 2. We propose a novel dynamic heterogeneous representation graph $G_d = (V_t, \mathcal{E}_t)$ with three enhanced node types, incorporating dual cultural-psychological pathways through innovative architectural design. The graph construction process comprises the following key components.

3.1 Dynamic Heterogeneous Graph Construction

Dynamic heterogeneous graphs are constructed using specialized nodes. Contextualized post nodes V_p^c derive from sliding window token sequences $s_i^{1:k}$, processed by BERT and aggregated via a hierarchical layer-wise attention mechanism as described by Eq. 1. Psycholinguistic-enhanced word nodes V_w^e augment BERT word embeddings e_j^{BERT} by projecting them into LWC psycholinguistic categories according to Eq. 2. Cultural category nodes V_c^h integrate LIWC-derived categories c_k^{LIWC} with external cultural knowledge $c_m^{Culture}$ via weighted concatenation defined by Eq. 3, where Υ_m defines cultural adaptation weights. An adaptive edge weight generator dynamically computes connection strengths ω_{ij}^t between nodes v_i^t and v_j^t using a learnable matrix W_ω and sigmoid activation σ applied to concatenated features as per Eq. 4, enabling topology refinement. The symbol $||$ semantic denotes concatenation throughout.

$$p_i^c = LayerAtt\left(BERT\left(s_i^{1:k}\right)\right) \tag{1}$$

$$w_j^e = ProjLIWC\left(e_j^{BERT}\right) \tag{2}$$

$$c_k^h = \sum_{m=1}^{M} \Upsilon_m \cdot MLP\left(c_k^{LIWC} || c_m^{Culture}\right) \tag{3}$$

$$\omega_{ij}^t = \sigma\left(W_\omega\left[v_i^t || v_j^t\right]\right) \tag{4}$$

3.2 Dual-Path Graph Learning

Dual-Path Graph Learning employs complementary message-passing pathways to disentangle cultural and psychological semantics in Chinese social media text, handling polysemy, cultural specificity, and syntactic dynamism. The Cultural-Aware Pathway models cultural correlations by propagating messages between contextualized post nodes and category nodes enriched with external cultural knowledge and LIWC psycholinguistics, retaining edges based on cultural relevance exceeding threshold τ using cosine similarity as specified in Eq. 5 with a culture-specific GAT. Simultaneously, the Psychological Reinforcement Pathway enhances psychological salience by aggregating features from words exceeding a psychological salience index threshold θ, implemented via Eq. 6 with a dedicated GAT. Features from both pathways are adaptively integrated through a dynamic gated fusion mechanism. This mechanism computes a gating value using a sigmoid-activated linear transformation of the concatenated pathway outputs Eq. 7, enabling context-aware prioritization of cultural or psychological signals based on syntactic ambiguity levels. The final fused representation is computed via element-wise multiplication as shown in Eq. 8, ensuring robust disambiguation and improved decoding of culturally-shaped implicit personality cues.

$$Path_{culture}:p_i^{l+1} = GAT_c\left(p_i^l, \left\{c_k^l | \mathcal{R}(w_j, c_k) > \tau\right\}\right) \tag{5}$$

$$Path_{psychology} : \boldsymbol{p}_i^{l+1} = GAT_p\left(\boldsymbol{p}_i^l, \left\{\boldsymbol{w}_j^l \mid PSI\left(w_j\right) < \theta\right\}\right) \tag{6}$$

$$g_i^l = \sigma\left(W_g\left[p_i^{l,c} \| p_i^{l,p}\right]\right) \tag{7}$$

$$p_i^{l+1} = g_i^l \odot p_i^{l,c} + \left(1 - g_i^l\right) \odot p_i^{l,p} \tag{8}$$

3.3 Optimization

The proposed personality detection model is optimized using a comprehensive training strategy that combines advanced optimization with architectural enhancements. Employing a compound loss of cross-entropy and adaptive L2 regularization, where coefficients adjust dynamically by layer depth to prevent over-parameterization, the model integrates dynamic graph structures, domain-specific lexicons, and dual-path learning.

4 Experiments

4.1 Experimental Environment and Dataset

Experiments utilized a computing platform with an AMD EPYC 7402 processor and NVIDIA RTX 3090 GPU, running Ubuntu 22.04 with PyTorch 2.2.0 accelerated via CUDA 11.6. Development employed Python 3.8. The study used the Chinese Multi-label Affective Computing Dataset (CMACD) [20], featuring multi-label annotations with verified intensity levels. To focus on personality traits, preprocessing retained only MBTI-related labels (I/E, S/N, T/F, P/J) while removing other emotional annotations. Subsequent analysis examined performance per personality trait as detailed in Table 1 (Table 2).

Table 1. Statistics of the CMACD dataset.

Dataset	Traits	Train(60%)	Valid(20%)	Test(20%)
CMACD	I/E	2570/4236	856/1411	856/1411
	S/N	2028/4778	675/1592	675/1592
	T/F	2008/4796	670/1598	670/1598
	P/J	3930/2874	1310/958	1310/958

Table 2. Performance comparison of personal detection methods (%)

Method	I/E (%)			S/N (%)			T/F (%)			P/J (%)		
	ACC	PRE	REC	ACC	PRE	REC	ACC	PRE	REC	ACC	PRE	REC
SVM	34.9	33.1	35.8	32.5	31.2	33.8	31.8	30.5	33.1	35.1	33.9	36.3
BiLSTM	58.2	56.8	59.4	54.6	53.1	56.2	53.2	51.8	54.6	57.8	56.3	59.3
BERT$_{att}$	68.8	67.9	69.6	66.4	65.3	67.5	65.7	64.4	67.0	67.9	66.8	69.0
D-DGCN	89.2	88.5	90.1	87.6	86.9	88.3	86.4	85.7	87.2	88.7	88.1	89.4
OUR	**94.5**	**93.8**	**95.2**	**93.1**	**92.4**	**93.8**	**92.3**	**91.6**	**93.0**	**93.9**	**93.2**	**94.6**

4.2 Baselines

To comprehensively evaluate our proposed approach, we implement four representative baseline models spanning traditional machine learning and deep learning paradigms. SVM [5] serves as a fundamental traditional machine learning baseline for affective computing, using linear classification with TF-IDF vectorization. BiLSTM [8] establishes a sequence modeling baseline for emotion recognition, employing bidirectional LSTM processing to capture contextual dependencies and a dense sigmoid output layer. BERTatt [2] represents state-of-the-art transformer approaches, enhancing contextual learning via multi-head self-attention within BERT-Base-Chinese and utilizing task-specific classifiers. D-DGCN [3] benchmarks graph-based multi-label classification strategies, constructing dynamic adjacency matrices from label co-occurrence and modeling label correlations through iterative message passing.

4.3 Result

The proposed DHGNN model demonstrates improved performance across all four MBTI dimensions compared to baseline methods, including SVM, BiLSTM, BERTatt, and the prior dynamic graph model D-DGCN. It achieves notably higher accuracy than D-DGCN. Both precision and recall remain consistently high across dimensions, with recall slightly higher. The model shows robust performance against class imbalance, particularly on the I/E and P/J dimensions. Comparatively lower metrics on the S/N and T/F dimensions likely reflect the inherent challenge of detecting subtle linguistic cues related to intuition and feeling, which require deeper semantic and cultural understanding. While this performance difference highlights the difficulty, the model still outperforms baselines. Its culture-aware pathway enhancement within the dynamic heterogeneous architecture aims to capture both explicit personality indicators and implicit cultural-linguistic patterns, suggesting these dimensions pose greater challenges (Fig. 3).

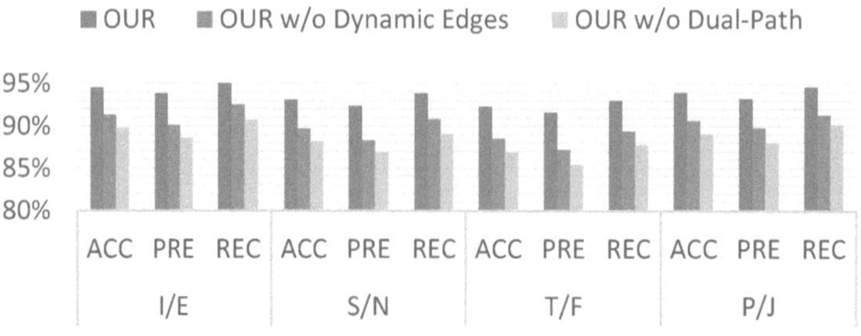

Fig. 3. Ablation study result

4.4 Ablation Study

Ablation studies confirm the necessity of key components in the Gd framework. Removing dynamic edge weights significantly reduces performance across all metrics, particularly in syntax-sensitive dimensions like I/E, demonstrating its critical role in capturing Chinese syntactic dynamics. Disabling the dual-path learning module causes substantial performance degradation, especially within cultural (S/N) and psychological (T/F) dimensions, as separate cultural-psychological pathways are essential for resolving semantic ambiguity. Both ablated variants still outperform the D-DGCN baseline, indicating the robustness of the heterogeneous graph structure. However, the observed performance gaps underscore that integrating dynamic edges and dual-path mechanisms is fundamental for effective Chinese personality detection.

5   Conclusion

This work proposes a novel graph neural network for personality detection in Chinese social media, addressing linguistic and cultural challenges. The model integrates BERT embeddings with LIWC features via a dynamic heterogeneous graph with contextualized post nodes, psychologically enriched word nodes, and cultural category nodes. Key contributions include dynamic cultural-psychological graph modeling, a culture-sensitive processing mechanism, and large-scale validation on Chinese corpora, suggesting potential utility for this task.

Acknowledgement. This work was supported by grants from the Hohhot Basic Research and Applied Basic Research Science and Technology Program Projects(2025-GUI-JI-44), Natural Science Foundation of Inner Mongolia (2023MS06016), Normal University 2023 College Student Innovation and Entrepreneurship Training Program (202310153007). We appreciate the valuable suggestions from anonymous reviewers.

References

1. Jiang, H., Zhang, X., Choi, J.D.: Automatic text based personality recognition on monologues and multiparty dialogues using attentive networks and contextual embeddings. arXiv preprint arXiv:1911.09304 (2019)

2. Lynn, V., Balasubramanian, N., Schwartz, H.A.: Hierarchical modeling for user personality prediction: the role of message-level attention. In: Proceedings of the 58th Annual Meeting of the Association for Computational Linguistics, pp. 5306–5316. ACL (2020)
3. Yang, T., et al.: Orders are unwanted: dynamic deep graph convolutional network for personality detection. In: Proceedings of the AAAI Conference on Artificial Intelligence, vol. 37, no. 11. AAAI Press (2023)
4. Cui, B., Qi, C.: Survey analysis of machine learning methods for natural language processing for MBTI personality type prediction. Final Report Stanford University (2017)
5. Tadesse, M.M., Lin, H., Xu, B., et al.: Personality predictions based on user behavior on the Facebook social media platform. IEEE Access **6**, 61959–61969 (2018)
6. Keh, S.S., Cheng, I.: Myers-Briggs personality classification and personality-specific language generation using pre-trained language models. arXiv preprint arXiv:1907.06333 (2019)
7. Tandera, T., Suhartono, D., Wongso, R., Prasetio, Y.L., et al.: Personality prediction system from Facebook users. Procedia Comput. Sci. **116**, 604–611 (2017)
8. Hochreiter, S., Schmidhuber, J.: Long short-term memory. Neural Comput. **9**(8), 1735–1780 (1997)
9. Cho, K., van Merrienboer, B., Gulcehre, C., et al.: Learning phrase representations using RNN encoder–decoder for statistical machine translation. In: Proceedings of the 2014 Conference on Empirical Methods in Natural Language Processing (EMNLP), pp. 1724–1734. ACL (2014)
10. Szegedy, C., Ioffe, S., Vanhoucke, V., Alemi, A.: Inception-v4, inception-resnet and the impact of residual connections on learning. In: Proceedings of the AAAI Conference on Artificial Intelligence, vol. 31. AAAI Press (2017)
11. Devlin, J., Chang, M.-W., Lee, K., Toutanova, K.: BERT: pre-training of deep bidirectional transformers for language understanding. In: Proceedings of the 2019 Conference of the North American Chapter of the Association for Computational Linguistics: Human Language Technologies, pp. 4171–4186. ACL (2019)
12. Jain, D., Kumar, A., Beniwal, R.: Personality BERT: a transformer-based model for personality detection from textual data. In: Bashir, A.K., Fortino, G., Khanna, A., Gupta, D. (eds.) Proceedings of International Conference on Computing and Communication Networks. Lecture Notes in Networks and Systems, vol. 394, pp. 515–522. Springer, Singapore (2022). https://doi.org/10.1007/978-981-19-0604-6_48
13. Cao, Y., Fang, M., Tao, D.: BAG: bi-directional attention entity graph convolutional network for multi-hop reasoning question answering. In: Proceedings of the 2019 Conference of the North American Chapter of the Association for Computational Linguistics: Human Language Technologies, pp. 357–362. ACL (2019)
14. Yao, L., Mao, C., Luo, Y.: Graph convolutional networks for text classification. In: Proceedings of the AAAI Conference on Artificial Intelligence, vol. 33. pp. 7370–7377. AAAI Press (2019)
15. Wang, K., Shen, W., Yang, Y., et al.: Relational graph attention network for aspect-based sentiment analysis. In: Proceedings of the 58th Annual Meeting of the Association for Computational Linguistics, pp. 3229–3238. ACL (2020)
16. Kömeçoglu, B.B., Yilmaz, B.: Event graph-based news clustering: the role of named entity-centered subgraphs. IEEE Access (2024)
17. Hua, J., Sun, D., Hu, Y., et al.: Heterogeneous graph-convolution-network-based short-text classification. Appl. Sci. **14**(6), 2279 (2024)
18. Yang, T., Yang, F., Ouyang, H., et al.: Psycholinguistic tripartite graph network for personality detection. arXiv preprint arXiv:2106.04963 (2021)
19. Tausczik, Y.R., Pennebaker, J.W.: The psychological meaning of words: LIWC and computerized text analysis methods. J. Lang. Soc. Psychol. **29**(1), 24–54 (2010)

20. Zhou, J., Luo, S., Chen, H.: A Chinese multi-label affective computing dataset based on social media network users. arXiv preprint arXiv:2411.08347 (2024). https://doi.org/10.48550/arXiv.2411.08347

DualCBR: Cross-Modal Collaborative Filtering with Bidirectional Alignment for Long-Tail Recommendation

Xin Li[1,2,3], Lei Zhao[1,2], Dekai Zhang[1,2], Dawei Zhao[1,2(✉)], Lijuan Xu[1,2], Chunhui Wang[3], and Fuqiang Yu[1,2]

[1] Key Laboratory of Computing Power Network and Information Security, Ministry of Education, Shandong Computer Science Center, National Supercomputer Center in Jinan, Qilu University of Technology Shandong Academy of Sciences, Jinan 250014, China
Zhaole10733@163.com
[2] Shandong Provincial Key Laboratory of Computer Networks, Shandong Fundamental Research Center for Computer Science, Jinan 250014, China
[3] Shandong Shen Qi Information Technology Co., LTD., Jinan 250013, China

Abstract. In the era of digital economy, recommendatory systems face the dual challenges of insufficient use of semantic information and limited generalization ability of long tail data. It is difficult for traditional collaborative filtering methods to excavate deep semantic associations of items, while existing sequential recommendation models have significant bottlenecks in heterogeneous feature fusion and multi-scale interest modeling. In this paper, a dual-way collaborative semantic recommendation framework DualCBR is proposed. First, the collaborative embedding based on ID-PCA and the semantic embedding driven by LLM are generated respectively through the heterogeneous feature coding layer to preserve the group behavior pattern and fine-grained attribute features. Secondly, a lightweight cross-modal interaction layer is designed to dynamically align synergistic signals and semantic signals using the bidirectional cross-attention mechanism to solve the feature spatial heterogeneity problem. Furthermore, the multi-scale hybrid encoder is proposed, and the advantages of Transformer's global dependency capture and RNN's local time series modeling are combined to realize the collaborative expression of users' long-term and short-term interests. Experiments on Amazon Beauty and Fashion datasets show that DualCBR achieves improvements of 5.7%–11.3% in NDCG@10 and HIT@10 compared with SASRec and other baseline models, while its bidirectional cross-attention mechanism increases the recommendation hit rate for long-tail items by 176%. The effectiveness of the model in alleviating the data sparsity problem through collaborative-semantic dual-path fusion is verified. This study provides a new technical path for semantic-enhanced personalized recommendation.

Keywords: Collaborative filtering · Semantic recommendation · Hybrid encoder · Long-tail recommendation

T. Zhu et al. (Eds.): KSEM 2025, LNAI 15923, pp. 237–247, 2026.
https://doi.org/10.1007/978-981-95-3061-8_25

1   Introduction

The rise of the digital economy has made recommendation systems the key to dealing with information overload and achieving personalized content distribution. The traditional collaborative filtering method relies on user-item interaction but makes insufficient use of rich semantic information such as text and images, resulting in poor performance when the data is sparse. Subsequent deep learning sequence models (such as GRU4Rec [20], SASRec [2], BERT4Rec [18]) have enhanced the temporal modeling ability of user interests through RNN or self-attention mechanisms, but still mainly rely on item ID sequences. It is difficult to effectively understand deep semantic attributes (such as associating "sports shoes" with "casual shoes"). The breakthrough of large language models (LLMS) provides a new path to solve the bottleneck of semantic understanding. The semantic embeddings generated by them can represent the fine-grained attributes [8,9] of items, and the cross-modal interaction [10] is also helpful for aligning behaviors with semantic features. However, the existing fusion works face two core challenges: First, the heterogeneity of collaborative signals (behaviors) and semantic signals (attributes) makes deep feature fusion difficult, and simple strategies are prone to introduce noise [16]; Second, user behaviors include long-term stable preferences and short-term temporary interests. It is difficult for a single modeling scale to effectively capture such complex multi-scale temporal patterns.

This paper proposes the dual-path collaborative semantic recommendation framework DualCBR, which collaboratively models user preferences through collaborative filtering and semantic analysis of user behaviors. Its core innovations include: (1) Heterogeneous feature coding layers, which generate collaborative embeddings and semantic embeddings respectively by using data Dimension reduction (ID-PCA) and large language models (LLM); (2) The bidirectional cross-attention mechanism aligns and collaborates with semantic signals to address feature differences; (3) A multi-scale hybrid encoder combining Transformer and RNN to collaboratively capture users' long-term and short-term interests.

2   Related Work

Early sequence recommendation studies were mainly based on the RNN architecture (such as GRU4Rec [20] by Hidasi et al.); Subsequently, Kang et al. 's SASRec introduced the Transformer self-attention mechanism to capture long-distance dependencies [2]; Sun et al. 's BERT4Rec further adopts bidirectional Transformer and mask prediction targets to enhance the modeling ability [18]. These works have laid the foundation for dual-path collaborative modeling.

For the long-tail recommendation problem in data-sparse scenarios, researchers have proposed multiple optimization ideas: Fan et al. 's DT4SR model [4] alleviates the cold start problem through distributed modeling; Zhang et al. The CDN network of [5] reduces probabilistic bias through decoupling modules; The TailNet framework of Liu et al. [17] introduces a preference mechanism to dynamically balance popular and long-tail items; The CSLP framework of Huang et al. [7] adopts a dual representation and scoring strategy to collaboratively solve the problems of long tail and bias. These methods provide references for improving the sparse data generalization ability of DualCBR.

Large language models bring new opportunities to recommendation systems: Harte et al. [8] significantly improved the performance of sequence recommendation models (such as BERT4Rec) by using LLM semantic embedding initialization; The LLM-ESR framework proposed by Liu et al. [9] optimizes the representation learning of long-tail items and users through dual-view representation; The Trans2D model of Singer et al. [10] fuses the multi-attribute features of objects with the help of the two-dimensional attention mechanism, coordinating the cooperative signal and the semantic signal. These works jointly inspired the design of DualCBR in the heterogeneous feature coding layer and the cross-modal interaction layer.

Meanwhile, the CITIES framework proposed by Jang et al. [11] realizes dynamic representation enhancement through contextual header item inference and tail item embedding, combined with collaborative filtering and semantic inference. Fang et al. [12] 's deep sequence recommendation review system analyzes the advantages of hybrid coding between Transformer and RNN, and points out that multi-scale timing pattern capture plays a key role in user preference modeling, which provides theoretical support for DualCBR's multi-scale hybrid encoder design.

3   Method

This section will introduce in detail the design and implementation of DualCBR (Dual-path Collaborative-Behavioral Recommender). This framework is mainly composed of three parts: the heterogeneous feature coding layer, the cross-modal interaction layer and the multi-scale hybrid encoder.

3.1   Input Representation and Embed Generation

In the input representation stage, the user behavior sequence $S_u = [v_1, v_2, \ldots, v_T]$ (uniformly processed to a fixed length of $T = 50$ through truncation or filling) and the item attribute text T_v are converted into standardized forms. Generate the item ID sequence $\tilde{S}_u \in \mathbb{Z}^T$ (where the fill position index is 0) and the lexical index sequence $\tilde{T}_v \in \mathbb{Z}^L$ based on the pre-trained vocabulary; Meanwhile, construct the binary matrix $M \in \{0, 1\}^{|\mathcal{U}| \times |\mathcal{V}|}$ representing the historical interaction (Fig. 1).

Entering the embedding generation stage, the system extracts two types of low-dimensional embeddings from these standardized inputs. Firstly, the collaborative embedding is obtained by applying PCA dimensionality reduction to the user-item interaction matrix M, capturing the co-occurrence patterns of

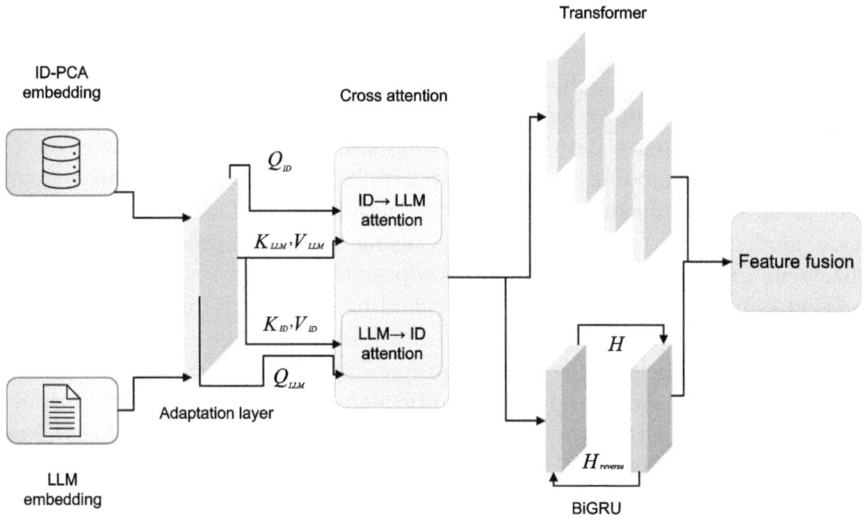

Fig. 1. Overall frame diagram

users and forming sequences representing behavioral patterns. Secondly, semantic embedding utilizes the frozen pre-trained large language model (such as LAMA-7B) [3] to parse $\tilde{T}_v$, generate the context hidden state of each lexical element, and obtain the lightweight global semantic embedding sequence through global average pooling and dimensionality reduction. Thus, while effectively retaining the semantics of key attributes (such as item functions), the computational burden is significantly reduced, achieving a balance between the expression of semantic information and the subsequent computational efficiency.

3.2 Dual Coding and Cross-Modal Interaction

This section introduces the implementation of dual-channel coding and cross-modal interaction, as follows:

The ID collaborative path focuses on mining explicit collaborative signals such as group preferences and item co-occurrence in users' historical behaviors [13]. It first linearly maps the 64-dimensional PCA co-embedding to 128 dimensions to align the dimensions of the LLM semantic paths, and encodes the alignment positions of the shared temporal position index superimposed on the two paths. After the path undergoes layer normalization and Dropout, the output of the ID path fuses the characteristics of cooperative attributes and behavioral timing sequences. LLM semantic paths handle lightweight text semantic embedding sequences, use the same alignment position encoding, and suppress semantic noise through a gating mechanism. Subsequently, the bidirectional cross-attention [6] realizes two-way interaction [1]: The ID feature is used as the Query to guide the semantic feature (ID → LLM, using group behavior to correct semantic deviation), and the semantic feature is used as the Query to explain the ID feature (LLM → ID, mining the semantic motivation of unconventional behaviors). The bidirectional attention head shares the subparameters of the projection matrix and fuses the correction values with the original features through residual connections to prevent excessive correction from losing important signals (such as the ID of long-tail items).

Algorithm 1: DualCBR Recommendation Framework

> **Input** : A collection of user behavior sequences S, Collection of item text attributes T, Position coding matrix P
> **Output**: Item recommendation probability vector $Prec$
> **Function** DUALCBR(S, T, P):
>> $\mathbf{E}_{co}, \mathbf{E}_{se} \leftarrow \varnothing$
>> **foreach** *User behavior sequence $s_i \in S$* **do**
>>> Generate the AST parse tree $a_i \leftarrow$ PARSES(s_i)
>>> $\mathbf{E}_{co} \leftarrow$ PCA(a_i) + $\mathbf{P}_{co}$
>>
>> **end**
>> **foreach** *Article text $t_j \in T$* **do**
>>> $\mathbf{E}_{se} \leftarrow$ LLAMA-7B(t_j) + $\mathbf{P}_{se}$
>>
>> **end**
>> **for** $k \leftarrow 1$ **to** 2 **do**
>>> **if** $k = 1$ **then**
>>>> $\mathbf{A}_{cross} \leftarrow$ CROSSATTN($\mathbf{E}_{co}, \mathbf{E}_{se}$)
>>>
>>> **else**
>>>> $\mathbf{A}_{cross} \leftarrow$ CROSSATTN($\mathbf{E}_{se}, \mathbf{E}_{co}$)
>>>
>>> **end**
>>> $\mathbf{E}_{co} \leftarrow \mathbf{E}_{co} + \mathbf{A}_{cross}$
>>
>> **end**
>> $\mathbf{Z}_{global} \leftarrow$ TRANSFORMER($\mathbf{E}_{co} \oplus \mathbf{E}_{se}$)
>> $\mathbf{Z}_{local} \leftarrow$ BIGRU($\mathbf{E}_{co}$) + BIGRU($\mathbf{E}_{se}$)
>> $\mathbf{Z}_{fused} \leftarrow \mathbf{Z}_{global} + \mathbf{Z}_{local}$
>> $Prec \leftarrow$ SOFTMAX(FC($\mathbf{Z}_{fused}$))
>> **return** $Prec$

3.3 Multi-scale Hybrid Encoder

The multi-scale hybrid encoder module consists of three parts: Transformer global modeling, RNN local modeling, and gated feature fusion.

1) Transformer global modeling: This part uses self-attention mechanism to tap cross-location dependencies of user behavior and capture long-term stable interest preferences.

Firstly, the synergistic feature $\tilde{H}^{id} \in \mathbb{R}^{50 \times 128}$ and semantic feature $\tilde{H}^{llm} \in \mathbb{R}^{50 \times 128}$ after cross-attention alignment are concatenated along the feature dimension to form a global input matrix:

$$H^{global} = \mathrm{Concat}\left(\tilde{H}^{id}, \tilde{H}^{llm} \right) \in \mathbb{R}^{50 \times 256} \tag{1}$$

A multi-head attention mechanism is then used, here using the 4-head attention mechanism as an example, to map inputs to different subspaces to capture diversified interest patterns:

$$\text{MultiHead}(Q, K, V) = \text{Concat}\left(\text{head}_1, \text{head}_2, \text{head}_3, \text{head}_4\right) W^O \tag{2}$$

where single-head attention is calculated as:

$$\text{head}_i = \text{Softmax}\left(\frac{QW^Q(KW_i^K)^{\mathsf{T}}}{\sqrt{d_k}}\right) VW_i^V \tag{3}$$

The projection matrices $W_i^Q, W_i^K, W_i^V \in \mathbb{R}^{256 \times 64}$, and $d_k = 64$ is used for scaling gradient stability.Then, the self-attention output is enhanced by a two-layer feedforward network (FFN) :

$$\text{FFN}(x) = W_2 \cdot \text{GELU}\left(W_1 x + b_1\right) + b_2 \tag{4}$$

where $W_1 \in \mathbb{R}^{256 \times 1024}$, $W_2 \in \mathbb{R}^{1024 \times 256}$. With residual connection and normalized stability training:

$$Z^{\text{global}} = \text{LayerNorm}\left(x + \text{Dropout}\left(\text{MultiHead}(x) + \text{FFN}(x)\right)\right) \tag{5}$$

The marker vector $z_{\text{cls}}^{\text{global}} \in \mathbb{R}^{256}$ at the beginning of the encoder output [CLS] is taken as the user's long-term interest representation.

2) RNN Local timing Modeling:First, the GRU dynamically adjusts the information flow through the update and reset gates.We adopted a bidirectional GRU,and generated the forward and backward hidden state sequences $\overrightarrow{H} \in \mathbb{R}^{B \times L \times 128}$ and $\overleftarrow{H} \in \mathbb{R}^{B \times L \times 128}$ respectively and concatenate them along the feature dimension to obtain the final local temporal feature:

$$Z^{\text{local}} = \left[\overrightarrow{H}; \overleftarrow{H}\right] \in \mathbb{R}^{B \times L \times 256} \tag{6}$$

3) Feature fusion and splicing: Finally, we add GRU output and Transformer output element by element to achieve global-local feature complementarity:

$$Z^{\text{fused}} = Z^{\text{global}} + Z^{\text{local}} \tag{7}$$

4   Experiment

In terms of the experimental setup, we adopted the public datasets of Amazon Fashion and Amazon Beauty, and referred to the SASRec method for prepro-cessing [2]. For data segmentation, the one-of-a-kind method [14] was used. Four representative models were selected for comparison in the experiment: SASRec, MELT_SASRec, CSLP_SASRec and Bert4Rec. For the Top-K recommendation task (K = 10) [15], multiple dimensions were evaluated using hit rate (Hit@10, H@10) and normalized discount cumulative gain (NDCG@10, N@10). All experiments were run in an environment equipped with NVIDIA GeForce RTX 3090 GPU and PyTorch.Text semantic embedding is achieved through the LLaMA-7B model (Tables 1 and 2).

Table 1. Improved performance of DualCBR compared to the benchmark model

Dataset	Overall	SASRec	BERT4Rec	MELT_SASRec	CSLP_SASRec	DualCBR
Beauty	HIT@10	0.4428	0.4005	0.4997	0.4985	**0.5598**
	NDCG@10	0.2983	0.2411	0.3303	0.3268	**0.3640**
Fashion	HIT@10	0.4882	0.4708	0.3260	0.3251	**0.5454**
	NDCG@10	0.4399	0.3583	0.2486	0.2330	**0.4650**

Table 2. DualCBR compares base model users, tail users, header items and tail items NDCG@10 and HIT@10

Dataset	Model	Tail Item		Head Item		Tail User		Head User	
		H@10	N@10	H@10	N@10	H@10	N@10	H@10	N@10
Beauty	DualICBR	**0.2194**	**0.0994**	0.7727	0.5553	**0.5488**	**.3552**	**0.6099**	**0.4042**
	CSLP SASRc	0.2089	0.0907	**0.7807**	**0.5568**	0.4830	0.3138	0.5664	0.3835
	MELT SASRec	0.1738	0.0829	0.6517	0.4310	0.4847	0.3179	0.5654	0.3849
	SASRec	0.0794	0.0608	0.5174	0.3623	0.4154	0.2330	0.4822	0.3530
	BERT4Rec	0.0965	0.0040	0.4876	0.3025	0.3918	0.2196	0.4607	0.2785
Fashion	DualICBR	**0.0957**	**0.0456**	0.7244	0.6319	**0.4569**	**0.3651**	**0.6603**	**0.5946**
	CSLP SARSc	0.0213	0.0068	**0.9575**	0.7040	0.2428	0.1576	0.6113	0.4953
	MELT SASRec	0.0286	0.0099	0.9452	**0.7457**	0.2448	0.1629	0.6085	0.5467
	SASRec	0.0519	0.0190	0.6824	0.5990	0.3904	0.3450	0.6182	0.5677
	BERT4Rec	0.0158	0.0075	0.6516	0.4933	0.3463	0.2296	0.6222	0.5314

4.1   Benchmark Performance Comparison

Experiments on the Amazon Beauty and Fashion datasets show that `DualCBR`, with its dual-path collaborative mechanism (integrating semantic information and user behavior modeling) and hybrid encoder (combining global and local time series features), It significantly outperformed all benchmark models in both NDCG@10 and HIT@10 metrics. The specific manifestations are as follows: On the Beauty dataset, it has increased by more than **10%** compared with MELT and CSLP, and on the Fashion dataset, it has increased by **5.7%** compared with `SASRec`. The deficiency of the benchmark model lies in: `SASRec` lacks semantic modeling and only relies on self-attention; The bidirectional mask training of `BERT4Rec` deviates from the real recommendation target. MELT and CSLP fail to explicitly fuse semantics, and the optimization strategies have limited effects when the long-tail distribution is severe (such as in the Fashion dataset). Overall, `DualCBR` has effectively broken through the performance ceiling, demonstrating its comprehensive advantages in modeling (Table 3).

Table 3. Ablation experiment of removing bidirectional cross attention layer

Dataset	Overall		Tail Item		Head Item		Tail User		Head User	
	H@10	ND@10	H@10	ND@10	H@10	ND@10	H@10	ND@10	H@10	ND@10
Beauty	0.4062	0.2405	0.0069	0.0025	0.5015	0.2973	0.3924	0.2313	0.4696	0.2827
Fashion	0.4736	0.3836	0.0232	0.0092	0.6529	0.5326	0.3661	0.2610	0.6130	0.5426

4.2 Long Tail Scenario Analysis

DualCBR performs exceptionally well in long-tail analysis of users and items. For the Short user group with sparse interaction behavior, it achieved 0.3552 and 0.5488 respectively on NDCG@10 and HR@10 on the Beauty dataset, significantly improving over the optimal benchmark without sacrificing the recommendation effect of the top user, and even outperforming all benchmark models in the metrics of the top user. For the low-frequency interaction Tail item group, it improves up to **26.3%** in Beauty from the benchmark, over **300%** in Fashion from HR@10 to MELT_SASRec, while maintaining competitive performance in the Popular item group (Table 4).

Table 4. Ablation experiment of removing RNN module from DualCBR model

Dataset	Overall		Tail Item		Head Item		Tail User		Head User	
	H@10	ND@10	H@10	ND@10	H@10	ND@10	H@10	ND@10	H@10	ND@10
Beauty	0.4326	0.2630	0.0393	0.0170	0.5264	0.3217	0.4188	0.2530	0.4959	0.3090
Fashion	0.4944	0.4232	0.0405	0.0200	0.6750	0.5839	0.3912	0.3100	0.6282	0.5702

4.3 Ablation Experiment

The core design of the DualCBR framework was verified for its necessity through ablation experiments. Cross-modal interaction layer: Removing it leads to a significant decline in system performance (particularly in long-tail item recommendations) on Beauty/Fashion datasets (e.g. NDCG@10 and HIT@10). Multi-scale hybrid encoder BiGRU overcomes the Transformer 's limitations in capturing the short-term evolution/emergent interests of sparse users (such as Short users) and Tail items, significantly enhancing local/event-driven interest representation capabilities (such as a **136.4%** improvement in HR@10 for tail items in Fashion) for adaptive modeling. Dual-path collaboration mechanism: Relying solely on the ID path significantly reduces the recommendation effect for head users (Long users) (e.g., HIT@10 by **34.2%**), and also limits the modeling of long tail/cold start users (e.g., NDCG@10 by **16.4%**); On the contrary, the LLM path recognizes long-tail demands by parsing commodity semantics, supports cold-start recommendations, and significantly improves accuracy, alleviates popularity bias, and enhances generalization after dynamic fusion with collaborative signals. Removing any core components will lead to significant degradation in key indicators or scenarios, highlighting their indivisible design value (Table 5).

Table 5. The DualCBR model retains only the ablation experiments of ID paths

Dataset	Overall		Tail Item		Head Item		Tail User		Head User	
	H@10	ND@10	H@10	ND@10	H@10	ND@10	H@10	ND@10	H@10	ND@10
Beauty	0.3690	0.2159	0.0493	0.0312	0.4452	0.2599	0.3624	0.2130	0.3991	0.2291
Fashion	0.4695	0.4161	0.0347	0.0156	0.6426	0.5755	0.3657	0.3054	0.6042	0.5597

5   Conclusion

The dual-path collaborative semantic recommendation framework DualCBR proposed in this paper effectively fuses the explicit collaborative signal and the implicit semantic features generated by LLM through the dual-path interaction of collaborative filtering and user behavior semantic analysis, combined with heterogeneous feature encoding and the bidirectional cross-attention module, and solves the problem of heterogeneous feature fusion noise. The framework also uses a multi-scale encoder with Transformer and BiGRU to capture user preferences at different granularities, significantly improving recommendation performance on several datasets (such as NDCG@10 with a **5.7%–11.3%** improvement), especially on long-tail user and item recommendations (with a hit rate increase of over **176%**). It has significantly alleviated the Matthew effect of the recommendation system and provided effective technical support for cross-category recommendations in e-commerce.

Acknowledgements. This work was supported in part by the National Key R&D Program of China (2023YFB3107303), in part by the National Natural Science Foundation of China (62172244), in part by the Innovation Ability Promotion Project for Small and Medium-sized Technology-based Enterprises of Shandong Province (2023TSGC0150, 2024TSGC126, 2023TSGC0163), in part by the Shandong Provincial Natural Science Foundation (ZR2020YQ06, ZR2024MF050), in part by the Taishan Scholars Program (tsqn202211210), and in part by the "20 New Universities" Project of Jinan City (202333023, 202333045), in part by the Pilot Project for Integrated Innovation of Science, Education and Industry of Qilu University of Technology (Shandong Academy of Sciences) (2023RCKY145).

References

1. Li, M., Ma, W., Chu, Z.: User preference interaction fusion and swap attention graph neural network for recommender system. Neural Netw. **184**, 107116 (2025)
2. Kang, W.C., McAuley, J.: Self-attentive sequential recommendation. In: Proceedings of the 2018 IEEE International Conference on Data Mining (ICDM 2018), pp. 197-206. IEEE (2018)
3. Lin, J., et al.: How can recommender systems benefit from large language models: a survey. ACM Trans. Inf. Syst. **43**(2), 1–47 (2025)
4. Fan, Z., Liu, Z., Wang, S., Zheng, L., Yu, P.S.: Modeling sequences as distributions with uncertainty for sequential recommendation. In: Proceedings of the 30th ACM International Conference on Information and Knowledge Management (CIKM 2021), pp. 3019-3023. ACM (2021)
5. Zhang, Y., et al.: Empowering long-tail item recommendation through cross decoupling network (CDN). In: Proceedings of the 29th ACM SIGKDD Conference on Knowledge Discovery and Data Mining (KDD 2023), pp. 5608–5617. ACM (2023)
6. Mateos, P., Bellogín, A.: A systematic literature review of recent advances on context-aware recommender systems. Artif. Intell. Rev. **58**(1), 1–53 (2025)
7. Huang, Y., Yang, Z., Hu, W., Xu, B., Zhang, Z.: CSLP: collaborative solution to long-tail problem and popularity bias in sequential recommendation. In: 2024 IEEE International Conference on Systems, Man, and Cybernetics (SMC 2024), pp. 4404–4411. IEEE (2024)
8. Harte, J., Zorgdrager, W., Louridas, P., Katsifodimos, A., Jannach, D., Fragkoulis, M.: Leveraging large language models for sequential recommendation. In: Proceedings of the 17th ACM Conference on Recommender Systems (RecSys 2023), pp. 1096–1102. ACM (2023)
9. Liu, Q., et al.: LLM-ESR: large language models enhancement for long-tailed sequential recommendation. In: Advances in Neural Information Processing Systems, vol. 37, pp. 26701–26727 (2024)
10. Singer, U., et al.: Sequential modeling with multiple attributes for watchlist recommendation in E-commerce. In: Proceedings of the Fifteenth ACM International Conference on Web Search and Data Mining (WSDM 2022), pp. 937-946. ACM (2022)
11. Jang, S., Lee, H., Cho, H., Chung, S.: Cities: contextual inference of tail-item embeddings for sequential recommendation. In: 2020 IEEE International Conference on Data Mining (ICDM 2020), pp. 202-211. IEEE (2020)
12. Fang, H., Zhang, D., Shu, Y., Guo, G.: Deep learning for sequential recommendation: algorithms, influential factors, and evaluations. ACM Trans. Inf. Syst. (TOIS) **39**(1), 1–42 (2020)
13. Sun, P., et al.: Collaborative-enhanced prediction of spending on newly downloaded mobile games under consumption uncertainty. In: Companion Proceedings of the ACM Web Conference 2024, pp. 10–19. ACM (2024)
14. Qin, J., et al.: Learning to retrieve user behaviors for click-through rate estimation. ACM Trans. Inf. Syst. **41**(4), 1–31 (2023)
15. Ciaccia, P., Martinenghi, D.: Directional queries: making top-K queries more effective in discovering relevant results. Proc. ACM Manag. Data **2024**2(6), 1–26 (2024)
16. Li, Y., Liu, K., Satapathy, R., Wang, S., Cambria, E.: Recent developments in recommender systems: a survey. IEEE Comput. Intell. Mag. **19**(2), 78–95 (2024)
17. Liu, S., Zheng, Y.: Long-tail session-based recommendation. In: Proceedings of the 14th ACM Conference on Recommender Systems (RecSys 2020), pp. 509–514. ACM (2020)

18. Sun, F., et al.: BERT4Rec: sequential recommendation with bidirectional encoder representations from transformer. In: Proceedings of the 28th ACM International Conference on Information and Knowledge Management (CIKM 2019), pp. 1441–1450. ACM (2019)
19. Lin, J., et al.: Large language models make sample-efficient recommender systems. Front. Comp. Sci. **19**(4), 194328 (2025)
20. Hidasi, B., Karatzoglou, A., Baltrunas, L., Tikk, D.: Session-based recommendations with recurrent neural networks. arXiv preprint arXiv:1511.06939 (2015)

Semantic Information Extraction with Language Models for Zero-Day Attack Detection

Shyamali Sinali Karunarathne[1,2], Sutharshan Rajasegarar[1(✉)], and Lei Pan[1,2]

[1] School of IT, Deakin University, Geelong, Australia
{s222518802,srajas,l.pan}@deakin.edu.au
[2] Deakin Cyber Research and Innovation Centre, Deakin University, Burwood, Australia

Abstract. Automatic extraction of Semantic information from documents or online resources, and incorporation of these patterns for tasks involving cyber attack detection, have recently gained significant attention. Semantic information plays a crucial role in enhancing the capability of zero-shot learning models, particularly in identifying previously unseen cyber attacks. Existing methods often use deep learning models with the aid of manually engineered semantics, which are time-consuming and scale poorly. To address these limitations, this paper proposes a zero-shot learning framework that integrates an autoencoder with a language model to extract semantic information and combine with network traffic information for accurate detection of novel attacks. Our experimental setup utilizes online articles to evaluate three approaches. Initially, the model's performance is tested without semantic embeddings. Subsequently, it is evaluated with attack-related embeddings and non-attack-related embeddings. Results from benchmark datasets demonstrate that the proposed model, incorporating automatically extracted semantic embeddings, significantly outperforms existing methods in accurately detecting zero-day attacks.

Keywords: Semantic information · language models · Zero-day attack · Zero-shot learning · cyber security

1 Introduction

The evolution of generative artificial intelligence, including large language models (LLMs), has revolutionized multiple fields [5]. With the impressive abilities of natural language processing (NLP) in understanding complex language patterns, security experts are empowered to explore a broader spectrum of attack vectors across different contexts associated with textual data. This enables deeper insights into potential threats and the development of more effective strategies for mitigating risks [13]. Anomaly-based attack detection aims to identify unusual

T. Zhu et al. (Eds.): KSEM 2025, LNAI 15923, pp. 248–256, 2026.
https://doi.org/10.1007/978-981-95-3061-8_26

patterns in network traffic [8,9,14]. The process starts with designing characteristics of network traffic before creating a model based on these features [3,10]. This model can recognize both normal traffic and attack traffic patterns. The main benefit of anomaly-based detection is its ability to identify unfamiliar and new attacks [7,12]. With the rapid advancement of technology, cyber attacks are continually changing their tactics and behaviors. This dynamic nature makes it challenging to stay up-to-date with evolving threats. Obtaining samples of each attack and training the model accordingly presents a significant challenge for cybersecurity professionals.

Zero-day attack detection [1,4] enables identification of emerging threats and novel attack vectors that may differ from traditional detection methods. By leveraging semantic information and transfer learning techniques, zero-shot learning empowers security systems to adapt and respond effectively to evolving cyber threats [11]. Various types of documents, including news articles, research papers, technical documents and blog posts are increasingly published daily about cyber attacks. These documents often detail the root causes of cyber attacks reported by organizations worldwide. The rapid growth makes the task of reading through and extracting root causes from each cyber attack document time-consuming and resource-intensive for organizations. While machine learning based models are deployed to monitor and prevent cyber attacks according to organizational security needs, security analysts must still extract up-to-date semantic information. This paper aims to automate the responsibilities of security analysts, including researching documented cyber-attacks and safeguarding organizational systems from both known and unknown threats.

In this paper, we propose a novel zero-shot framework that can automatically learn an embedding using natural language models from various information, such as online documents. These learned embeddings provide semantic information that aids in detecting new attacks more accurately. The embeddings are integrated into an autoencoder-based deep learning framework that combines network traffic data with semantic embeddings to learn normal and known attack behaviors. The learned encoder is used to detect zero-day attacks. Our proposed framework functions as a 'co-cyber security analyst' within an organization, supporting security analysts in capturing large volumes of document-based information as semantic data for effective cyber attack detection and mitigation.

2   Proposed Methodology

Our proposed framework comprises two components; semantic information extraction and model building, as shown in Fig. 1. The utilization of semantic information as an intermediate layer facilitates the connection between known attack patterns and emerging zero-day attacks. Integrating semantic embeddings into the model-building process enables the system to make accurate predictions about previously unseen attacks.

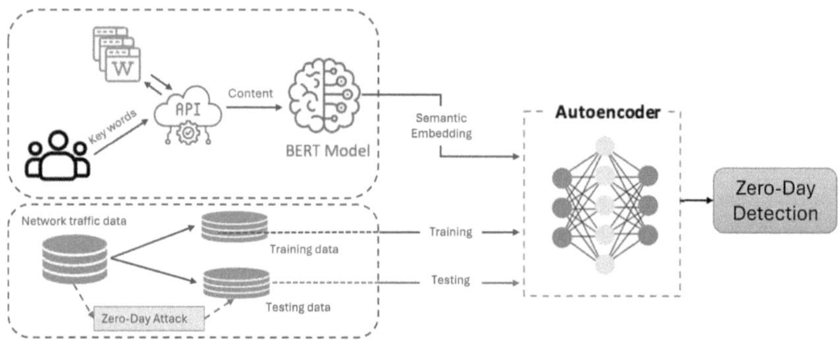

Fig. 1. Proposed Framework comprises a semantic embedding generator and an autoencoder that integrates network traffic information for zero-day attack detection.

Extracting Semantic Information. Semantic information, comprising contextual meaning and relationships, is crucial for understanding the characteristics and behavior of both known and unknown attacks. Semantic information can be gathered through various methods, including extracting data from Wikipedia articles, using Google, and referencing cyber attack-related publications [15]. This information enriches the knowledge base and bridges the gap by linking known attack patterns with emerging threats.

In our research, we prioritized automating the collection of semantic information over manual processes. Automation ensures continuous updates and refinement of the semantic knowledge base. Semantic information extraction is pivotal to our methodology, forming the foundation for establishing relationships between known and unknown attacks. Manually gathering and creating semantic information is time-intensive, limiting its practicality in dynamic cybersecurity contexts. Given the rapidly evolving cyber threat landscape, relying solely on manual approaches is impractical. To address this, our methodology incorporates an automated semantic embedding generation process, leveraging semantic information from known attacks to detect unseen threats effectively.

To extract semantic information and convert it into a machine-readable format, the BERT model is used. BERT, stands for Bidirectional Encoder Representations from Transformers, is a pre-trained natural language processing (NLP) model developed by Google. Semantic content is extracted from Wikipedia articles, which are gathered based on keywords related to the topic. Initially, topic-related keywords are provided, and relevant articles are collected using the googlesearch and beautifulsoup libraries to form a corpus. The content is then segmented into sentences, and each sentence is tokenized using the BERT tokenizer. Processing steps are applied to generate machine-readable BERT embeddings, including flattening the embeddings and converting them into a Numpy array. In the final step, embeddings are flattened, converting multi-dimensional arrays into one-dimensional vectors. This operation simplifies the structure of the embeddings, making them easier to manipulate and analyze. Finally, the flattened embeddings are converted into a Numpy array, a common data structure

---

Algorithm 1. Semantic Embeddings Generation

Initialize: $bert\_embeddings\_array = []$, $valid\_sources = []$, $corpus = []$, $tokenized\_corpus = []$,
$bert\_embeddings = []$
Input: $sources = [article\ titles,\ URLs]$
for all source **in** $valid\_sources$ **do**
    content $= get\_content(source)$
    if content **is not** $None$ **then** $corpus.append(content)$
    end if
end for
for all doc **in** $corpus$ **do**
    sentences $= tokenize\_sentences(doc)$
    for all sentence **in** $sentences$ **do**
        tokens $= tokenize\_with\_bert\_tokenizer(sentence)$
        $tokenized\_corpus.append(tokens)$
    end for
end for
for all tokens **in** $tokenized\_corpus$ **do**
    inputs $= create\_bert\_inputs(tokens)$
    outputs $= generate\_bert\_outputs(inputs)$
    embeddings $= extract\_bert\_embeddings(outputs)$
    pooled_embedding $= apply\_max\_pooling(embeddings)$
    $bert\_embeds.append(pooled\_embedd)$
end for
for all embedding **in** $bert\_embeddings$ **do** $bert\_embeds\_flat.append(flatten(embedd))$
end for
Output: $bert\_embeddings\_array$

---

for numerical computations and machine learning tasks. Algorithm 1 outlines the process for generating semantic embeddings.

Model Building. The second component of the framework involves an autoencoder. The autoencoder consists of an encoder and a decoder: the encoder compresses the input data into a lower-dimensional representation, and the decoder reconstructs the original inputs from these representations. Both the encoder and decoder are composed of multiple dense layers, each utilizing rectified linear unit (ReLU) activation functions, batch normalization, and dropout regularization to improve model generalization and prevent overfitting.

Encoder: The encoder comprises three dense layers with ReLU activation functions to reduce the dimensionality of the input data. Batch normalization is applied after each dense layer to stabilize the training process, while dropout regularization is incorporated to prevent overfitting by randomly deactivating a fraction of the units during training.

Decoder Layers: The decoder comprises dense layers designed to reconstruct the original input data from the compressed representation generated by the encoder. The output layer of the decoder uses a sigmoid activation function to scale the output values to the range $[0, 1]$.

The process begins by specifying keywords related to each attack, which are then utilized by a language model to locate and extract relevant articles containing semantic information. This semantic information is integrated into the autoencoder model during training, enabling a comprehensive understanding of the patterns and relationships associated with known attacks. To evaluate the model's efficacy in detecting unseen attacks, one attack type is systematically excluded from the training data while being included in the testing dataset, and the model is evaluated accordingly. With the rapid advancement of technology and the growing interest in cybersecurity, numerous research articles are published on emerging attacks and threats. Consequently, the proposed method is well-equipped to effectively extract semantic information and prepare for potential unseen attacks.

3   Evaluation and Discussion

Datasets: The proposed methodology is evaluated using two distinct datasets. The NSL-KDD dataset [2] consists of four main attack categories (see Table 1 The second dataset, CICIoT2023, is a benchmark for assessing large-scale attacks on the IoT ecosystem. It comprises 46,686,579 samples generated by 105 interconnected IoT devices [6] having 33 distinct attack types. For this work, a sample subset of the CICIoT2023 dataset is utilized (see Table 1).

Table 1. Datasets

CICIoT2023	Category	Normal	DDoS	DoS	Recon	Exploit	Malware	Other	Total
	Training	22,484	756,395	166,679	6,563	1,258	68	10,326	963,773
	Testing	11,173	366,209	81,327	3,257	582	38	4,951	467,537
NSL KDD	Category	Normal	DoS	U2R	R2L	Probe	Total		
	Training	67,343	45,927	52	2,885	11,656	127,863		
	Testing	9,711	7,460	67	995	2,421	20,654		

Experimental Set Up: In the proposed experiment, the performance of detecting unseen attacks with the aid of learned semantics is analyzed. Initially, keywords related to unknown attacks are provided to the model to extract semantic embeddings. To achieve zero-shot learning, each attack type is systematically excluded from the training phase. The model is trained on the remaining attack types and their corresponding semantic embeddings. Subsequently, the excluded attack type is incorporated into the testing phase to evaluate the model's ability to detect it. In the proposed experiments, three architectures (as mentioned below) are implemented to provide a comprehensive overview of the impact of the semantic information derived from the BERT model.

Model with Autoencoder: This architecture employs an autoencoder to reconstruct the input data, focusing on evaluating its effectiveness in reconstructing the input without incorporating additional relevant semantic information. The pre-processed training data is provided to the model, with each attack type systematically excluded to achieve zero-shot learning. The model is then tested using a dataset that includes zero-day attacks, and its performance in detecting unseen attacks is evaluated.

Model with Related Embedding: This architecture integrates semantic embeddings obtained from the language model, specifically related to a particular zero-day attack. The objective is to investigate the impact of incorporating relevant attack-related semantic information on the model's detection capabilities. By leveraging the semantic information embedded within the embeddings, the model enhances its ability to detect previously unseen attacks by referencing the relevant documents. Each attack type is systematically excluded from the training dataset. Articles about the excluded zero-day attack are retrieved using the Google API based on the provided keywords. The model is then trained using the remaining training data and the generated semantic embeddings, and its performance is evaluated on a testing set to understand the impact of semantic information on its ability to detect previously unseen attacks.

Model with Non-related Embeddings: This architecture represents an approach that incorporates semantic embeddings derived from the language model, unrelated to the specific zero-day attack. The objective is to analyze the performance of the autoencoder in reconstructing the input data with the assistance of additional semantic information from other attacks.

Results and Discussion. Three sets of comparative experiments are conducted using two datasets. Anomalies are detected as those samples with mean squared error values exceed a given threshold.

Evaluation using NSL-KDD. The experimental results for NSL-KDD data are shown in Table 2. Across all attack types, models incorporating additional embeddings (AE with related embeddings and AE with non-related embeddings) generally outperform the baseline AE model in terms of precision and F1 score. All models achieve perfect recall (1.0) for all attack types, demonstrating their ability to identify all instances of attacks. The F1 scores are consistently high across all models and attack types, reflecting a strong balance between precision and recall. For instance, in the case of DoS attacks, precision improves from 0.69 with the baseline AE model to 0.73 with `AE + related embeddings`, resulting in an F1 score increase from 0.82 to 0.84. Similarly, for U2R attacks, precision increases from 0.69 to 0.74, leading to an F1 score improvement from 0.82 to 0.85. Probe attacks also show gains, with the F1 score rising from 0.83 to 0.85. However, the consistent performance across R2L attacks suggests that additional techniques or features may be required to effectively address this specific attack type. The observed improvements in precision and F1 score with additional embeddings highlight the value of incorporating supplementary features in enhancing the model's classification performance. Notably, the performance for the 'R2L' (Remote-to-Local) attack type remains unchanged across all models.

   The results demonstrate that incorporating semantic information enhances the model's ability to recognize unseen attacks. The impact of semantic embeddings is evident when comparing the autoencoder-only model to the one with semantic integration. Wikipedia articles serve as the primary source of semantics, but limited availability for certain attacks may affect performance.

Table 2. Results: RE - related embedding, NRE- non-related embedding.

Dataset	Type	AE			AE+RE			AE+NRE		
		Prec	Recall	F1	Prec	Recall	F1	Prec	Recall	F1
NSL KDD	**Dos**	0.69	1	0.82	0.73	1	0.84	0.71	1	0.83
	U2R	0.69	1	0.82	0.74	1	0.85	0.72	1	0.84
	Probe	0.7	1	0.83	0.73	1	0.85	0.72	1	0.83
	R2L	0.72	1	0.83	0.72	1	0.83	0.72	1	0.83
CICIOT2023	**DoS**	0.96	0.64	0.77	0.96	0.64	0.77	0.96	0.64	0.77
	DDoS	0.96	0.63	0.77	0.96	0.67	0.79	0.96	0.67	0.79
	Exploit	0.96	0.57	0.72	0.96	0.57	0.71	0.96	0.58	0.72
	Recon	0.96	0.57	0.72	0.96	0.57	0.72	0.96	0.57	0.72

Evaluation using CICIOT2023. The experimental results for the CICIoT2023 dataset are presented in Table 2. Precision, recall, and F1 scores are calculated for various attack types, including Denial of Service (DoS), Distributed Dos, Exploit, and Reconnaissance (Recon), across all scenarios. For DDoS attacks, precision remains consistently high across all models at 0.96. However, recall and F1 scores show noticeable improvements when related embeddings are incorporated. Specifically, the baseline autoencoder (AE) model achieves a recall of 0.63 and an F1 score of 0.77 for DDoS attacks. With the inclusion of related embeddings (AE + Related Embeddings), the recall increases to 0.67, and the F1 score improves to 0.79. These results highlight the enhanced capability of the model to detect DDoS attacks when leveraging relevant semantic information, demonstrating its ability to extract and utilize meaningful content effectively.

In summary, the results suggest that the detection of attacks is enhanced by the inclusion of related embeddings, as reflected in the improvements in recall and F1 scores. The importance of contextually relevant semantic information is highlighted, as it improves the model's ability to detect previously unseen or more complex attacks, such as DDoS. In general, the use of non-related embeddings can negatively impact model performance. While semantic embeddings are intended to provide additional context and improve the detection of patterns, non-related embeddings; those misaligned with the specific task or context may introduce irrelevant or misleading information. It is indicated that the ability of the model to correctly identify relevant content is compromised when non-related embeddings are incorporated.

4   Conclusion

Zero-shot learning approaches enable detection of novel cyber threats that emerge in a network. Moreover, the growth in language models enable efficient understanding of complex contents. Recognizing the critical role of semantics in enhancing model performance, this paper proposes a novel semantic information extraction framework utilizing language models and integrating with the network traffic information to improve cyber attack detection. Evaluation on benchmark datasets demonstrate the potential of extracting relevant content and incorporating semantic embeddings into models for zero-day attack detection. The BERT-based embeddings balances efficiency and accuracy, revealing its potential for improving cyber attack detection. Future work include exploration of more advanced language models, such as GPT or domain-specific large language models, to capture deeper contextual patterns and further enhance detection capabilities.

References

1. Bilge, L., Dumitraş, T.: Before we knew it: an empirical study of zero-day attacks in the real world. In: Proc. of the ACM Conf. on Computer and Communications Security, pp. 833–844 (2012)
2. Elkan, C.: Results of the kdd'99 classifier learning. ACM SIGKDD Explorations Newsl **1**(2), 63–64 (2000)
3. Hdaib, M., Rajasegarar, S., Pan, L.: Quantum deep learning-based anomaly detection for enhanced network security. Quantum Mach. Intell. **6**(1), 26 (2024)
4. Miao, Y., Pan, L., Rajasegarar, S., Zhang, J., Leckie, C., Xiang, Y.: Distributed detection of zero-day network traffic flows. In: 15th Australasian Conf. on Data Mining, AusDM, pp. 173–191. Springer (2018)
5. Motlagh, F.N., Hajizadeh, M., Majd, M., Najafi, P., Cheng, F., Meinel, C.: Large language models in cybersecurity: State-of-the-art. arXiv preprint arXiv:2402.00891 (2024)
6. Neto, E.C.P., Dadkhah, S., Ferreira, R., Zohourian, A., Lu, R., Ghorbani, A.A.: Ciciot 2023: a real-time dataset and benchmark for large-scale attacks in iot environment. Sensors **23**(13), 5941 (2023)
7. O'Reilly, C., Gluhak, A., Imran, M.A., Rajasegarar, S.: Anomaly detection in wireless sensor networks in a non-stationary environment. IEEE Commun. Surv. Tutorials **16**(3), 1413–1432 (2014)
8. Pokhrel, S.R., Yang, L., Rajasegarar, S., Li, G.: Robust zero trust architecture: Joint blockchain based federated learning and anomaly detection based framework. In: Proc. of the SIGCOMM Workshop on Zero Trust Arch. for Next Gen. Comm., pp. 7–12 (2024)
9. Rajasegarar, S., Leckie, C., Palaniswami, M.: Anomaly detection in wireless sensor networks. IEEE Wirel. Commun. **15**(4), 34–40 (2008)
10. Shilton, A., Rajasegarar, S., Palaniswami, M.: Multiclass anomaly detector: the cs++ support vector machine. Int. Mach. Learn. Res. **21**(213), 1–39 (2020)
11. Wang, H., Wang, Y., Guo, Y.: Unknown network attack detection method based on reinforcement zero-shot learning. J. Phys. Conf. Ser. **2303**, 012008. IOP Publishing (2022)
12. Wang, W., Sheng, Y., Wang, J., Zeng, X., Ye, X., Huang, Y., Zhu, M.: Hast-ids: learning hierarchical spatial-temporal features using deep neural networks to improve intrusion detection. IEEE access **6**, 1792–1806 (2017)
13. Yang, J., Jin, H., Tang, R., Han, X., Feng, Q., Jiang, H., Zhong, S., Yin, B., Hu, X.: Harnessing the power of llms in practice: a survey on chatgpt and beyond. ACM Trans. Knowl. Discov. Data **18**(6), 1–32 (2024)

14. Yi, T., Chen, X., Zhu, Y., Ge, W., Han, Z.: Review on the application of deep learning in network attack detection. J. Netw. Comput. Appl. **212**, 103580 (2023)
15. Zhang, Z., Liu, Q., Qiu, S., Zhou, S., Zhang, C.: Unknown attack detection based on zero-shot learning. IEEE Access **8**, 193981–193991 (2020)

A Review of Optimization Techniques for Large Language Model Inference

Yujia Cao[iD], Xi Tao[✉][iD], Weipeng Cao, Chuanfei Xu, and Zhong Ming

Guangdong Laboratory of Artificial Intelligence and Digital Economy (SZ),
Shenzhen, Guangdong, China
2400811011@mails.szu.edu.cn, {taoxi,caoweipeng,xuchuanfei}@gml.ac.cn,
mingz@szu.edu.cn

Abstract. Large Language Models (LLMs) have demonstrated impressive capabilities across a wide range of tasks; however, these models face critical efficiency challenges due to their resource-intensive nature. This paper presents a comprehensive analysis of recent advances in LLM inference optimization, systematically categorizing optimization techniques into three fundamental domains: computation, memory, and system-level enhancements. We examine key approaches including attention mechanism improvements, key-value cache optimizations, efficient decoding strategies, batching techniques, and model compression methods. These innovations directly address critical performance bottlenecks in memory utilization, computational efficiency, and response latency. Breakthrough technologies such as FlashAttention, PagedAttention, speculative decoding, and advanced quantization methods have demonstrated substantial improvements in inference performance. Our analysis further explores the inherent trade-offs between various optimization strategies and their practical implications for deploying LLMs in production environments.

Keywords: Large Language Models · Inference Optimization · Computation Optimization · Memory Optimization · System Optimization

1 Introduction

As Large Language Models (LLMs) continue to grow in complexity and capability, optimizing their inference processes has become paramount for practical deployment. This optimization challenge encompasses multiple critical objectives: enhancing computational efficiency, minimizing response latency, and achieving effective resource management. The research community has explored various strategies for optimizing LLM inference. The survey by Cheng et al. [3] offers a detailed examination of quantization and model compression techniques; however, it leaves significant gaps in the analysis of computational efficiency and

T. Zhu et al. (Eds.): KSEM 2025, LNAI 15923, pp. 257–265, 2026.
https://doi.org/10.1007/978-981-95-3061-8_27

system-level optimization strategies. Although Shi et al. [13] present a comprehensive analysis of algorithmic and system-level optimizations for model training, their work peripherally addresses inference optimization challenges. While Mishra et al. [11] deliver a comprehensive survey of compression techniques, their analysis does not extend to the crucial domains of computational efficiency and system-level optimizations. The distinctive contribution of this survey lies in its three-tiered analytical framework, which systematically categorizes LLM inference optimization techniques. By organizing methods across computation, memory, and system-level domains, we provide a unified perspective on the complex landscape of LLM optimization strategies. An overview of these optimization techniques is presented in Table 1.

Table 1. Overview of the Optimization Techniques

Category	Key Technologies
computation optimization	attention mechanism, decoding strategies
memory optimization	key-value cache managements, compression
system optimization	batching strategies, distributed inference

The remainder of this review is organized as follows: Sect. 2 explores computation optimization techniques; Sect. 3 analyzes memory optimization methods; Sect. 4 presents system-level optimizations; Sect. 5 concludes this paper.

2   Computation Optimization

While LLMs have become indispensable across numerous applications, their practical deployment presents significant performance challenges due to substantial computational overhead. This section focuses on two fundamental approaches to LLM inference optimization: attention mechanisms and decoding strategies.

2.1   Attention Mechanisms

The attention is a pivotal concept in machine learning, enabling models to focus on specific parts of input data in order to process information more effectively. It has revolutionized deep learning architectures, especially with the advent of transformer architecture [14], which consists of multiple stacked blocks. Each block comprises several key components including self-attention and feedforward network. Optimization of the self-attention mechanism is the key to solving the bottleneck of LLM long context processing, as its computational complexity grows quadratically with the context length.

Sharing-Based Attention Optimization. To address these challenges, one optimization approach is sharing-based attention, such as Multi-Query Attention (MQA) [12] and Grouped-Query Attention (GQA) [2]. These methods significantly reduce memory usage and computational overhead by sharing the key and value matrices across attention heads. Specifically, MQA allows all attention heads to share a single set of Key-Value (KV) matrices, reducing the memory requirement from being linearly proportional to the number of attention heads to a constant level. This optimization can improve decoding speed by over 30%. However, it may introduce a slight performance degradation, typically reflected in a 2–5% increase in perplexity. In contrast, GQA builds upon MQA by introducing a grouped sharing mechanism, further balancing performance and efficiency. By significantly reducing memory and computational demands, these techniques enable high-performance models to run on resource-constrained hardware such as single GPUs, with only minor trade-offs in model quality. The gains in speed and resource efficiency far outweigh the slight increase in perplexity.

FlashAttention. FlashAttention (FA) [5] represents a significant advancement in optimizing the attention mechanism. In conventional attention computation, the input matrices $Q, K, V \in \mathbb{R}^{N \times d}$ are used to compute intermediate results, specifically the attention scores:

$$S = QK^T \in \mathbb{R}^{N \times N}, \quad P = \mathrm{softmax}(S) \in \mathbb{R}^{N \times N}. \tag{1}$$

As sequence lengths increase from 2K tokens in GPT-3 to 1M tokens in Gemini 1.5, the memory consumption of the $N \times N$ intermediate tensors becomes prohibitively large.

To address this issue, FA implements a block-based tiling approach where matrices Q, K, V (each with dimension $N \times d$) are processed systematically through nested inner and outer loops. The computation pipeline is structured in distinct phases: initially, blocks of K^T are transferred from high-bandwidth memory (HBM) to on-chip Static Random-Access Memory(SRAM); subsequently, for each block of Q processed within the inner loop iteration, corresponding data blocks are loaded to SRAM where localized attention computations are performed in the designated compute block region. The diagram delineates the precise data movement patterns between memory hierarchies through strategic copy operations, with the final attention output $\mathrm{sm}(QK^T)V$ (softmax-normalized attention scores multiplied by values) ultimately written back to HBM. This methodical tiled execution architecture circumvents the explicit materialization of the complete $N \times N$ attention matrix, thus achieving optimal memory utilization while maintaining computational efficiency for attention mechanism calculations. As a result, FA achieves a 2–4 times speedup over standard attention while reducing memory usage by 10–20 times.

FA significantly improves attention computation by reducing memory usage and increasing efficiency through tiling and online softmax techniques. However, it still involves non-trivial memory management and non-GEMM overheads. FlashAttention-2 (FA2) [4] further optimizes FA by refining softmax computation, enhancing parallelism, and leveraging specialized hardware features such as Tensor Memory Accelerator (TMA) and Warp Group Matrix Multiply-Accumulate (WGMMA), achieving up to 2 times speedup over FA. While FA2 maximizes performance on modern GPUs, its reliance on advanced hardware limits its applicability on older devices. Both methods offer substantial efficiency gains, but future work should focus on improving hardware adaptability and reducing memory bottlenecks.

2.2   Decoding Strategies

Token-level early exit is an important research direction in decoding optimization, with its core idea being to reduce the overall computational burden by allowing simpler samples to complete computation at the shallow layers of the model. This approach is based on a key observation: not all tokens require full-depth network processing to achieve accurate predictions. Traditional decoding methods process all tokens with the same depth, whereas early exit technology introduces dynamic decision mechanisms based on heuristic metrics such as entropy or hash mapping, providing different processing depths for tokens of varying complexity.

Among numerous implementations, the SkipDecode [6] method has achieved significant breakthroughs. It not only inherits the fundamental principles of early exit but also deeply integrates this mechanism with batch processing and KV cache optimization. SkipDecode designs a sophisticated confidence scoring system that accurately determines when specific tokens can exit the computation process early. It innovatively introduces a token grouping mechanism, intelligently aggregating tokens with similar exit points, which significantly enhances operational efficiency in batch processing scenarios. Additionally, SkipDecode optimizes KV cache management. Traditional transformer decoders maintain complete key-value pair caches for each token at every layer, leading to substantial memory usage and redundant computations. SkipDecode dynamically optimizes the KV cache by precisely managing the cache states of early-exit tokens, effectively reducing memory usage and improving computational efficiency. Experiments show that SkipDecode can reduce inference latency by 20–30% while maintaining nearly unchanged model accuracy (with errors controlled within 1%). In scenarios with highly variable input complexity, it can cut computational costs by up to 40% and reduce memory usage by 15–20%.

3   Memory Optimization

Optimizing memory usage in LLM inference is essential for enhancing performance and efficiency. In this section, we review the memory optimization of LLM inference from two perspectives: KV cache managements and model compression.

3.1 KV Cache Managements

KV cache is a key optimization technology in LLM inference, enabling the avoidance of repeated calculations by caching the keys and values of generated tokens. Although it significantly improves inference performance, this technique typically consumes around 30% of the total memory, prompting various research efforts on its optimization.

PagedAttention. Inspired by the operating system paged virtual memory, vLLM [8] proposes the page attention mechanism, which uses non-contiguous memory space to store contiguous KV caches. A contiguous piece of memory space is allocated on a GPU node and divided into a number of physical KV blocks of the same specification. Accordingly, vLLM also represents the KV cache for each request sequence as a series of logical KV blocks, similar to pages in virtual memory, each containing the KV tensor generated by a fixed number of tokens.

During the pre-population phase, vLLM reserves only the necessary KV blocks for storing the KV cache without reserving the explicit memory for the maximum sequence length that may be generated. After generating the KV cache for the 1st output tag, the vLLM stores it in the preallocated logical KV block and updates the block table to record the mapping relationship between the logical KV block and the physical KV block as well as the number of its populated locations. Then, the virtual memory is mapped to the physical memory through the page table, completing the conversion from logical to physical addresses.

During the decoding process, vLLM flexibly allocates a new physical KV block for each logical KV block as new tokens and their corresponding KV caches are generated. At the same time, vLLM keeps track of the fill position of each logical KV block and its associated physical KV block. All physical KV blocks are populated from left to right, and the next block is allocated only if all previous physical blocks are filled. This approach limits the memory wastage per request to a single physical block, thus effectively reducing the generation of internal fragmentation. This optimization is crucial for long sequences or concurrent requests such as beam search, improving scalability and performance for real-world applications with high memory demands.

3.2 Model Compression

The compression technology used in LLMs primarily focuses on low-precision inference and quantization techniques, which are critical for reducing computational and memory costs while maintaining model performance. Among these, quantization has emerged as a key enabler of efficient inference, particularly for large-scale models.

Quantization. Quantization reduces the precision of model weights and activations, enabling faster computation and lower memory usage. SmoothQuant [15] addresses the challenge of quantizing activations by mathematically shifting the quantization difficulty to the weights. It demonstrates that this approach achieves 8-bit quantization with minimal accuracy loss across models such as LLaMA and GPT-3. The experiments show latency reductions of 20–30% while maintaining model accuracy within 1% of the original full-precision performance. KVQuant [7] focuses specifically on compressing the KV cache to 3 bits for long sequences. The comprehensive evaluations show this technique reduces KV cache memory footprint by 4 times, enabling longer context lengths with the same memory constraints. Across multiple benchmarks, KVQuant maintains perplexity within 0.5% of baseline while achieving 15–20% reduction in total memory usage, making it particularly valuable for long-context reasoning tasks such as document summarization and multi-turn dialogue. ZeroQuant [16] combines group weight quantization with low-rank compensation techniques to achieve 4-bit quantization with minimal accuracy degradation. Its methodology reduces model size by 4 times while improving inference speed by approximately 2 times. Extensive evaluations on BERT and GPT-2 demonstrate that ZeroQuant preserves 99% of the original model's accuracy while significantly reducing computational requirements.

4   System Optimization

This section explores system-level optimizations in LLM inference, including batching strategies and distributed inference. These techniques can enhance the throughput and scalability of LLM inference systems.

4.1   Batching Strategies

Batching strategies are essential in LLM inference for improving system throughput, particularly when handling small request sizes. Among these strategies, continuous batch processing has emerged as a highly effective approach for optimizing real-time inference by dynamically adjusting batches during token generation.

Continuous Batch Processing. Continuous batch processing holds its core value in dynamically adjusting batch sizes to enhance computational resource utilization and reduce request wait times. Orca [17] optimizes batch organization through iteration-level scheduling, allowing different requests to interleave execution within a single generation cycle. The core idea is to break the limitation of static batching, which requires waiting for all requests to complete, and instead adopt a finer-grained scheduling approach that enables new requests to be inserted into the current computation stream. This method offers significant advantages in high-concurrency environments, reducing idle time of computational units and improving GPU efficiency.

In contrast, SARATHI [1] introduces stall-free batching, further refining the request scheduling strategy in continuous batch processing. Its main improvement lies in decoupling the prefill and decode phases, allowing the system to continue accepting new requests for the prefill computation while processing the decode phase of current requests. This approach effectively reduces computational unit idling caused by uneven request completion times, enhancing system throughput.

4.2 Distributed Inference

Distributed inference has become essential for scaling LLMs across multiple devices or data centers, addressing the massive computational and memory demands of these systems. Among recent advancements, ring attention and DistAttention have emerged as particularly innovative solutions for long-sequence processing and memory optimization in distributed environments.

Ring attention [10] addresses the limitations of traditional attention mechanisms by dividing long sequences into smaller blocks distributed across devices in a ring-like topology. Each device processes its local block while exchanging intermediate results with neighbors, enabling efficient handling of sequences beyond individual device memory limits. This approach reduces memory overhead and improves throughput, particularly benefiting tasks like document summarization and genomic analysis.

DistAttention [9] optimizes KV cache management across distributed systems, a major memory bottleneck in large models. It intelligently partitions the KV cache across devices, minimizing data movement and communication overhead. A specialized memory manager tracks cache utilization, enabling dynamic scaling and efficient resource allocation. While effective in reducing memory usage and improving performance, DistAttention may struggle with highly dynamic workloads or uneven access patterns, and its implementation complexity can pose challenges in resource-constrained environments.

5   Conclusion

Efficient LLM inference reduces computational, memory, and storage costs while improving latency, throughput, and energy efficiency. This review highlights advancements in computational, memory, and system-level optimizations. The rapid growth of LLMs presents several challenges and future research should focus on addressing these challenges. For attention mechanisms, hybrid approaches or hardware-specific optimizations could further reduce memory and computational costs. In model compression, adaptive quantization or hybrid methods could balance precision and efficiency. For distributed inference, hierarchical systems or federated learning could optimize workloads across devices. By tackling these challenges, researchers can unlock the full potential of LLMs, enabling real-time, energy-efficient, and scalable solutions for diverse applications.

Acknowledgments. This work was supported by GuangDong Basic and Applied Basic Research Foundation (2025A1515011259) and Director Fund of Guangdong Laboratory of Artificial Intelligence and Digital Economy (Shenzhen) (24420001).

References

1. Agrawal, A., Panwar, A., Mohan, J., Kwatra, N., Gulavani, B.S., Ramjee, R.: SARATHI: efficient LLM inference by piggybacking decodes with chunked prefills. arXiv preprint arXiv:2308.16369 (2023)
2. Ainslie, J., Lee-Thorp, J., de Jong, M., Zemlyanskiy, Y., Lebron, F., Sanghai, S.: GQA: training generalized multi-query transformer models from multi-head checkpoints. In: Proceedings of the 2023 Conference on Empirical Methods in Natural Language Processing, pp. 4895–4901 (2023)
3. Cheng, Y., Wang, D., Zhou, P., Zhang, T.: Model compression and acceleration for deep neural networks: the principles, progress, and challenges. IEEE Signal Process. Mag. **35**(1), 126–136 (2018)
4. Dao, T.: FlashAttention-2: faster attention with better parallelism and work partitioning. arXiv preprint arXiv:2307.08691 (2023)
5. Dao, T., Fu, D., Ermon, S., Rudra, A., Ré, C.: FlashAttention: fast and memory-efficient exact attention with IO-awareness. In: Advances in Neural Information Processing Systems, vol. 35, pp. 16344–16359 (2022)
6. Del Corro, L., Del Giorno, A., Agarwal, S., Yu, B., Awadallah, A., Mukherjee, S.: SkipDecode: autoregressive skip decoding with batching and caching for efficient LLM inference. arXiv preprint arXiv:2307.02628 (2023)
7. Hooper, C., et al.: KVQuant: towards 10 million context length LLM inference with KV cache quantization. In: Advances in Neural Information Processing Systems, vol. 37, pp. 1270–1303 (2024)
8. Kwon, W., et al.: Efficient memory management for large language model serving with PagedAttention. In: Proceedings of the 29th Symposium on Operating Systems Principles, pp. 611–626 (2023)
9. Lin, B., et al.: Infinite-LLM: efficient LLM service for long context with DistAttention and distributed KVCache. arXiv preprint cs.DC/2401.02669 (2024)
10. Liu, H., Zaharia, M., Abbeel, P.: Ring attention with blockwise transformers for near-infinite context. arXiv preprint arXiv:2310.01889 (2023)
11. Mishra, R., Gupta, H.P., Dutta, T.: A survey on deep neural network compression: challenges, overview, and solutions. arXiv preprint arXiv:2010.03954 (2020)
12. Shazeer, N.: Fast transformer decoding: one write-head is all you need. arXiv preprint arXiv:1911.02150 (2019)
13. Shi, Y., Yang, K., Jiang, T., Zhang, J., Letaief, K.B.: Communication-efficient edge AI: algorithms and systems. IEEE Commun. Surv. Tutorials **22**(4), 2167–2191 (2020)
14. Vaswani, A., et al.: Attention is all you need. In: Advances in Neural Information Processing Systems, vol. 30 (2017)
15. Xiao, G., Lin, J., Seznec, M., Wu, H., Demouth, J., Han, S.: SmoothQuant: accurate and efficient post-training quantization for large language models. In: International Conference on Machine Learning, pp. 38087–38099. PMLR (2023)

16. Yao, Z., Yazdani Aminabadi, R., Zhang, M., Wu, X., Li, C., He, Y.: ZeroQuant: efficient and affordable post-training quantization for large-scale transformers. In: Advances in Neural Information Processing Systems, vol. 35, pp. 27168–27183 (2022)
17. Yu, G.I., Jeong, J.S., Kim, G.W., Kim, S., Chun, B.G.: ORCA: a distributed serving system for transformer-based generative models. In: 16th USENIX Symposium on Operating Systems Design and Implementation (OSDI 22), pp. 521–538 (2022)

GeoER: A Challenging Benchmark for Geometric Element Recognition

Jiamin Tang[1], Chao Zhang[1], Xudong Zhu[2], and Mengchi Liu[1(✉)]

[1] School of Computer Science, South China Normal University, Guangzhou, China
{jiamin,zhangchao}@m.scnu.edu.cn, liumengchi@scnu.edu.cn
[2] School of Information and Artificial Intelligence, Anhui Agricultural University,
Hefei, China

Abstract. Recent advancements in Large Multimodal Models (LMMs) have enabled them to tackle complex visual-mathematical reasoning tasks. However, their ability to recognize geometric elements remains underexplored. To address this gap, we introduce **GeoER**, a novel benchmark designed for evaluating LMMs on **Geo**metric **E**lement **R**ecognition. GeoER consists of 1,080 diverse geometric diagrams sourced from primary and secondary school exams, competitions, and textbooks, ranging from simple geometric shapes to complex combinations. Each diagram is paired with four questions, resulting in 4,320 visual-question-answer pairs. Unlike existing benchmarks focusing on higher-level cognition, GeoER emphasizes recognizing geometric elements through a "simple but interesting" counting task. Evaluation of 12 prominent LMMs, including GPT-4o and Claude 3.5 Sonnet, reveals that these models still struggle with even seemingly simple tasks. Notably, the top-performing model achieved an overall accuracy of only 53.0%, far below human-level performance. These findings will inspire the development of expert-level multimodal foundational models.

Keywords: Large Multimodal Models · Geometric Element Recognition · Visual-mathematical Reasoning · Benchmark Evaluation · Multimodal Foundational Models

1 Introduction

Large multimodal models (LMMs) such as GPT-4o [7] and Claude 3.5 Sonnet [2] have demonstrated exceptional capabilities across various tasks. However, their performance on multimodal mathematical reasoning, particularly geometry problems, remains significantly below human level. Current benchmarks like MathVista [6], MATH-Vision [11], and GeoEval [12] reveal that state-of-the-art models achieve only 51–56% accuracy on geometry tasks.

As illustrated in Fig. 1, even advanced LMMs struggle with basic geometric diagram understanding. We argue that accurate recognition of geometric elements is a fundamental prerequisite for geometric reasoning. Without properly

© The Author(s), under exclusive license to Springer Nature Singapore Pte Ltd. 2026
T. Zhu et al. (Eds.): KSEM 2025, LNAI 15923, pp. 266–273, 2026.
https://doi.org/10.1007/978-981-95-3061-8_28

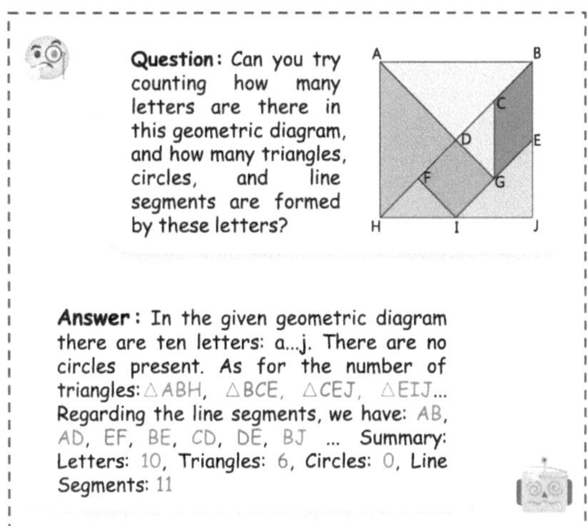

Fig. 1. GPT-4o's errors in recognizing geometric elements, with correct answers in green and errors in red. (Color figure online)

identifying points, lines, circles, and triangles in diagrams, models cannot perform effective mathematical reasoning on geometric problems.

To address this gap, we introduce **GeoER**, a novel benchmark for **Geo**metric **E**lement **R**ecognition. It consists of 1,080 geometric diagrams with 4,320 questions, focusing on counting basic geometric elements. Unlike existing benchmarks that emphasize complex reasoning, It evaluates the fundamental ability to recognize and count geometric components.

Our evaluation of 12 prominent LMMs reveals significant limitations: the best-performing model (GPT-4o) achieves only 53.0% accuracy, far below human performance (93.6% for students, 99.5% for experts). These findings highlight a critical weakness in current LMMs and provide insights for developing more capable multimodal models.

In summary, our contributions are: (1) We propose GeoER, the first benchmark specifically designed for geometric element recognition. (2) We conduct comprehensive experiments showing that current LMMs struggle with fundamental geometric understanding, revealing substantial room for improvement in multimodal mathematical reasoning.

2   The GeoER Benchmark

GeoER consists of 1,080 geometric diagrams with 4,320 visual-question-answer pairs. As shown in Fig. 2, each diagram is annotated with counts of geometric elements and paired with four related questions. GeoER includes both plane and solid geometric diagrams, requiring models to count points, triangles, circles, and line segments.

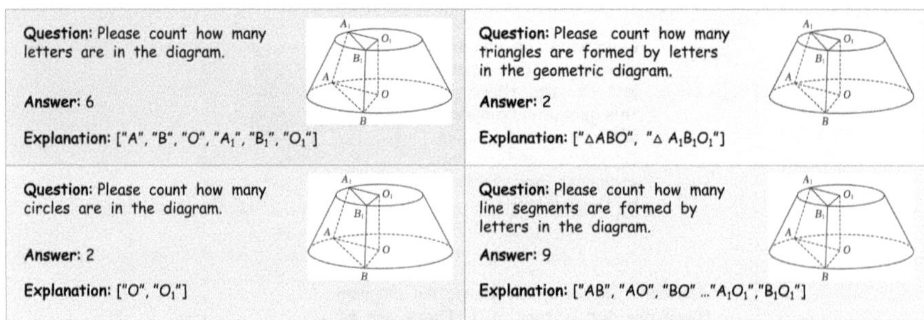

Fig. 2. An example from GeoER showing four counting questions for geometric elements including letters, circles, triangles and line segments.

	Easy		Medium		Hard
Letter	4	Letter	6	Letter	7
Triangle	1	Triangle	2	Triangle	10
Circle	1	Circle	0	Circle	0
Line segment	3	Line segment	9	Line segment	15
Sum of all	9	Sum of all	17	Sum of all	32

Fig. 3. Examples of geometric diagrams categorized by difficulty level.

2.1 Motivation

Current LMMs achieve only 51–55% accuracy on geometry benchmarks like MathVerse [13], MathVista [6], and GeoEval [12]. We argue that accurately understanding geometric elements is crucial before tackling complex reasoning tasks. As the Chinese proverb says, *A journey of a thousand miles begins with a single step.* For geometry problems involving diagrams, identifying elements within the diagram is a fundamental prerequisite for effective reasoning.

2.2 Data Collection and Difficulty Classification

We collect 3,197 geometry problems from educational websites and textbooks [4], filtering them to retain 1,080 diagrams containing identifiable geometric elements. Ten mathematics graduate students annotated each diagram using a double-checking mechanism with three independent annotators per diagram.

We categorize diagrams into three difficulty levels based on total element count: *Easy* (≤ 15 elements, 488 diagrams), *Medium* (15–30 elements, 459 diagrams), and *Hard* (>30 elements, 133 diagrams), as shown in Fig. 3 and Table 1.

Table 1. Statistics of GeoER across three difficulty levels.

Sum of elements	Difficulty	Diagram	Question
$0 < x \leq 15$	Easy	488	1,952
$15 < x \leq 30$	Medium	459	1,836
$30 < x$	Hard	133	532

2.3 Key Features

GeoER has three distinctive features: (1) **Diverse Content**: includes both solid and plane geometry with various geometric elements; (2) **Uncontaminated Data**: all questions are newly constructed to prevent data leakage; (3) **Graded Difficulty**: three complexity levels enable comprehensive evaluation of LMMs' geometric recognition capabilities.

3 Experiments

In this section, we present systematic experiments on GeoER, evaluating both open-source and closed-source large multimodal models (LMMs). Our results show that, even for simple counting tasks that humans can easily perform, the accuracy of the most advanced LMMs remains low.

3.1 Evaluation Metric

We use accuracy as the evaluation metric to fairly compare the performance of various models on the GeoER benchmark. Following MathVista [6], we extract answers from the models' responses using GPT-4o [7] with an accuracy exceeding 98%. We then compare the extracted results with the benchmark's standard answers to calculate the final accuracy.

3.2 Experimental Setup

LMMs. We evaluate both open-source and closed-source models on GeoER. For closed-source models, we select GPT-4o [7], Gemini 1.5 Pro [8], Claude 3.5 Sonnet [2], Qwen-VL-Plus [3], and Qwen-VL-Max [3]. For open-source models, we consider models ranging from 7B to 76B parameters, including LLaVA-v1.6 [10], Yi-VL-34B [1], and InternVL2 [9] series. We adopt a zero-shot setting across all LMMs, and additionally evaluate closed-source models under Zero-shot-CoT [5] setting.

Human Performance. We recruited ten middle school students to complete element-counting tasks on 108 geometric diagrams (*Human-student*), and three graduate students in mathematics as expert annotators (*Human-expert*).

Table 2. Accuracy(%) scores of models on our GeoER ALL: overall accuracy. §: Letter; ≡: Line Segment; ⊙: Circle; △: Triangle. The highest accuracy for open-source, closed-source and closed-source(Zero-shot-CoT) LMMs is marked in blue , red and green respectively.

Model	All	GeoER–*Easy*					GeoER–*Medium*					GeoER–*Hard*				
		All	§	≡	⊙	△	All	§	≡	⊙	△	All	§	≡	⊙	△
Open-source LMMs																
LLaVA-v1.6-13B	20.6	22.2	26.4	8.2	36.3	18.0	20.8	9.8	1.1	58.4	13.7	18.8	6.8	0.0	64.7	3.8
InternVL2-26B	23.4	32.7	36.1	18.6	70.1	6.1	22.5	32.5	5.9	43.4	8.5	14.8	25.6	3.0	26.3	4.5
LLaVA-v1.6-7B	24.2	25.6	19.3	7.8	52.9	22.5	24.1	7.0	1.7	74.7	12.9	22.9	0.0	0.0	88.0	3.8
Yi-VL-34B	28.4	41.2	49.0	14.8	74.6	26.6	28.4	30.1	0.0	71.7	12.0	15.6	12.0	0.0	43.6	6.8
InternVL2-76B	37.2	50.5	83.6	28.1	81.1	9.0	38.0	64.7	10.2	69.5	7.4	23.3	45.9	3.8	43.6	0.0
InternVL2-40B	39.1	46.5	62.3	26.8	88.1	8.6	37.5	46.6	10.7	85.2	7.2	33.5	42.1	6.8	81.2	3.8
InternVL2-8B	42.1	50.1	90.8	21.3	78.3	10.0	42.4	87.6	5.7	64.1	12.4	33.6	63.2	3.0	66.2	2.3
Closed-source LMMs																
Qwen-VL-Plus	30.3	36.2	6.4	19.5	95.9	23.0	29.4	6.1	0.0	94.1	17.4	25.4	6.8	0.0	94.0	0.8
Qwen-VL-Max	35.7	40.7	40.6	31.3	88.3	2.7	37.8	43.6	6.1	89.3	12.2	28.8	20.3	3.0	88.7	3.0
GPT-4o	39.4	44.7	45.3	29.9	92.2	11.3	39.4	41.4	14.8	94.1	7.2	34.0	24.1	13.5	93.2	5.3
Gemini 1.5 Pro	43.6	53.2	79.7	27.7	92.4	13.1	44.2	69.9	10.7	89.8	6.5	33.3	35.3	3.0	89.5	5.3
Claude 3.5 Sonnet	47.1	55.3	86.7	28.1	90.8	15.8	47.8	77.8	11.3	90.0	12.0	38.2	52.6	2.3	90.2	7.5
Closed-source LMMs (Zero-shot-CoT)																
Qwen-VL-Plus	29.5	33.7	30.5	9.6	70.1	24.4	27.8	30.3	3.3	65.1	12.3	20.0	15.8	0.0	60.2	3.8
Qwen-VL-Max	34.2	39.9	46.9	14.1	78.3	20.1	31.7	46.6	4.6	60.8	14.8	24.0	38.1	0.0	56.4	1.5
Claude 3.5 Sonnet	40.0	50.4	86.7	24.0	79.9	11.1	41.3	79.1	10.5	63.0	12.6	28.4	61.7	3.8	42.1	6.0
Gemini 1.5 Pro	51.9	58.1	97.1	28.1	92.8	14.5	51.5	94.3	9.6	93.7	8.3	46.1	80.5	3.0	94.0	6.8
GPT-4o	53.0	57.0	98.6	27.5	93.4	8.6	53.3	95.6	13.9	95.2	8.3	48.7	88.7	6.0	97.0	3.0
Human performance																
Human-student	93.6	96.5	98.7	94.8	100	92.4	93.8	96.4	90.5	100	88.3	90.7	94.2	85.6	100	98.1
Human-expert	99.5	99.9	100	99.8	100	99.7	99.6	100	99.5	100	98.9	99.1	99.9	98.3	100	98.1

Human. We recruited ten middle school students, each of whom completed element-counting tasks on 108 geometric diagrams. The results of these participants are labeled as *Human-student* in our experimental results. Additionally, three graduate students majoring in mathematics were recruited to complete the tasks, and their results are labeled as *Human-expert*.

3.3   Experimental Results

Table 2 presents the overall experimental results. Based on these results, our key findings can be summarized as follows:

Challenging Nature of GeoER. Table 2 demonstrates the challenges posed by GeoER for current Large Multimodal Models (LMMs). While GPT-4o achieves the best performance with an accuracy of 53.0%, there remains a significant gap compared to *Human-student* (93.6%) and an even larger gap compared to *Human-expert* (99.5%).

Table 3. Recognition accuracy (%) of closed-source LMMs on plane and solid diagrams.

Closed-source LMMs	Plane	Solid
Claude 3.5 Sonnet	51.8	40.8 ($-$11.0)
Gemini 1.5 Pro	49.3	35.1 ($-$14.2)
GPT-4o	42.2	35.5 ($-$6.7)
Qwen-VL-Max	38.9	33.4 ($-$5.5)
Qwen-VL-Plus	32.7	28.2 ($-$4.5)

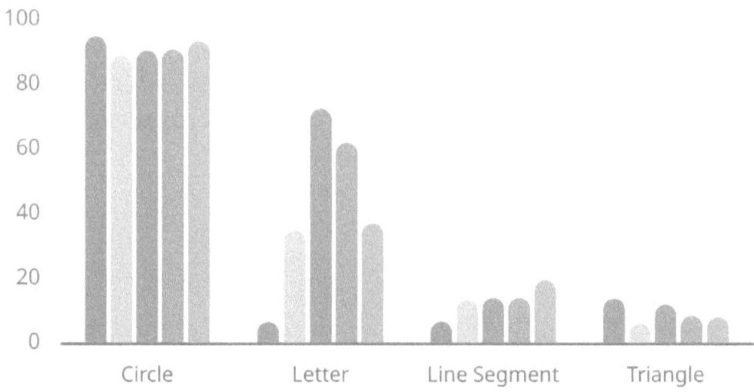

Fig. 4. Performance of models on different types of geometric elements.

Closed-Source LMMs are Better-Performed. According to the experimental results, closed-source models generally outperform open-source models. Notably, InternVL-8B achieves an accuracy of 42.1%, approaching the 43.6% accuracy of Gemini 1.5 Pro. Additionally, InternVL-8B outperforms closed-source models such as Qwen-VL-Plus, Qwen-VL-Max, and even GPT-4o. These findings suggest that while open-source models have made substantial progress, there remains significant room for improvement. Overall, closed-source models exhibit an average accuracy of 39.2%, which is 9.5% higher than the 29.7% average accuracy of open-source models.

Performance Across Different Geometric Elements. Each diagram in GeoER contains various geometric elements, and LMMs exhibit significant variation in their ability to recognize these elements. As shown in Fig. 4, the recognition accuracy for line segments and triangles is consistently lower than for circles and letters. As the complexity of the diagram increases, the accuracy for line segments and triangles drops sharply. We speculate that this is due to the frequent overlap of triangles and lines within a single diagram, which becomes more pronounced as the diagram's complexity rises. This finding suggests that current LMMs struggle with recognizing overlapping elements. Furthermore, as shown in Table 3, model accuracy on solid geometric diagrams is significantly lower than on plane diagrams. This may be because solid geometry is generally more complex and abstract, making it more challenging for models to interpret.

Chain-of-Thought Prompting is Useful But Limited. Following the chain-of-thought (CoT) [5] template, we append "Let's think step by step" to the original prompt to encourage structured reasoning. As shown in Table 2, using CoT prompting results in an improvement for most models, indicating that CoT facilitates more structured and thorough reasoning. Notably, these improvements are most pronounced in tasks involving simpler geometric elements, such as recognizing letters and circles, where models like GPT-4o and Claude 3.5 Sonnet show significant progress.

Impact of Model Scale. Experiments with the InternVL2 model family reveal that performance generally improves with increasing model size, though the degree varies across geometric elements. Letter recognition significantly improves from 36.1% (26B) to 83.6% (76B), while improvements for line segments and triangles are less pronounced, indicating that model scale alone may not address the complexity of overlapping geometric elements.

4   Conclusion

In this paper, we introduce GeoER, a benchmark designed to assess the ability of large multimodal models (LMMs) to recognize geometric elements. The benchmark consists of 1,080 geometric diagrams and 4,320 questions, with each diagram categorized into one of three difficulty levels. Experiments with both open-source and closed-source models reveal a consistent decline in recognition accuracy as diagram complexity increases. Moreover, a significant performance gap remains between LMMs and human annotators on GeoER, highlighting the need for further advancements in LMMs' visual comprehension. GeoER also underscores that most existing LMMs struggle with accurately recognizing geometric diagrams, particularly when overlapping elements are involved. We hope this work will provide valuable insights into multimodal mathematical reasoning and contribute to improving the visual comprehension capabilities of LMMs.

5   Limitations

There are two limitations of our work. Firstly, the experiments conducted in this paper were based on the API versions of closed-source models available at that time. However, with the advancement of technology, these APIs may be updated or deprecated in the future. This means that our experimental results may be difficult to replicate using the same API settings, which could have a certain impact on the reproducibility of our findings. Secondly, Our evaluation method employs a coarse-grained comparison, focusing solely on the number of geometric elements and not delving into the detailed matching between them. This binary classification-based assessment may, to some extent, overestimate the model's accuracy. Since our dataset includes detailed annotation information, future research will explore and adopt more refined evaluation criteria to provide more accurate performance assessments.

Acknowledgments. This work is supported by the National Natural Science Foundation of China (Grant No. 61672389), and Guangzhou Key Laboratory of Big Data and Intelligent Education (Grant No. 201905010009).

References

1. Young, A., et al.: Yi: open foundation models by 01.AI (2024)
2. Anthropic: Claude 3.5 Sonnet (2024). https://www.anthropic.com/news/claude-3-5-sonnet
3. Bai, J., et al.: Qwen-VL: a frontier large vision-language model with versatile abilities. CoRR abs/2308.12966 (2023)
4. Gu, J. (ed.): Geometry Problems for Math Competitions. Independently Published (2021)
5. Kojima, T., Gu, S.S., Reid, M., Matsuo, Y., Iwasawa, Y.: Large language models are zero-shot reasoners. In: Advances in Neural Information Processing Systems 35: Annual Conference on Neural Information Processing Systems 2022, NeurIPS 2022, New Orleans, LA, USA, 28 November–9 December 2022 (2022). http://papers.nips.cc/paper_files/paper/2022/hash/8bb0d291acd4acf06ef112099c16f326-Abstract-Conference.html
6. Lu, P., et al.: MathVista: evaluating mathematical reasoning of foundation models in visual contexts. In: The Twelfth International Conference on Learning Representations, ICLR 2024, Vienna, Austria, 7–11 May 2024 (2024)
7. OpenAI: GPT-4o system card. Technical report, OpenAI (2024). https://cdn.openai.com/gpt-4o-system-card.pdf
8. Team, G., et al.: Gemini 1.5: unlocking multimodal understanding across millions of tokens of context (2024). https://arxiv.org/abs/2403.05530
9. OpenGVLab Team: InternVL2 (2024). https://internvl.github.io/blog/2024-07-02-InternVL-2.0/
10. Wang, J., Ming, Y., Shi, Z., Vineet, V., Wang, X., Joshi, N.: Is a picture worth a thousand words? Delving into spatial reasoning for vision language models. arXiv preprint arXiv:2406.14852 (2024)
11. Wang, K., Pan, J., Shi, W., Lu, Z., Zhan, M., Li, H.: Measuring multimodal mathematical reasoning with math-vision dataset (2024)
12. Zhang, J., Li, Z., Zhang, M., Yin, F., Liu, C., Moshfeghi, Y.: GeoEval: benchmark for evaluating LLMs and multi-modal models on geometry problem-solving (2024)
13. Zhang, R., et al.: MathVerse: does your multi-modal LLM truly see the diagrams in visual math problems? (2024). https://doi.org/10.48550/ARXIV.2403.14624

SocioSupplyAlert: Comprehensive Supply Chain Crisis Prediction Using LLMs and Social Media Data

Meixuan Chen[1], Chen Wang[1], Yujun Wu[1], Wei Kang[2(✉)],
and Zaiwen Feng[1,3,4(✉)]

[1] Huazhong Agricultural University, Wuhan, China
`zaiwen.feng@mail.hzau.edu.cn`
[2] Hangzhou Galaxy AI Co., Ltd, Hangzhou, China
`kangw-galaxyai@outlook.com`
[3] Hubei Key Laboratory of Agricultural Bioinformatics, Wuhan, China
[4] Engineering Research Center of Agricultural Intelligent Technology, Ministry of Education, Wuhan, China

Abstract. Supply chain crisis prediction is a crucial task in business operations and risk management. However, existing research mainly focuses on identifying risk signals or predicting specific aspects of the supply chain, with relatively little emphasis on comprehensive crisis prediction. This challenge is further exacerbated by the scarcity of existing datasets. Moreover, when analyzing social media data, existing methods face challenges of noise and context specificity, affecting the accuracy of the prediction. To address these challenges, we propose SocioSupplyAlert (SSA), an innovative supply chain crisis prediction framework and create three domain-specific datasets based on X (formerly known as Twitter). SSA employs large language models (LLMs) for dynamic topic extraction and updating, enabling the precise identification of key topics that trigger supply chain crises. Furthermore, SSA utilizes LLMs for multidimensional topic classification and sentiment analysis of tweets, incorporating news data for crisis labeling. By leveraging a Voting Classifier to integrate multiple traditional machine learning and deep learning models, SSA can effectively predict the probability of supply chain crises. Experimental results on the datasets demonstrate that SSA outperforms baseline models, showcasing its outstanding generalizability and broad applicability. The dataset and code will be released upon paper acceptance.

Keywords: Large language models · Supply chain crisis prediction · Social media data · Machine learning models

---

M. Chen and C. Wang contributed equally to this work.

The original version of the chapter has been revised. A correction to this chapter can be found at https://doi.org/10.1007/978-981-95-3061-8_35

T. Zhu et al. (Eds.): KSEM 2025, LNAI 15923, pp. 274–281, 2026.
https://doi.org/10.1007/978-981-95-3061-8_29

1   Introduction

Stable supply chains underpin global competitiveness, yet disruptions in procurement, production, or logistics can rapidly erode profitability and threaten firm survival. Real-time social media streams constitute a rich and timely source for anticipating supply-chain crises. Recent studies have begun to exploit these data for supply-chain management [1,5,15], while most existing research remains confined to extracting local risk cues or analysing a single operational aspect by applying sentiment, trend, or topic mining techniques [4,7,8,10,11]. Consequently, four critical gaps persist in current research: (1) Most existing approaches focus on detecting isolated risk signals or predicting individual operational variables rather than delivering forecasts of supply-chain crises. (2) Prevailing topic- and sentiment-analysis pipelines lack robustness to the noise, irony, and domain shifts that pervade social-media text, limiting their contextual adaptability. (3) By modeling only a single explanatory factor, current methods overlook interacting drivers. (4) Progress is further constrained by the absence of publicly available social-media corpora annotated for supply-chain crisis events. To address these limitations, we propose **SocioSupplyAlert** (SSA), a novel large-language-model framework for holistic supply-chain crisis prediction from social media. SSA employs LLMs to extract domain-specific topic sets, perform joint topic and sentiment classification effectively addressing data noise and contextual specificity issues. Our contributions are as follows:

- To our knowledge, we are the first to apply large language models to supply chain crisis prediction, proposing the innovative SSA framework that overcomes limitations of previous research by accurately forecasting supply chain crises using social media data.
- We create three social media datasets specifically designed for supply chain crisis prediction, covering fields from high-tech products to apparel and food, and will be released publicly to facilitate future research in this area.
- Experimental results demonstrate that SSA outperforms on three datasets, showing strong generalization capabilities and confirming the model's effectiveness and reliability in practical applications.

2   Problem Definition

Definition 1 (Tweet). Each tweet is represented as a tuple:

$$t_i = \left(t_i^T, t_i^C, t_i^L, t_i^R, t_i^M\right), \tag{1}$$

where t_i^T represents the posting time of the tweet, t_i^C represents the content of the tweet, and t_i^L, t_i^R, and t_i^M indicate the numbers of likes, retweets, and comments respectively.

Definition 2 (Feature Vector). The feature vector F_m for the m-th month includes relevant characteristics derived from tweet data, such as topic frequency and sentiment scores, which are used to predict supply chain crises.

Problem Definition: Supply Chain Crisis Prediction. Given the feature vector F_m for month m, our model is to predict the probability $\hat{y}_{m+1}$ of a company experiencing a supply chain crisis in month $m+1$, which can be expressed as follows:

$$\hat{y}_{m+1} = f(F_m, \psi), \tag{2}$$

where $0 \leq \hat{y}_{m+1} \leq 1$ and ψ denotes the set of learnable parameters of the function f.

3   Method

In this section, we presents the SSA framework as shown in Fig. 1. To process social media data, we leverage LLMs for extracting salient topics from textual content. Subsequently, we utilize LLMs for topic classification and sentiment analysis to handle complex contexts and capturing deep semantic information of social media data. Finally, we employ a Voting Classifier for prediction and use SHAP for result interpretation, offering valuable insights into the factors driving the predictions.

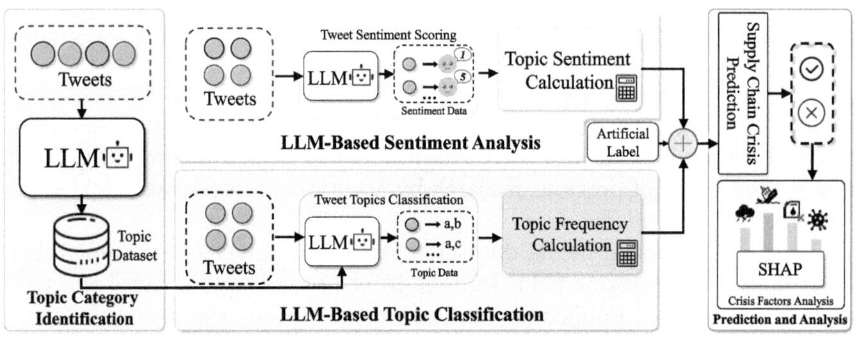

Fig. 1. The overall pipeline of our proposed SSA framework.

3.1   Topic Category Identification

We analyze a large volume of news media data to establish a comprehensive crisis theme library $\mathcal{K}$, with each theme representing a key factor affecting supply chain crisis. This library systematically organizes and monitors risk signals related to the supply chain. To capture the latest trends and emerging topics, we define a topic set X, encompassing themes such as key raw material supply, regional stability, demand fluctuations, and global events impacting supply chains.

We employ GPT4o for initial topic extraction from the entire tweet set and introduce a dynamic updating mechanism to refine the topic set X and maintain the theme library $\mathcal{K}$.

3.2 LLM-Based Topic Classification and Sentiment Analysis

Given the topic set X, we employ LLMs for multidimensional topic classification on tweets to identify complex patterns indicative of supply chain crises.

1. **Topic assignment.** Each tweet t_i is mapped to one or more topics,

$$t_i^S = \{\, X_j \in X \mid t_i \text{ semantically matches } X_j \,\}.$$

2. **Topic prevalence.** Monthly counts and relative frequencies are

$$|T_{m,j}| = \sum_{t_i \in T_m} \mathbf{1}_{\{X_j \in t_i^S\}}, \qquad c_{m,j} = \frac{|T_{m,j}|}{|T_m|},$$

where $c_{m,j}$ traces the salience of topic X_j over time and highlights emerging supply-chain risk factors.

Subsequently, we apply the same LLM to sentiment analysis on the topic-labeled tweets.

1. **Sentiment scoring.** The LLM assigns each t_i an affective score $t_i^E \in [1,10]$.
2. **Engagement-aware aggregation.** To reduce popularity bias, we weight tweets by their engagement vector (t_i^L, t_i^R, t_i^M) of likes, retweets, and replies:

$$w_i = \frac{\alpha t_i^L + \beta t_i^R + \gamma t_i^M + \varepsilon}{\sum_{t_k \in T_{m,j}} \left(\alpha t_k^L + \beta t_k^R + \gamma t_k^M\right) + |T_{m,j}|\varepsilon},$$

where α, β, γ are empirically calibrated and $\varepsilon \ll 1$. The engagement-adjusted mean sentiment for topic X_j in month m is

$$\bar{e}_{m,j} = \sum_{t_i \in T_{m,j}} w_i\, t_i^E.$$

Joint trends in $\{c_{m,j}, \bar{e}_{m,j}\}$ provide a unified view of both topical prominence and public mood, enabling early detection of supply-chain crises.

3.3 Feature Engineering

Given the topic set $X = \{X_j \mid j = 1, 2, \ldots, n\}$, we construct feature representations that capture both temporal dynamics and topical patterns. For each topic X_j and month m, we compute frequency $c_{m,j}$ and sentiment score $\bar{e}_{m,j}$, augmented with moving averages MA_w and standard deviations SD_w over windows $w \in \{3, 6\}$ to capture trends and volatility. Additionally, we extract time features (month, quarter) to capture cyclical and seasonal patterns.

The feature vector for month m is defined as:

$$F_m = \{(c_{m,j}, \bar{e}_{m,j}, MA_w, SD_w) \mid j = 1, \ldots, n\}. \tag{3}$$

The complete feature matrix aggregates all monthly representations:

$$F = \{F_1, F_2, \ldots, F_M\}, \tag{4}$$

where M denotes the total number of months in the dataset. This multi-scale temporal representation provides the foundation for supply chain crisis prediction.

3.4 Prediction and Analysis

To enhance prediction performance and generalization capability, we adopt ensemble learning approach using a Voting Classifier [6,9,14,17]. We frame the task as binary classification to predict supply chain crisis occurrence and estimate associated probabilities. We integrate two models that excel at handling binary classification tasks: Support Vector Machine (SVM) [3] and eXtreme Gradient Boosting (XGBoost) [2]. Additionally, we incorporated the Multilayer Perceptron (MLP) [16] and Convolutional Neural Network (CNN) [12], to capture both long-term dependencies and short-term trends in time series data. Given feature matrix F and crisis labels Y, the model predicts crisis probability for month $m + 1$:

$$P(y_{m+1} = 1 \mid F_m) = \text{VotingClassifier}(F_m), \tag{5}$$

where $y_{m+1} \in \{0, 1\}$ indicates crisis occurrence.

After obtaining the prediction results, we employ SHAP analysis [13] for feature importance interpretation to identify key contributing factors.

4   Experiments

4.1   Experimental Setup

Table 1. Comparison results (%) between single prediction models and our prediction model approach for supply chain crisis prediction across three datasets: Apple, Adidas, and Tyson.

Dataset	Apple				Adidas				Tyson			
Method	**Pre**	**Rec**	**F1**	**Acc**	**Pre**	**Rec**	**F1**	**Acc**	**Pre**	**Rec**	**F1**	**Acc**
MLP	84.12	90.14	87.03	87.95	85.23	90.11	87.60	83.78	88.11	91.14	89.60	87.95
CNN	75.63	83.93	79.56	73.71	71.20	70.06	70.63	72.46	82.35	91.11	86.51	83.57
Linear	80.59	83.57	82.05	80.38	57.15	55.38	56.25	58.77	54.68	60.67	57.52	53.22
LSTM	61.77	61.79	61.78	59.81	66.55	67.46	67.00	67.53	74.55	81.11	77.69	77.31
GRU	67.12	75.71	71.16	65.43	70.11	77.51	73.62	67.49	72.33	72.22	72.27	75.20
SVM	85.23	91.33	88.17	86.18	81.62	82.48	82.05	81.26	88.64	91.33	89.96	89.18
RF	85.97	90.56	88.21	87.89	87.52	77.52	82.22	82.52	85.56	92.56	88.92	87.89
Ours	**87.14**	**91.43**	**89.23**	**88.67**	**89.82**	**95.24**	**92.45**	**91.24**	**89.78**	**95.56**	**92.58**	**92.28**

Datasets. We manually curated three datasets focusing on Apple, Adidas, and Tyson, corresponding to the high-technology, apparel, and food industries, respectively. Specifically, we utilized the X API to retrieve tweets associated with supply chain crises for each company between January 1, 2019, and December 31, 2023. Collectively, these datasets comprise a corpus of approximately 200,000 tweets.

Supply Chain Crisis Labeling. We collected supply chain crisis news reports via Bing search engine from January 2019 to December 2023. Five annotators independently classified monthly news as"crisis" (1) or "non-crisis" (0) following standardized labeling principles. Discrepancies were resolved through majority voting to ensure consistency and minimize individual bias, yielding the label set Y.

Table 2. Results (%) of comparisons between traditional topic modeling, sentiment analysis methods, and our LLM approach for supply chain crisis prediction on three datasets: Apple, Adidas, and Tyson.

Dataset	Method	Pre	Rec	F1	Acc
Apple	LDA+BERT	85.45	74.64	79.68	78.95
	Ours	**87.14**	**91.43**	**89.23**	**88.67**
Adidas	LDA+BERT	80.12	72.50	76.12	73.75
	Ours	**89.82**	**95.24**	**92.45**	**91.24**
Tyson	LDA+BERT	86.58	89.33	87.93	84.80
	Ours	**89.78**	**95.56**	**92.58**	**92.28**

Baseline. We introduce SSA as the first social media-based framework for supply chain crisis prediction. Given the absence of existing baseline methods in this domain, we compare the key components of SSA with classical methods: (1) We compare our method against classical classifiers. (2) We evaluate GPT-4 against traditional methods (LDA, BERT) for feature extraction.

4.2 Experimental Results

Prediction Model. Table 1 displays the comparison results of our method with various single prediction models on the Apple, Adidas, and Tyson datasets. The results indicate that our method excels across all datasets and evaluation metrics. Notably, on the Adidas and Tyson datasets, our method achieves over 90% in Recall, F1 score, and Accuracy, demonstrating its exceptional performance in crisis prediction within both the apparel and food industries. A more detailed explanation of the results can be found in the materials.

Topic Classification and Sentiment Analysis. Table 2 presents the comparison results of our method with traditional LDA and BERT models on the Apple, Adidas, and Tyson datasets. Our method performs best across all datasets and metrics, demonstrating that when handling social media data, LLMs can effectively resolve issues such as noise and context specificity, thereby possessing significant advantages.

Table 3. The result (%) of ablation experiments.

Dataset	Method	Pre	Rec	F1	Acc
Apple	w/o SA-LLM	79.12	80.36	79.74	79.05
	w/o TC-LLM	77.98	84.43	81.08	80.38
	SSA	**87.14**	**91.43**	**89.23**	**88.67**
Adidas	w/o SA-LLM	85.15	87.50	86.31	85.00
	w/o TC-LLM	85.66	91.50	88.48	87.50
	SSA	**89.82**	**95.24**	**92.45**	**91.24**
Tyson	w/o SA-LLM	87.05	91.11	89.03	89.06
	w/o TC-LLM	86.74	91.11	88.87	87.89
	SSA	**89.78**	**95.56**	**92.58**	**92.28**

4.3 Ablation Study

We perform ablation experiments as shown in Table 3. Omitting the sentiment-analysis module (w/o SA-LLM) produces marked drops in performance. Removing topic classification (w/o TC-LLM) likewise degrades performance. The results show that the complete *SSA* framework outperforms all other variants while eliminating key modules such as SA-LLM or TC-LLM causes a significant decrease in predictive performance, highlighting the critical role these components play in boosting overall model effectiveness.

5   Conclusion

In this paper, we propose a robust framework, SocioSupplyAlert (SSA), to predict supply chain crisis using social media data. SSA effectively extracts topics through LLMs, integrates large language models for multidimensional classification and sentiment analysis, and employs a Voting Classifier to provide accurate predictions. We also contribute three datasets, addressing a significant gap in existing resources. Experimental results demonstrate that our framework performs excellently across these datasets and is widely applicable. Although the models used in the prediction module are straightforward, their effectiveness has been thoroughly validated. Future work will focus on optimizing the prediction models and expanding the framework's capabilities to enable the monitoring and prediction of specific crisis types.

Acknowledgements. This work is supported in part by the National Undergraduate Innovation and Entrepreneurship Training Program of China under Grant 202410504100, and the Hubei Key Research and Development Program of China under Grant 2024BAA008, and in part by the Fundamental Research Funds for the Chinese Central Universities under Grant 2662025XXPY005.

References

1. Chae, B.K.: Insights from hashtag# supplychain and twitter analytics: Considering twitter and twitter data for supply chain practice and research. Int. J. Prod. Econ. **165**, 247–259 (2015)
2. Chen, T., Guestrin, C.: Xgboost: A scalable tree boosting system. In: Proceedings of the 22nd ACM SIGKDD International Conference on Knowledge Discovery and Data Mining, pp. 785–794 (2016)
3. Cortes, C., Vapnik, V.: Support-vector networks. Mach. Learn. **20**, 273–297 (1995)
4. Cui, R., Gallino, S., Moreno, A., Zhang, D.J.: The operational value of social media information. Prod. Oper. Manag. **27**(10), 1749–1769 (2018)
5. Deiva Ganesh, A., Kalpana, P.: Supply chain risk identification: a real-time data-mining approach. Ind. Manage. Data Syst. **122**(5), 1333–1354 (2022)
6. Dhar, P., Suganya Devi, K., Satti, S.K., Srinivasan, P.: An hybrid soft attention based xgboost model for classification of poikilocytosis blood cells. Evol. Syst. **15**(2), 523–539 (2024)
7. El Filali, A., Lahmer, E.H.B., El Filali, S., Kasbouya, M., Ajouary, M.A., Akantous, S.: Machine learning applications in supply chain management: a deep learning model using an optimized LSTM network for demand forecasting. Int. J. Intell. Eng. Syst. **15**(2) (2022)
8. Ga, S.F., Prakashb, N.: Machine learning in demand forecasting-a review. In: Proceedings of the 2nd International Conference on IoT, Social, Mobile, Analytics & Cloud in Computational Vision & Bio-Engineering (2020)
9. Gao, X., Jamil, N., Ramli, M.I., Ariffin, S.M.Z.S.Z.: A comparative analysis of combination of CNN-based models with ensemble learning on imbalanced data. JOIV: Int. J. Inform. Visual. **8**(1), 456–464 (2024)
10. Iftikhar, R., Khan, M.S.: Social media big data analytics for demand forecasting: development and case implementation of an innovative framework. In: Research Anthology on Big Data Analytics, Architectures, and Applications, pp. 902–920. IGI Global (2022)
11. Lau, R.Y.K., Zhang, W., Xu, W.: Parallel aspect-oriented sentiment analysis for sales forecasting with big data. Prod. Oper. Manag. **27**(10), 1775–1794 (2018)
12. LeCun, Y., Bottou, L., Bengio, Y., Haffner, P.: Gradient-based learning applied to document recognition. Proc. IEEE **86**(11), 2278–2324 (1998)
13. Lundberg, S.M., Lee, S.I.: A unified approach to interpreting model predictions. Adv. Neural Inf. Process. Syst. **30** (2017)
14. Mienye, I.D., Sun, Y.: A survey of ensemble learning: concepts, algorithms, applications, and prospects. IEEE Access **10**, 99129–99149 (2022)
15. Pohl, D., Bouchachia, A., Hellwagner, H.: Active online learning for social media analysis to support crisis management. IEEE Trans. Knowl. Data Eng. **32**(8), 1445–1458 (2019)
16. Rosenblatt, F.: The perceptron: a probabilistic model for information storage and organization in the brain. Psychol. Rev. **65**(6), 386 (1958)
17. Shi, Z., Hu, Y., Mo, G., Wu, J.: Attention-based CNN-LSTM and xgboost hybrid model for stock prediction. arXiv preprint arXiv:2204.02623 (2022)

SKG-LLM: Enhancing Large Language Models with Sentiment Knowledge Graphs for Fine-Grained Sentiment Analysis

Yixuan Yuan$^{(\boxtimes)}$ (iD) and Bixuan Li (iD)

Institute of Collaborative Innovation, University of Macau, Macau, China
{mc46536,mc36529}@um.edu.mo

Abstract. This study presents a sentiment-analysis framework that integrates a large language model with a structured sentiment knowledge graph to evaluate smart-home product reviews. Moving beyond the conventional three-class scheme of positive, negative, and neutral sentiment, the framework adopts an eight-emotion taxonomy that captures fine-grained affective variation. Product features and their associated emotions are automatically extracted from reviews and encoded as nodes and edges in a graph, whose prior information is subsequently injected into the language model through prompt optimization and adaptive weighting. On a manually annotated test set the proposed method attains an accuracy of 82.05%, exceeding the performance of all baseline models. The results demonstrate that coupling graph-based priors with a modern language model improves the detection of domain-specific sentiments, providing consumers with precise insight into product perception and offering manufacturers reliable evidence for product refinement.

Keywords: Sentiment Analysis · Sentiment Knowledge Graph · Large Language Model

1 Introduction

Sentiment analysis is a critical NLP task for assessing the sentiment polarity in textual content [2]. The rapid growth of textual data has made comprehending embedded sentiments a key research focus. While traditional approaches are effective under standard conditions, they encounter significant limitations with long-form text, implicit sentiment, or domain-specific contextual variations [7]. Deep learning models learn patterns directly from text, improving emotion classification. However, these models rely on statistical correlations from large datasets, and these datasets usually lack structured domain-specific knowledge. This also limits their effectiveness in specialized tasks [6].

Knowledge graphs (KGs), a structured form of knowledge representation, have received attention in addressing these challenges. Using knowledge graphs can strengthen the performance of sentiment classification tasks [5] because they offer reliable prior knowledge through structured relationships between entities and expressed

T. Zhu et al. (Eds.): KSEM 2025, LNAI 15923, pp. 282–290, 2026.
https://doi.org/10.1007/978-981-95-3061-8_30

sentiments. Sentiment Knowledge Graph (SKG) provides aspect-centric sentiment knowledge in a structured format, showing which aspects in the text are correlated to which sentiment terms, enabling a more accurate and contextual-aware sentiment classification process [11]. Traditional SKGs often require extensive manual curation or rule-based extraction approaches. However, LLMs could efficiently alleviate these issues through their knowledge representation capability, allowing the automatic extraction and construction of knowledge graphs from text, enhancing the quality of the knowledge base [9].

In this paper, we investigate how LLMs can be leveraged to efficiently build SKGs and evaluate the influence of prior knowledge on sentiment classification performance and robustness. LLMs automatically extract sentiment knowledge from smart home product reviews to construct a domain-specific SKG. Then, SKG-encoded knowledge is integrated into LLMs through prompt-based knowledge augmentation to enhance classification. Finally, we systematically evaluate the impact by comparing pure LLM-based, SKG-enhanced LLM-based, and traditional sentiment classification models. Experiments show that SKG integration improves accuracy and robustness, particularly for implicit and domain-specific expressions.

This study makes three key contributions. (1) A methodology for LLM-based SKG construction, automatically extracting and organizing sentiment attributes from large-scale product reviews. (2) A knowledge-enhanced sentiment classification framework, demonstrating how SKGs improve LLM-based sentiment analysis through structured prior knowledge. (3) A comprehensive evaluation highlighting the advantages of integrating structured knowledge with LLMs.

2   Related Work

2.1   Large Language Models (LLMs) in Sentiment Analysis

Large language models (LLMs) including BERT, GPT series, and DeepSeek have greatly enhanced sentiment analysis accuracy and efficiency. They outperform traditional methods in understanding long-form text and capturing nuanced sentiments [12]. Krugmann and Hartmann (2024) tested state-of-the-art LLMs, such as GPT-3. 5, GPT-4, and Llama 2, exceeded traditional transfer learning approaches in zero-shot binary and ternary sentiment classification [4]. Despite their great potential in sentiment analysis, LLMs still struggle with implicit sentiment expressions and lack domain-specific knowledge [3].

2.2   Knowledge Graph-Enhanced LLMs for Sentiment Analysis

To overcome these drawbacks, recent research has investigated knowledge injection techniques that combine structured knowledge graphs (KGs) with black-box LLMs [1, 10]. KGs provide structured prior knowledge of entities, attributes, and relationships that improve sentiment analysis [5]. Sentiment knowledge graphs (SKGs) capture domain-specific sentiment trends and help LLMs comprehend complex emotional contexts [11]. For instance, the SAKG-BERT model incorporates KG-enhanced representations into BERT, greatly increasing Chinese sentiment classification accuracy [11].

Despite the demonstrated potential of KG-LLM integration, current approaches still face considerable challenges. KG construction often relies on manual annotation or rule-based extraction, which hinder scalability and domain adaptability [11]. Additionally, these methods are costly and difficult to maintain with evolving datasets [13].

3 Methodology

3.1 Semantic Features of Texts from Smart Home Communities

Posts in smart-home forums are linguistically atypical: dense jargon (e.g., mesh routing, Zigbee gateway), cyber-slang ("the speaker bombed", "super slick"), and noisy symbols. A further challenge is that multiple product functions are interleaved within one post; a camera review may praise image quality yet criticize subscription cloud storage in the same sentence. Such aspect-mixing obscures the polarity–aspect link and easily misleads single-aspect sentiment classifiers. Consequently, context-aware methods with domain knowledge are required to uncover users' true attitudes.

3.2 Coupling Large Language Models with the Sentiment Knowledge Graph

Large Language Models (LLMs) demonstrate outstanding contextual reasoning and comprehension in natural-language processing. To enhance sentiment detection in smart-home community reviews, we integrate an LLM with a sentiment knowledge graph through three consecutive stages: Step 1 Input and Retrieval, Step 2 Knowledge-Graph Augmentation, and Step 3 LLM Analysis. The following subsections provide a theoretical explanation of each stage (Fig. 1).

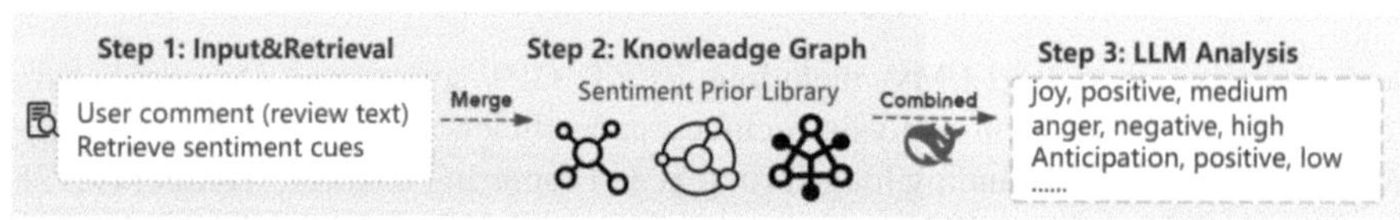

Fig. 1. Overview of the Proposed LLM–Sentiment Knowledge Approach.

Step 1: Input and Sentiment Cue Retrieval. A review C is tokenized and normalized. Candidate sentiment cues

$$\text{Retrieve}(C) = \{t_1, t_2, \ldots, t_k\}, \tag{1}$$

are extracted, retaining only device features and opinion terms after frequency and lexicon filtering.

Step 2: Knowledge Base Matching and Prior Integration. In the second stage, every feature cue is first aligned with its node in the SKG, from which the corpus statistics p_f^+ and μ_f are retrieved. If the cue is an opinion term associated with that feature, the system additionally fetches its SenticNet polarity score and VAD vector and attaches these values to the edge $(f, \textit{expresses}, e)$. To highlight dominant feature-emotion combinations, a salience weight is calculated as

$$w(f, e) = \frac{\text{count}(f, e)}{\sum_{e'} \text{count}(f, e')},\tag{2}$$

after which all collected figures are concatenated into a structured hint that precedes the review text.

Step 3: LLM-Based Sentiment Analysis. The hint and the original review are jointly processed by the LLM. Textual and graph embeddings are blended through

$$\mathbf{h}_{\text{final}} = \alpha \cdot \mathbf{h}_{\text{LLM}} + (1 - \alpha)\mathbf{h}_{\text{KG}},\tag{3}$$

where α is tuned on a development set. Because $\mathbf{h}_{\text{KG}}$ now encodes corpus-level statistics and SenticNet attributes, the fused vector enables the model to identify the predominant emotion linked to any feature, or conversely to trace an emotion back to its most salient features, thereby improving fine-grained sentiment classification and interpretability.

4   Experiment Design

4.1   Proposed Methodology

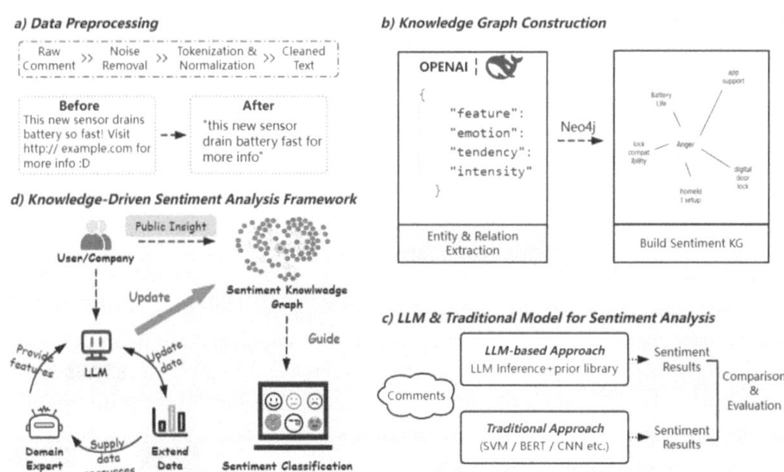

Fig. 2. Overview of the Proposed EKG–LLM Framework.

This paper proposes an SKG-LLM framework that integrates a Sentiment Knowledge Graph (SKG) with a Large Language Model (LLM) to achieve fine-grained sentiment analysis of smart-home reviews (Fig. 2). Raw comments are first cleaned, de-noised, tokenised, and normalised; domain-specific product features and sentiment cues are then extracted automatically. Each feature–emotion pair is written to a Neo4j SKG whose nodes and edges store corpus-level statistics and SenticNet affective attributes. During inference the SKG supplies these structured priors to the LLM through prompt engineering, allowing the model to reason explicitly over feature–emotion associations. The resulting knowledge-enhanced LLM is evaluated in an ablation setting that includes a vanilla few-shot LLM and a chain-of-thought (CoT) prompt variant; a single BERT classifier serves as a classical reference model. This design isolates the incremental benefit conferred by SKG guidance while preserving comparability with a well-established neural baseline.

4.2 Data Preprocessing

From Reddit's "smart home" forum we collected 21,116 raw comments. To prepare them for analysis, the text was standardised by converting full-width characters to half-width, normalising case, and eliminating URLs, special symbols, and non-semantic numeric strings with regular expressions; comments that were excessively short or incomplete were discarded. Internet slang and abbreviations were expanded to their full forms using an externally compiled "Abbreviation List for NLP Studies." After these procedures, 12,531 high-quality comments remained, supplying a reliable foundation for SKG construction and subsequent sentiment-classification experiments.

4.3 Construction of the Prior Knowledge Base and Sentiment Knowledge Graph

The sentiment knowledge graph is constructed in three successive stages, namely automatic information extraction, prior-knowledge consolidation, and graph instantiation.

Step 1: Automatic Information Extraction. We begin by selecting 80% of the 12 531 cleaned comments as the construction set. A task-specific prompt instructs the LLM to parse each review and output structured feature–emotion pairs together with sentiment polarity and intensity. Manual spot-checks confirm extraction consistency and provide the raw material for the graph.

Step 2: Construction of the Prior Sentiment Library. For every extracted pair (f, e) we record its co-occurrence frequency and derive the salience weight according to Eq. (2). Each feature node is annotated with the corpus statistics p_f^+ and μ_f, whereas the corresponding feature–emotion edge receives polarity scores and VAD vectors from SenticNet 6. The resulting prior sentiment library is organized around the eight primary emotions defined in Plutchik's psycho-evolutionary model [8]; Table 1 lists these emotions together with brief descriptions used in this study.

Step 3: Building the Sentiment Knowledge Graph. All entities and weighted relations are imported into Neo4j, producing the sentiment knowledge graph. Nodes represent product features or one of the eight Plutchik emotions; edges store the attribute set $\{w_{f,e}, p_f^+, \mu_f, \text{VAD}\}$. This graph provides explicit, quarriable priors for the downstream classification experiments.

Table 1. Definitions of the eight primary emotions.

Sentiment	Contextual Description
Sadness	Product fails to meet a key need, leading to disappointment
Fear	Worry about potential risks or future costs
Disgust	Strong aversion caused by poor quality or unfair pricing
Anger	Frustration with malfunctions or unmet promises
Trust	Confidence built through reliable performance
Anticipation	Excitement or anxiety about forthcoming features
Joy	Satisfaction resulting from comfort or convenience
Surprise	Brief, intense reaction to unexpected added value

4.4 Sentiment Classification

The remaining 20% of the corpus, manually annotated at sentence level, is used as the evaluation set. For each review, the system queries the sentiment knowledge graph and retrieves, for every referenced product feature, a structured prior that includes the emotion label, polarity, intensity, salience weight, VAD vector, the feature's positive-occurrence ratio p_f^+, and its mean emotional intensity μ_f. This prior information is appended to the original text through knowledge injection and the combined prompt is fed to the large language model. The model jointly encodes the review context and the injected priors to produce a sentiment label, which is then compared against the gold annotations. Evaluation is conducted with accuracy, precision, recall, and F1 score.

5 Results and Discussion

5.1 Prior Knowledge Base and Sentiment Knowledge Graph

This section presents the sentiment knowledge graph built from smart-home reviews and describes how it represents feature–emotion relations. Figure 3(a) depicts the full graph, whose dense node–edge structure reflects the breadth of automatically extracted relations. A clearer illustration appears in Fig. 3(b), which isolates the subgraph centered on Anger and reveals the product features most frequently linked to that emotion. Together, the global and local views confirm that our pipeline captures domain-wide sentiment associations while preserving the fine-grained links required for downstream classification.

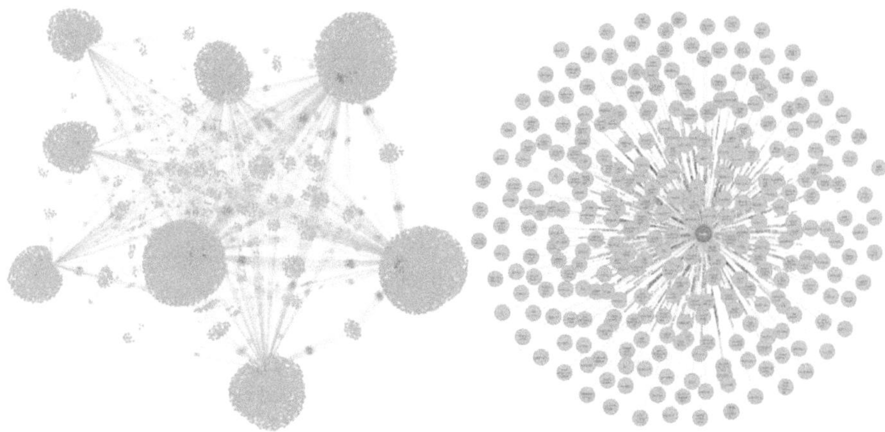

(a) Overall Sentiment Knowledge Graph   (b) Sentiment Subgraph

Fig. 3. Sentiment Knowledge Graph.

5.2 Sentiment Classification Results

In the sentiment classification phase, we used the remaining 20% of the reviews from the dataset that were not used for constructing the emotion knowledge graph; these reviews were manually annotated and cross-verified twice to form the test set. We then applied our proposed approach, which integrates a Large Language Model with prior knowledge injection, to classify these reviews, and compared its performance with three baseline models: a zero shot LLM, a chain of thought LLM, and a traditional BERT classifier. During inference, we applied dynamic weighting and prompt optimization strategies to the LLM, thereby leveraging prior knowledge to enhance sentiment-classification accuracy for ambiguous or polysemous expressions.

Table 2. Comparative Sentiment Classification Results.

Model	Metrics	Sadness	Fear	Disgust	Anger	Trust	Anticipation	Joy	Surprise
Bert	Accuracy	0.619							
	Precision	0.631	0.605	0.659	0.675	0.589	0.645	0.704	0.608
	Recall	0.615	0.651	0.613	0.698	0.577	0.664	0.738	0.593
	F1-score	0.623	0.627	0.635	0.686	0.583	0.654	0.721	0.600
Zero-shot LLM	Accuracy	0.641							
	Precision	0.641	0.661	0.602	0.614	0.651	0.685	0.693	0.564
	Recall	0.683	0.674	0.625	0.559	0.634	0.701	0.744	0.615
	F1-score	0.661	0.667	0.613	0.585	0.642	0.693	0.718	0.588
Cot-LLM	Accuracy	0.776							
	Precision	0.658	0.845	0.998	0.938	0.542	0.771	0.781	0.402
	Recall	0.891	0.715	0.381	0.811	0.620	0.852	0.762	0.418

(continued)

Table 2. (*continued*)

Model	Metrics	Sadness	Fear	Disgust	Anger	Trust	Anticipation	Joy	Surprise
	F1-score	0.757	0.775	0.552	0.870	0.578	0.810	0.771	0.410
SKG-LLM	Accuracy	0.821							
	Precision	0.786	0.781	0.778	0.789	0.762	0.968	0.778	0.788
	Recall	0.880	0.568	0.875	0.965	0.851	0.674	0.928	0.743
	F1-score	0.830	0.658	0.824	0.868	0.804	0.795	0.846	0.765

Table 2 indicates that the traditional BERT classifier attains roughly 0.62 accuracy, confirming its utility for general sentiment recognition. The zero-shot LLM surpasses BERT, and the addition of chain-of-thought prompting yields a further improvement. The proposed SKG-LLM achieves the highest scores across almost all emotion categories, with especially pronounced gains on the rarer classes. These findings show that incorporating domain-specific prior knowledge allows the LLM to distinguish subtle emotional differences that prompt engineering alone cannot reliably address.

6   Conclusion

This study introduces a SKG-LLM framework that couples a sentiment knowledge graph with a large language model to perform eight-class, fine-grained sentiment analysis on smart-home reviews. Experimental results demonstrate that the model captures implicit, domain-specific emotions more accurately than prompt-only or traditional baselines, confirming the benefit of explicit prior knowledge. The contributions are twofold. For consumers, the framework retrieves nuanced public opinion on individual product features, thereby supporting more informed purchase decisions. For companies, the detailed emotion taxonomy reveals concrete weaknesses in products and services, guiding targeted improvements. Future work will test the approach on larger and cross-domain corpora, extend it to multilingual and multimodal inputs, and explore adversarial-robust training to strengthen its capacity for interpreting complex emotional cues.

Disclosure of Interests.   The authors have no competing interests to declare that are relevant to the content of this article.

References

1. Bai, X., et al.: Construction of a knowledge graph for framework material enabled by large language models and its application. NPJ Comput. Mater. **11** (2025)
2. Liu, B.: Sentiment Analysis and Opinion Mining. Morgan And Claypool, San Rafael (2012)
3. Chochlakis, G., Potamianos, A., Lerman, K., Narayanan, S.: The strong pull of prior knowledge in large language models and its impact on emotion recognition. arXiv (Cornell University) (2024)

4. Krugmann, J.O., Hartmann, J.: Sentiment analysis in the age of generative AI. Customer Needs Solutions **11** (2024)
5. Ji, S., Pan, S., Cambria, E., Marttinen, P., Yu, P.S.: A survey on knowledge graphs: representation, acquisition, and applications. IEEE Trans. Neural Netw. Learn. Syst. **33**, 494–514 (2021)
6. Liu, W., et al.: K-BERT: enabling language representation with knowledge graph. arXiv (Cornell University) (2019)
7. Pang, B., Lee, L., Vaithyanathan, S.: Thumbs up? Sentiment classification using machine learning techniques. In: Proceedings of the ACL-02 Conference on Empirical Methods in Natural Language Processing - EMNLP 2002, vol. 10 (2002)
8. Plutchik, R.: A general psychoevolutionary theory of emotion. In: Theories of Emotion, pp. 3–33. Academic Press, New York (1980)
9. Wang, X., et al.: KEPLER: a unified model for knowledge embedding and pre-trained language representation. Trans. Assoc. Comput. Linguist. **9**, 176–194 (2021)
10. Wang, Z., et al.: ECoK: emotional commonsense knowledge graph for mining emotional gold. Find. Assoc. Comput. Linguist. ACL **2024**, 8055–8074 (2024)
11. Yan, X., Jian, F., Sun, B.: SAKG-BERT: enabling language representation with knowledge graphs for Chinese sentiment analysis. IEEE Access **9**, 101695–101701 (2021)
12. Yang, J., et al.: Harnessing the power of LLMs in practice: a survey on ChatGPT and beyond (2023)
13. Zhu, Y., et al.: LLMs for knowledge graph construction and reasoning: recent capabilities and future opportunities (2023)

Harnessing Heterogeneous Social Networks for Better Group Recommendations: An Integrated Approach Towards Cold-Start Problem

Yunwei Zhao[1], Songtao Peng[2], Linbo Qiao[3(✉)], Qiwei Ye[3], Han Han[1], and Shanqing Yu[2]

[1] CNCERT/CC, Beijing 100094, China
{zhaoyw,hanh}@cert.org.cn
[2] Institute of Cyberspace Security, Zhejiang University of Technology, Hangzhou 310023, China
{pengst,yushanqing}@zjut.edu.cn
[3] College of Computer Science and Technology, National University of Defense Technology, Changsha 410073, China
{qiao.linbo,yeqiwei}@nudt.edu.cn

Abstract. The cold-start problem caused by data sparsity remains a significant challenge in recommendation systems. In this paper, we propose DiGcl-H, a data integration approach based on graph contrastive learning, designed to enhance recommendations for sparse groups by addressing both item cold-start and user cold-start challenges. Our integration approach innovatively captures the latent individual-group correlations in heterogeneous social networks by leveraging the user-item bipartite graph and the user social network graph. Additionally, it refines the cold item/user fusion optimization strategy through contrastive learning, effectively improving the integration of cold items and users within the same group without adversely affecting other group recommendations. Extensive experiment results on two real-world social recommender benchmark datasets, Filmtrust and Epinions, demonstrate that DiGcl-H is competitive with other state-of-the-art methods in cold-start scenarios, with Hit Ratio@50 increased by around 20%.

Keywords: Cold-start · Data integration · Heterogeneous social network · Graph contrastive learning · Group recommendation

1 Introduction

Group Recommendation (GR) has achieved distinctive performance in suggesting relevant items or events that are consumed socially by groups of people. GR is the task of recommending relevant items/events to a group of users in online systems, making it efficient and effortless for a group to identify a broad spectrum of suitable activities to participate in. However, the widespread adoption of

T. Zhu et al. (Eds.): KSEM 2025, LNAI 15923, pp. 291–301, 2026.
https://doi.org/10.1007/978-981-95-3061-8_31

this technology remains hindered by the persistent cold-start problem: new users face distorted interest modeling due to a lack of behavioral data [23]; new items are constrained by the "long-tail dilemma" due to insufficient exposure [11]; and cold communities encounter difficulties in accessing personalized services due to data sparsity [22].

To tackle the cold-start problem, existing research can be broadly classified into two main categories: data-driven methods [3] and method-driven approaches [19,20]. Data-driven methods primarily include Auxiliary Information-Driven Methods [10,18,21] and Interactive Strategies & Active Learning-based methods [4,8]. Auxiliary Information-Driven Methods leverage side data (e.g., user demographics, item metadata) to infer user preferences, but the data may not be available due to incomplete item descriptions or noisy user profiles. Interactive Strategies & Active Learning-based methods proactively engage users to reduce uncertainty by such measures as soliciting feedback, though real-time updates as feedback arrives can be computationally complex. Method-driven approaches mainly comprise Meta-Learning & Transfer Learning based methods [5,9] and Emerging Approaches [1,7,16,17] based on Generative AI. Meta-Learning & Transfer-Learning methods transfer knowledge from warm-start domains to new users/items, but Meta-Learning requires diverse training tasks, and transferred knowledge often suffers from domain mismatch issues. Generative AI Approaches employ generative models to infer user preferences, although such models may generate unrealistic user or item profiles.

However, there are two issues that still need to be addressed in these state-of-the-art methods. Firstly, due to the extreme sparsity of historical interactions for cold-start users/items, the complex and correlated interactions within the local subgraph are often overlooked. Secondly, while primarily focusing on leveraging the relationships among individual node embeddings, these methods fail to capture group-wise collective behaviors within the heterogeneous graph.

To address the aforementioned challenges, this work introduces an innovative approach to tackle the cold-start problem in group recommendation. By fine-tuning a small amount of selected users' heterogeneous types of interaction, DiGcl-H effectively reduces the implicit distance between a specific item and the relevant user group, while simultaneously accentuating the differences with other groups. More specifically, to efficiently capture the latent group-wise correlations, a contrastive learning strategy is utilized to learn the similarity of the (item, group) pairs, enabling the dynamic identification and reinforcement of high-value behavioral patterns within the group. In essence, the integration optimization approach orchestrates lightweight behavior generation, facilitating sparse data enhancement for specific groups and boosting exposure for cold items.

The contributions of our work are summarized as follows:

- A novel data integration framework is introduced, namely DiGcl-H, which synergizes graph contrastive learning and bi-level optimization to mitigate cold-start problems. By leveraging heterogeneous types of social network edges, DiGcl-H captures both user-item and user-user interactions/edges to enhance cold item/user recommendation effectiveness.

- A novel and effective metric, named WHOS (Weighted Hit-Overflow Score), is proposed to score of the data integration method towards solving the cold-start problem. It balances the recommendation accuracy of cold items/users to the integration user group and the risk of impacting other user groups.
- Extensive numerical experiments were conducted on two widely used real-world datasets, FilmTrust and Epinions, under cold-start scenarios to demonstrate the effectiveness of the proposed approach. Additionally, an ablation study was performed to analyze the effectiveness of different modules in the proposed solution framework. By integrating both user-item and user-user interactive relationships, the framework effectively captures and leverages the latent information embedded within the heterogeneous social network, thus enhancing the fusion of cold items/users within the same group.

2 Methodology

2.1 Problem Formulation

We formalize the "cold-start" problem for social recommendation under few-shot link prediction and graph modeling [15]. Let U and I denote the sets of users and items of an black-boxed social recommender, and $I_m \subseteq I$ the set of cold items to be integrated. Let $G = (U \cup I, E)$ denote the heterogeneous social network graph, where $E = \{E_{UI}, E_{UU}\}$ represents the edges, with E_{UI} the user-item interaction links/edges (e.g., ratings, clicks, or purchases by users on items, etc.), and E_{UU} the user-user interaction inks/edges (e.g. follow, etc.), respectively. That is, $G = G_{UI} \cup G_{UU}$, where G_{UI} denotes the bipartite graph between users and items, and G_{UU} denotes the user social network graph. A new interaction graph $\hat{G}_I = (\hat{U} \cup I, \hat{E})$ is obtained by introducing side information, and thus enhancing the density of the graph G. We have $\hat{U} = \{U_c, U_i, U_n\}$, where U_i represents the integrated user group, and U_n represents the other normal group, and U_c represents the selected users. $\hat{G}_I = \hat{G}_{UI} \cup \hat{G}_{UU}$ is then constructed by integrating the interactions of the selected users U_c with items (update E_{UI}) and users (update E_{UU}), that is, $\hat{E} = \{\hat{E}_{UI}, \hat{E}_{UU}\}$, $\hat{E}_{UI} = \{(u_i, i_k) \mid u_i \in U_c, i_k \in I\}$, $\hat{E}_{UU} = \{(u_i, u_j) \mid u_i \in U_c, u_j \in U\}$.

Now, the cold-start problem of recommending specific items I_m for a specific group U_i can be viewed as a dual-objective optimization problem that gives accurate link prediction between I_m and U_i of $\hat{G}$ by optimizing the followings:

$$\max_{U_c} \left\{ \mathbb{E}_{u_i \in U_i, i_k \in I_m} \left[R(u_i, i_k \mid \hat{G}, \theta) \right] - \lambda \cdot \mathbb{E}_{u_n \in U_n, i_k \in I_m} \left[R(u_n, i_k \mid \hat{G}, \theta) \right] \right\}$$
$$\text{s.t.}\quad \hat{e}(u_n, u_t) = \emptyset, u_t \notin N(u_n), \hat{e} \in \hat{E} \tag{1}$$

where $R(\cdot)$ represents the surrogate social recommendation model[1], θ denotes the model parameters, $N(u)$ represent the set of neighbors of user u in G, $\mathbb{E}$ represents the expected value of the model $R(\cdot)$ with respect to u_i and i_k.

---

[1] Without loss of generality, we employ SocialMF (Social Matrix Factorization), a social recommendation model based on matrix factorization [6], as our surrogate model.

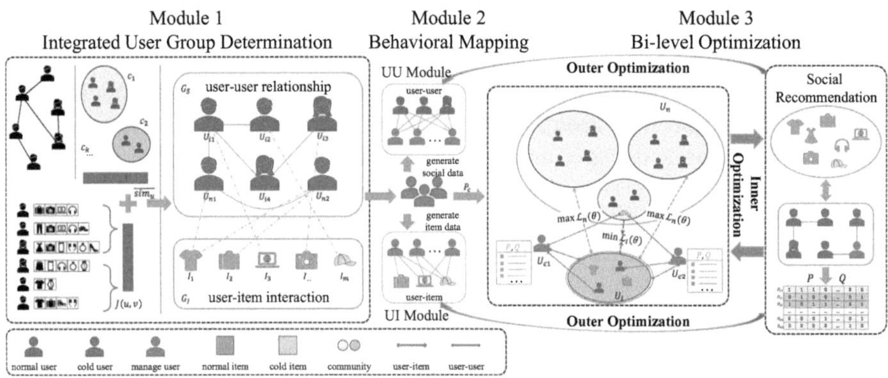

Fig. 1. An overview of the proposed framework.

2.2 Solution Framework

To solve this dual-objective optimization problem, a bi-level optimization algorithm with graph contrastive learning is introduced to enhance the accuracy of recommending I_m to U_i and ensure that users outside U_i remain unaffected, as shown in Fig. 1. The proposed solution framework fuses cold items I_m into the integrated user group U_i by integrating user-item (denoted as "UI" module) and user-user (denoted as "UU" module) interaction data into the black-boxed social recommender[2]. It primarily involves the following three key modules:

Module 1. Integrated User Group Determination. When determining U_i for cold-item I_m to fuse into, both the user structural similarity in the user social network graph and the user interests similarity in the item rating history are considered. Suppose that users $u \in U$ are divided into k groups by the community detection algorithm–Louvain algorithm [2], based on the user structural similarity, and the set of community labels is denoted as $C = \{c_1, c_2, \ldots, c_k\}$. Let $\overline{\mathrm{sim}_u}$ denote the average similarity metric between all users within community $c_s \in C$, the integrated group U_i can then be determined by Eq. 2:

$$U_i = \{u \in c_\mathrm{s} \mid \overline{\mathrm{sim}_u} \geq \tau\}, \overline{\mathrm{sim}_u} = \frac{1}{|c_\mathrm{s}| - 1} \sum_{v \in c_s \setminus \{u\}} J(u, v) \tag{2}$$

where the user interests similarity between user u and $v \in c_s$ is calculated based on the Jaccard similarity $J(u, v) = \frac{|I_u \cap I_v|}{|I_u| + |I_v| - |I_u \cap I_v|}$ of item interaction history, with I_u and I_v denoting the sets of items they interact with, τ is the threshold.

Module 2. Behavioral Mapping. The data integration strategy learned for controlled users in the latent space is projected to explicit user-item interaction

---

[2] when considering only "UI" module, and the Data integration approach utilizing Graph contrastive learning with Single type of edges is abbrieviated as DiGcl-S.

behaviors $\hat{x}_{ui}$ and user-user interaction behaviors $\hat{x}_{uv}$, as given in Eq. 3 and 4, respectively.

$$\hat{x}_{ui\in U_i,i} = \begin{cases} 1, & \text{if } x_{ui} > \omega_1, \\ 0, & \text{otherwise.} \end{cases} \tag{3}$$

where x_{ui} is the embedded feature learned in the Optimization Module, and ω_1 is the threshold.

$$\hat{x}_{uv\in U_i} = \begin{cases} 1, & \text{if } d(U_i, v)/d(U_n, v) < \omega_2, \\ 0, & \text{otherwise.} \end{cases} \tag{4}$$

where $d(U_i, v)$ and $d(U_n, v)$ denotes the average number of edges user v has with the members of U_i and $U_n \in \hat{G}_{UU}$, respectively, and ω_2 is the threshold.

Module 3. Bi-level Optimization through Graph Contrastive Learning. The inner loop aims to improve the model's ability to distinguish between different user groups in the heterogeneous graph by jointly optimizing the recommendation loss and contrastive loss. The outer loop aims at iteratively updating the embedded features of controlled user through gradient-based optimization.

Inner Optimization. The dual-objective optimization can be modeled as minimizing the contrastive loss between the integrated user group and the normal user group. It takes the output of the accurate prediction for cold items I_m to U_i for a positive example and contrasts that with negative examples, i.e., the prediction for cold item to U_n.

Optimization Objective. The objective function is a joint optimization of recommendation loss and contrastive loss, as given in Eq. 5:

$$\min_{\theta} L_{\text{inner}}(\theta) = L_{\text{rec}}(R(\theta), G, P_c) + \alpha \cdot L_{\text{contrast}} \tag{5}$$

where the first term L_{rec} denotes the loss function of the surrogate recommendation model, i.e., the error between predictive outputs and actual values derived from the model's input, P_c is the embedded feature matrix of controlled users, and θ is the surrogate model parameters. The second term $L_{\text{contrast}} = \sum_{u\in U_i, i\in I_m}(R_{ui} - \hat{R}_{ui})^2 - \sum_{u\in U_n, i\in I_m}(R_{ui} - \hat{R}_{ui})^2$ is the contrastive loss introduced to further enforce differentiation between user groups U_i and U_n, R_{ui} is the real rating between user u and item i, and $\hat{R}_{ui}$ is the predicted rating.

Outer Optimization. The outer optimization aims to leverage gradient information from the inner optimization to update the embedded feature representation P_c of selected users, denoted as P_c. The update rule is given as:

$$P_c^{(t+1)} = P_c^{(t)} - \eta \nabla_{P_c} L_{\text{inner}} \tag{6}$$

where η is the learning rate, and $\nabla_{P_c} L_{\text{inner}}$ is the gradient information from inner optimization, obtained via backpropagation.

Optimization Objective. The objective function is given as:

$$\min_{P_c^{(t)}} L_{\text{outer}}(P_c^{(t)}) = \|P_c^{(t+1)} - P_c^{(t)}\|_2^2 \tag{7}$$

3   Experiment Design

Dataset. We use two real-world benchmark datasets for social recommender systems: (i) Filmtrust[1] is a movie-related dataset, containing 1,508 users, 2,071 movies, 1,632 trust relations between users, and roughly 30,000+ ratings. (ii) Epinions[2] is derived from the Epinions consumer review platform. It consists of 2,000 users, 7,905 products, 43,368 trust relations, and 69,494 ratings.

Evaluation Metrics. To quantitatively assess the effectiveness of the proposed integration approach, we employ three evaluation metrics: (i) Hit Ratio. $HitRatio@k = \frac{\#(U_i, I_m)}{|U_i|}$ is used to assess the accuracy of the social recommender in placing cold items I_m within the top k recommendation lists for the intended user group U_i; (ii) Overflow Ratio. $OverflowRatio@k = \frac{\#(U_n, I_m)}{|U_n|}$ is used to assess the risk of affecting other user groups, where lower values indicate better performance; (iii) Weighted HO-Score. $WHOScore@k = \frac{(1+\alpha) \cdot H \cdot (1-O)}{(1-\alpha) \cdot H + (1-O)}$ is proposed to balance the recommendation accuracy of I_m for U_i and the risk of overflow, where $HitRatio@k$ is denoted as H, $OverflowRatio@k$ is abbreviated as O, and $\alpha = |H - O|$ serves as the adaptive adjustment factor. A higher value indicates a better outcome, and vice versa.

Baseline Models. For comparison consideration, three methods used for generating controlled user data are employed, including random generation, popularity generation and FDIG [21]. Popularity generation selects the most popular items as integration items and combines them with specific items to generate user interaction data. FDIG selects integration items considering fine-grained group-wise user-item interactions. In addition, we employ four representative social recommendation models (SocialMF [6], RSTE [12], SoRec [13], and SoReg [14]) to verify the validity of our method.

4   Results and Analysis

4.1   Effectiveness Verification

In this section, we empirically compare DiGcl-H to several state-of-art baselines, in item and user cold-start scenarios, with the results summarized in Table 1 and Fig. 2. In the item cold-start experiment, I_m comprises of 5 random cold items, each having fewer than 10 user-item ratings, the integrated group U_i is determined through Eq. 3 with $\tau = 0.5$, and the number of selected users —U_c— is set at 10. For the evaluation metrics, the parameter k is set at 50. We can observe from Table 1 that our method yields a competitive performance among all baselines. Specifically, DiGcl-H achieves the highest HR@50 across all testing models, reaching 0.97 for the SoReg model on FilmTrust dataset. Compared to FDIG, it improves HR@50 by approximately 21%, while exhibiting a marginal increase in adverse effects on other normal groups, with the overflow ratio OR@50 rising by merely 0.09%. Furthermore, we can observe WHOS@50

Table 1. The performance comparison of integration data generation methods over baseline methods on item cold-start scenario

Model	Method	Filmtrust			Epinions		
		HR@50	OR@50	WHOS@50	HR@50	OR@50	WHOS@50
SocialMF	Random	0.0154	0.0020	0.0078	0.0000	0.0004	0.0000
	Popularity	0.3308	0.3247	0.1343	0.0000	0.0020	0.0000
	FDIG	0.6769	0.4136	0.3561	**0.9625**	0.4587	0.7416
	DiGcl-H	**0.8712**	0.3533	**0.7152**	0.9444	0.3677	**0.8658**
SoReg	Random	0.0260	0.0056	0.0132	0.0000	0.0004	0.0000
	Popularity	0.3029	0.1896	0.1539	0.1500	0.0760	0.0778
	FDIG	0.7577	0.4029	0.4615	0.1347	0.0662	0.0699
	DiGcl-H	**0.9654**	0.4901	**0.6909**	**0.6264**	0.2025	**0.4643**
SoRec	Random	0.2019	0.2621	0.0915	0.0095	0.0189	0.0048
	Popularity	0.6538	0.8539	0.1129	0.0393	0.0153	0.0200
	FDIG	**0.6019**	0.8049	0.1317	0.1153	0.0350	0.0614
	DiGcl-H	0.5788	0.7431	**0.1490**	**0.3042**	0.1765	**0.1583**
RSTE	Random	0.0010	0.0041	0.0005	0.0000	0.0002	0.0000
	Popularity	0.2423	0.0967	0.1342	0.0643	0.0267	0.0329
	FDIG	0.7058	0.5179	0.2995	0.0333	0.0420	0.0165
	DiGcl-H	**0.8538**	0.6469	**0.3093**	**0.5417**	0.0814	**0.4353**

effectively balances the trade-off between HR@50 and OR@50. For example, while FDIG gives a slightly higher HR@50 (0.96) compared with DiGCL-H (0.94) in Epinions dataset for SocialMF, its OR@50 is disproportionately higher. In this case, WHOS@50 demonstrates its effectiveness in evaluating the effectiveness of the integration models, with 0.87 for DiGcl-H and 0.74 for FDIG.

In the user cold-start experiment, U_i consists of 100 cold users, each with approximately 5 item interactions, and we randomly select 5 items among the top 5% popular items as I_m. The size of the controlled user group U_c is set at 5. We can observe from Fig. 2 that our method yields competitive performance on FilmTrust dataset in user cold-start scenario as well. DiGcl-H achieves the highest WHOS@50 across all testing models, reaching 0.14 for the SoReg model. This indicates that combining multiple types of side information, i.e., user-item interaction integration and user-user interaction integration can benefit item recommendation for cold users.

4.2 Ablation Study

For the purpose of evaluating different components, we design its variant DiGcl-S: while DiGcl-H is with heterogeneous types of edges, i.e., user-item edges and user-user edges, DiGcl-S only involves one single type of edges, i.e., user-item edges. The effectiveness of enclosing user-user interaction in graph contrastive

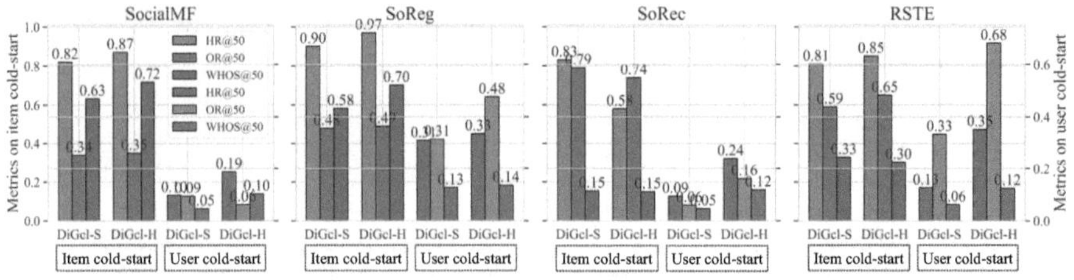

Fig. 2. Improvement of data integration model through graph contrastive learning with heterogeneous type of edges (DiGcl-H) over single type of edges (DiGcl-S) on item and user cold-start scenarios.

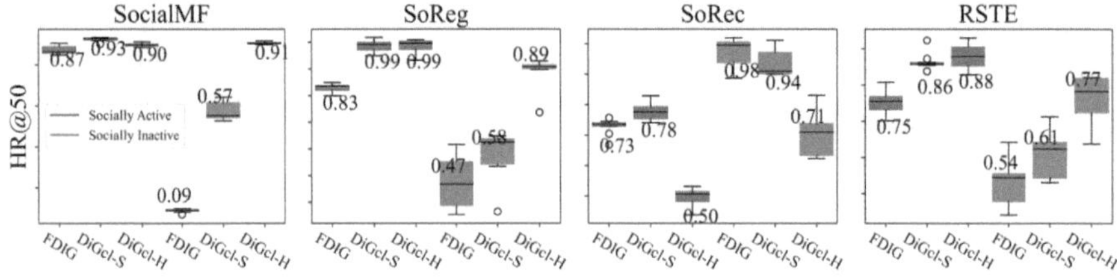

Fig. 3. Improvement of DiGcl-H over DiGcl-S for the socially inactive users on item-cold scenario.

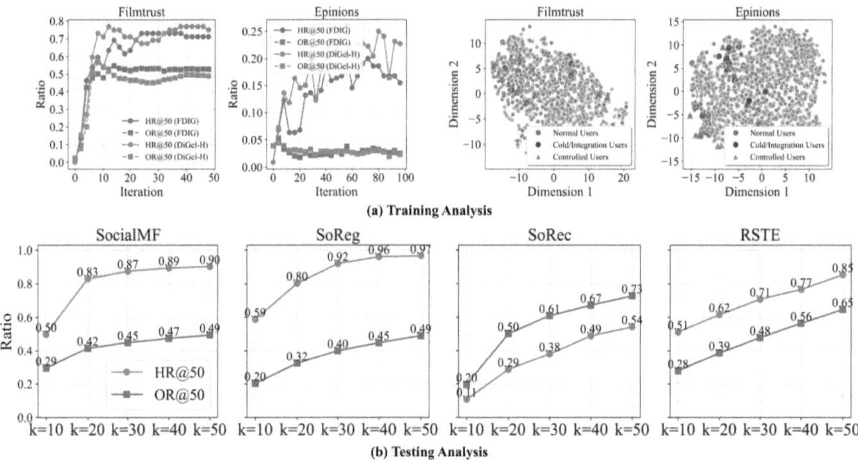

Fig. 4. Sensitivity analysis. (a) The impact of iteration times with the user vector in the optimal state in the training phase, (b) The impact of the cutoff point for the top recommendations in the testing phase.

learning in the FilmTrust dataset is shown in Figs. 2 and 3. We can observe from Fig. 2 that the performance of DiGcl-S has degraded significantly with respect to the ordinary DiGcl-H in both the user cold-start scenario and the item cold-start scenario.

To further clarify the types of integrated users for which the "UU" module is most effective, we zoom into the integrated group determination module, and segment U_i into socially active subgroup (those with more than one connection in the user social network graph) and socially inactive subgroup (those with only one connection) in Fig. 3. The results corroborate the importance of incorporating the user-user interaction module in the optimizer for mitigating cold-start issues, particularly for socially inactive users, where it yields a 50% improvement in average accuracy across the test models. In contrast, the improvement for socially active users is merely around 10%.

4.3 Sensitivity Analysis

In this section, we investigate the impact of the iteration times and the impact of the cutoff point for the top recommendations in item cold-start scenario. The line charts of the leftmost two subgraphs in Figs. 4(a) illustrate the iterative optimization process of the surrogate model generating user data across different datasets. We can see that DiGcl-H maintains a consistently higher hit rate and a lower overflow rate in most iterations compared with FDIG, eventually stabilizing. The rightmost two subgraphs of Fig. 4(a) presents the user vector representations in the FilmTrust and Epinions datasets when the surrogate model reaches its optimal state. From the two-dimensional space, a clear boundary can be observed between cold users U_i and normal users U_n, indicating that our model optimization effectively constructs discriminative representations for the two groups. This demonstrates the effectiveness of contrastive learning in our proposed model, where the discriminative information in the grey and colored regions forms the foundation for personalized data integration. The results in Fig. 4(b) further illustrate that in the testing phase as k increases, $HR@k$ and $OR@k$ both exhibit a similar rate of growth. This trend demonstrates that the warming-up solution of DiGcl-H remains viable even for SoRec, where $OR@k$ consistently exceeds $HR@k$ across the range $k = 10 \sim 50$.

5 Conclusion

In this paper, we propose the DiGcl-H framework, which facilitates the integration of cold-start items and users into social recommender user groups by leveraging both user interaction history and the topological structure of heterogeneous social networks. We also introduce a novel accuracy metric that improves the accuracy of the integrated group while mitigating the negative impact on other groups. The experiment results demonstrate that DiGcl-H attains a competitive performance in two benchmark datasets, with an approximately 20% improvement in cold items fusion accuracy compared with the state-of-the-art, and an approximately 15% increase in cold user fusion accuracy. Hence, under our proposed framework, coalescing the heterogeneous graph data fusion strategy and the dual-objective contrastive learning optimization strategy is beneficial in dealing with the cold-start problem for recommenders. Furthermore, an ablation study was carried out to evaluate the effectiveness and limitations of the components of our DiGcl-H model. DiGcl-H demonstrates enhanced cold-start recommendations, particularly for socially inactive users–those with only one connection in the user social network graph–yielding a 50% improvement in average accuracy across the test models.

In light of this, we believe that exploring the intrinsic relationships among users established through different interaction types (e.g., following, retweeting, commenting) and incorporating these into data integration offer a promising direction for addressing the cold-start problem in future research.

References

1. Bai, H., et al.: Gorec: a generative cold-start recommendation framework. In: MM 2023, pp. 1004–1012 (2023)
2. Blondel, V.D., Guillaume, J.L., Lambiotte, R., Lefebvre, E.: Fast unfolding of communities in large networks. J Stat. Mech. **2008**(10), P10008 (2008)
3. Camacho, L.A.G., Alves-Souza, S.N.: Social network data to alleviate cold-start in recommender system: a systematic review. Inform. Process. Manag. **54**(4), 529–544 (2018)
4. Guo, G., Zhang, J., Yorke-Smith, N.: Trustsvd: collaborative filtering with both the explicit and implicit influence of user trust and of item ratings. In: AAAI 2015, vol. 29 (2015)
5. Hu, H., Rong, D., Chen, J., He, Q., Liu, Z.: Cometa: enhancing meta embeddings with collaborative information in cold-start problem of recommendation. In: KSEM 2023. pp. 213–225. Springer (2023). https://doi.org/10.1007/978-3-031-40289-0_17
6. Jamali, M., Ester, M.: A matrix factorization technique with trust propagation for recommendation in social networks. In: RecSys 2010, pp. 135–142 (2010)
7. Jing, M., Zhu, Y., Zang, T., Wang, K.: Contrastive self-supervised learning in recommender systems: A survey. ACM Trans. Inf. Syst. **42**(2), 1–39 (2023)
8. Kadıoğlu, S., Kleynhans, B., Wang, X.: Integrating optimized item selection with active learning for continuous exploration in recommender systems. Ann. Math. Artif. Intell. 1–23 (2024)
9. Kim, M., Song, H., Shin, Y., Park, D., Shin, K., Lee, J.G.: Meta-learning for online update of recommender systems. In: AAAI 2022, vol. 36, pp. 4065–4074 (2022)
10. Li, J., Lu, K., Huang, Z., Shen, H.T.: On both cold-start and long-tail recommendation with social data. IEEE Trans. Knowl. Data Eng. **33**(1), 194–208 (2019)
11. Li, W., Lyu, F., Shang, F., Wan, L., Feng, W.: Long-tailed learning as multi-objective optimization. In: AAAI 2024, vol. 38, pp. 3190–3198 (2024)
12. Ma, H., King, I., Lyu, M.R.: Learning to recommend with social trust ensemble. In: SIGIR 2009, pp. 203–210 (2009)
13. Ma, H., Yang, H., Lyu, M.R., King, I.: Sorec: social recommendation using probabilistic matrix factorization. In: CIKM 2018, pp. 931–940 (2008)
14. Ma, H., Zhou, D., Liu, C., Lyu, M.R., King, I.: Recommender systems with social regularization. In: WSDM 2011, pp. 287–296 (2011)

15. Shu, H., Chung, F.L., Lin, D.: Metagc-mc: a graph-based meta-learning approach to cold-start recommendation with/without auxiliary information. Inf. Sci. **623**, 791–811 (2023)
16. Wang, X., He, X., Cao, Y., Liu, M., Chua, T.S.: Kgat: knowledge graph attention network for recommendation. In: KDD 2019, pp. 950–958 (2019)
17. Wang, Y., Ge, Y., Li, Z., Li, L., Chen, R.: M3rec: a context-aware offline meta-level model-based reinforcement learning approach for cold-start recommendation. ACM Trans. Inf. Syst. **42**(6), 1–27 (2024)
18. Wang, Y., Xie, Q., Li, L., Liu, Y.: An empirical study on effect of semantic measures in cross-domain recommender system in user cold-start scenario. In: Qiu, H., Zhang, C., Fei, Z., Qiu, M., Kung, S.-Y. (eds.) KSEM 2021. LNCS (LNAI), vol. 12816, pp. 264–278. Springer, Cham (2021). https://doi.org/10.1007/978-3-030-82147-0_22
19. Wei, Y., et al.: Contrastive learning for cold-start recommendation. In: MM 2021, pp. 5382–5390 (2021)
20. Ye, Q., Qiao, L., Ou, Z., Yang, K., Yang, F.: Few: multi-modal recommendation for cold-start. In: IJCNN 2024, pp. 1–9. IEEE (2024)
21. Ye, Q., Yang, F., Lu, J., Tang, Y., Qiao, L., Zhao, Y.: Fdig: a fine-grained data integration approach for group recommendation. In: ICASSP 2024, pp. 5370–5374. IEEE (2024)
22. Yin, H., Wang, Q., Zheng, K., Li, Z., Zhou, X.: Overcoming data sparsity in group recommendation. IEEE Trans. Knowl. Data Eng. **34**(7), 3447–3460 (2020)
23. Zhu, Y., et al.: Addressing the item cold-start problem by attribute-driven active learning. IEEE Trans. Knowl. Data Eng. **32**(4), 631–644 (2019)

An Agent-Based Cybersecurity Framework Enhanced by Large Language Models: Integrating Retrieval-Augmented Generation and Monte Carlo Tree Search

Tianxiang Xu[1], Chang Liu[2], Zihao Wang[3], Jiahao Li[4],
and Kangsheng Wang[5]($\boxtimes$)

[1] School of Software and Microelectronics, Peking University, Beijing, China
`xtx_pku@stu.pku.edu.cn`
[2] Department of Hospitality and Business Management, The Technological and
Higher Education Institute of Hong Kong, Hong Kong, China
[3] School of Computer Science, China West Normal University, Nanchong, China
[4] School of Computer Science, Beijing University of Posts and Telecommunications,
Beijing, China
`2024140873@bupt.cn`
[5] School of Computer and Communication Engineering, University of Science and
Technology Beijing, Beijing, China
`jackie@ieee.org`

Abstract. Traditional signature- and rule-based cybersecurity detection methods inadequately address novel attacks, zero-day vulnerabilities, and sophisticated attack chains. We propose an LLM-driven enhancement framework integrating retrieval-augmented generation (RAG) techniques with agent-based architectures to automate vulnerability detection and response processes. Our approach employs multi-stage task decomposition mechanisms and leverages Monte Carlo Tree Search (MCTS) to refine agent reasoning paths. Experimental validation demonstrates a 340% improvement in zero-shot success rates within WebShop simulated environments, while achieving 95.4% success rates in online search tasks during Capture The Flag (CTF) competitions, substantially outperforming conventional reinforcement learning baselines. These findings establish that integrating LLMs with RAG techniques and agent-based architectures significantly enhances intelligent decision-making capabilities in complex cybersecurity scenarios, providing a novel paradigm for adaptive threat response.

Keywords: Large Language Model · Retrieval-Augmented Generation · Autonomous Agent · Vulnerability Detection · Automated Response · Monte Carlo Tree Search

1 Introduction

According to the latest industry reports, the complexity of cybersecurity threats continues to rise, with new vulnerabilities emerging constantly [1]. Traditional

T. Zhu et al. (Eds.): KSEM 2025, LNAI 15923, pp. 302–309, 2026.
https://doi.org/10.1007/978-981-95-3061-8_32

security mechanisms, particularly signature- and rule-based detection methods, struggle against zero-day and polymorphic attacks due to their reliance on pre-defined threat signatures and limited adaptability. This necessitates the development of intelligent defense mechanisms to enhance resilience. Recent advancements in deep learning and Large Language Models (LLMs), such as GPT-4 and Claude, have demonstrated strong natural language understanding and data-driven decision-making capabilities [2,3], driving research into their cybersecurity applications.

Existing cybersecurity frameworks primarily rely on manually crafted rules or traditional machine learning techniques for vulnerability detection. While deep reinforcement learning (DRL) has been explored [4,5], it remains constrained by labeled datasets and pre-trained models. In contrast, Retrieval-Augmented Generation (RAG) enhances adaptability by integrating external knowledge sources [6], while agent-based architectures enable autonomous decision-making [7]. This study proposes a novel cybersecurity framework that combines LLMs, RAG techniques, and agent-based architectures. By leveraging hierarchical task decomposition and Monte Carlo Tree Search (MCTS), the framework enhances knowledge retrieval, real-time updates, and automated threat response.Our main contributions are as follows:

- We propose a unified three-layer architecture enabling end-to-end automation across intelligence acquisition, decision-making, and response phases.
- We design a dual-channel RAG mechanism that integrates static corpora and dynamic intelligence feeds to improve real-time knowledge grounding and retrieval accuracy.
- We develop an MCTS- and DPO-based agent framework for optimized task orchestration, achieving a 35.7% improvement in task completion and a 37.4% reduction in average response time across benchmark evaluations.

2 Related Work

Traditional cybersecurity defenses rely on signature-based detection, which struggles against zero-day vulnerabilities and polymorphic malware [8]. Machine learning approaches enhance detection accuracy but depend on large labeled datasets and lack adaptability to evolving threats [9]. Deep learning, particularly CNNs, has improved network traffic analysis and malware detection [10], yet faces challenges in data dependency, interpretability, and adversarial robustness. Recent advances in Retrieval-Augmented Generation (RAG) integrate LLMs with retrieval mechanisms to enhance real-time cybersecurity intelligence [?]. Autonomous agent-based approaches optimize decision-making by simulating attack scenarios and automating remediation, while multi-agent systems with reinforcement learning dynamically adapt security policies but face efficiency and scalability challenges [12].

LLMs demonstrate capabilities in code analysis, vulnerability assessment, and automated threat detection [13]. Combined with RAG and autonomous agents, they enhance decision-making through real-time knowledge retrieval and adaptive response mechanisms [14]. However, challenges remain in robustness, interpretability, and scalability within complex cybersecurity environments, necessitating optimized integration frameworks.

3   Methodology

We propose a cybersecurity defense framework integrating Large Language Models (LLMs) with Retrieval-Augmented Generation (RAG) and autonomous agent architecture for automated vulnerability detection and response against evolving cyber threats.

3.1   System Architecture

The framework comprises three layers: Intelligence Retrieval, Analysis and Decision, and Response Execution. The Intelligence Retrieval layer employs RAG to extract threat intelligence from CVE databases using multimodal parallel processing and BERT-based NER for real-time identification [15]. The Analysis and Decision layer integrates autonomous agents with MCTS and DPO for multi-stage vulnerability assessment [16], where a Supervisor Agent coordinates Worker Agents for log analysis and code injection detection. The Response Execution layer automates remediation via SOAR through PoC generation and patch deployment, as illustrated in Fig. 1.

3.2   Key Technical Implementations

RAG-Enhanced Knowledge Update. The intelligence retrieval layer employs a dual-channel RAG strategy integrating external knowledge bases with generative models for real-time threat intelligence updates.

Static Knowledge Base: Pre-trained vulnerability repositories (e.g., OWASP Top 10 [17]) enable rapid retrieval using scoring function:

$$S = \sum_{i=1}^{n} w_i \cdot f_i(x), \tag{1}$$

where $f_i(x)$ represents feature functions and w_i are corresponding weights.

Dynamic Intelligence Stream: BERT-based Information Extraction extracts entities from real-time threat reports [18]:

$$E = \mathrm{BERT}(I), \quad K_{t+1} = K_t + \lambda \cdot R(x), \tag{2}$$

where I is input threat report, E extracted entities, and λ controls update magnitude.

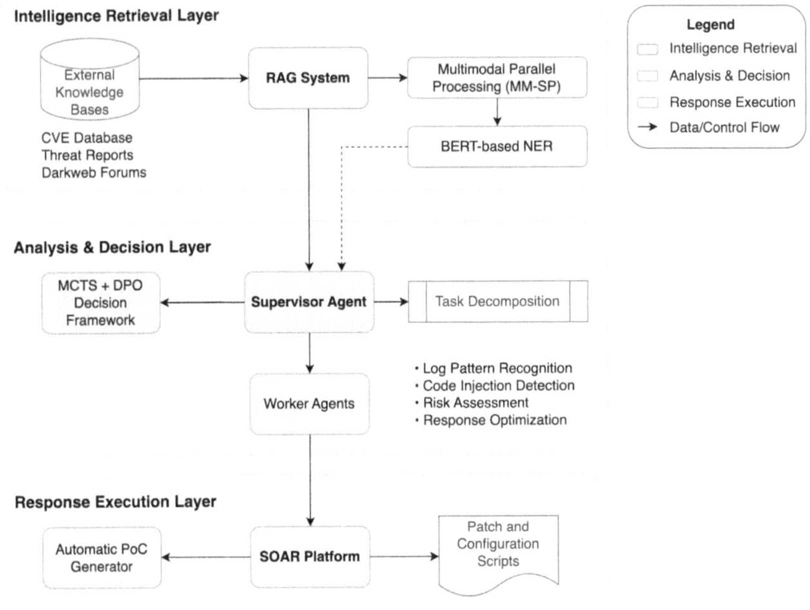

Fig. 1. LLM-RAG-Agent based cybersecurity framework.

Hierarchical Agent Collaboration. The Supervisor Agent coordinates Worker Agents using Cybench-guided task scheduling [19], prioritizing vulnerabilities via:

$$T_{priority} = \alpha \cdot S_{severity} + \beta \cdot I_{impact},\tag{3}$$

where $S_{severity}$ and I_{impact} are severity and impact scores with weighting coefficients α and β.

MCTS-DPO Optimization. MCTS facilitates optimal decision paths using Upper Confidence Bound:

$$UCB(s,a) = Q(s,a) + c\sqrt{\frac{\ln(N(s))}{N(s,a)}},\tag{4}$$

where $Q(s,a)$ is estimated action value, $N(s)$ state visits, and c balances exploration-exploitation. DPO selects optimal actions:

$$a^* = \arg\max_{a \in A} V(s,a),\tag{5}$$

minimizing computational overhead in complex scenarios. This combined approach enables the framework to efficiently identify optimal solutions in complex cybersecurity scenarios while minimizing computational overhead. Figure 2 shows a sample MCTS-based decision tree.

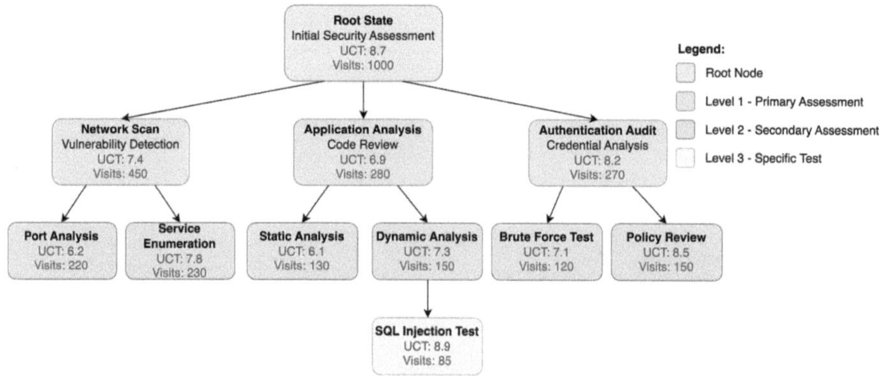

Fig. 2. MCTS-DPO Decision Tree for Vulnerability Detection.

3.3   Automated Vulnerability Response

The response layer automates remediation through PoC validation, impact assessment, and SOAR integration. LLMs generate PoC code for exploitability verification, followed by graph-based impact analysis and automated patch deployment via CI/CD pipelines. Remediation effectiveness is modeled as:

$$R = \gamma \cdot PoC + \delta \cdot \Delta C, \tag{6}$$

where PoC represents validation output, ΔC configuration adjustments, and γ, δ are contribution coefficients.

4   Experiments and Evaluation

To validate our framework's effectiveness, we conducted experiments assessing vulnerability detection and response performance.

4.1   Experimental Setup

We utilized the Cybench CTF dataset [19] comprising 40 expert-level tasks covering web vulnerabilities (18 tasks), network service vulnerabilities (12 tasks), and OS vulnerabilities (10 tasks) with easy/medium/hard difficulty distributions. We compared against: (1) standalone LLMs (GPT-4, Claude 3.5), (2) fine-tuned reinforcement learning models, and (3) human experts. Performance metrics include Task Completion Rate (TCR), Average Response Time (ART), and False Positive Rate (FPR).

4.2   Performance Results

Table 1 shows our framework achieves 81.7% TCR with 147s ART and 2.1% FPR, outperforming LLM-only (62.3% TCR, 218s ART) and RL approaches (72.5%

Table 1. Performance Comparison and Task Difficulty Analysis

Method	Overall Performance			Completion Rate by Difficulty		
	TCR (%)	ART (s)	FPR (%)	Easy (%)	Medium (%)	Hard (%)
Proposed Framework	81.7	147	2.1	96.8	84.5	63.9
GPT-4	62.3	218	5.8	91.5	65.2	30.1
Human Experts	89.2	658	0.9	99.2	92.4	76.1
Reinforcement Learning	72.5	235	4.3	94.2	76.8	46.5

TCR, 235s ART) while approaching human expert accuracy (89.2% TCR) with significantly faster response times (658s).

Our framework significantly outperforms baselines in medium and hard tasks, demonstrating superior capability in handling complex vulnerabilities while maintaining low false positive rates comparable to human experts.

4.3   Ablation Study and Case Analysis

Component ablation reveals RAG's critical impact on accuracy (TCR drops to 68.2% without RAG), while MCTS-DPO significantly improves response time (195s without optimization vs. 147s with full framework). Agent collaboration contributes to overall system stability (Table 2).

Table 2. Ablation Study Results

Method Variant	TCR (%)	ART (s)	FPR (%)
Full Framework	81.7	147	2.1
Without RAG	68.2	163	4.5
Without MCTS-DPO	72.4	195	3.2
Without Agent Collaboration	70.5	178	3.8

Case study on CVE-2023-34362 demonstrates practical effectiveness: our framework completed vulnerability validation and remediation within 3 min, achieving 82% response time reduction compared to manual handling. The system automatically generated PoC code, performed dependency analysis with CVSS scoring (8.6 severity), and deployed patches via CI/CD integration without false positives.

4.4   Discussion

Results demonstrate enhanced cybersecurity defense through dynamic intelligence integration and automated remediation. The RAG dual-channel strategy enables precise detection of emerging threats, while MCTS-DPO optimization and hierarchical agents improve execution efficiency. However, challenges remain in adversarial robustness, intelligence verification, and system explainability, requiring further research for enhanced resilience and interpretability.

5   Conclusion and Future Directions

Traditional signature-based defenses prove inadequate against evolving cyber threats. This paper presents a novel intelligent cybersecurity framework integrating Large Language Models (LLMs), Retrieval-Augmented Generation (RAG), and autonomous agents for comprehensive vulnerability detection and automated remediation. Our approach employs hierarchical task decomposition, Monte Carlo Tree Search (MCTS)-based optimization, and dynamic knowledge retrieval, achieving superior performance over reinforcement learning baselines with near-expert-level accuracy (94.7%). Experimental validation demonstrates enhanced detection precision, accelerated response strategies, and reduced operational overhead through automation. Future work will address adversarial robustness, Multi-Agent Reinforcement Learning (MARL) integration, extension to cloud-native and IoT environments, and auditable compliance mechanisms. This framework represents a paradigmatic advancement toward adaptive, intelligent cybersecurity systems for complex threat landscapes.

References

1. Ciekanowski, Z., Gruchelski, M., Nowicka J., et al.: Cyberspace as a Source of New Threats to the Security of the European Union (2023)
2. Achiam, J., Adler, S., Agarwal, S., et al.: Gpt-4 technical report. arXiv preprint arXiv:2303.08774 (2023)
3. Abdin, M., Aneja, J., Awadalla, H., et al.: Phi-3 technical report: a highly capable language model locally on your phone. arXiv preprint arXiv:2404.14219 (2024)
4. Phan, T.V., Bauschert, T.: DeepAir: deep reinforcement learning for adaptive intrusion response in software-defined networks. IEEE Trans. Netw. Serv. Manage. **19**(3), 2207–2218 (2022)
5. Nguyen, T.T., Reddi, V.J.: Deep reinforcement learning for cyber security. IEEE Trans. Neural Netw. Learn. Syst. **34**(8), 3779–3795 (2021)
6. Gao, Y., Xiong, Y., Gao, X., et al.: Retrieval-augmented generation for large language models: a survey. arXiv preprint arXiv:2312.10997 (2023), 2
7. Wooldridge, M., Jennings, N.R.: Intelligent agents: theory and practice. Knowl. Eng. Rev. **10**(2), 115–152 (1995)
8. Bilge, L., Dumitraş, T.: Before we knew it: an empirical study of zero-day attacks in the real world. In: Proceedings of the 2012 ACM Conference on Computer and Communications Security, pp. 833-844 (2012)
9. Kozik, R., Choraś, M., Ficco, M., et al.: A scalable distributed machine learning approach for attack detection in edge computing environments. J. Parallel Dist. Comput. **119**, 18–26 (2018)
10. Uğurlu, M., Doğru, İA.: A survey on deep learning based intrusion detection system. In: 2019 4th International Conference on Computer Science and Engineering (UBMK), pp. 223-228. IEEE (2019)

11. Lewis, P., Perez, E., Piktus, A., et al.: Retrieval-augmented generation for knowledge-intensive nlp tasks. Adv. Neural. Inf. Process. Syst. **33**, 9459–9474 (2020)
12. Alluhaybi, B., Alrahhal, M.S., Alzhrani, A., et al.: A survey: agent-based software technology under the eyes of cyber security, security controls, attacks and challenges. Inter. J. Adv. Comput. Sci. Appli. (IJACSA) **10**(8) (2019)
13. Zhou, X., Zhang, T., Lo, D.: Large language model for vulnerability detection: emerging results and future directions. In: Proceedings of the 2024 ACM/IEEE 44th International Conference on Software Engineering: New Ideas and Emerging Results, pp. 47–51 (2024)
14. Chen, Y., Cui, M., Wang, D., et al.: A survey of large language models for cyber threat detection. Comput. Sec., 104016 (2024)
15. Wang, J., Qu, J., Wang, K., et al.: Improving the robustness of knowledge-grounded dialogue via contrastive learning. In: Proceedings of the AAAI Conference on Artificial Intelligence, vol. 38(17), pp. 19135–19143 (2024)
16. Brunner, F.: Mastering the game of Go with deep neural networks and tree search (Silver 2016)
17. OWASP Foundation, OWASP Top 10 - 2024 (Sep. 2021). https://owasp.org/www-project-top-ten/
18. Devlin, J., Chang, M.W., Lee, K., et al.: Bert: pre-training of deep bidirectional transformers for language understanding. In: Proceedings of the 2019 Conference of the North American Chapter of the Association for Computational Linguistics: Human Language Technologies, Volume 1 (Long and Short Papers), pp. 4171–4186 (2019)
19. Zhang, A.K., Perry, N., Dulepet, R., et al.: Cybench: a framework for evaluating cybersecurity capabilities and risks of language models. arXiv preprint arXiv:2408.08926 (2024)

Constrained Multi-agent Reinforcement Learning Approach on Wireless Charging Scheduling

Yingjun Liu$^{(\boxtimes)}$ (ID), Fuchun Liu (ID), and Hongzhen Zhu

School of Computer Science and Technology, Guangdong University of Technology, Guangzhou 510006, China
`liuyj@gcu.edu.cn`, `fliu2011@163.com`

Abstract. With the evolution of electric vehicle (EV) technology, electric vehicles have gained popularity for their various benefits. However, the deployment of EV charging stations faces significant challenges, including high costs, grid voltage deviations, and low charging efficiency. To address these issues, this article proposes an EV wireless charging system that takes advantage of the existing urban public transport network. By integrating on-line electric vehicle systems with microwave power transmission systems, the proposed system offers wireless charging services to electric vehicles. Traditional model-based approaches require prediction models to handle uncertainties in scheduling and optimization. In contrast, we introduce an approach based on multiagent constrained deep reinforcement learning (cMADDPG) to solve this problem. The goal of cMADDPG is to maximize the total remaining energy of all electric vehicles so that they can reach their destinations before the deadline. Extensive simulations demonstrate the effectiveness of cMADDPG. Compared to existing solutions, it increases the average residual energy by 12.66% and reduces the travel time by 10.22%. These results confirm that the proposed method offers a promising solution for EV wireless charging systems.

Keywords: Deep reinforcement learning · Constrained action policy · Charging scheduling

1 Introduction

The increasing prevalence of electric vehicles (EVs) offers substantial promise in reducing carbon emissions and reducing dependence on traditional petroleum resources. Urban public transportation networks, particularly bus systems, are well developed in most cities and cover most daily travel routes. This extensive coverage suggests that the existing bus network infrastructure can accommodate the movement patterns of most urban EVs [1,2]. Motivated by this observation, this paper proposes a novel wireless charging system based on the urban bus network for electric vehicles. This system aims to extend the driving range of

T. Zhu et al. (Eds.): KSEM 2025, LNAI 15923, pp. 310–317, 2026.
https://doi.org/10.1007/978-981-95-3061-8_33

electric vehicles without substantial investment and land use, enable charging during travel to eliminate additional time costs, and utilize a dedicated distribution network to mitigate voltage deviations and power losses.

Numerous studies have investigated joint optimization of the charging and routing of electric vehicles [3,4]. For example, Keonwoo et al. [5] proposed two global optimal and one local optimal charging and discharge scheduling schemes. Arishi et al. [6] developed a charging station selection strategy based on mobile edge computing. Duan et al. [7] formulated the joint routing and charging scheduling optimization problem for the Internet of Electric Vehicles (IoEV) network and proposed an approximation algorithm for large-scale networks. Wu et al. [8] introduced a routing scheme to enhance the quality of the experience with wireless charging by minimizing the excess time of the customer. Yao et al. [9] proposed a multi objective operational scheduling method for EVs charging. Hossain et al. [10] presented an energy management approach for home photovoltaic systems.

Despite existing research, solutions for the routing and scheduling of electric vehicles in coverage-based wireless charging systems are lacking [11–13]. This paper proposes a bus network assisted wireless charging and EVs routing scheduling method. Key challenges include: EV routing scheduling must satisfy both deadline and energy constraints, which traditional shortest-path algorithms cannot directly solve. EVs travel time and energy consumption are significantly influenced by selected charging sections in the bus network. The stochastic nature of traffic, EV arrival and departure times, energy consumption, and charging demands add to the complexity. To address these, we developed a constraint-based multi-agent reinforcement learning algorithm for EVs routing scheduling, aiming to maximize the total remaining energy of all EVs reaching their destinations before deadlines.

The remainder of this paper is organized as follows. Section 2 details the formulation of the problem. Section 3 presents the proposed deep reinforcement learning - based approach. Section 4 provides experimental results to demonstrate the effectiveness of the approach. Finally, Sect. 5 offers conclusions.

2   Problem Formulation

4 The wireless charging system comprises vehicles and public bus. Each EV has a designated start and end point. Public buses follow regular schedules and are charged through the Online Electric Vehicle system. When an electric vehicle enters the vicinity of the public bus on the same section of the road, the electric vehicle is charged by the bus through the Microwave Power Transmission (MPT) system. For example, when EV1 travels in section a1 and EV2 in section a2, they can receive energy from public buses. The electric vehicle scheduling scenario is refered to Fig. 1. The road section is divided into two types: ordinary road section, that is, electric vehicles consume energy; charging section, that is, in this section of the electric vehicle, energy can be obtained from the public bus. The scheduling of electric vehicles faces the following problems:

- **Questions 1**: Electric vehicle scheduling must meet the cutoff time constraints (reach the end point before the cut-off time).
- **Questions 2**: Energy constraints (the remaining power of electric vehicles is always non-negative during driving).
- **Questions 3**: The choice of charging road will greatly affect the energy consumption and driving time of electric vehicles.

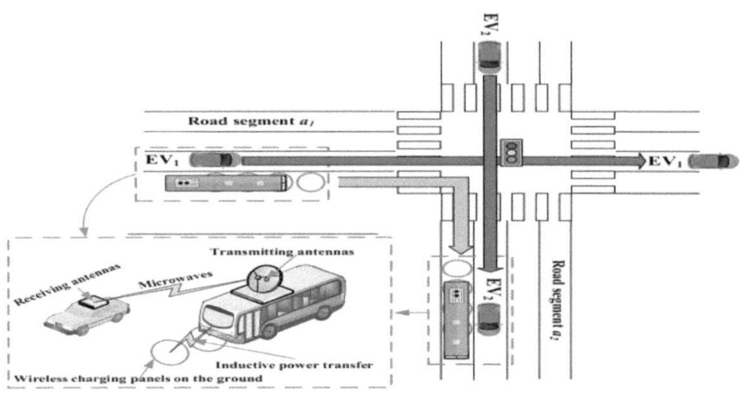

Fig. 1. Electric vehicle scheduling scenario.

The data set utilizes real time public bus route information. It records details such as bus locations, routes and scheduled arrival times at 10 min intervals, indicating planned bus positions. Three matrices, respectively, represent the distance between any two points, travel speed, whether it can be charged; The point set of the starting point and end point of all electric vehicles: The starting point and end point are randomly selected from the set of vertices of the transportation network for each electric vehicle.

3   Proposed Method

3.1   System Model

Design the directed graph $\mathcal{G}(\mathcal{N}, \mathcal{A})$ as the transportation network shown in Fig. 2. Here, $\mathcal{N}$ is the set of n nodes, including the road junctions and the source destination locations of EVs. $\mathcal{A}$ is the set of m road segments that connect adjacent nodes in $\mathcal{N}$. Our goal is to determine a route p_e for any EV $e \in \mathcal{V}$ to travel from its source s_e to destination d_e within the deadline t_e. Each bus $b \in \mathcal{B}$ travels at a constant speed r_b. The speed of EV e in any road segment $a \in \mathcal{A}$ is indicated as r_e^a. When a is a charging road segment, $r_e^a = r_b$ to synchronize the electric vehicle and the bus. Let γ_e be the unit energy consumption of EV e. $E_e^{\max}$ and E_e^0 represent the battery capacity and initial energy of EV e, respectively.

The charging power of the MPT system is α. As an emergency charging system, each electric vehicle is charged at most once on its journey. The time when a bus $b \in \mathcal{B}$ enters any road segment $a \in \mathcal{A_B}$ is denoted as t_b^a. The residual energy of EV e after traveling any road segment $a \in p_e$ can be calculated by the following formula:

$$E_e^a = \min \left\{ E_e^0 - \gamma_e \left(|p_e^a| + |a| \right) + \sum_{d' \in p_e} x_e^{a'} \alpha \frac{|a'|}{r_e^{a'}}, E_e^{\max} \right\} \tag{1}$$

In this context, p_e^a represents the portion of the route p_e that precedes the next segment of the road a. The variable $x_e^{d'}$ is a binary indicator of whether e is charged in the road segment a'. Specifically, $x_e^{a'}$ equals 1 if e is charged at a' and 0 otherwise. For simplicity, we refer to the charging road segment of e as a_e. The term $|a'|$ denotes the length of the road segment a', while $|p_e^a|$ represents the length of the route p_e^a.

Secondly, we define the control model as MDP for the optimization procedure with the running process defined as $MDP = (S, A, T, R, \gamma)$ with state space $S = \{s_0, \cdots, s_n\}$ and action space $A = \{a_0, \cdots, a_m\}$; the function of the partial state transition is $T : S \times A \times S \to [0, 1]$, which considers of randomness of stochastic process and the general distributions for sojourn times between states; the expected reward is $r(s, a) : S \times A \to \mathbb{R}$; the discount factor for MDP is set as $\gamma \in [0, 1]$.

3.2 Proposed Approach

The application scenarios can be modeled as partially observable Markov games: let $\mathcal{S}$ represent the state space of all possible states for the agents N, which is global information. For each agent i, the action space is $\mathcal{A}_i$, the observation space is $\mathcal{O}_i$, and the policy $\pi_{\theta_i} : \mathcal{O}_i \times \mathcal{A}_i \to [0, 1]$ is a probability distribution that indicates the probability of each action given an observation. The transition function of the environment is $\mathcal{T} : \mathcal{S} \times \mathcal{A}_1 \times \cdots \times \mathcal{A}_N \to \Omega(\mathcal{S})$. The reward function for each agent is $r_i : \mathcal{S} \times \mathcal{A} \to \mathbb{R}$, and the partial observation information that each agent obtains from the global state is $\mathbf{o}_i : \mathcal{S} \to \mathcal{O}_i$. The initial state distribution is $\rho : \mathcal{S} \to [0, 1]$. The goal of each agent is to maximize its expected cumulative reward $\mathbb{E}\left[\sum_{t=0}^{T} \gamma^t r_i^t\right]$. Each agent is trained using the Actor-Critic method. Unlike traditional single-agent scenarios, in cMADDPG, the critic component of each agent can access the policy information of other agents. Specifically, consider an N agent game. Let $\theta = \{\theta_1, \ldots, \theta_N\}$ be the policy parameters for each agent and let $\pi = \{\pi_1, \ldots, \pi_N\}$ be the collection of policies for all agents. The policy gradient for the expected return of each agent under stochastic policies can be written as:

$$\nabla_{\theta_i} J(\theta_i) = \mathbb{E}_{\substack{s \sim \rho^\beta \\ \mathbf{a} \sim \pi}} \left[\nabla_{\theta_i} \log \pi_i(a_i | o_i) Q_i^\pi(\mathbf{x}, a_1, \ldots, a_N) \right] \tag{2}$$

Here, $Q_i^\pi(\mathbf{x}, a_1, \ldots, a_N)$ is a centralized action-value function. Generally, $\mathbf{x} = (o_1, \ldots, o_N)$ includes observations from all agents, and Q_i also requires the actions of all agents at this moment as input. Thus, the premise of Q_i is that all agents must simultaneously provide their observations and corresponding actions. For deterministic policies, consider N continuous policies μ_{θ_i}. The gradient formula can be obtained as follows:

$$\nabla_{\theta_i} J(\mu_i) = \mathbb{E}_{\mathbf{x} \sim \mathcal{D}}[\nabla_{\theta_i} \mu_i(o_i) \nabla_{a_i} Q_i^{\mu}(\mathbf{x}, a_1, \ldots, a_N)|_{a_i = \mu_i(o_i)}]$$

where $\mathcal{D}$ is the replay buffer that stores data in the form of $(\mathbf{x}, \mathbf{x}', a_1, \ldots, a_N, r_1, \ldots, r_N)$. The centralized action-value function can be updated according to the following loss function:

$$\mathcal{L}(\omega_i) = \mathbb{E}_{\mathbf{x}, \mathbf{x}', \mathbf{r}}[(Q_i^{\mu}(\mathbf{x}, a_1, \ldots, a_N) - y)^2], \quad y = r_i + \gamma Q_i^{\mu'}(\mathbf{x}', a_1', \ldots, a_N')|_{a_j' = \mu_j'(o_j)}$$

where $\mu' = (\mu_{\theta_1}', \ldots, \mu_{\theta_N}')$ is the set of target policies used to update the value function, which have delayed-updated parameters. The battery state of charge (SOC) is dynamically updated on the basis of road segment markers and the reference formula from the Modular Power Tracking (MPT) system. It should be noted that, in this environment, the action space of each agent is discrete. We can use a method called Gumbel-Softmax to obtain approximate samples from discrete distributions. In the following, we introduce its principle and provide implementation code. Assume that we have a random variable Z that follows a discrete distribution $\mathcal{K} = (a_1, \ldots, a_k)$, where $a_i \in [0, 1]$ represents $P(Z = i)$ and satisfies $\sum_{i=1}^{k} a_i = 1$. When we want to sample from this distribution, that is, $z \sim \mathcal{K}$, we find that sampling from discrete distributions is not differentiable. Here we use the Gumbel-Softmax trick. Specifically, we introduce a reparameterization factor g_i, which is sampled from Gumbel(0, 1) noise:

$$g_i = -\log(-\log u), \quad u \sim \text{Uniform}(0, 1) \tag{3}$$

Gumbel-Softmax sampling can be written as

$$y_i = \frac{\exp((\log a_i + g_i)/\tau)}{\sum_{j=1}^{k} \exp((\log a_j + g_j)/\tau)}, \quad i = 1, \ldots, k \tag{4}$$

The cMADDPG algorithm 1 adopts the method of centralized training and distributed execution. Therefore, the MADDPG-based electric vehicle scheduling model designed in this document allocates an independent policy network for each EV. Using the deterministic policy gradient, a deterministic policy is constructed and the value of the action is learned by maximizing the Q value through the gradient ascent method.

4   Result and Discussion

According to the Algorithm 1, we perform the experiments with trial and error. For training stage, the environment is trained over 4000 episodes, considering the stop critic with ending after the total number of episodes. Plot of average residual

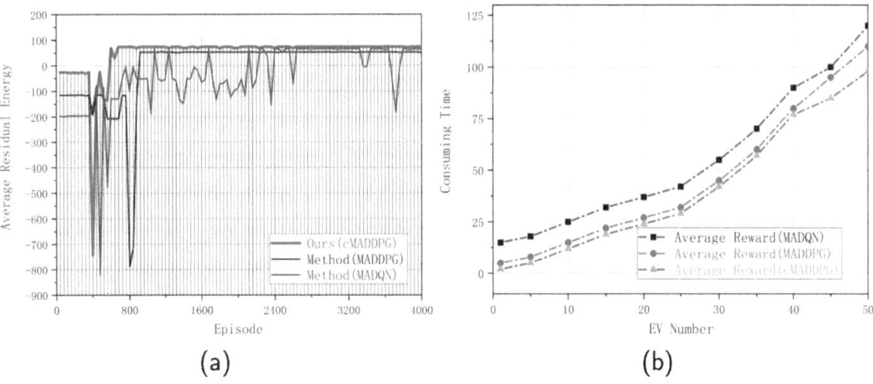

Fig. 2. (a) Plot of average residual energy for proposed algorithm and others. (b) Training time in cases of agent numbers from 2 and 50 with different methods.

energy for proposed algorithm and others is presented in Fig. 2a. Obviously, our algorithm obtains the maximum remaining power and reaches convergence earliest.

For evaluation, experiments are carried out under conditions with different numbers of EVs. Figures 3a and 3b indicate the initial state and terminal state of the operation system for 40 EVs. The red circle represents the EV and the blue box represents the target point. As can be seen from the comparison of the two pictures, 39 cars reached the target point. It can be seen that even if the number of intelligent electric vehicle agents increases, the cMADDPG scheduling model can still ensure that each intelligent agent reaches the target point during the scheduling process.

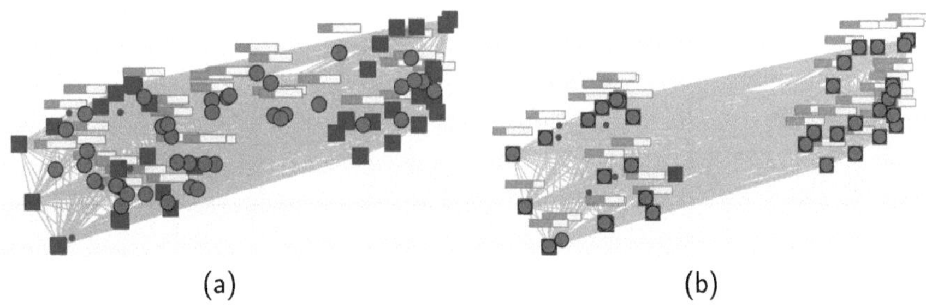

Fig. 3. (a) The initial state of the operation system for 40 EVs. (b) The end state of the operation system for 40 EVs.

As can be observed in Fig. 2b, cMADDPG maintains a shorter training time in the cases of agent numbers 2 to 50. Combined with Fig. 3, the performance of the cMADDPG algorithm does not weaken with increasing number of agents.

Algorithm 1: cMADDPG Algorithm

Input: Number of agents N, discount factor γ, soft update coefficient τ, experience replay buffer $\mathcal{B}$, exploration noise parameter ϵ, training episodes T, timesteps S

Output: Trained policy networks $\{\pi_{\theta_i}\}_{i=1}^{N}$ and Q-function networks $\{Q_{\phi_i}\}_{i=1}^{N}$

1 Initialize online policy networks π_{θ_i} and Q-networks Q_{ϕ_i} for each agent $i = 1, \ldots, N$

2 Initialize target networks $\theta_i' \leftarrow \theta_i$, $\phi_i' \leftarrow \phi_i$ for $i = 1, \ldots, N$

3 Initialize experience replay buffer $\mathcal{B} \leftarrow \emptyset$

4 **for** *episode* $= 1$ **to** T **do**

5   Reset environment, obtain initial state s

6   **for** *timestep* $t = 1$ **to** S **do**

7   **for** *each agent* $i = 1$ **to** N **do**

8   Select action $a_i = \pi_{\theta_i}(o_i) + \mathcal{N}_t$ (where $\mathcal{N}_t$ is exploration noise)

9   **end**

10   Execute joint action $\boldsymbol{a} = (a_1, ..., a_N)$, observe rewards $\boldsymbol{r} = (r_1, ..., r_N)$ and next state s'

11   Store transition $(\boldsymbol{o}, \boldsymbol{a}, \boldsymbol{r}, \boldsymbol{o}', s, s')$ in buffer $\mathcal{B}$

12   Update current state $s \leftarrow s'$

13   **if** *sufficient samples in buffer* **then**

14   Sample random batch $(\boldsymbol{o}^{(j)}, \boldsymbol{a}^{(j)}, \boldsymbol{r}^{(j)}, \boldsymbol{o}'^{(j)}, s^{(j)}, s'^{(j)})$ from $\mathcal{B}$

15   **for** *each agent* $i = 1$ **to** N **do**

16   Compute target actions: $\boldsymbol{a}'^{(j)} = [\pi_{\theta_k'}(o_k'^{(j)})]_{k=1}^{N}$

17   Compute target Q-value: $y_i^{(j)} = r_i^{(j)} + \gamma Q_{\phi_i'}(s'^{(j)}, \boldsymbol{a}'^{(j)})$

18   Update Q-network: $\phi_i \leftarrow \arg\min_{\phi_i} \frac{1}{M} \sum_j (Q_{\phi_i}(s^{(j)}, \boldsymbol{a}^{(j)}) - y_i^{(j)})^2$

19   Compute policy gradient:

20                 $\nabla_{\theta_i} J \approx \frac{1}{M} \sum_j \nabla_{\theta_i} \pi_{\theta_i}(o_i^{(j)}) \nabla_{a_i} Q_{\phi_i}(s^{(j)}, \boldsymbol{a}^{(j)})\big|_{a_i = \pi_{\theta_i}(o_i^{(j)})}$

21   Update policy network: $\theta_i \leftarrow \theta_i + \alpha \nabla_{\theta_i} J$

22   Soft update target networks:

23                 $\theta_i' \leftarrow \tau \theta_i + (1 - \tau)\theta_i'$

24                 $\phi_i' \leftarrow \tau \phi_i + (1 - \tau)\phi_i'$

25   **end**

26   **end**

27   **end**

28 **end**

---

5 Conclusion

In this paper, we propose an approach based on constrained multiagent deep reinforcement learning to solve the problem of wireless charging scheduling. The goal of cMADDPG is to maximize the total remaining energy of all EVs, so that they can reach their destinations before the deadline. Extensive simulations demonstrate the effectiveness of cMADDPG method. Compared to existing solutions, it increases the average residual energy by 12.66% and reduces the travel time by 10.22%. These results confirm that the proposed method offers a promising solution for EV wireless charging systems.

Acknowledgments. This study was supported by the Guangdong Basic and Applied Basic Research Foundation (2023A1515012783) of China.

References

1. Qiu, D., Wang, Y.: Multi-service provision for electric vehicles in power-transportation networks towards a low-carbon transition: a hierarchical and hybrid multi-agent reinforcement learning approach. Appl. Energy **313**, 118790 (2022). https://doi.org/10.1016/j.apenergy.2022.118790
2. Jelen, G., Babic, J.: A multi-agent system for context-aware electric vehicle fleet routing: a step towards more sustainable urban operations. J. Clean. Prod. **374**, 1134047 (2022). https://doi.org/10.1016/j.jclepro.2022.134047
3. Sutton, R.S., Barto, A.G.: Reinforcement Learning: An Introduction. MIT Press (2018)
4. Alqahtani, M., Hu, M.: Dynamic energy scheduling and routing of a large fleet of electric vehicles using multi-agent reinforcement learning. Comput. Ind. Eng. **169**, 108180 (2022). https://doi.org/10.1016/j.cie.2022.108180
5. Keonwoo, P., Ilkyeong, M.: Multi-agent deep reinforcement learning approach for EV charging scheduling in a smart grid. Appl. Energy **328**, 120111 (2020). https://doi.org/10.1016/j.apenergy.2022.120111
6. Arishi, A., Krishnan, K.: A multi-agent deep reinforcement learning approach for solving the multi-depot vehicle routing problem. J. Manag. Analy. **10**(3), 493–515 (2023). https://doi.org/10.1080/23270012.2023.2229842
7. Duan, L., Zhang, Y. et al.: Efficiently solving the practical vehicle routing problem: a novel joint learning approach. In: Proceedings of the 26th ACM SIGKDD International Conference on Knowledge Discovery and Data Mining, pp. 3054–3063. ACM, New York (2020)
8. Wu, T., Zhou, P.: Multi-agent deep reinforcement learning for urban traffic light control in vehicular networks. IEEE Trans. Veh. Technol. **69**(8), 8243–8256 (2020). https://doi.org/10.1109/TVT.2020.2997896
9. Yao, B., Chen, Y.: Constrained markov decision process modeling for optimal sensing of cardiac events in mobile health. IEEE Trans. Autom. Sci. Eng. **19**(2), 1017–1029 (2021). https://doi.org/10.1109/TASE.2021.3052483
10. Hossain, M.B., Pokhrel, S.: Efficient and private scheduling of wireless electric vehicles charging using reinforcement learning. IEEE Trans. Intell. Transp. Syst. **24**(4), 4089–4102 (2023). https://doi.org/10.1109/TITS.2022.3230012
11. Mnih, V., Kavukcuoglu, K., Silver, D.: Human-level control through deep reinforcement learning. Nature **518**(7540), 529–533 (2015). https://doi.org/10.1038/nature14236
12. Lillicrap, T.P., Hunt, J.J., Pritzel, A.: Continuous control with deep reinforcement learning. arXiv preprint arXiv:1509.02971 (2016)
13. Li, Y.J., Su, S., Zhang, M.H.: Multi-agent graph reinforcement learning method for electric vehicle on-route charging guidance in coupled transportation electrification. IEEE Trans. Sustainable Energy **15**(2), 1180–1193 (2023). https://doi.org/10.1038/nature14236

A Dual-Module System Design and Application for Digital Payment Fraud Detection

Yingxin Hong[1], Qingqing Ren[2(✉)], Shijie Cao[1], and Hualing Liu[1]

[1] Shanghai University of International Business and Economics, Shanghai, China
24349026@suibe.edu.cn
[2] Independent researcher, New York, USA
qr2129@columbia.edu

Abstract. The rapid development of digital payment systems has brought great convenience but also introduced significant fraud risks. Current fraud detection systems face two major challenges: difficulty with identification of overlapping samples due to data imbalance, and low sensitivity to emerging new fraud patterns. To address these issues, this paper proposes an intelligent fraud detection system based on a dual-module architecture (OS-DFDA). The main innovations include: (1) Design of an OV-WGAN data balancing preprocessing module that precisely models samples in overlapping regions by integrating Wasserstein distance and overlapping coefficients, effectively improving the quality and reliability of balanced samples; (2) Development of a dual-module detection framework that combines Decision Tree and autoencoders, enabling collaborative detection of both known and unknown fraud patterns while maintaining high precision and significantly improving recall rate. Experiments on real-world digital payment datasets demonstrate that the system achieves an F1-score of 86%, outperforming the existing mainstream methods.

Keywords: System design · Digital payment · Fraud detection · Intelligent recognition · Data balancing · Emerging fraud pattern detection

1 Introduction

Online consumer lending and digital payments have gained increasing popularity thanks to the development of financial technology, which not only brings enhanced convenience and efficiency, but also creates a rich environment for fraudsters [1]. The frequency of digital payment fraud incidents has soared and the frauds have also become more concealed, causing annual losses of billions of dollars worldwide [2,3].

While machine learning and deep learning have shown promising results in fraud detection, three significant challenges persist. First, the exponential growth

T. Zhu et al. (Eds.): KSEM 2025, LNAI 15923, pp. 318–326, 2026.
https://doi.org/10.1007/978-981-95-3061-8_34

in transaction volume and feature dimensionality has rendered traditional audit methods inadequate [4]. Second, current models struggle with transactions that exhibit highly similar behavioral characteristics despite belonging to different categories, particularly where feature distributions overlap and datasets are severely imbalanced [5]. Third, existing supervised learning approaches, which rely on historical fraud patterns, often fail to identify emerging new fraud patterns not present in training data [6].

To address these challenges, we propose OS-DFDA (Overlapping Samples-focused Dual-module Fraud Detection Algorithm), with two key innovations:

- We introduce an overlapping coefficient as a quantitative metric for dataset structural analysis and develop a locally optimized WGAN (Wasserstein Generative Adversarial Network) for data equalization. This approach minimizes Wasserstein distance to enhance learning effectiveness in overlapping regions [8].
- We present a DT-AE-OSVM dual-module detection framework that combines supervised and unsupervised learning. This hybrid approach can simultaneously identify known fraud patterns and detect emerging fraudulent behaviors that deviate from existing security patterns.

2 Related Work

Data equalization techniques in fraudulent transaction identification aim to supplement minority fraud samples to mitigate the negative impact of imbalanced data distribution [5], enabling traditional classification algorithms to perform effectively. Early resampling methods like random oversampling and undersampling faced challenges of overfitting and information loss. The SMOTE algorithm, proposed by Chawla and Bowyer [7], addressed these issues by generating synthetic samples from local neighborhoods. However, it treated all minority samples as seed nodes without considering outliers, potentially reducing sample distinguishability. Recent years have witnessed growing interest in GAN-based equalization methods. Pioneering work by Fiore [8] applied GAN to fraud detection, generating pseudo-fraud samples while comparing performance with SMOTE. The introduction of WGAN by Arjovsky [6], which incorporates Wasserstein distance metrics, significantly improved training stability by addressing issues like gradient vanishing and mode collapse.

Recent advances focus on adaptive loss functions. Yang and Shi [9] enhanced detection performance by combining Focal Loss with the deviation between BPNN recognition results and true labels. Liu [10] proposed Adaptive Focal Loss (AFL), dynamically adjusting weights based on classification difficulty and confidence.

3 OV-WGAN Data Equalization Techniques

3.1 Sample Overlap Coefficient and Overlapping Samples

We propose the sample overlap coefficient based on the K-nearest neighbor algorithm to quantify the neighborhood distribution of samples. The relevant definitions are as follows:

Definition 1 (K-Nearest Neighbor Count). For sample $d_{i,n}$ representing the nth sample in the ith category, where $i \in \{0,1\}$ denotes normal and fraudulent transactions respectively, $n \in \{1,2,\ldots,|C_i|\}$ is the sample index within category i, and C_i represents the set of all samples belonging to category i:

$$K(d_{i,n}) = |\{x \in \mathrm{KNN}_k(d_{i,n}) : x \in \overline{C_i}\}| \tag{1}$$

where $\mathrm{KNN}_k(d_{i,n})$ returns the set of k nearest neighbors of $d_{i,n}$ based on Euclidean distance, $\overline{C_i}$ represents the complement set of category i, and $k \in \mathbb{N}^+$ is the neighborhood size parameter.

Definition 2 (Sample Overlap Coefficient). The overlap coefficient measures the proportion of heterogeneous neighbors:

$$\mathrm{Overlap}_{i,n} = \frac{K(d_{i,n})}{k} \in [0,1] \tag{2}$$

where $k \geq 2$ to ensure meaningful neighborhood analysis and avoid logical contradictions.

Based on the overlap coefficient, samples are classified into three types: *safe samples* ($\mathrm{Overlap}_{i,n} \in [0, \frac{1}{k}]$) with clear class membership, *overlapping samples* ($\mathrm{Overlap}_{i,n} \in (\frac{1}{k}, 1)$) in ambiguous boundary regions, and *noise samples* ($\mathrm{Overlap}_{i,n} = 1$) potentially mislabeled or outliers.

Lemma 1 (Theoretical Constraint for k). The constraint $k \geq 2$ is necessary and sufficient for meaningful sample classification based on overlap coefficients. *Proof* When $k = 1$, the overlap coefficient $\mathrm{Overlap}_{i,n} \in \{0,1\}$ can only take binary values. This creates a degenerate case where:

- If the single nearest neighbor belongs to the same class, $\mathrm{Overlap}_{i,n} = 0$ (safe sample)
- If the single nearest neighbor belongs to a different class, $\mathrm{Overlap}_{i,n} = 1$ (noise sample)

This binary classification fails to capture the nuanced neighborhood structures necessary for identifying overlapping samples that lie in ambiguous regions between classes. When $k \geq 2$, the overlap coefficient can take values in $\{0, \frac{1}{k}, \frac{2}{k}, \ldots, 1\}$, enabling the detection of overlapping samples with $\mathrm{Overlap}_{i,n} \in (\frac{1}{k}, 1)$. Therefore, $k \geq 2$ is essential for effective three-way sample classification.

Theorem 1 (Sample Classification by Overlap). Given the overlap coefficient $\mathrm{Overlap}_{i,n}$ and neighborhood parameter $k \geq 2$, the dataset is partitioned into three disjoint subsets:

$$\mathrm{Type}(d_{i,n}) = \begin{cases} \text{Noise sample} & \text{if } \mathrm{Overlap}_{i,n} = 1 \\ \text{Overlapping sample} & \text{if } \mathrm{Overlap}_{i,n} \in (\frac{1}{k}, 1) \\ \text{Safe sample} & \text{if } \mathrm{Overlap}_{i,n} \in [0, \frac{1}{k}] \end{cases} \tag{3}$$

The theoretical constraint $k \geq 2$ prevents degeneracy as demonstrated in Lemma 1. This three-way classification enables OV-WGAN to focus data generation efforts on overlapping regions where traditional methods struggle, while filtering out noise samples that could degrade model performance.

3.2 OV-WGAN Algorithm

The OV-WGAN algorithm addresses issues brought by unbalanced data and high proportion of overlapping samples in fraudulent transactions. The construction follows three steps: data screening, distribution fitting, and data equalization. The specific process is shown in Algorithm 1.

Algorithm 1. Data Equalization Algorithm based on OV-WGAN

Require: The class imbalanced dataset after calculating overlap coefficient D_1
Ensure: Dataset D_{balanced} after data equalization
 1: **Data screening:** Remove noise samples in normal transactions and under-sample safe samples in normal transactions, retaining only 1% of original size. Result: filtered dataset D_2.
 2: **Distribution fitting:** Construct OV-WGAN algorithm
 3: **Training Critic:**
 4: **for** $i = 1$ to 5 **do**
 5:    Extract m real samples: $\{(x^1, l^1), (x^2, l^2), \ldots, (x^m, l^m)\}$
 6:    Draw m noise samples with labels: $Z = \{(z^1, l^1), (z^2, l^2), \ldots, (z^m, l^m)\}$
 7:    Generate fake samples: $\hat{X} = G(Z)$
 8:    Calculate Wasserstein loss and update critic parameters:

$$\mathrm{Loss}_C = \frac{1}{m} \sum_{i=1}^{m} [D(x_i) - D(\hat{x}_i)] + \lambda GP \tag{4}$$

    where $GP = \mathbb{E}_{(\tilde{x})} \left[(\|\nabla_{\tilde{x}} D(\tilde{x})\|_2 - 1)^2 \right]$
 9: **end for**
10: **Training Generator:**
11: Generate samples and update generator parameters:

$$E_G = -\frac{1}{m} \sum_{i=1}^{m} D(\hat{x}_i) \tag{5}$$

12: **Data balance:** Use trained generator to supplement fraudulent transaction samples

---

4 DT-AE-OSVM Dual Module Framework

4.1 Architecture Design

The DT-AE-OSVM algorithm consists of two complementary modules:

Module 1: Historical Fraud Pattern Recognition (DT). We choose the Decision Tree algorithm for identifying historical fraudulent behavior patterns due to two advantages: (1) significantly improved performance with balanced samples; (2) highly interpretable classification rules that intuitively show reasons for transaction approval or rejection.

Module 2: New Fraud Transaction Prediction (AE-OSVM). This module combines autoencoder with One-Class Support Vector Machine to detect emerging fraud patterns not present in training data.

The architecture of the new fraud transaction prediction module is illustrated in Fig. 1, which shows the integration of autoencoder and One-Class SVM components for detecting anomalous patterns in transaction data.

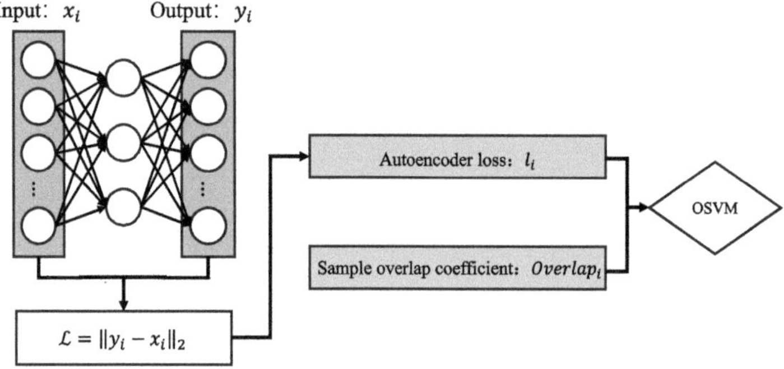

Fig. 1. New fraud transaction prediction module based on AE-OSVM architecture.

Algorithm 2. AE-OSVM Training Algorithm

Require: Normal transaction dataset D_{normal} from D_{balanced}
Ensure: Trained AE-OSVM model
1: **Normal transaction behavior pattern extraction:**
2: Train autoencoder on D_{normal}:

$$\text{Loss}_{AE} = \sum_{i=1}^{n_{\text{batch}}} (y_i - x_i)^2 \tag{6}$$

3: **Calculate reconstruction loss:**
4: **for** every x_i in D_{normal} **do**
5:     Compute: $l_i = \|y_i - x_i\|_2$
6: **end for**
7: **Hypersphere construction:**
8: Train OSVM using reconstruction loss and overlap coefficient features

---

5   Experiments and Results

5.1   Experimental Setup

Dataset. We use the Kaggle European credit transaction dataset containing 284,807 transactions over two days, with 492 fraudulent transactions (0.172%).

The dataset includes 30 anonymized features: Time interval, V1-V28 (PCA-reduced features), Amount, and Class label.

Implementation. Python 3.9 with PyTorch 1.10.0 for OV-WGAN implementation. Five-fold cross-validation ensures robustness while maintaining 0.172% fraud proportion in train/test splits.

Hyperparameters. Table 1 shows the OV-WGAN parameter settings. For DT-AE-OSVM: decision tree max depth 5, autoencoder architecture [32,32,10,32,32, input_dim] with 300 training epochs and batch size 512, OSVM using RBF kernel with nu = 0.003.

Table 1. OV-WGAN Hyperparameter Settings

Parameter	Value/Range
Neighbor parameter k	[3, 5, 7, 9]
Generator network nodes	[512, 256, feature_dim]
Discriminator network nodes	[512, 256, 1]
Training epochs	500
Batch size	64
Noise dimensions	100
Balance sample ratio	[0.2, 0.5, 0.75, 1, 2, 4, 6, 10]
Gradient penalty λ_{gp}	10
Learning rate	1e-4

5.2   Performance Analysis

Robustness Test of OV-WGAN Algorithm. As the balanced sample ratio ranges from 0.2 to 4 times, the recall rates of all algorithm combinations show improvement, indicating that the supplemented balanced samples help models better learn fraud transaction patterns. However, when the balance ratio exceeds 4 times, resampling methods (SMOTE, ADASYN) and generative adversarial network methods show significant divergence in precision performance. In contrast, GAN-based methods like WGAN and OV-WGAN demonstrate better stability, maintaining high precision even at high sample ratios, with OV-WGAN exhibiting optimal performance stability across various models.

Dual-Module Framework Results. Figure 2 illustrates the performance comparison of AE-OSVM (unsupervised), DT (supervised), and our proposed DT-AE-OSVM (dual-module) algorithms on the European credit card transaction dataset using five-fold cross-validation. The evaluation metrics include precision, recall, and F1-score. The results demonstrate that while the unsupervised AE-OSVM effectively identifies more potential fraud cases, it suffers from high false positive rates, making it impractical for direct decision-making. Our dual-module DT-AE-OSVM strategy combines the strengths of both approaches, achieving an average increase of 6.65% in precision and 15.83% in recall compared to the baseline DT model.

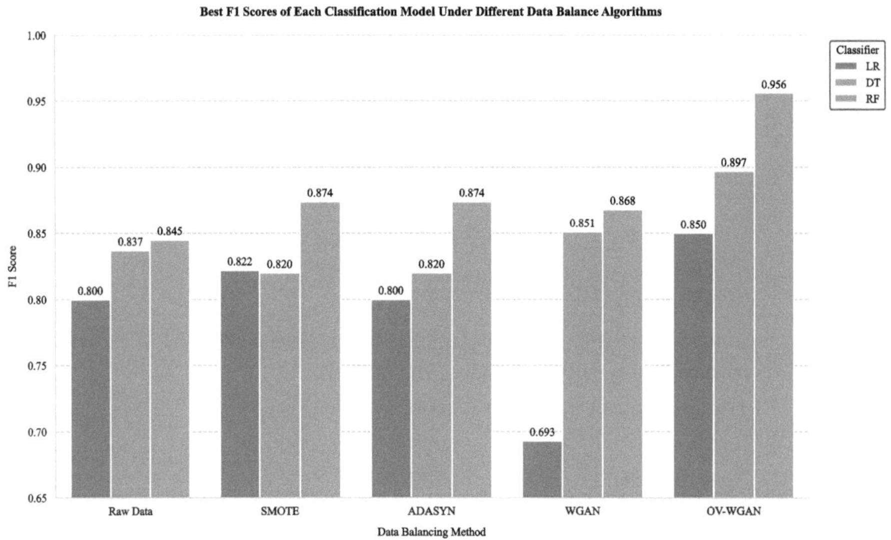

Fig. 2. Model Performance Comparison showing precision, recall and F1-score metrics for different approaches.

Comprehensive Performance. Table 2 presents detailed performance metrics across various algorithms. The prefix "OV-WGAN" indicates models trained on our balanced data. Our proposed OV-WGAN + Dual Module approach achieves superior performance with 91.74% precision, 80.87% recall, and 85.98% F1-score.

Statistical Significance Analysis. We conducted comprehensive statistical analysis to validate our approach using the K-S (Kolmogorov-Smirnov) metric calculated as $K - S = \max |F_1(x) - F_0(x)|$, where $F_0(x)$ and $F_1(x)$ represent the cumulative distribution functions of normal and fraudulent transactions respectively. Ablation studies show: removing overlap coefficient calculation reduces F1-score by 4.2%, our WGAN-based approach outperforms traditional GAN by 8.1% in F1-score, and the combined dual-module approach achieves 12.3% improvement over single DT.

Table 2. Performance metrics of different algorithms

Algorithm	Precision	Recall	F1-score	K-S
AE-OSVM	0.2341	0.8392	0.3659	0.2487
DT	0.7087	0.6823	0.6952	0.3512
LGB	0.7834	0.6841	0.7306	0.3623
RF	0.7976	0.7084	0.7508	0.3681
XGBoost	0.7913	0.6947	0.7404	0.3658
DNN	0.8127	0.7139	0.7604	0.3724
OV-WGAN + DT	0.8284	0.7372	0.7806	0.3773
OV-WGAN + LGB	0.8791	0.7693	0.8206	0.3891
OV-WGAN + RF	0.8912	0.7761	0.8298	0.3926
OV-WGAN + XGBoost	0.8836	0.7749	0.8259	0.3902
OV-WGAN + DNN	0.8983	0.7892	0.8406	0.3951
OV-WGAN + Dual Module	**0.9174**	**0.8087**	**0.8598**	**0.4018**

6 Conclusion

This paper presents the OS-DFDA algorithm with two key contributions: Development of OV-WGAN, a local data perspective-based equalization algorithm derived from structural dataset analysis, and construction of an interpretable dual-module fraud detection framework (DT-AE-OSVM) that combines supervised and unsupervised learning to enhance sensitivity to novel fraud patterns.

Experimental results demonstrate that our OV-WGAN algorithm generates robust balanced samples and maintains stable performance across sampling ratios. The dual-module DT-AE-OSVM architecture achieves 85.98% F1-score, substantially outperforming existing methods.

References

1. Zhou, Z.H.: Three stages of digital economy development: digital payment, digital legal currency and digital finance. Tsinghua Financ. Rev. **04**, 63–64 (2018)
2. People's Bank of China: The overall operation of the payment system in 2020. Financ. Acc. **04**, 77–80 (2021)
3. Zheng, P., Yuan, S., Wu, X.: One-class adversarial nets for fraud detection. In: Proceedings of the AAAI Conference on Artificial Intelligence, vol. 33, pp. 1286–1293 (2019)
4. Khan, S., Hayat, M., Bennamoun, M.: Cost-sensitive learning of deep feature representations from imbalanced data. IEEE Trans. Neural Netw. Learn. Syst. **29**(8), 3573–3587 (2018)
5. Zhang, T., Wang, Y.H., Li, K.: Credit scoring of small and micro enterprises based on sample-dependent cost matrix. J. Tongji Univ. (Nat. Sci.) **48**(01), 149 (2020)
6. Arjovsky, M., Chintala, S., Bottou, L.: Wasserstein generative adversarial networks. In: Proceedings of Machine Learning Research, vol. 70, pp. 214–223 (2017)

7. Chawla, N.V., Bowyer, K.W., Hall, L.O., Kegelmeyer, W.P.: SMOTE: synthetic minority over-sampling technique. J. Artifi. Intell. Res. **16**, 321–357 (2002)
8. Fiore, U., De Santis, A., Perla, F.: Using generative adversarial networks for improving classification effectiveness in credit card fraud detection. Inf. Sci. **479**, 448–455 (2019)
9. Yang, Y., Wu, Q., Wang, Y.: Research on LSTM with focal loss for credit card fraud detection. Neural Comput. Appl. **33**(14), 8645–8657 (2021)
10. Liu, Y., Zhang, H., Chen, C.: Adaptive focal loss: learning where to look in credit card fraud detection. IEEE Access **8**, 73898–73911 (2020)

Correction to: SocioSupplyAlert: Comprehensive Supply Chain Crisis Prediction Using LLMs and Social Media Data

Meixuan Chen, Chen Wang, Yujun Wu, Wei Kang, and Zaiwen Feng

Correction to:
Chapter 29 in: T. Zhu et al. (Eds.): *Knowledge*
Science, Engineering and Management, **LNAI 15923,**
https://doi.org/10.1007/978-981-95-3061-8_29

In the original version of this chapter, equal-contribution statement of the authors were wrong and also contains a typographical error. This has been corrected. Correctly it should be read as: "M. Chen and C. Wang contributed equally to this work".

The updated version of this chapter can be found at
https://doi.org/10.1007/978-981-95-3061-8_29

Author Index

B

Bai, Jinyin 85

C

Cao, Shijie 318
Cao, Weipeng 257
Cao, Yujia 257
Chen, Junyu 156
Chen, Meixuan 274
Chen, Shouyi 67
Cheng, Jiangmai 105
Chu, Chiawei 67
Cui, Wenfeng 156

D

Dong, Jiming 198
Duan, Xuliang 165

F

Feng, Ling 165
Feng, Zaiwen 274
Fu, Chenhan 1

G

Gong, Youdi 25
Guo, Yanfei 67

H

Han, Han 291
He, Yiyi 67
Hong, Yingxin 318
Hou, Zhehao 210
Hu, Haoji 219
Hu, Wei 210
Hu, Zhangxiang 97
Hu, Zhongjian 77
Huang, Weide 134

J

Jiang, Bo 105
Jiang, Cheng 190
Jiang, Chi 17
Jiang, Hezhong 210
Jiang, Yunan 134
Jing, Zhi 165

K

Kang, Wei 274
Karunarathne, Shyamali Sinali 248
Ke, Xikai 210

L

Li, Bixuan 282
Li, Dandan 59
Li, Guoyu 59
Li, Jiahao 302
Li, Kaiwen 59
Li, Lei 46
Li, Qingru 143
Li, Tongliang 210
Li, Xin 198, 237
Liang, Xiaoyu 219
Liu, Baojing 9
Liu, Chang 302
Liu, Fang 210
Liu, Fangxiang 36
Liu, Fuchun 310
Liu, Hualing 318
Liu, Linlan 134
Liu, Mengchi 266
Liu, Shengyao 59
Liu, Yingjun 310
Liu, Yuchong 46
Lu, Rongxing 1
Lu, Yanjun 116
Luo, Xiaorui 17

T. Zhu et al. (Eds.): KSEM 2025, LNAI 15923, pp. 327–329, 2026.
https://doi.org/10.1007/978-981-95-3061-8

M
Ma, Wei   67
Ma, Yuxi   25
Meng, Fanjun   156, 228
Meng, Lingzhong   25
Meng, Xiangbin   97
Ming, Zhong   257
Mu, Lianrui   219

O
Ou, Hongze   219

P
Pan, Lei   248
Peng, Songtao   291

Q
Qiao, Linbo   291
Qin, Xuanli   97

R
Rajasegarar, Sutharshan   248
Ren, Qingqing   318
Ren, Xiangrong   165

S
Shi, Yuting   176
Shu, Jian   134
Shuai, Zhihao   59
Song, Kun   77
Song, Xinyi   116
Su, Bing   46
Sun, Tianfang   105

T
Tang, Jiamin   266
Tang, Naisheng   59
Tang, Siliang   1
Tao, Xi   257
Tong, Fenghua   198

W
Wang, Boyu   105
Wang, Changguang   143
Wang, Chen   274
Wang, Chun   190
Wang, Chunhui   237
Wang, Dong   124
Wang, Fangwei   143

Wang, Guoming   1
Wang, Hongxuan   143
Wang, Jiabao   25
Wang, Kangsheng   302
Wang, Qingren   36
Wang, Ranran   17
Wang, Te   228
Wang, Xiangchen   85
Wang, Xiaole   36
Wang, Yiran   17
Wang, Yuting   36
Wang, Zihao   302
Wei, Chung-Lun   67
Wei, Zhenghao   134
Wen, Xu   36
Wu, Peng   124
Wu, Tianhao   165
Wu, Yujun   274

X
Xia, Weike   210
Xiang, Wenkang   198
Xu, Anyang   124
Xu, Chuanfei   257
Xu, Lijuan   198, 237
Xu, Qinglin   85
Xu, Tianxiang   302
Xu, Xianjun   97
Xu, Xingjian   156, 228

Y
Yan, Dengcheng   36
Yang, Bowen   124
Yang, Guang   25
Yang, Jing   97
Yang, Peng   77
Ye, Qiwei   291
You, Haochen   9
Yu, Fuqiang   237
Yu, Shanqing   291
Yuan, Yixuan   282

Z
Zhang, Chao   266
Zhang, Chuan   46
Zhang, Dekai   237
Zhang, Heng   36
Zhang, Shichao   46
Zhang, Xi   143

Zhang, Yin   17
Zhang, Zhaokang   17
Zhao, Dawei   198, 237
Zhao, Lei   237
Zhao, Yunwei   291
Zheng, Jianchao   46

Zheng, Peng   85
Zhou, Tianwai   77
Zhu, Hongzhen   310
Zhu, Liehuang   46
Zhu, Wei   85
Zhu, Xudong   266